# Advanced Applied
# PSYCHOLOGY

# Advanced Applied PSYCHOLOGY

Psychology Applied to Education, Human Development and Psychological Disorders

Volume-1

Ram Nath Sharma
Rachana Sharma

Published by

**ATLANTIC**

**PUBLISHERS & DISTRIBUTORS (P) LTD**

7/22, Ansari Road, Darya Ganj, New Delhi-110002
Phones : +91-11-40775252, 40775214, 23273880, 23275880
Fax: +91-11-23285873
Web: www.atlanticbooks.com
E-mail: orders@atlanticbooks.com



Printed & bound in India by Atlantic Print Services

# Preface

Advanced Applied Psychology is the most important branch of Psychology encompassing applications of psychological knowledge in all areas of psychology. Though several books are available on Applied Psychology, there is hardly any book covering the entire spectrum of psychology applied to various areas of life. This book entitled *Advanced Applied Psychology* has been designed to fill up this gap. Published in two volumes, its Vol. I deals with Psychology Applied to Education, Human Development and Psychological Disorders, while Vol. II covers Psychology Applied to Crime, Society and Industry. Within the scope of these two volumes the book covers the courses of all the Indian Universities for undergraduate and postgraduate degrees in Psychology.

Written in simple language, with examples drawn from Indian life, presenting authentic material with latest data and explaining the subject matter through central, side and running headings, this book is a must on the desk of every teacher and student of psychology. The book will also be a major source of information for professional practitioners and researchers in the domain of psychology.

I am thankful to Dr. K.R. Gupta, Chairman of M/s Atlantic Publishers and Distributors, New Delhi, for publishing the book.

Suggestions, if any, for the improvement of the book in the next edition, will be gratefully acknowledged.

RAM NATH SHARMA
RACHANA SHARMA

# Contents

## PART IV — CLINICAL PSYCHOLOGY

# Part I

# General Principles

# 1

# Introduction

Psychology is not only a theoretical study but also helps in the solution of various problems concerning different aspects of human behaviour. This is known as applied psychology. Applied psychology today is, however, divided into different special branches *e.g.*, clinical psychology, educational psychology, legal psychology, industrial psychology, etc. To have an idea of the scope of applied psychology, a brief survey of its important branches is as follows :

1. **Clinical Psychology.** Clinical psychology is concerned with the cure of various types of abnormalities, psychoses, neuroses, etc. One of the pioneers in this field was Sigmund Freud. Since his time clinical psychology has progressed so much that now every next modern hospital in the Western countries has a clinical psychologist attached to it. An American survey in 1951 showed that clinical psychology is being used in about 43 per cent of the American hospitals.

2. **Counselling and vocational guidance.** One of the most valuable applications of psychology is in this field of vocational guidance. Psychology helps young men and women to choose their career according to their capacities and talents. Thus, the universities, the colleges, the industrial centres and the employment exchanges profit by the counselling of the psychologist. This helps them in finding the right man for the right job. Besides giving guidance to the youth in vocations, the psychologist also guides the parents in tackling the problems of the child, truancy, delinquency, etc.

3. **Educational Psychology.** Psychology has almost revolutionised our approach to education. Not only the teacher but also the taught and the parents have profited by psychology.

As Clifford T. Morgan points out, "The study of the development of the child shows us what to teach, when to teach and how to teach." Educational psychology helps the teachers to bring about the utmost development of the faculties of the educated and to educate him according to his psychological capacities.

**4. Selection for Government services.** Modern Governments employ the service of the psychologist for the selection of suitable personnel for different public services, specially, in navy, army and air force. In the Second World War, army alpha tests and army beta tests were utilised for the recruitment of men in army and soldiers were given work according to the results of these tests. In the Second World War, engineering psychology, a new branch of psychology, was developed. Engineering psychology helps to devise such machinery as may be operated with the least fatigue. Thus, it has helped men in designing the auto-vehicles, engines, etc.

**5. Industrial Psychology and commercial Psychology.** The most useful application of psychology has been in the field of industry and commerce. By the study of the psychology of the commerce, the industrialists can know about the requisite qualities of the articles as well as the methods of buying selling and advertising. It is in the field of advertisement that one notices most interesting application of psychology. Psychology has helped the industrialists in their relation with the labourers as well as in the recruitment of the labourers and in finding the suitable jobs for them. In the modern factories one finds wide use of different types of tests *e.g.*, tests of steadiness, tests of alertness, tests of special abilities, etc.

**6. Legal Psychology.** Psychology has been used in the field of law and justice. It is useful for judges, lawyers, witnesses and all others who are concerned with the law or justice. It has helped in the detection of crimes, false witnesses and other complex phenomena.

Besides the above application of psychology, it is being very much used in almost every branch of the political field. In elections, administration, legislation and all other fields, the knowledge of psychology is paying good dividends. As a matter of fact as psychology will grow, its applications in different fields of human activities will also grow. The scope of psychology, theoretical as well as applied, includes every aspect of human behaviour. Thus the scope of psychology includes the study of conscious, unconscious, subconscious; child, adolescent, adult; individual, mob and audience; leaders and followers; labourers, students and men in all walks of life and different types of animal behaviour. In short, where there is behaviour there is field of psychology and this field is widening with the ever increasing knowledge of the psychologist.

## DEFINITION OF APPLIED PSYCHOLOGY

Applied psychology, as is evident from the nomenclature, is the applied or practical aspect of psychology. In the words of Hepner, "The aims of applied psychology are the description, prediction and control of human activities in order that we may understand and direct intelligently our lives and influence the lives of others." Hence, instead of considering applied psychology as a branch of psychology, it would perhaps be better to look upon it as an aspect of the general science. Just as every science has the theoretical and the practical aspects, psychology also has a practical or applied aspect of its theoretical research. Discoveries of the various sciences such as chemistry, physics and sociology have been found fit to be applied to practical life. In the secluded atmosphere of his laboratory, the scientist searches for general principles through his experiment in particular cases, but the utility or applicability of these principles is not limited only to the sphere of the laboratory. After all, the main concern of the human race is to ensure its longevity, and to continue to do so in the manner of human beings and not insects. Man is a special being in as much as he has been favoured with brain or mind, which he can use to comprehend the various objects that constitute his environment, to discover the general laws that underlie their existence and co-relations, to apply these discoveries to the intended betterment of his own lot. This is the fundamental source of all science. Thus, psychology too, like all other sciences, aims at the improvement of the man's life on earth. This, of course, does not imply that no search for truth is intended merely to add to existing knowledge, or that there is no significant place for theoretical study in human life. The truth of the matter is that in human life, the difference between the theoretical and the practical or applied is merely relative as the same thing viewed from one standpoint has seemed theoretical while from a different perspective it has exhibited very practical soundness. It need not be mentioned that the facts discovered in the pursuit of theoretical science are used in practical life as much as possible, and one can only hope for such application increasing in the future.

## HISTORY OF APPLIED PSYCHOLOGY

In the historical cycle, theoretical study precedes practical application of discovery. In like manner psychology, too, started with the discovery of many theoretical principles, which were subsequently put to practical use. It is evident that applied psychology, as a branch of the main subject, sprung up after general psychology. In his essay entitled Applied Psychology Comes of Age, Paterson divides the history of its development into the following four parts :

**1. Pregnancy.** The period 1882 to 1917 was the period of pregnancy for applied psychology, a time in which the contributions of Galton, Cattell and Binet were of importance. And during this period the United States was engaged in the world war.

**2. Birth.** According to Paterson, the period from 1917 to 1937 should be regarded as the prolonged period of the science's birth and emergence from the womb. In this period psychology was used to examine individuals regarding their fitness for service in the armed forces. Army alpha and army beta tests were devised to select desirable soldiers.

**3. Infancy.** The period 1918 to 1937 is of the science's infancy. The year 1937 saw the establishment of a National Institute of Applied Psychology in the United States, the institute promoting the application of psychology to the task of emancipating the nation.

**4. Adolescence or youth.** Following this, applied psychology enters into its youth, and from that day to this its scope and sphere have both been considerably enlarged, with no end in sight. History of the development of applied psychology is the history of its development in the United States of America, since it cannot be questioned that the recent development of applied psychology has all taken place there.

### Testing of Individual Differences

The discovery of psychology that has been most encouraged by applied psychology is concerned with individual differences. Psychological testing revealed the existence of wide differences of intelligence, capability and personality besides other qualities between different individuals. It became quite obvious that all people could not do the same work or do it equally efficiently. Modern age lays much emphasis upon the division of labour. In all modern nations, the entire structure of economic policy and political efficacy rests upon division of labour. The very principle of division of labour is based on the psychological fact that every person is not capable of performing any function. And any nation can derive the benefit from division of labour only when it makes a study of individual differences among its population at the national level, and arranges to have the right man in the right job, and the right task for the right individual. This will help to make the maximum utilisation of the manpower that is available to the nation, avoiding entirely unnecessary wastage in energy. To take a simple but salient example, if a person interested in the manipulation of machinery is forced to take up an academic career, then the nation is not only deprived of an enthusiastic and devoted engineer but it also stands in danger of having a bad teacher foisted upon some part of its population. Having come to this realisation of stark fact, most progressive nations are doing their best to make vocational guidance popular among the masses. Evidently, applied psychology is needed almost at every step.

## NEED FOR APPLIED PSYCHOLOGY IN INDIA

India is a newly created democratic republic, power in which is vested in the public. And public is a term denoting the entire population of the country. These citizens are possessed of various skills and capabilities. Development and progress of the democracy depend upon these citizens. Hence, if the future of India is to be bright, it is essential that these people be given jobs and occupations that accord with their innate abilities, and that conditions be created under which they can give their very best. Here, the need for applied psychology becomes fairly evident. It is only recently that the study of applied psychology was initiated in the country, but this branch of psychology is becoming popular and useful at a rapid pace. It is becoming increasingly apparent that the application of psychological methods is essential in the fields of education, industry, prevention of crime, elections, propaganda, advertising, etc. One established fact that now goes unchallenged is that in these spheres there is considerable scope for application of psychological methods, tests and observations, research and discovery. If only the field of education is taken into immediate consideration then in India there are a few million children who are sorely in need of psychologically determined and fashioned education. Present education, or what passes for education, in this country, neither builds the character of the youth nor provides him with skill enough to get suitable employment, besides denying them the ability to think of what they are capable of doing and what they should actually do. For all this and more, psychology is completely essential and absolutely indispensable. Not very long ago, our country achieved its independence, but already many reactionary and destructive forces have started working. Some people have raised the banner of casteism, while other people are agitating for separate states on the ground that bilingualism and multilingual conditions are creating many problems. Regionalism is not unknown to this country, and religious flags have invaded the field of politics. Class struggle and consciousness are very strong. Selfishness, corruption, inactivity or the negative attitude, disgust with life in general and frustration are common places of life in this country. Psychological discoveries can help much towards the solution of this depressing state of affairs. Realising the imperative need for immediate remedial measures the present administration is superintending the establishment of psychological bureaus at various places where expert advice will be available easily. People can bring problems of adjustment and vocational guidance to these experts and get advice.

## PROBLEMS OF APPLIED PSYCHOLOGY

To have a view of the problem of applied psychology, a brief survey of its application in different fields of human life is helpful :

**1. Educational problems.** Applied Psychology has made radical reforms in the field of education and revolutionised the syllabi and methods of education. The rule of cane has been substituted by psychological methods of persuasion, encouragement, sympathy, etc. Thus psychology has made education more natural, easy and useful. It has helped in the all-round development of the educated and in sweet relation between the teacher and the taught.

**2. Problems of crime detection and justice.** Applied Psychology has been very helpful in understanding the causes of crimes and also their cures. In modern states, step have been taken to reform the criminals and to restore them to the society by removing the psychological causes of crimes. It is due to the influence of psychology that one finds new experiments in the field of criminology *e.g.*, probation, reformatories, borstal schools, open air jails, etc. Psychology has made it clear that the criminal alone is not responsible for his crimes but much of the responsibility rests with his social situations as well. This has changed our attitude towards the criminal. In the present theory of punishment, revenge has been substituted by reform. Separate arrangements have been made for the juvenile delinquents and juvenile delinquency has become a separate study. Applied Psychology has helped the judges to distinguish criminals from non-criminals and to devise suitable punishment in various cases. Thus in the field of justice as well as of crime detection, the study of psychology is gradually proving more and more helpful.

**3. Cure of abnormal diseases.** Applied Psychology has proved very valuable in the field of medicine. According to present day psychology, every somatic disease is psychological and hence requires not only physical but also psychological treatment. According to Brown, the author of the *Psycho Dynamics of Abnormal Behaviour*, every man stands in need of periodical check up. It has been found that 10 per cent of the population in America at one time or another suffers from some serious type of mental diseases. According to an estimate, 45 per cent of American colleges under graduates require the services of mental hygienist. Roughly, it can be said without exaggeration that almost every man needs the guidance of the clinical psychology at some time or the other to keep his mental health. The psychologist has been instrumental removing the chains of the insanes in asylums. The insanes today are no more treated as sinners, but sympathised with those who have failed to accommodate themselves to their circumstances. Thus psychology has removed a lot of superstitions about the mental diseases and also helped in their cures.

**4. Problems of industry and trade.** One of the most important factors in modern trade is advertisement and it is here that one finds widest application of psychology. Applied Psychology studies the interests and reactions and helps the industrialists to manufacture according to tastes. Psychology has made selling an art, if not a science. It has helped in the solution of the industrial disputes, the problems of strikes and lockouts and all other problems between mill owners and labour welfare in modern countries.

**5. Recruitment in services.** Applied Psychology has helped the employers in finding out suitable men for different kinds of work. It has helped the employee to secure work suited to his capacities and talents. It has helped in minimising the fatigue and using human capabilities with utmost efficiency. It is due to the advice of the psychologist that one finds numerous schemes of labour welfare in modern countries.

**6. Problems of human relations.** Applied Psychology has been instrumental in bringing about adjustment in society. It has enabled men to understand each other and thus to improve their relations. Thus, it has helped the sociologists and the social reformers to solve various problems of society.

**7. Personal problems.** Applied Psychology has not only helped in the solution of the social problems, but also in that of the problems of the individual. Psychology makes man understand himself. Self-understanding is the way to self-control. Self-control helps one in future progress. Again, psychology has removed many superstitions regarding various phenomena in human psychology *e.g.*, the meaning of dreams, daydreams and various abnormal phenomena, etc. Applied Psychology has helped man to form his character, to change his habits, to control his conduct and finally to adjust himself to new situations. It has warned him against dangerous activities and showed him the way to integral development of his personality.

**8. Problems of understanding of others.** Just as Applied

Psychology helps in the understanding of oneself, so it leads one to the understanding of others. It removes prejudices and eliminates hatred, because one can understand the cause of differences in behaviour. Thus psychology has been helpful in all types of primary and secondary relations *e.g.*, family, clubs, schools, colleges, playgrounds etc. Applied Psychology helps the parents to understand the child and the teacher to understand the taught. It helps in maintaining harmony between husband and wife, friends and lovers. In brief, psychology helps in the understanding of every type of human relation and solving its difficulties.

**9. Political problems.** Psychology has been widely applied in the political field. Social psychology has helped the leaders to understand the masses and control them. Government which rules in defiance of the psychology of the public cannot stay long. Hence, modern democratic Governments have a keen eye on different tendencies in the public. A democratic Government is formed by the people's representatives. These representatives are elected by the masses. Modern election depends upon the success of propaganda and the success of propaganda depends upon its psychological appeal. Thus modern politics very much depends upon psychology. Legislation, unless based upon psychological principles has scant chances of success. Even the reforms should be devised according to the psychology of the public. The administrator, without the knowledge of psychology, shall be a complete failure. History is a witness to the fact that the great rulers have always been masters of human psychology. Thus in every branch of Government and politics, the knowledge of psychology has been valuable.

**10. Problems of wartime.** In the times of war, the value of Applied Psychology becomes even more. The cold wars almost entirely depend upon psychological propaganda. Victory in war depends as much on self-confidence as on equipment. Psychology maintains the self-confidence in the army. It also helps in the recruitment of different men for different posts in navy, air and land forces. In the time of war the leaders arc chosen according to their psychological insight and influence on the masses. In the time of an attack by the enemy the reactions of the public are observed and confidence is maintained with the help of psychological suggestions. The art of diplomacy very much depends upon the knowledge of psychological facts.

**11. Problems concerning world peace.** Not only in the time of war, but also in the time of peace Applied Psychology has its own importance. The problem of peace is in fact the problem of human adjustment. The world peace depends upon the adjustment of men and women of different nationalities to one another. It is here that psychology plays a vital role. The knowledge of individual differences helps persons of different nationalities to understand one another. It helps to realise ideal fraternity among men. It helps in the understanding of aggressive tendencies, their control as well as in finding suitable outlets for them. The realisation of the cherished idea of world peace depends to a great extent upon finding suitable outlets of the various tendencies in men and women.

Thus, in the ultimate analysis, one finds that Applied psychology is concerned with almost all the psychological problems in human life.

## QUESTIONS FOR EXERCISE

1. Discuss the nature and scope of Applied Psychology.
2. Define Applied Psychology and discuss its history.
3. What is the need of Applied Psychology in India? Discuss problems of Applied Psychology.

# 2

# Relation with Other Branches of Psychology

## RELATION WITH GENERAL PSYCHOLOGY

### General Psychology

Psychology is the normative science of behaviour, having two aspects as has every other science — the theoretical and the practical or applied. In this theoretical aspect, the most extensive branch is the general psychology, a branch that includes the general principles of almost each and every one of its various branches. It studies the nature of psychology, its methods and relations to other sciences, learning, thinking, memory, sensation, perception, feeling, volition, emotion, imagination, personality, or rather the general principles governing these phenomena.

### Use of Psychology

Science is a theoretical pursuit, an objective investigation of factual laws that has nothing to do directly with the utility of these investigations. The psychologist is not the social reformer nor is he the mental doctor. His only concern is the study and objective investigation of the laws that govern human conduct, and the discovery of general principles from this study. From this viewpoint, psychology is a theoretical science. Yet, psychology is not exclusively a theoretical science or study. Actually, there is no way in which theory and application can be rigidly separated. Hence, psychology helps in understanding and solving problems of human relationships that exist in various spheres, thereby helping in the better adjustment of individuals. Psychology is extensively employed in education, business, trade, family, social, and individual life, war, peace, and elsewhere.

**Development of Psychology**

In this manner, the scope of applied psychology widened with the advance of general psychology. The year 1905 saw the construction of the Binet Simon Intelligence Test. Subsequently, in 1908 and 1911, revised and improved versions of the same intelligence tests were published. In 1855, Ebbinghaus put forward his discoveries concerning the phenomenon of memory while in 1889, Thorndike made known his views on the subject of learning. The principle of conditioned response came to light in 1902 through the efforts of the Russian psychologist Pavlov. First World War occasioned the development and application of army alpha and army beta group intelligence tests. In addition to this, the needs of the armed forces were met by the application and modification of tests of interest, rating scales, neurotic inventories, etc. At the same time, the statistical methods were also developed to be used in the aptitude tests. Attainment tests were devised to suit various aspects of education. Development and successful functioning of these tests resulted in research in the direction of job analysis. Lists of professions were made, and the various professions divided into families. Other kind of tests that became prevalent at or about this time are many, the important among them being General classification test, Mechanical aptitude test, Clerical aptitude test, Radio-operator aptitude test, Non-language tests, etc. Vocational counselling became the vogue after the Second World War, at the time when many psychologists turned their attention to the treatment of patients confined to lunatic asylums also many psychologists established private clinics that made a special point of attending to and providing cure for problem children, backward children, morons, and juvenile delinquents, etc. Applied psychology made further invasions into the industrial territory, besides advances into the field of politics, prevention of crime, etc.

Progress of both general as well as applied psychology is outlined in the above historical perspective. Once a new principle is discovered through some research, and it becomes established, it naturally increases the existing stock of psychological knowledge. But when the same new principle is put to practical application, it becomes a part and parcel of applied psychology. Hence, it is only too evident that general and applied psychology are distinct and separate branches of psychology. General psychology is theoretical while applied psychology is allegedly practical. The former elucidates the psychological principles of behaviour while the latter tests their practical validity and utility.

Munsterberg has divided psychology into three parts — theoretical psychology, applied psychology and psycho-technik. The first, apparently, is general psychology. In the case of the second classification, it studies occurrence and facts of other sciences from psychological viewpoint. For example, if the physics of colour are examined on the basis of psychological principles, such an examination would be called applied psychology. If these principles were to be used in the actual manufacture and actual use of colours and medicines, then it would be within the province of psycho-technik. In this way, Munsterberg believes the use of psychology, in the solution of practical problems, to be within the scope of psycho-technik. But this view does not appear to be quite tenable, since a close examination will reveal no actual difference between applied psychology and psycho-technik.

### Difference between General Psychology and Applied Psychology

On the other hand, many psychologists are not inclined to credit that there is any difference between applied psychology and general psychology when there is actually a definite distinction between the two branches. General psychology develops within the traditions and limitations of the laboratory while applied psychology invades the various fields of active life for actual application and development. It breathes the fresh air outside the boundaries of the laboratory. For example, it would be well within the scope of general psychology to test the effect of colours within the controlled environment of the laboratory. At a later stage, when the conclusions drawn from such tests are used in advertising in the field of industry and commerce, applied psychology is involved.

In this way, the problems of applied psychology and general psychology are different. In the words of Poffenberger, "The problem of applied psychology is so to adjust differentially endowed individuals by training them, by selection of their environment and by the control of this environment that they may attain the maximum social productivity and the maximum of personal satisfaction."[1] Evidently, then, the problems and viewpoint of applied psychology do not coincide with those of general psychology.

The points of distinction between general and applied psychology are fairly evident from the preceding discussion. The truth of the matter is that applied psychology begins to function where general psychology leaves off. For example, general psychology elucidates such a condition as communal tension, and searches for the causes inherent in it, but here its involvement in the subject is complete. Applied psychology takes over at this stage, moves into the actual living world with this knowledge as its equipment and tries to reduce this tension.

Applied is the practical aspect of psychology. No science retains its theoretical nature permanently. In its gradual development, it makes some definite suggestions for the improvement of mankind in respect of happiness, synthesis, comfort and prosperity. In this manner, every science has a definite applied aspect. Since the practical aspects of all sciences are concerned with the betterment of human life and general prosperity, it is essential that there be adjustment and synthesis between them. Looked at from this viewpoint, all sciences, theoretical and practical, are related. And applied psychology is no exception to the rule. It is intimately related to political science, sociology, medicine, economics, jurisprudence, etc. But its nearest and most important relationships are with the various other branches of psychology. The present chapter includes discussion of its relationships with experimental psychology and child psychology.

## RELATION WITH EXPERIMENTAL PSYCHOLOGY

### What is Experimental Psychology?

The most important field of psychology is that of experimental psychology. It is this aspect which is responsible for having won recognition for psychology in the field of science.

---

1. Proffenberger, A. T., *Principles of Applied Psychology*, Applied Pacific (1961), p. 13.

It uses the experimental method, by reason of which it is called experimental psychology. This branch makes a study of the external behaviour, such as speaking, learning, etc. and such internal behaviour as attitude, etc. of infants, children, adolescents, adults, as well as animals; for this purpose it conducts experiments upon them. Almost every branch and aspect of psychology makes some or the other use of experiment. Experiment helps in the study of various faculties such as intelligence, memory, imagination, logic, etc., and various capabilities in human beings. Experiments of all kinds — qualitative as well as quantitative — are conducted. In experiments, the subject under study is examined under controlled condition. Experimental psychology has its own laboratories, and its results have no less validity and veracity than the various physical sciences. The scope of this branch of psychology is constantly increasing.

**Objectives of Applied Psychology**

In the words of Poffenberger, "...the essence of applied psychology, namely the recognition of individual differences in endowment and in training and the need for the adjustment of each individual in life so as to furnish to him the maximum of satisfaction and to society the maximum of desirable goods."[2] In this manner, it is evident that the fundamental assumption of applied psychology is that individuals differ from fellow beings in respect of interests, tendencies, capabilities, etc., and that this difference is reflected in their training. This individual difference creates the problem of adjustment, since similarity to individual would have made it possible to find one single solution and adjust them all. But since this is nothing more than wishful thinking and individuals are widely different, it is necessary for applied psychology to help individuals in their adjustment in life, in all its various aspects and spheres. Adjustment of this kind is required in all human relationships. Family, society, trade, industry, political sphere, the field of economic endeavour, are all in need of this adjustment and guidance. Such adjustment helps the individual to make his best efforts in any field of activity, and assists him in the achievement of the greatest possible satisfaction. On the other

2. *Ibid.*, p. 2.

hand, adjustment between individuals leads to the maximum production of desired goods.

**Relation between Applied Psychology and Experimental Psychology**

Experimental psychology helps applied psychology achieve this objective. In this science, the various aspects of human behaviour and conduct are studied in laboratory conditions, and on this basis general principles are discovered. It is only after this that the facts discovered in the quiet conditions of the laboratory can be put to use in actual life. It is unquestionable that in actual life there are many conditions dissimilar to situation within the laboratory, and many of the living situations are not amenable to control, yet even in life many situations can be brought under sufficient control to admit of the application of principles discovered in the laboratory. In fact, applied psychology cannot maintain its scientific nature without the presence and active cooperation of experimental psychology. It is experimental psychology that provides applied psychology with the data that it utilizes in mental disease, personal, educational and vocational guidance, education, selection of government officials at a high level, trade, industry, commerce, prevention of crime etc.

**Difference between Applied and Experimental Psychology**

Despite the above points of coordination between applied and experimental psychology, there are important points of difference. Points worth mentioning in this respect are the following :

**1. Difference of aim.** The objective of experimental psychology is the discovery of real concerning some subject by examining it under controlled circumstances. On the other hand, the objective of applied psychology is the practical utilisation of these facts towards the better adjustment of individuals. In this way, while the aim of experimental psychology is apparently theoretical that of applied psychology is essentially and primarily practical.

**2. Difference of scope.** The scope of experimental psychology is limited to those subjects that permit of control and modification to suit the requirements of the laboratory. They must allow study under controlled circumstances. On the other hand, the field of applied psychology is much wider as it includes both subjects that can be controlled as well as subjects that do not admit of such discipline, to a greater or lesser extent. Many subjects can be examined at length within the limits of the laboratory, but then they cannot be examined in the same form in actual life. Similarly, there are certain experiments the conclusions of which do not find direct application to life, and a certain degree of ingenuity is required to benefit from them. Evidently, then though such experiments do fall within the scope of experimental psychology, they are not included in applied psychology. Reciprocally there are other subjects that are the subject matter of applied psychology, but are not such as to submit easily to experimental study and hence they evade the field of experimental psychology.

**3. Difference of viewpoint.** A description of the objectives of applied as well as experimental psychology must have made it clear that their respective viewpoints have little in common with each other. The latter is more theoretical and factual while the former is predominantly of a utilitarian and practical viewpoint.

**4. Difference in methodology.** Experimental psychology makes the greatest use of the experimental method while in the case of applied psychology the main methods are testing methods, evaluative approaches, etc.

It is evident from the preceding account of the differences and similarities between applied and experimental psychology that applied psychology is a complement to experimental psychology. As long as the facts discovered by experimental psychology are not put to practical use by applied psychology, they are incomplete and inconsequential. On the other hand, the new problems that arise in the path of applied psychology are promptly referred to experimental psychology which analyses and studies them in the safety and quiet of the laboratory.

## RELATION WITH CHILD PSYCHOLOGY

### What is Child Psychology?

One important aspect of psychology is child psychology. It makes a study of the child's development, the origination and evolution of mental processes such as feeling, perception, memory, imagination, etc., in the child. The field of this branch extends from the embryo in the womb till the child attains the age of twelve. It studies the child's development, language, mental processes, personality, intelligence, learning, etc. Psychology has proved its utility by solving the various problems that arise in the course of child's education, improvement, physical and mental health, and other aspects of his development.

**Relation between Applied and Child Psychology**

Making the best use of the principles discovered in the research carried out by child psychology towards the child's best adjustment is within the function designated to applied psychology. In other words, child psychology is proved to have utility through applied psychology. In this manner, there is a very intimate relationship between child psychology and applied psychology. One principal objective of applied psychology is attaining the individual's best adjustment in the various situations of life, keeping in mind his personal qualities, interests, capabilities, etc. Mental hygiene or cure is one major aspect of applied psychology. And in this role, applied psychology makes use of the principles discovered by child psychology in curing moron children, backward or problem children and securing for them a better adjustment towards their environment. Juvenile delinquency having proved a very serious and potent threat to social peace, all governments now provide for the psychological treatment of such individuals so that their mental defects can be removed and their criminal tendencies sublimated. And the need for a child psychologist is felt very acutely in the child's educative process since it is here that the most complex problems arise. Applied psychology is concerned with providing educational and general guidance in personal matters to children. But the scientific information required for providing this guidance is provided by child psychology which makes it a point to study children. Such childish problems as the method of education, the curriculum, improvement in children's habits and personalities, extracurricular programmes, cultural programmes, instilling discipline in the children, etc., can be solved only with the help of child psychology. Hence, applied psychology requires the assistance of child psychology in solving the child's problems of adjustment in his family, school, neighbourhood, the playground, etc. On the other hand, the very purpose of child psychology is defeated if principles discovered by it are not employed to improve children by solving their practical problems. Then while one is solving problems posed by children, other difficulties arise that require patient research and theoretical analysis at the hand of the child psychologist. In this manner, applied psychology and child psychology are mutually complementary.

**Difference between Child Psychology and Applied Psychology**

Despite such a close intimacy between child psychology and applied psychology, the note of discord is apparent in the following respects :

**1. Difference of scope.** It has been pointed out earlier in the discussion that child psychology is limited exclusively to elements related to the psychology of children. On the other hand, the scope of applied psychology is almost incomparably vast. It comprehends the study and solution of such problems as suggestion and guidance, mental health and hygiene, education, commerce and industry, personal and social problems and difficulties, selection in government and semi-government institutions, prevention of crime and legal and political problems, etc. Suggestion and guidance are not given to children alone but also to adolescents, adults and senile people. Educational problems of adolescents as well as adults are dealt with, in addition to the problems of children. Similarly, the treatment and curing of backward, moron, juvenile delinquent, and problem children are no more than a small part of mental health and hygiene. Besides these, the clinical psychologist also treats the mental diseases and personality disorders of young as well as old people.

**2. Difference of objective.** The aim of child psychology is the theoretical study of the child's development, tendencies, mental faculties, and various aspects of its psychology. Applied psychology utilizes these to solve the problems that the children pose before it. In this manner, its objective is the utilization of facts of child psychology towards the adjustment of children.

**3. Difference of viewpoint.** Evidently, the viewpoint of child psychology is theoretical and factual, while that of applied psychology is practical and utilitarian.

**4. Difference of methods.** Methods peculiar to experimental sciences, such as the observation, experimental methods, etc., are used in child psychology whereas in the case of applied psychology, the main methods are of an evaluative and tentative nature.

Although child psychology and applied psychology are independent of each other, there is an important relationship between them. As child psychology progresses, the scope of applied psychology in that direction improves. Every further experimentation on the part of applied psychology leads to a further problem which the child psychologist has to ponder over. He is further enlightened thereby, and so applied psychology. In this manner, each helps the other to progress.

## QUESTIONS FOR EXERCISE

1. Show the relationship of General and Applied Psychology.
2. How is Applied Psychology related to Experimental Psychology?
3. Describe the application of Applied Psychology to children's problems.

# PART II

# PSYCHOLOGY APPLIED TO EDUCATION

# 3

# Psychology in Education

Educational psychology is a branch of the practical aspect of psychology, in which capacity it is intimately concerned with facts of human behaviour and experience. Being a branch of practical psychology, it applies these facts of actual conditions of teaching. Hence Skinner is eminently correct when he says that educational psychology makes use, in educational conditions, of facts that are specifically concerned with the behaviour and experiences of human beings. The educational circumstance is a state of learning, or one in which the main activity that is inherent is that of learning. Hence, educational psychology is mainly concerned with finding solutions to the problem of how human beings learn. The process of learning helps the individual to develop, and this is the aim of all education. Consequently, the most important subject in educational psychology concerns the development of a balanced personality in the child. The reason why so much emphasis is laid on development in the field of educational psychology is that all other problems confronting the science are fundamentally based on various different aspects of this single aim. It is for the development of the child's personality that the teacher makes use of facts gleaned from human behaviour and experience in conditions of education. Consideration of the various problems with which educational psychology deals will make these thoughts all the more clear.

## PROBLEMS OF EDUCATIONAL PSYCHOLOGY

Of course, there can be many problems in educational psychology, but the main one are the following :

**1. Development of a balanced personality.** The main problem that engages the attention of educational psychology is the development of a balanced personality in the child. And, generally speaking, a balanced personality is one in which the intellectual, emotional, aesthetic and moral aspects are properly blended and synthesized, functioning properly. It is a common thing for the child to pick up many quirks and faults of personality in the conditions within and without the home. One of the common experiences of life is that a child develops a faulty and imperfect personality, one in which some one aspect of his being is exaggerated while another equally vital is suppressed, if the, coordination between his parents is not all that is desirable or if he belongs to an extremely poor family, or if he is a spoilt child, spoilt with exaggerated affection and love. There are many thousands of such social and even physical conditions that result in the child's avoiding the society of his equals or indulging in excessive daydreaming. Educational psychology studies the characteristics of the child's adjustment, diagnoses the basic causes leading to it and finally searches for ways and means of correcting this error.

**2. Motivation.** Often enough, the problems that are at the root of various adjustment defects are problems of motivation. Progress is always slow in the absence of any rotation. Lack of enthusiasm is a bar to effective progress. A child cannot be developed unless he is given the appropriate and adequate motivation. You may take the horse to the pond but you cannot make it drink water. In the same way, unless some motivation is awakened in the child, the teacher cannot succeed in his work. The problem of creating motivation in the child is a difficult one. It is educational psychology that attempts the solution of this problem. Observation shows that sometimes progress has been accelerated by 20 to 30 per cent by the simple expedients of praise or blame or by creating competition among the children. Problems such as selection of curriculum, choice of various activities within the process of education or learning, etc., are all problems concerned with motivation.

**3. Increase in understanding and meaning.** Another factor at the root of the motivation problem is sometimes a deficient understanding and an inability to comprehend and implications of the problems existing. It is to this end that the material chosen in teaching nowadays is such as is drawn from an environment with which the child is reasonably familiar and with which he is conversant enough not to be embarrassed by it. A simple example would be the creation of a model government within the class in order to explain the working of the actual government of the country to the students. In democratic societies the students usually understand the functioning of a democratic system in their student groups.

**4. Individual importance of heredity and environment in individual differences.** The aim of education is the development of the child. Hence, one of the important problem facing the educational psychologist is the determination of the relative importance of heredity and environment in the child's development and in causing individual difference among children. Can education change the inherited qualities? Can children reach an adequate stage of development on their inherited qualities if they are placed in a common environment? Is it possible to make a child into anything on the basis of education irrespective of his heredity? It is questions of this nature that encourage and inspire the educational psychologist to make comparative study of hereditary and environmental factors. For example, one important question is the extent to which intelligence can be developed through education regarding which educational psychologists have discovered numerous facts after much investigation.

**5. Methods for maximum progress in learning.** Fundamentally, the process of education advances with learning. The most prominent question that interests the educational psychologist in this regard is what methods of learning can most facilitate learning and achieve the maximum progress? One such question could be : is there any conflict between imitation and creation? Should education pay more attention to the collection of factual details or concentrate on creative activities? Psychology has made considerable experiments with such methods as imitation, conditioned response, trial and error and insight, and has tried to discover the conditions that are best attuned to the application of these methods, the coordination between the condition and method being productive of the best results.

**6. Education of emotions.** The proper and adequate development of personality demands the proper and complete development of emotions. An absence of such education of emotions results in many mental diseases such as indiscipline, split personality, etc.

**7. Measurement and development of intelligence and attainment.** Education develops intelligence and attainment. Educational psychologists search for and discover methods and measures where-by one can know how this development can be achieved and once it has been achieved, to know how much development in the child has taken place.

**8. Individual differences.** Practical psychology is based on the fact of individual differences. Educational psychology, a knowledge that makes practical use of psychology in the field of education, finds out why and in what respects individual beings differ from each other. These differences are so obtrusive and well-defined that the skilled teacher cannot function properly unless he can understand them. For example, the mental level of some individuals is so low that they can be taught even fundamental activities such as wearing clothes and eating only with the greatest of difficulty, while some children, precocious ones, are so intelligent and quick minded that the normal teaching and study level of the class are not enough to occupy them so that they soon tire of it. Hence, the educational psychologists attempt to discover the limits, if any, of these individual differences, and even evolve methods for their measurement in exceptional children. The modern teacher discovers these individual differences and then makes efforts to help the children progress individually.

**9. Problems relating to learning.** Many of the problems of educational psychology are concerned with learning. The main among them are :

(a) nature of the process of learning,

(b) relation between level of maturity and learning,

(c) importance of individual differences to the speed of learning and limits of learning,

(d) internal changes taking place within the process of learning,

(e) relation between the methods of teaching and the results of learning,

(f) modes of evaluating the process of learning,

(g) relative importance of the formal and informal methods of the education or learning and

(h) psychological effect of social conditions upon the learner.

**10. Practical problems.** Educational psychology is no less a practical science than it is a critical one. Hence, in it one comes across many problems that arise before the teacher when he is teaching normally. Such problems would be — (i) knowledge of the nature of every student and of the possibilities of his development, (ii) individual and social adaptation necessary for adjustment in modern culture and (iii) search for the fundamental psychological causes at the root of the processes of learning and teaching.

As educational psychology progresses, it comes face to face with newer problems. In modern democratic societies, educational psychology is engaged in adapting education to democracy. And it has the services of psychology on the one hand and many other social sciences on the other at its disposal in the solving of any problems that it comes across in such an effort. And it is on the solution of these problems that the future of democratic societies depends.

## NATURE OF EDUCATIONAL PSYCHOLOGY

Educational psychology is a normative science and as a science, like any other science, it has its objectives of forecasting and control of its subject matter. Psychology strives to discover the fundamental principles that govern the interaction between the human being and his environment. In this search psychology employs scientific methodology. And such a methodology helps to reach psychological conclusion. Psychology is a normative science. Its scope and field of operation have been constantly increasing for the last fifty years, and the use of psychology in different spheres led to the development of various branches of the science. It was the use of psychology in the field of education that led to the development of educational psychology. As it progressed, educational psychologists became alive to the fact that they were not to apply psychological principles to their field without giving them a thought but they were actually to put these principles to test their validity. Consequently, the educational psychologists developed a critical approach and attitude to general psychology. This has in its turn led to educational psychology being regarded as an independent science. The nature of educational psychology is scientific. It employs methods approved by science and on the basis of conclusions reached thereby makes tentative forecasts as to human behaviour in educational conditions. It is the research that is being carried on in the field of educational psychology that has made it possible today to make some definite and reliable forecasts concerning learning and other elements in education. In this manner educational psychology is constantly progressing towards an ever greater objectivity.

## ASPECTS OF EDUCATIONAL PSYCHOLOGY

**1. Social aspect.** The object of educational psychology is to assist the teacher in his effort to achieve comprehensive development of the child's personality. Often, and most commonly, children are adequately influenced by their social circumstances. The process of education entails a constant interaction between the teacher and the taught. The taught receives both an inspiration for study and material for study from his teacher. Working in the guise of a social engineer the teacher strives to make the child an ideal citizen in the context of modern democratic societies. If the student develops obstinacy towards the teacher, he may in time arrive at a condition where he may feel safe in disregarding and refuting the power of society and government. In the social sphere, the student is accompanied by his fellow students apart from the teacher. The social status of the family is also an important influence. But children who attend the kindergarten bring very little influence of the home with them. Fundamentally they are not socialised and the teacher has to socialise them by putting them in an adequate and proper social environment. And this socialisation is very important for the democratic nations. The child acquires his position within the group through constant trial and error and learns to work accordingly.

**2. Abnormal aspect**. As a general rule, every teacher can confidently expect to find some antisocial and anarchist children in his class. These children, for one reason or the other, have failed to adapt themselves and adjust to the social environment in which they have been placed. To effect any improvement in their mental attitude to their environment, it is essential that the teacher be in a position to understand their mental aberrations. It is here that the teacher gets some very definite assistance from abnormal psychology. In the schools at present many psychologists assist the teacher in curing the abnormalities of many children. At the same time, the teacher and the psychologist cooperate to rid the child of his feeling of inferiority, excessive daydreaming and general abnormality or unsociability.

**3. Individual aspect**. Apart from and distinctly more important than either the social or abnormal aspect is the individual aspect. Educational psychology lays great emphasis upon individual differences in education and the science has also devised methods whereby these deviations from the average can be measured and evaluated. In modern educational psychology, three kinds of psychological measures in particular have been developed — (i) intelligence, (ii) attainment and (iii) personality. The individual abnormalities of different children can be discovered by the use of these measurements and tests so that they can be taught accordingly.

**4. Genetic aspect.** Merely understanding the social, individual and abnormal aspect of a child's development is insufficient for a complete understanding of the child. For this comprehensive understanding it is necessary to supplement his personal history with his case history. This refers to the genetic aspect of educational psychology. In this practice, a careful record of the child's daily life and his progress is maintained. In this respect it differs from a life history. In clinical psychology the life history of the child is studied with a view to solving some definite problem whereas in the genetic aspect of educational psychology the progress of the child is noted in terms of hours and days. Educational psychologists have conducted many such studies.

## SCOPE OF EDUCATIONAL PSYCHOLOGY

Though educational psychology is an independent science, the limits of its field of operation have not yet been determined as the history of development extends back only forty or fifty years. Nevertheless, the subject matter of educational psychology can be studied in three different aspects — educand, process of learning and conditions of learning as under :

**1. Educand.** The term educand applies to students who individually or collectively participate in the educational programmes. These students taken collectively constitute the class. And in fact the behaviour of the class is none other than the behaviour of these students. Modern psychology gives the teacher an opportunity of improving the behaviour of students whence they can progress in the class. In order to provide proper education, the teacher should possess as much knowledge of the educand as is possible for him. For example, the teacher should be aware of the various stages of the educand's maturity since different subjects can be taught more fruitfully than others in different definite stages of maturity. The possession of such extensive knowledge makes it indispensable for the teacher to study the various aspects and stages in the child's development from birth to adulthood. In this way, while he makes psychological study of the child's progress through childhood, adolescence and adulthood, he also makes a study of the child's progress in physical, mental, emotional, moral and aesthetic aspects, and in the process makes notes of the changes that have taken place constantly in this development. The teacher should also be aware of the individual differences of the child. And for a knowledge of his individual differences the teacher must also have some knowledge of the relative influences of heredity and environment upon the developing child. And to gain this essential knowledge of individual quirks and peculiarities the modern educational psychologists makes use of many kinds of measurements and tests. Of the many kinds of tests in use in present-day psychology, the main ones are concerned with intelligence, character, personality and vocational abilities. The results of these tests form the basis of the child's education and later on his vocation regarding which he is guided. In using these methods of measurement, the data has to be tabulated, following which informative conclusions are drawn that help in teaching. This is the statistical aspect of educational psychology. Knowledge of the child's intelligence, personality and abilities is essential for the teacher. The measurement of all such factors falls within the scope of educational psychology.

**2. Process of learning.** The process of learning means the process in evidence at the time when teaching or learning is in progress. The question is what happens within the child when he is learning? All children learn something either through themselves or through the teacher's teaching. Many of the things that a child learns are often not taught in the class, neither are they comprehended under the curriculum, yet the child grasps them. The educational psychologist tries to discover exactly what occurs within the child during his learning, why the children grasp the things the teacher teaches them and even more, why or how they learn things that the teacher would prevent them from knowing. The constant effort has led the educational psychologists to the discovery of many a principle and concepts that may be of considerable value to the teacher. One of them concerns the complexity of the process of education which leads to removing the difficulty in solving its problems. Hence modern educational psychology is concerned with the psychological problem of learning various subjects, progress in learning them, evaluation of the progress, obstacles that hinder it and ways and mean of removing such obstacles.

**3. Conditions of learning.** This phrase implies the factors or conditions that influence the educand and the process of learning. Some of these factors may concern the classroom, being purely physical such as the quantity and direction of light, normal air and humidity, acoustic conditions, etc. All these apparently minor considerations influence the child's learning but the most important factor among the conditions of learning is the teacher himself. Besides these rather obvious factors, there are many other influential factors that are neither visible nor readily apparent but are none the less effective and important for all their invisibility. Of the many such conditions an important one is the attitude of the child's parents to a collective education or learning in a group. Yet such a condition is not generally apparent. If they do not hold the work of the school and education in any very high regard, then this inimical attitude may be harmful to school study. It is even more potent an influence in its effect upon the enthusiasm and interest of teacher which it may adversely affect. Although this condition does not invade the classroom and as a rule is existing only outside it, yet the teacher has to face it and battle against it within the four walls of the classroom.

Generally speaking, it is this third aspect of educational psychology that is commonly identified with education. Most of the people are in the habit of confusing education with a condition of learning within the classroom and the school in which the teacher is understood to be the creator and manipulator of the conditions of learning. It is true that of the three aspects of educational psychology described above, it is only the third that can at all adequately be controlled by the teacher, and yet it can never be regulated to quite the extent to which people normally believe it to be amenable to control. Nevertheless, by confusing education exclusively with this third aspect, people overlook the significance of the other two aspects. Such an attitude tends to make education mechanical and even to oversimplify it. It overlooks and violates the actual dynamic aspect of education in which learning is a conscious process and the educand a progressive and changeable being. While educational psychology has helped both the teacher and taught it has also acquainted the general masses with the real meaning of education so that they may contribute their little mite to the process education by helping the teacher and the students.

**Expanding Scope of Educational Psychology**

It was only in 1920 that educational psychology attained a definite form Since then its scope has been changing continually as the discovery of new concepts and new instruments in educational psychology has coincided with the introduction of new objectives of education in democratic societies. The search for possibilities of education in nursery schools has led to the opening up of new vistas in educational psychology. Similarly, a view recently voiced by educationists to the effect that children should be taught the democratic mode of life in schools has proved to be revolutionary in educational psychology. In this way, the scope and limits of educational psychology undergo continual change as it is influenced by new discoveries in the fields of psychology and other social sciences on the one hand, and the new concepts and views of educational philosophers on the other. Hence, its limits are indefinite and changeable. This led some authors and teachers to call a meeting to determine the field of educational psychology, but meetings of this nature cannot have any real value. On the other hand, as Gates and others have suggested, a meeting that makes suggestions on new needs and problems in the field of educational psychology from time to time can be of more use. When the famous psychologist Cattell, who has done work of considerable value and importance in the field of educational psychology, was asked to define psychology he enigmatically replied that psychology is what the psychologists do. On similar lines it can reasonably and equally enigmatically be commented that educational psychology is what the educational psychologists do. The researches, experiments, studies and similar activities of educational psychologists determine the scope of educational psychology. As these change, the scope of the subject also widens. Finally, it must also be kept in mind that educational psychology is definitely a developing science. Educational psychology concerns itself with new and every new research as new problems appear in education and new concepts come to light in the theory of education, with the result that there is no saying what form the science will have after ten years and hence what will its scope be.

## QUESTIONS FOR EXERCISE

1. "Educational Psychology utilises those findings that deal specifically with the experiences and behaviour of human beings in educational situations" (Skinner).

   Evaluate this statement and discuss the main problems with which Educational Psychology is concerned.
2. Discuss the nature and aspects of Educational Psychology.
3. Define the scope of Educational Psychology and show how this science affects educational practice.

# 4

# Individual Differences

## MEANING OF INDIVIDUAL DIFFERENCES

In education, even from the most ancient times, students have been differentiated on the basis of age as difference in age levels entitles the children to differing levels of education. As the child's age gradually increases, the subject of his education can be made more complex and difficult. In addition to differences in age, another factor that was partly taken into consideration was the differences in levels of intelligence. Besides this, educational attainments were also considered to be important. In this manner, during the ancient and the medieval periods, individual difference was believed to be the capacity of attaining skill in a particular subject. In modern schools, other kinds of skills and abilities, and peculiarities of personality in individuals are also taken into consideration. According to Skinner, "Today we think of individual differences as including any measurable aspect of the total personality." From this definition of individual differences it is evident that it comprehends every aspect of the human personality, albeit all aspects that are in some manner measurable. Aspects of this nature can be many such as variability, conformity, difference in the rate of learning and development, relationship between the various characteristics of the personality, etc. In this manner, various individuals exhibit differences of physical and mental development, nature, rate of learning, ability, specific abilities, interest and personality, etc.

## TYPES OF INDIVIDUAL DIFFERENCES

**1. Average intelligence.** The following brief description may serve to make individual differences a simple concept that can easily be grasped. Individuals are seen differing in considerable measure in respect of their quotient of below 50 to schools. Children with a higher intelligence quotient go to school. Children with intelligence quotients between 50 and 70 can learn only the simplest tasks. Even the small schools trouble children whose intelligence quotient varies between 70 and 80. Children between 75 and 90 I.Q. are considered morons, and they have considerable difficulty in progressing, along with the other children, in their learning. Generally, 40 to 60 percent of the children in school have I.Qs. varying between 95 and 105, being the children with average intelligence who form the basis for the formulation of the syllabus and curriculum as well as the method of teaching. Children who are either above or below this level of intelligence require special educational methods and conditions. Children with intelligence quotients varying between 115 and 120 are considered brilliant or intelligent. The following facts have come to light concerning individual differences of intelligence in children :

(a) However good and beneficial the environment and the method of education, the moron invariably reaches his highest level of learning before the average or the intelligent child.

(b) In favourable circumstances the average child generally gives a good account of himself in his academic pursuits.

(c) If the circumstances are favourable, the intelligent child shows great alacrity in the process of learning.

(d) Adverse circumstances have the worse effect on all children, and their learning activities are hindered.

**2. Special abilities.** During the junior and senior high school as well as the college stage, the individual differences in respect of special abilities, in addition to the general intelligence, are also important since special professions and specialised fields of vocation all need certain specific abilities. Abilities of this kind are concerned with mental, artistic, personality or motor ability.

**3. Differences of background.** In school, the differences that the children exhibit are the outcome of their different families and their communities. Attitudes towards education and authority differ in each family, culture and class. Some of these attitudes are favourable while others are unfavourable to education. In either condition, the difference of attitudes results in differences among children. Besides these attitudes, the child's emotional, social, aesthetic and moral development is influenced by his family and the neighbourhood. Hence, differences of background are also manifest in individual differences.

**4. Alacrity in learning.** Difference in the quickness or alacrity in learning is visible not only in children of different ages but also among children in the same age group. This difference is dependent upon their maturity and educational background. Differences in the alacrity of learning result in benefits accruing from formal education.

**5. Mental age.** Children of differing ages as well as children of the same age show differences in their respective mental ages. Generally speaking, all students studying in the same class differ according to their mental ages. It has been observed that at the age of 6, differences in mental age range up to 5 years. Mental age and education are intimately related. The child's level of education is determined according to his mental age.

**6. Motor ability.** The individual's movements of the hand and feet and other physical abilities are seen to be very individual, as they do not resemble another's to any great extent. Till the individual attains adulthood, his manual dexterity, rate of muscular movement and resistance to fatigue develop continually. In this manner, the same individual in different age groups manifests considerable differences in manual dexterity.

**7. Sex differences.** Makneimer and Terman discovered the following differences between men and women, on the basis of some studies :

(a) Women have greater skill in memory while men have greater motor ability.

(b) Female handwriting is superior while men excel in mathematical logic.

(c) Women show greater skill making sensory distinctions of taste, touch, smell, etc., while men show greater reaction and consciousness of size-weight illusion.

(d) Possessing greater linguistic ability women are superior to men in languages, similitudes, work building, compositions and use of long sentences, etc. On the other hand, men are superior in physics and chemistry.

(e) Women are better than men in mirror drawing. Faults of speech, etc., in men were found to be three times of such faults in women.

(f) Women are more susceptible to suggestion while there are three times as many colour-blind men as there are women.

(g) Young girls take interest in stories of love, fairy-tales, stories of the school and home and day-dreaming, and show various levels in their play. On the other, boys take interest in stories of bravery, science, war and scouting, stories of games and sports, occupation and skill.

**8. Racial difference.** Many scientific studies have indicated the presence of various kinds of differences between individuals of different races, although differences of environment are a normal factor in causing these differences. Karl Brigham has composed a list on the basis of differences in levels of intelligence among people who have migrated to United States from other countries.

**9. Nationality.** Many studies have led to the conclusion that individuals of different nations differ in respect of nature, physical and mental differences, interest and personality, etc. Such a difference is only natural since their cultural and geographic environment is distinctive.

**10. Economic situation.** Economic differences are seen causing differences in the children's interests, tendencies, character, etc.

**11. Differences relating to learning.** In respect of learning, children manifest such differences as past experience and learning, ability in the use of various kinds of apparatus, rate of learning, interest in learning, etc.

**12. Difference in respect of development.** Difference in development is in evidence not only in individuals of different age groups but also between individuals of the same age.

**13. Difference of interests.** As has been pointed out, the difference in sex leads to a difference in interests. Similarly, factors such as family background, level of development, differences of nationality and race, etc., cause difference of interests.

**14. Personality.** Differences in respect of personality have led psychologists to much study, and on the basis of this study individuals have been classified into many groups. Jung, for example, has divided individuals into three groups — (a) Introvert, (b) Extrovert and (c) Ambivert. This is the psychological classification of people. Stephenson has divided human beings into two categories — preserver and non-preserver. In this division, people of the first group are very sensitive and susceptible to experience while people of the second group are not influenced by it to quite that extent. Cattell has put people into the Surgent and the Surgeless or Non-surgent classes. The former is similar to Jung's extrovert while the surgeless resembles his introvert individual. Terman has put people into nine classes according to their level of intelligence — (a) Genius, (b) Near-genius, (c) Very superior intelligence, (d) Superior, (e) Average, (f) Backward, (g) Feeble-minded, (h) Dull and (i) Idiot.

Thorndike has divided people into four categories on the basis of thinking — (a) Abstract thinkers, (b) Ideational thinkers, (c) Object thinkers and (d) Thinkers in whom sensory experience is predominant. These names indicate the peculiarities of thinking in these individuals.

From the viewpoint of nature, personality has been divided into three classes — (a) Thought dominant, (b) Emotion dominant and (c) Action dominant.

Concerning these classifications of the human personality, it should be remembered that although one specific person may exhibit the main broad characteristics of one class of personality, he cannot be said to belong to only that class of personality as the differences between various personalities are so subtle and minute that it is not scientifically feasible to divide them into classes.

### Teacher's Advantage in Knowing Individual Differences

One object of modern education is the complete development of the child. In this connection, the teacher has the following advantages to derive from a knowledge of individual differences :

1. This can help him to form the proper attitude towards the brilliant and the dull-witted students. It is only too evident that very good results cannot be expected from dull-witted or mediocre students.

2. Any effort to bring all or a majority of the students in the class to the same level is futile since 50 or odd percentage of them will invariably be below this level.

3. Improvements in atmosphere, method of teaching, and the apparatus of education cannot lead to the satisfactory teaching of all students since their individual ability to learn differs widely.

4. Knowing the presence of individual differences, the teacher is not perturbed at the failure of some of his students since such failures are only to be expected from below-average students.

5. The teacher does not come to expect successes that are impossible. Individual difference makes it clear that all aspects of the personality are mutually related and to develop any one aspect it is essential that all the aspects be developed.

## INDIVIDUAL DIFFERENCES AND EDUCATION

From the above account of the benefits that a teacher can derive from a knowledge of individual difference it is evident that he can make use of it in education and teaching. The main features in this connection are the following :

**1. Curriculum.** In school, the curriculum should be modified to suit the needs of the dull-witted children. Failure to achieve this adversely affects the development of all the three kinds of children. Whereas the backward students start playing truant from school, the brilliant children find the studies inadequate and turn their intellect to more perverse uses.

**2. Limited size of the class.** Keeping in mind the individual differences of the students, it is advisable that if they are to be taught properly a class should not include more than 20 students. With 50 or more students it is impossible to teach them keeping in mind their specific requirements.

**3. Method of education.** It is never advisable or efficacious to use the same method of education in the case of all children. It should be varied to suit and conform to their individual differences and mental requirements.

**4. Educational guidance.** Knowing the personal differences between his students, the teacher can render them signal service by guiding them in their educational career. It is the teacher who can tell them the subjects they must choose to pursue in their higher studies if they are not to do violence to their natures.

**5. Vocational guidance.** Different professions require some specific physical, mental and personality qualities of the individual. Hence, knowing their peculiar mental make up and their tendencies, the teacher can guide the students in the vocation that they should adopt.

**6. Contribution of school, family and community in education.** Knowledge of individual differences among children determines that education in school is not sufficient since many differences are due to the family and the community. Hence, according to modern educational psychologists, to attain the objective of complete development of individuals, prescribed by modern education, the cooperation of school, family, community and religious institutions is sought.

**7. Individual training.** Having knowledge of individual differences, now many methods of individual training have been devised. In America the Dalton plan, project method, Winnetka method, contract plan and activity programme methods have been devised for individual training. A brief resume of the various methods is given below :

(a) ***Dalton plan :*** In this, children are not taught in classrooms. They are given subjects that suit their interests and they are given a project that covers a period of 15 days to a month. Such treatment leads to the development of naturality, independence, cooperation, sociability, etc.

(b) ***Project method :*** In this the children are required to do work of every day requirements, such as cooking, stitching, furniture making, etc. And in the process of this work, they are taught novel things.

(c) ***Winnetka plan :*** In this method, the student on his own tries to attain a certain definite objective and the teacher offers very little assistance. Later on, through some tests, the extent to which the student has attained his goal is discovered.

(d) ***Contract plan :*** In this, similar to the Dalton method, the subjects of study are determined and similar to the Winnetka method, the student's progress is measured through tests. In this manner it is a synthesis of the Dalton and Winnetka methods.

(e) ***Activity programme :*** In this method, keeping in mind the interests and requirements of the students, activities are prescribed in order to define the curriculum. These activities are based on democratic principles. This helps to develop democratic notions in the children.

It is evident from the foregoing description that modern education makes proper arrangements for a child's education, keeping in view his peculiar nature and special abilities. In a democratic society every individual has the right to achieve a definite level of development. Hence, even more essential is it that individual difference be kept in mind while educating people of democratic countries.

Two facts emerge when human development is studied. One, that the development of separate individuals exhibits certain similarities. Two, that different individuals show differences from the biological and social viewpoint. Generally speaking, these differences are quantitative rather than qualitative. In other words, the same traits are to be found in most individuals but it is the quality or intensity of these traits that differs in these individuals. And this difference leads to considerable difference in the education of different individuals. Hence, the teacher should keep in mind the differences between various boys and girls and he should make the necessary arrangements so that everyone be educated properly.

## CAUSES OF INDIVIDUAL DIFFERENCES

It is not even within the bonds of possibility to describe all the causes of individual differences in children, yet the main ones are the following :

**1. Age.** It is a matter of common knowledge that age creates differences of intelligence, abilities, physical capacity, maturity, etc., in different children.

**2. Physical development.** Differences in height, weight, physical structure, and the state and quality of development of the various parts of the body lead to differences between individuals.

**3. Heredity.** It has now been established that heredity differences result in the quantity and rate of physical as well as mental development being different in different individuals. Many physical as well as mental diseases are the result of heredity in persons. According to many scientists, a person inherits many mental peculiarities from his parents.

**4. Environment or atmosphere.** Modern psychologists do not believe heredity to be the only cause of individual differences. Personality is the outcome of mutual intersection between heredity and environment. Hence, the influence of environment on individual differences is no less than the influence of heredity. Gradual changes in a child's environment can be seen reflected in the changes in his personality. An individual exhibits good and bad qualities as accruing from a good or bad environment. Generally speaking, environment comprehends family, school, neighbourhood, society and culture. The child is open to a very wide range of influences such as the social and economic level, standard of living, education, profession of parents, their mutual relationships, their relations with their children, their attitudes and personalities, nature of other people's character, personality and attitudes, etc.

**5. Effect of race and nation.** Although modern psychologists believe that race does not lead to differences in the mental structure of individuals, yet it cannot be denied that individuals of different races exhibit very pronounced differences, even though it may be induced by the environment. Similarly, individuals of different nations show differences in respect of their personality, character, and mental abilities. These are the outcome of their geographical, social and cultural environment. Many scientific tests have established the existence of differences between Eastern and Western, Negro and American, Chinese and Japanese, English and Indian individuals.

**6. Sex differences.** Although modern psychologists are not prepared to accept sex differences as the basis of differentiation between boys and girls, yet sex does lead to differences between individuals, even though the family, social and cultural environment may play a major part in it. Development of boys and girls exhibits difference due to difference in sex.

**7. Intelligence and mental age.** Many studies have indicated that many individuals differ because the difference of intelligence and mental ages, and environment cannot be accepted to account for majority of such differences. Individuals who are well below the average in intelligence and mental age find much difficulty in learning and acquiring some training that the average intelligent person can pick up easily.

**8. Emotional stability.** Due to many physical, mental and environmental factors, the emotional stability of individuals is differently affected, and this leads to differences in their respective nature.

**9. Temperament.** Medicine men, and in particular Indians believe that individuals have different temperaments. Some people are by temperament quick and short-tempered, while others are serious, some active and others inactive.

**10. Difference relating to learning.** Individuals differ from each other because of their attitude to learning, their zeal, rate of progress, transfer of training, etc.

## QUESTION FOR EXERCISE

1. What do you understand by individual differences? How can their knowledge help the teacher in his work?

# 5

# Education of Problem, Backward and Gifted Children

## PROBLEM CHILDREN

In the words of Valentine, "Problem children is generally used to describe children whose behaviour or personality in something is seriously abnormal". In this manner the class of problem children includes all those juveniles whose character or personality shows some signs of abnormality. Some behavioural abnormalities that seem to indicate this condition are — stealing, lying, annoying children weaker and younger than themselves, not doing home assignments, running away from school, or arriving late at school. They can also be called defects or abnormalities concerning character or personality because conduct of this nature indicates shortcomings in both personality as well as character.

### Causes of Problematic Behaviour

Problematic behaviour can have two kinds of causes — (l) hereditary and (2) environmental. Hereditary causes include physical, emotional or nervous defects, but sometimes these may also be the result of weakness. The environmental factors are the following :

**1. Atmosphere of home.** One major cause of problematic behaviour is the contaminated behaviour that exists in many homes. A large majority of problem children come from broken families of divorced persons. In a study conducted by Bannister and Rooder it became known that 66 per cent of the children come from homes that have an improper atmosphere. Certain other studies traced abnormal behaviour to such diverse cases as poverty, lack of recreation, absence of care, almost complete absence of affection and love, cruel behaviour of step-mothers or other relatives, too much cinema seeing, etc. Where the entire family is compelled to live in a small house with only two rooms, the child may have occasion to see his parents behaving towards each other in a manner the witnessing of which has the worst influence upon his undeveloped mind and leads him to forming bad sexual habits. Signs of problematic behaviour are also generated in children who come from homes the atmosphere in which is either strictly disciplinarian or completely lax and uninhibited.

**2. Bad company.** Besides the family, another agency that plays an important role in developing signs of abnormal behaviour in the child is his companionship. Falling into bad company the best of children learn stealing, smoking, physical outrage, cruelty or sex habits of a bad nature.

**3. Atmosphere in school.** Another important case of problematic behaviour is the defective and contaminated atmosphere of the school. It is only natural for children to show signs of abnormal behaviour when they are compelled to study in schools in which the teachers present improper and immoral ideals before them, the method of teaching is disgusting or uninteresting, and where there is absence of wholesome recreation, etc.

### Cure of Problem Children

Hence, the cure of problematic children demands the removal of all objectionable elements from the atmosphere at home and in college as well as from the child's company. The main facts to be noted in this connection are the following :

(a) **Measures concerning the family.** Valentine has made the following suggestions concerning the administration of discipline in the family :

1. Discipline should not take the form of pressure or fear but should aim at ultimate self control in the child.
2. Level of conduct should not be too high.
3. The behaviour of parents should be benevolent, and there should be every possible co-operation between the home and school.

4. Discipline and rules should be relative.
5. The child should never be allowed to feel that he is not loved by anyone.

Following these suggestions it will be possible to improve the atmosphere in the family. Residence of families should normally be as far as possible from prostitution houses, gambling dens and factories, etc. Children should not be allowed to view very inflammatory or highly sexually arousing films. Parents should be affectionate and understanding in their behaviour, as the child's behaviour, character and personality depend upon these corresponding elements in themselves. Thus, they must present the best ideals to the children, and if the child develops any undesirable symptoms it should be dealt with psychologically rather than having recourse to physical punishment.

(b) **Good company.** The company that a student keeps outside the house, in the college or in the neighbourhood should be carefully studied and kept in mind. If he has had the misfortune of falling into had company, tactful methods should be employed to wean him of it and introduce him into better circle of friends. It is equally improper and unjustified to give the child too much pocket money or to give him none at all. There should be adequate arrangement for his recreation.

(c) **Methods adopted by school.** Schools can adopt the following measures for the prevention or cure of problematic behaviour in their students :

1. ***Presentation of high ideals by teachers*** : In the school the teacher is no less than an ideal to the student or child, hence it is essential that the teacher's character, personality and conduct should be of the highest order and exemplary so that the best ideals become personified in him.

2. ***Interesting method of education*** : If the method of education or teaching be not interesting, the children run away from school and fall into very bad habits. If they are taught by more interesting methods they will be interested and thereby prevented or protected from many ill-usages.

3. ***Proper use of educational apparatus*** : In schools through the medium of libraries and reading rooms, children and

students should get healthy literatures so that their thinking may take on a healthy hue and proper form.

4. ***Balanced curriculum :*** The curriculum in various classes for students should be so designed as not to strain the student too much, but at the same time provide him with a variety of knowledge.

5. ***Arrangement of extracurricular programmes :*** Where the question of preventing problematic behaviour in children is concerned, much more can be gained by extracurricular activities such as picnics, touring camps, scouting, community, singing and dancing and debate, etc. than can be achieved through the formal curriculum.

6. ***Means of healthy recreation :*** If the child is to be persuaded to avoid any unhealthy means of entertainment, it is necessary that various kinds of games and means of recreation be available to him so that he can enjoy himself without injuring his development.

7. ***Self-discipline :*** Discipline in the college should not be foisted upon the student but should take the form of autonomous or self-discipline. This will help to increase a sense of responsibility without being a burden upon them.

8. ***Harmony between family and school :*** In order to prevent or to cure problematic behaviour in the child, it is essential that the teacher and parents should jointly endeavour to achieve it. Hence, family and school should be harmonised.

9. ***Guidance :*** Children are often faced with problems the solution of which is beyond their own ability, and this results in difficulty that manifests itself in the form of symptoms of problematic behaviour. Hence, the school should provide for individual, educational as well as vocational guidance.

## BACKWARD CHILDREN

### Who can be called a Backward Child?

Generally speaking, no mother or father is easily prepared to accept that their child is mentally backward. But modern intelligence test techniques have indubitably established that some children are mentally backward. A backward child is more in need of assistance than one with average or above average intelligence, hence in modern schools, teachers are expected to pay particular attention to the weak students in their classes. A backward child, evidently, is one who has an intelligence quotient lower than the average child. In the words of Cyril Burt, "A backward child is one, who, in the middle of the school career, is unable to do the work of the class below that which is normal for his age." In this way, the backward child falls far behind other children of his age in matters of study. In school, such children remain in the same class for many years, and fail to progress upward. Educational psychologists have no single opinion on the intelligence quotient below which a child can definitely be called backward. Yet, generally, psychologists classify those children as backward whose intelligence quotient falls below 85.

**Problems of Backward Children**

Children who are backward have certain problems that are peculiarly their own. Having a very low intelligence quotient, they require to be taught many things by others. A backward child cannot lead; he is more in a position to need the help and sympathy of friends and relatives. A child who is very feeble-minded, having an intelligence quotient of 70 or less, cannot obtain education in the ordinary schools, and has to be sent to special institutions. Emotional adjustment of the child is completely disintegrated if he fails in the same class time after time. In a class, teaching approximates to be average level of students. Hence, it is only natural for the backward child to meet with failure in life. His ambitions are thwarted, and he becomes hopeless.

Backward child also faces difficulties in social adjustment. In the group he does not easily grasp even the smallest thing, and rules of play have to be repeated for his benefit. His colleagues naturally heckle him. It is possible that a spark of leadership may be ignited in him if he communicates with youngers than himself but on the same intelligence level. But there he is unwelcome since other children steer clear of him because of his physical superiority. Adults pay him little or no attention; instead he is sculled from time to time. In adolescence and adulthood, too, the situation of this child does not improve. He is made the butt of every joke. Activities of the group are usually on a higher level, so that he does not fit in them either.

## Causes of Backwardness

It is not even possible to recount all the various causes of backwardness, but the main causes are the following :

**1. Physical causes.** Due to many physical defects and abnormalities, the child lags behind other average children. Such physical conditions would be weakness of the eyes, deafness or being hard of hearing, stuttering, being weak or crippled, etc. This also has an adverse effect upon his social adjustment.

**2. Mental defects.** It has been indicated earlier that the backward child has a very low intelligence quotient, as compared with that of an average child. Having a low intelligence his other mental characteristics and abilities also do not compare favourably with the average child.

**3. Educational immaturity.** Physical and metal shortcomings in the child result in educational maturity. Putting it differently, he has not adequate maturity to grasp the teaching that is customary for his age level.

**4. Emotional factors.** The child's social adjustment is marred by his mental and physical abnormalities, and he meets with successive failures. He meets with criticism on every account. Here, it is natural for him to manifest anxiety, tension, depression and other emotional factors. Sometimes, though every other defect is absent, the child is backward in his class for no better reason than these psychological or emotional factors.

**5. Atmosphere in the home.** One reason of backwardness is the atmosphere in the home. Proper development of the child cannot occur in a virulent family atmosphere. Hence, he falls behind children of his age group. And among the factors that contribute to the defective atmosphere in the home are constant quarrelling and fighting between parents and children, unbalanced diet, strict discipline, absence of all peace and calm, poverty, etc.

**6. Lack of interest.** Sometimes, even though the child is free from all the defects and shortcomings mentioned above and even those that have not been mentioned, he falls behind the rest of the class for the simple reason that he cannot stir any interest in the various subjects being taught. This causes repeated failure.

**7. Factors concerning the school.** The school can be a veritable storehouse of factors that inhibit the child's development such as inadequate method of teaching, uneducated teacher, undesirable atmosphere, inadequate curriculum, defective time tide, disgusting relations between students and teachers, etc. All these causes conspire to make even the average child look backward.

### Selection of Backward Children

Modern schools are led to believe that the backward children in a class should be specially attended to. Hence the teacher must know how to distinguish and identity a backward child. This can be done in four steps :

**1. Discovering the child's A.Q.** Test in arithmetic, language and general knowledge can be used for discovering the child's A.Q.

**2. Discovering I.Q.** Selecting children with an intelligence quotient of bestow 85, their exact I.Q. should then be calculated.

**3. Individual intelligence test.** Now the result obtained from the group intelligence tests should be examined for their reliability by obtaining results through individual intelligence tests and coinciding the two conclusions.

**4. Rating by teacher.** Following this, rating by teachers should be sought concerning children who appear to be backward so that the results of tests are confirmed by educated insight.

**5. Case history.** After all the above tests have been completed, the child's detailed life history should be prepared.

### Solution of the Problem of Backwardness

Most of the so-called backward children can be improved. In the case of children with intelligence quotient below 70, no improvement is possible through education in the ordinary schools since they need to be sent to specialised schools and institutions. In children with intelligence quotients between 70 and 85, considerable improvement is possible even in the regular educational institutions. Many of these children can be raised to the level of average normality through many cures so that they can find success in school and later life. If they are given some encouragement and are shown some success, they learn many simple activities. But this requires modification of the curriculum, the teacher's method of teaching, and conduct. For children with intelligence quotients between 70 to 85, separate educational establishments are not essential as they require only special attention and periodical expert examination. But with children of intelligence quotients bestow 70, separate arrangements are unavoidable.

**1. Curriculum.** Often many children fail repeatedly in the same class for the simple reason that the curriculum does not suit them. Consequently, the teacher must modify his curriculum to meet the requirements of backward children so that it contains only those subjects that have some utility for them, excluding all subtle subjects. The entire curriculum should be so fashioned that when the backward child completes his course, he should be able to adopt some particular profession. Basic education should be emphasized in the curriculum. Children can also be trained for some specific professions and vocations.

**2. Method of teaching.** The sole quality of a teaching method is that the student should grasp what it has to teach. Hence, there should be different methods of teaching for students on different levels. It is evident that backward children will not gain much if they are taught by a method that is found suitable for average children. For them, there should be a special method of teaching, with the following :

(a) Rate of teaching should be slow.

(b) Lesson should be repeated more than once.

## DEFECTS AND ABNORMALITIES

Children can have both defects and abnormalities. The general system of education is devised for the average and normally healthy children, as a result of which it cannot incorporate the development of abnormal children since they need special arrangements. One has to speak louder than when one is speaking to a normal person if one wants to communicate with a deaf individual. A modern teacher is concerned not only with the development of a majority of average children, but also with the development of brilliant, backward, defective and abnormal children. Hence the system of education should also provide for such individuals. Unfortunately, many circumstances conspire to make provision of such facilities impossible in all schools. Nevertheless, the teacher should definitely be aware of the defects and abnormalities that mar the development of a child, or arise during its progress. Hence, these defects will be divided into various categories concerning physical, mental, character, etc.

**Physical Defects and Abnormalities**

Almost any and every organ of the body can be deformed through defects, and it is not possible to list all such defects. Secondly, all of them do not have any effect on education. Thus, the physical defects and abnormalities that are to be treated of here, are specifically those that are particularly important from the point of view of educational process.

**1. Defects of the head.** Of all parts of the body, the head is most important since it houses the brain. Hence, removing defects of the head is the most important thing. Common defects of the head are the presence of leeches, skin eruptions, pus, etc., that are mainly caused through the head being left unclean. A child cannot himself keep his head clean. Parents should keep an eye on its cleanliness. One definite measure that must be taken very regularly is that it should be cleared with soap or other cleaning ingredient, and another is its regular massage with oil, and proper hair combing. It is always advisable for young students to keep hair short and trimmed. This both avoids putting much weight on the head and also makes for easier cleaning and maintenance. Oils that are used for lubricating the head should be those that have a good effect on the head and brain. Application of the oil itself should not involve mere smearing of it on the head but be more of the nature of a massage. There are a variety of oils available for the purpose, but only the best should invariably be preferred. If the child develops some disease of the skin on the head or acquires leeches, his head should be shaved clean following which he should be submitted to expert medical advice and care. The teacher should invite dirty children's parents to school, and point out the desirability of cleanliness and personal hygiene.

**2. Defects of the eye.** Another organ of the body that has considerable importance from the educational viewpoint is the eye. It, too, is another organ that is prone to many defects in the case of children. Some defects are innate, and even hereditary, but many others are the result of excessive strain on the eye.

Schools should provide facilities for regular periodical checks of the children's eyes so that it should be possible to know of a defect as soon as possible. Besides making arrangements for having any such defects cured, the teacher should also advise the student as to the proper mode of eye care. Power of the eyes can be maintained and increased through such expedients as splashing cold water on the eyes, standing facing the sun early in the morning with closed eyes, palming, deep breathing, consuming almonds, white pepper, etc., and other things that increase the power of the brain. Students should never be careless on this score since it is on this that their entire future is based.

**3. Defects of the ear.** After defects of the eye, come the defects of the ear that are no less harmful. Some children are born deaf, with the result that they also remain dumb since language cannot be learned without hearing. Being deaf, they cannot profit by studying in the normal kinds of schools. Special schools have now been provided for the education of such handicapped children where the deaf can learn many things that the normal people know. Consequently, they are also in a position to achieve a good status in society. Another defect that afflicts the ear is a difficulty to hear low sound. Their problem resembles the problems of the deaf to some extent. But in their case this shortcoming can either be cured or made less obnoxious through the use of some mechanical devices. Social adjustment is a problem for deaf children and for those who are hard of hearing. Teachers and other well-wishers must devote some of their attention to these problems. It usually happens that in large classes, teachers, have no way of knowing the various physical ailments that are affecting their students. Hence, it is for them to examine their students from time to time through tests, and to advise their guardians of their condition periodically. It is as necessary to cure defects of the ear as it is to provide for their general care. Living continuously in an area that is very noisy may lead to serious additional consequences since such conditions can cause deafness. There have been definite cases of traffic policemen in big cities going deaf through being constantly in the centre of extreme noise. When the ear accumulates dirt, most people are in the habit of cleaning it with some sharp-edged instrument, a practice that is most deprecate as it endangers the ear drum. If there is dirt within the ear, then it should be removed in such a manner that it does not endanger ear drum. Itching in the ear can be cured or at least relieved by putting lukewarm castor oil or oil of neem in it. And even otherwise, if some oil is put in the ear from time to time, it prevents extreme dryness of the ear. Too much dirt or any disease of the ear is a condition that only expert physician or ear specialist can treat. Considerable damage can result in such cases even from the least evidence of carelessness. Students who are hard of hearing should be given place in front of the class so that they may not miss too much of what the teacher says.

**4. Defects of the teeth**. Dental care is as important as the care of any other part of the body. Usually, parents pay little attention to the care of the children's teeth. Carelessness can lead to serious diseases such as pyorrhea, that can lead to serious general complications apart from irreparably damaging the teeth. This happens as food reaches the stomach through the teeth. It is for the teachers to arrange for periodical checking of childern's teeth, and for instructing them and their careless parents in the care of teeth. Cleanliness of teeth can be achieved through very regular brushing with some good dental cream or delicate branches of the neem tree. Wherever something is eaten, it should be followed by a careful gargling of the mouth so that all residue that is embedded in the teeth is eliminated. Decay of teeth often results from children drinking sweetened milk at night immediately before going to sleep since they do not then wash their mouths. Even if every meal is not succeeded by brushing of the teeth, they can be cursorily cleaned by carefully running a finger over them and removing any matter that sticks between the teeth.

**5. Defects of speech**. Some children are afflicted by defects of speech, such as stumbling over words, mispronunciation, etc. Many of these defects can be got rid of through the simple expedient of regular practice. Demosthenes, a famous speaker of Greece, stuttered from birth. He made a habit of going to the seashore and speaking with pebbles in his mouth, a habit that finally cured him of the trouble after he had persisted with it for a long time. Children who falter and stutter are usually teased and laughed at by other children with the result that their social adjustment is considerably hindered. The child himself develops many undesirable attitudes. Presence of such defects makes it imperative that the advice of a good physician be sought in order to remove them. Sometimes a condition of stuttering is actually induced by parents who first imitate children because the child's faltering tongue is pleasant to listen to. And, they often try to remind children of the manner in which they used to speak. In fact, even when the child pronounces incorrectly, parents should encourage them patiently to speak correctly so that the wrong pronunciations should not become a habit. Defects of speech can be more easily corrected in childhood than at a later stage. Yet, it is not quite right to plunge the child into complexities very early, since such a method can affect the emotional development adversely. A child's pronunciation depends to a considerable extent upon the pronunciation of other family members. Hence, teachers and parents should take care to pronounce words correctly when speaking in the presence of children. If the child persists in stuttering and faltering, he should be sympathetically assisted rather than criticised or looked down upon. In this respect, family members are particularly responsible.

**6. Defects of the nose.** Concerning children, parents should remember that cleaning of the nose is also important. Lack of proper care can lead to serious complications and consequences. A child himself cannot keep his nose properly clean, so that all responsibility of his hygiene is upon his parents. As soon as any disease of the nose such as difficulty in breathing is discovered, the child should be submitted to the care of an expert.

**7. Extreme delicacy of the body.** Another defect of the body is its extreme delicacy or weakness. A weak child finds social adjustment difficult since other children take advantage of his capacity and bother him. General weakness of the child's body can normally be alleviated through proper food and exercise. Hence, parents should see to it that other children do not worry their weak friends, and at the same time to do their best to improve the general health and debility of the children.

**8. Crippled children.** Some children become crippled either through some accident or even in pregnancy. Some children experience difficulty in social adjustment and adaptation since other children are prone to make fun of the cripple. Some parents develop a habit of mentioning the child's crippled condition in front of him, and showing their disgust at it. This has the worst possible effect upon the child's mind. In fact, children of this kind should be treated with more love and care than normal children, though it should be remembered that he should not be reduced to complete helplessness and dependence where he can do nothing on his own, but needs the assistance of his parents. Sensible parents can help in the adjustment of their children. Becoming crippled, the child's education should not be reduced in any measure as adequate and proper education can lead even cripples to considerable achievement and progress.

**9. Other physical defects.** In order to preserve the children from normal defects, teachers should train them to walk, sit, read, write, etc., in the correct manner. Many physical defects can result if the child forms a habit of walking crookedly, sitting in a doubled up position, or reading in a reclined position. Eyes can be adversely affected if the child develops a habit of reading with the book either too close or too far from the eyes. Furniture in the classroom should be comfortable and well-designed. Teachers should interrupt the students to point out defects and faults in their posture, their manner of reading, the angle of light, etc. Girls who do not know the way of carrying themselves gracefully, unwittingly deprive themselves of much of their natural charm and poise. The truth of the matter is that the right sort of carriage hides many defects while it brings into prominence all the good qualities of the individual.

### Mental Defects and Abnormalities

Besides the physical defects and abnormalities, one also finds mental shortcomings and abnormalities in children. For example, some children have very low intelligence quotient while those with below 70 are regarded as mentally retarded. On the other hand, some children show abnormal intelligence quotients, while those with scores of 130 and above are considered abnormal and gifted. Besides these aberrations, mental complexes, inferiority complexes, and superiority complexes are among the more normally found conditions of the mind in children, although their being found commonly does not reduce the ill-effects that they have upon the personality. Some children are also subject to epileptic and other kinds of fits. Fainting fits also are not quite unknown. Some children are oversexed in that the sexual urge is very intense in them. Other children give evidence of neuroses and psychoses. Such mental diseases can only be cured under expert medical advice and care. Sometimes, manifestations of mental diseases are misinterpreted as extreme obstinacy in the child, for which he is severely castigated and punished by the parents and even teachers. This does not cure the child, but rather further precipitates the conditions of illness. If the child is to be protected from emotional complexes, it is essential that he be treated with sympathy, love and understanding, with a little bit of common sense being thrown in for good measure. His problems be understood and he should be assisted in his efforts to overcome them. Every school curriculum should make the proper provision for education of backward as well as exceptionally intelligent children. Extracurricular programmes should also be adequately modified to suit the need of children.

### Defects and Abnormalities of Character

Children exhibit defects and abnormalities concerning character, in addition to defects and complications in the physical and mental aspects of their being. Development of child's character is an essential part of the educative process. Character is evident in conduct, and conduct is formed of habits that are acquired in childhood. Hence, proper care and attention to the child can save him from forming harmful habits that become permanent in the form of character elements. Faults of character usually have their origin in sex motivated activity. And in this, much of the responsibility can be placed squarely upon the shoulders of teachers and parents. Actually speaking, it is the parents, and not the children who are to be blamed for these bad habits since it is for them to satisfy the child's curiosity on all fronts, to explain everything to him sympathetically rather than beating him to develop an affectionate atmosphere in the home so that a healthy development of the child's character is almost ensured. Once the presence of some criminal streak in the child's character is discovered, it can be eliminated through some illuminated and sensible manoeuvring. Once the sense of self regard is developed in a child, his character then usually progresses in the right and desired direction.

## STEALING

Some children start on a career of crime by stealing when they are only 5 or 6 years of age. They begin with stealing thing from the house, stealing food and other domestic things. Then, gaining in confidence, they extend the sphere of their activity to the neighbourhood. Such children are often apprehended stealing books from other children when they go to school, with the result that their well-wishers and parents have sometimes to stand for much disgrace and embarrassment in front of strangers. Knowing of the child's activity, they give him a sound beating, but once the habit of stealing has set in, there is no getting rid of it, at least not so easily. Hence, what is more important is that they should not be given an opportunity to acquire any such habit in the first place. Yet, if he does form any such habit, it is essential that efforts at destroying a habit should be very tactful and imaginative. In either condition, it is essential to divine the reason why any child steals. Modern educational psychologists have discovered why children steal, and in this connection have shed some light on the psychological factors involved. Knowledge of these elements will help teachers and parents to solve the problem of stealing by children.

### Causes of Stealing

Main causes as to why children steal are the following :

**1. Sense of insecurity.** Children develop a sense of insecurity when the family is in turmoil, when children are indifferently treated by the parents or when they are frequently punished by them. If parents lie to their children, and the children manage to find out that the parents have been misleading them, they feel insecure. And this sense of insecurity sometimes induces the child to steal. Hence, it is essential that the calm and peace of family life be maintained intact, children should be told the truth as far as is practicable and they should be treated with love.

**2. Spoiling through excessive love.** Love and affection are things for which the child rightly yearns, but too much of them can spoil him and make him very obstinate. A child who has his full of love and affection has far too many needs, and while these needs can be satisfied in a family that is financially strong, in poor families this creates a problem. Descent from a strong financial position to an inferior level of income also creates a problem, and the child begins to steal. It is, of course, not inevitable that members of poor families steal. On the contrary, one finds habits of stealing in children who come from the richer families. Stealing or not is more positively concerned with the child being spoiled. Hence, it is essential that the child should be scolded if he does anything undesirable.

**3. Strict discipline.** Presence of extreme discipline in the family leads the child to complete repression of many of his tendencies. And repression leads to the formation of sentimental complexes that complicate his adjustment activity, for the fulfilment of which he turns to theft. Too much beating and punishing also instigates the child to stealing since this gives him a sense of independence. Hence, where discipline in the family is concerned, it is always desirable to wield the whippy by a liberal hand.

**4. Dissatisfaction of needs.** The basic cause why a child steals is that his needs are not satisfied. If a child gets enough to eat, wear and play within the home, he has no need for stealing. Generally, a child should also be given some pocket money when he goes to school. What actually happens is that when the child sees other children spending money on all kinds of things, it is natural for him to want the same things. When he finds no resources to do so, he steals things from school and money from his own home. It should also be remembered that if all the child's demands are promptly met with, instead of breaking of the habit of stealing, there is every possibility that it will be intensified. Lack of control spoils the child so that he has no compunctions in stealing.

**5. Sex problems.** Psychological studies have revealed that a child steals because of an unconscious desire to satisfy his repressed sexual desires. Scolding and punishing the child if he enquires after his curiosity on matters of sex leads to the formation of a guilt complex in the child, and he learns stealing, lying and other bad habits.

**6. Sense of adventure.** Some children find stealing an adventure, and the excitement involved is the main consideration. Plucking flowers where it is prohibited gives them a sense of thrill.

**7. Imitation.** Where children observe other members of the family stealing, it is comparatively more natural for them to adopt such activities. Some women surreptitiously remove money from their husband's pockets; some older children in the family are prone to stealing. And the child imitates them.

### Eliminating the Habit of Stealing

On the basis of the above-mentioned causes of stealing among children, the teacher can discover the cause of stealing in the case of an individual child with the parents, help. In fact, a child's stealing is less a crime but more a bad and defect of character. In order to kill this habit in the child, a teacher will advise the parents to maintain an atmosphere of peace and calm within the family, to love the child, to provide him with a reasonable amount of spending money, and to look after him carefully. Children who find stealing thrilling because of the adventure involved can be broken of the habit by being busied in games that involved adventure and require courage. Children who steal because of an unconscious desire arising out of the repression of sexual impulses can be guided into the right mode of behaviour. Actually, within the family a system should be developed whereby the children should use only what is theirs and not to pick up anything belonging to any other family member. Such a step will develop his sense of possession over what is admittedly his, and will also develop in him a habit of keeping his hands off from things that do not belong to him. Scolding or punishing a child after his stealing has come to one's notice is not a very constructive measure, neither is there anything to be gained by ignoring theft. If such a condition is precipitated, the teacher can coolly discuss things with the parents and discover the causes that lead the child to crime, and will remove them before trying to break him of the habit.

## LYING

### Meaning and Kinds of Lying

Conscious and wilful saying of a thing that is known to be incorrect is called lying. If a child says something that is incorrect but is not aware of its invalidity, it is incorrect to call him a liar. He is a liar only when he has knowingly said something that is untenable. Habits of lying of this type must be removed. Lying can be of many kinds. The famous criminologist Cyril Burt has classified lying in the following manner :

1. **Playful lies.** In infancy and childhood, sometimes the child tells a lie just for the fun of it. It is no crime, it is just wantonness.

2. **Lie of confusion.** When something is in doubt, the child fails to distinguish between true and false, and says that which is false.

3. **Lie of vanity.** Some children lie for the sake of false vanity. They talk of things that they have never done. Such lying satisfies their false vanity.

4. **Lie of revenge.** Sometimes the child who has been defeated and has no means of wreaking revenge upon the winner, turns up spreading false gossip and creating all kinds of false information to manifest his superiority over his adversary.

5. **Selfish lies.** Telling a deliberate lie in order to conceal some fault of one's own doing is called a selfish lie. For example, when some children are caught being naughty, they invent all kinds of false reasons to escape the natural reckoning.

6. **Lie of loyalty.** A child is very loyal to his group and tries to cover up its objectionable activities by telling lies.

7. **Pathological lie.** Some lying is the result of many abnormalities and mental complexes in the individual. Such lies resulting from mental diseases can arise due to following causes :

(a) Over-active imagination,

(b) Facility in the use words and

(c) To hide certain bad sex habits.

**Cure of Lying**

Once the child evinces the habits of telling lies, the teacher must endeavour to end it, since its persistence will adversely affect the development of his character and leave incomplete the function of education. Hence, teachers who catch their students telling lies, use many ways of curing them. Some of the main methods are the following :

**1. Psychological treatment.** In psychological treatment, the child is treated with love and affection in order to discover the cause of his lying. Having discovered them, the teacher tries to persuade the child and also causes such changes in his environment that the need for telling lies ceases to exist.

**2. Indirect punishment.** According to modern educational psychologists, direct punishment of the child leads to development of feelings of hatred and revolt against his teacher, hence this mode of retribution is not desirable. As an alternative, some forms of indirect punishment can be used that prove to be more effective even than direct punishment. Some such methods are not talking with the child, ignoring him, being indifferent towards him.

**3. Avoid provocative occasions.** Generally speaking the teacher should always try to avoid all occasions that may provoke the child into lying. Testing the child by deliberate creation of such situations is not very expedient since there is no bad habit that the child is incapable of picking up. Hence, as far as is practically possible and feasible, one should avoid all occasions that provoke lying in children.

**4. Confession.** When a lie is detected the first time, one must try to make the child confess that he is in the wrong. This inspires him to repent, and the embarrassment involved acts as a sufficient deterrent in case of future provocation. His self-respect is injured, if he has to confess. Secondly, having confessed to his fault and having promised not to repeat it, the child himself does his best to avoid all such occasions.

**5. Positive instructions.** According to modern educational psychologists, a teacher should avoid negative instructions and directions as far as possible, and try to make his directive positive. It is more expedient to say always tell the truth than to order the student to avoid lying. Childern have an almost natural tendency of contradicting all negative orders being more prone to accepting positively worded requests and orders.

**6. Rational attitude towards the child's imagination.** A child is naturally imaginative. He imagines all sorts of things by imaginatively putting himself in different situations. Sometimes he fails to do these things in the concrete, he boasts that he has done this or that, and that he has been on this or that plane. Hence, realising the child's sensitivity with regard to imagination, one should take the child to see new places, give him the independence and freedom to play all kinds of games, give him new things. When this is done, he will not tell lies among his friends for the simple reason that there will be no need to do it.

Finally, it can be said that successful elimination of the child's lying habits depends upon the teacher's psychological insight, patience, and tactful behaviour. He can benefit in his efforts by the suggestions of educational psychologists.

## (A) ANNOYING YOUNGER CHILDREN

Some children are prone to cause pain to other children junior to themselves. The teacher observes that one child is annoying a younger without any apparent reason. On the other hand, one student comes to him with the report that a class-fellow has beaten him up. Sometimes, reports of this kind are untrue and maliciously reported. But whether the report is a lie or a fact, it is for the teacher to investigate and find out, otherwise his wards are inclined to lose faith in him, and the discipline of the school is seriously jeopardized. The child making the complaint should be sympathetically treated and made to understand that his problem will be solved and in future he will not be molested. Now, the major problem that remains is how to prevent some children from annoying others without reason. Usually, teachers punish and thrash youngsters who do these wanton things with the result that the student awed and under the influence he is not prone to repeat his exploits. Yet, though this helps to maintain the proper discipline in the class, it defeats the purpose of education. The teacher's subject is not to prevent the children from being naughty but eliminating the causes that lead him to undesirable behaviour. Hence, if he is to completely cure the child of his habit of wantonly causing pain to his juniors, it is essential that he discovers the basic causes that originated the tendency.

**Causes of Annoying other Children**

The tendency of annoying other children want only is one that reveals a streak of cruelty in the child. And in this the environment in the family plays a large part. Main causes in this connection can be the following :

**1. Cruel behaviour on the part of family members.** The Child has an invariable tendency to imitate the conduct of family members. If members of the family quarrel with each other and the stronger and older beat the youngest in the family the child will follow suit.

**2. Absence of discipline in the family.** Lack of discipline in the family permits the children to quarrel with each other, the seniors almost invariably triumphing over the juniors by beating them. And many parents have not the strength of will to prevent such insane behaviour. Hence it can only be expected that children from such families will injure smaller children in school. It is sometimes seen that the parents take a hand in the punishing to stop their children behaviour in this manner. This may create a state of enforced peace and acquiescence in the home, but when in school, the child will imitate his parents and injure and beat children younger and weaker than himself.

**3. Relations between parents and child.** If the relations between parents and children are not loving and confident, the child becomes irritable, quarrelsome and selfish. He will manifest these qualities in fighting children younger than himself. The tendency towards cruelty is further promoted by the prejudiced behaviour of parents towards their children.

**4. Lack of discipline in schools**. In schools where senior students are seen beating and overpowering youngsters, there is little or no discipline. Teachers must adopt psychological means to create an atmosphere of discipline and rational obedience in the school.

There can be some other reasons, besides those mentioned above, why big children may injure and worry the smaller children. For example, being oversexed, some children annoy their juniors. Whatever the situation, the teacher must try to discover the causes involved in the situation and then try to eliminate them. Acting on two fronts, the teacher must use love and affection to persuade the student while he tries to eliminate the causes that have led to the formation of such a habit in him. Half of his battle is won if he can convince the child's parents of the need of improving the atmosphere at home. He must also try to make the student realise that it is indecent to bother smaller children. Secondly, it is for him to train the children to cooperate and work in an atmosphere of mutual confidence, love and sympathy. Once such an atmosphere has been successfully created in the school, incidents of big boys worrying small ones will be reduced. Teachers should keep an eye on such various tendencies as over sexuality, aggressiveness, false vanity, and criminal tendency that arise in children from time to time, and should also resort to tactful behaviour in trying to eliminate them.

### (B) AVOIDING TASK ALLOCATED FOR HOME WORK

In most schools, teachers allot some work to the students to complete at home. Sometimes, due to various causes that create unpredictable circumstances, the child fails to do this, but he is not to blame. But, if a child makes it a habit to avoid doing the allotted work, the teacher must do his best to break the child of such a habit. This habit can be caused by anyone of the following :

**1. Improper atmosphere in the home.** The atmosphere in some children's houses is not at all conductive to any sort of serious effort, as a consequence of too much noise and lack of any quiet corner.

**2. Lack of interest and enthusiasm.** Children who are not interested in academic pursuits and have no enthusiasm for it, usually do not complete the work allotted to them.

**3. Little respect and awe of teacher.** If a child does not respect a particular teacher and holds him in no awe whatsoever, then that teacher's commands have no particular value for him. In fact, he does the very contrary of what is required of him. His neglecting the work allotted for completion at home is all that can be expected from the child under the circumstances.

**4. Other causes.** In addition to the above causes, there can be many other reasons why a student may fail to complete the work required of him. For example, if the child has failed to understand a particular lesson taught in school, how can he be expected to solve any problems pertaining to it?

### Solution and Cure

Keeping in mind these various causes, the teacher should see to it that students do the work that he allots to them as their homework. In this effort he can, on the one hand, request the childern's parents to improve the atmosphere at home, and, on the other, he can improve his own conduct in the classroom. He must be able to win the respect and admiration of his students. Having done this, it will be easy for him to have his orders obeyed. Nevertheless, if some student persists in disobeying the instructions of the teacher, then it becomes necessary to administer some indirect punishment to persuade the student to abandon his lax ways. Among them is indifference to the particular student, abstaining from holding conversations with him, and other means whereby the student himself should realise the teacher's displeasure. A teacher must invariably avoid any situation that may lead students to develop feelings of antipathy and hatred towards him, or to feel that the work allocated for home is an unnecessary burden forced upon him. Proper method of education and desirable behaviour on the teacher's part coupled with adequate interest and inspiration in the work cause students to do their homework enthusiastically, and sometimes even go to the length of doing work on their own initiative if the teacher does not allot any, and showing it to him. Such children should be praised in front of the whole class. This will have the twofold effect of adding to their already exuberant enthusiasm, as well as inspiring the other students to emulate them and win the teacher's admiration.

## (C) ABSCONDING FROM MATHEMATICS CLASS

### Causes

Mathematics is one subject that has created aversion in more than one student, and they all do their best to avoid it. Some of these children are enterprising enough to run away from the mathematics class. If this sort of truant behaviour is constantly noted, then the teacher is compelled to take note and solve it. He must first of all uncover the causes that induce the child to have such responsibility. Main causes could be from among the following :

**1. Low level of maturity.** Mathematics is one subject that essentially requires the presence of a certain level of maturity in its students. At different levels of maturity, the curriculum relating to mathematics should be different.

**2. Defects of educational method.** If the teacher takes it upon himself to teach mathematics by a method that makes the subject appear easy to the student, he will not play truant from the class. Hence, sometimes, one of the reasons why students avoid the mathematics class could be a defective and unimaginative method of teaching.

**3. Student's personal difficulties.** If the student has no interest in academic study, lacks enthusiasm and inspiration regarding it, a subject as notoriously dry as mathematics is the least likely to hold his attention. Repeated failure is another thing that may discourage him. There can be numerous other similar problems that may prompt the student to avoid the mathematics class. And for this, attitudes, mental abilities and qualities of personality have a special significance.

### Solution and Cure

The teacher should try to discover the cause of a student's running away from the mathematics class, and having done so, should try to remove it. The child should constantly practise in this difficult subject. Lessons should start with simple questions that are comparatively easy to delve into more difficult problems. In teaching mathematics the teacher should adopt a method that makes it easy to grasp so that students achieve a kind of auto-inspiration in learning it. Besides this, if the children are found avoiding these classes through some personality defects, then the teacher should consult their parents, and through loving and affectionate behaviour, try to eliminate these shortcomings.

## (D) BEING LATE FOR SCHOOL

### Causes

Being occasionally late for the class is nothing unusual.

But if a student persists in being late for the school, the teacher has of necessity to investigate and find out the cause for it, since the punctuality is an important asset and a part of personality development. There can be many causes why a child is consistently late for the class, main ones among them being the following.

**1. Parents' carelessness.** Children can be punctual in reaching school only if their parents prepare them for school well in time. If they are careless in this respect, it is only natural that their children should be late for school.

**2. Aimless wandering.** Another reason why children, who are prepared for school in time by their parents, reach the school late is that they fall into bad company and play on the wayside or roam around before reaching the school. Once a child falls into a company of vagrants, it is only natural for him to develop a liking for wandering. It is a kind of wanderlust.

**3. Tendency to avoid classes.** The fundamental reason why the child is always late for school is that there is nothing in the class to interest him, and he wants to avoid it, any way. Tendency to run away from classes can be inspired by many things, among them uninteresting methods of teaching, strict discipline, level of education being higher than the child's level of mental development, bad atmosphere in the classroom, very strict administration in school, etc.

**4. Other causes.** There cannot be the same reason for children being late for school. Due to different reasons and under different circumstances, children do this. It is quite possible that a child may have a special passion for some particular form of exhibition and that this exhibition may be situated on his way to school so that he may be tempted to spend a few hours there everyday.

**5. Cure and solution.** Whatever it may be, the teacher must begin his investigation by examining the reasons why a student is delayed on his way to school. And then, efforts can be made to eliminate these causes, a venture that requires the cooperation of the parents. Parents and teachers can cooperate to punish the child indirectly and thus break him of his habit. Parents must do their bit by preparing the child for school with a good bit of time to spare. If the atmosphere in school and the method of teaching are defective, it can be removed and education made more interesting. It is the duty of his seniors to save the youngster from bad company. A child naturally likes to live in the group, be it a group of good children, or one of bad children. The sole method of having the child avoid bad company is that he be put in good company. Then, he will not try to go to bad company. Parents should communicate with the teacher at regular intervals to find out whether their child is reaching the school in time. If this is not done, it is up to the teacher to immediately inform them if he thinks it fit. Such cooperation and sensible behaviour can help to rid the child of his bad habit. Secondly, this problem can also be solved by teaching the child all the virtues of time allotted for their doing. Punctuality is a quality that is developed both in school and at home. Having become habituated to having meals, getting up, going to sleep at appointed hour and doing many things by the clock will develop into such a strong habit that he will be instinctively compelled to get to school in time. Otherwise, he is apt to reason out the little difference it makes by being late for school. But, before inculcating the wisdom of punctuality in children, it is essential that the parents and teachers themselves be very punctual. Teachers who themselves are usually late for their class can hardly expect to convince their students that punctuality is a virtue. Punctuality is a thing that is best learned by imitating one's seniors. If parents and teachers themselves are very punctual, the child will drop the habit of being late for school.

## GIFTED CHILDREN

### Who is a Gifted Child?

Many studies have indicated that the intelligence quotient of children differs from one individual to another. This difference is seen not only among children of different ages but between children of the same age group also. On the basis of this children are classified into the average, the backward and the gifted group. All psychologists do not agree about the level of intelligence required for a child to be considered gifted. Some psychologists believe that an intelligence quotient of 120 denotes exceptional gifts while others believe that the gifted child must have an I.Q. of 140. Children with an intelligence quotient even higher than 140 can be accepted as exceptionally gifted. It has been calculated that only one out of 400 children belongs to this category. Such exceptionally gifted children have an intelligence quotient ranging between 140 and 150. But an I.Q. of 170 or more is rarely seen, while an I.Q. between 140 and 150 is more common.

## Characteristics of the Gifted Child

The gifted child differs from the average child in other respects also, in addition to his greater intelligence. Physiologically, the gifted child is frequently better built, emotionally better balanced than the average child. Leaving aside the exceptions, it is often seen that the child is gifted not only in terms of intelligence but also in terms of other individual qualities, in which he is more developed. Apparently, the gifted children enjoy the benefits of nature and environment. Most of such children are born into families with a fairly high social and economic level. They, therefore, belong to the more well-to-do group of families with the result that the care lavished on them, the food provided, the education, etc., are all considerably better than that enjoyed by the average child. Besides, they also get good training in controlling their habits and emotions, which helps in developing many exceptional qualities of character and personality.

Frequently, the gifted child is one to two inches taller and a few pounds heavier than average child. At the time of joining school, such children are seen to be 4 or 5 pounds heavier than the others. At the age of 15, such children are 10 to 15 pounds heavier. In addition to this the gifted children do not normally suffer from headaches, they have clearer skins, they are less irritable, less inclined to exhaustion and less susceptible to such common maladies as cold. In one study, a group of 220 successful and 170 unsuccessful candidates was compared, and it was found that the successful candidates suffered from fewer physical defects than the unsuccessful ones. In this case there was one exception, since the gifted competitors were found to suffer from a higher incidence of visual defects. One possible explanation of this may be their excessive use of the eyes in reading and study. But physiologically they were neither weak nor dwarfed. In fact, they were taller and heavier.

It should be remembered that all gifted children are not better than the average child in their physiological characteristics, emotional stability or social adjustment. In fact, quite a few of the gifted children are below the average in this respect. In actual fact, gifted children differ from each other very much in these respects. As a general rule, all that can be said is that defects lead to more defects while good qualities generate more good qualities, although this, too, cannot be accepted as a universal rule. For this reason, it is desirable that each gifted child should be studied individually.

### Problems of the Gifted Child

As in the case of the backward child, the gifted child is also unlike the average child. As a result, certain problems arise in his case also. These problems should also be tackled with the same care and attention as is accorded to the backward child, sooner than he can recognise the gifted one. It may also happen that the teacher may completely fail to observe the qualities of the gifted child, and may even consider him backward. Such a situation is extremely harmful because it hinders the gifted child's proper development, and at the same time creates administrative problems for the school and the class. The future of any nation depends upon the proper development of all the gifted children born in it. Hence, schools should make special provisions for their training. But the parents also must accept responsibility for their training and education.

### The Education of Gifted Children

The following suggestions have been given for the education of gifted children :

**1. Selection**. The first step in their education is to find out which child is gifted. This selection can be made with the help of marks obtained at previous examination, the advice of the class teachers, the results of psychological tests and the reports given by parents.

**2. No separate classes**. Some psychologists have suggested that the gifted child should be taught in separate classes set apart for them. But this is not a very psychological suggestion for this may engender a feeling of vanity and superiority in them.

**3. Curriculum**. Many psychologists have suggested that the gifted child should be made to study some subjects in addition to the normal syllabi intended for the average class. This is a more practical suggestion because the gifted child's abilities can be better developed by the more comprehensive syllabus. It will also help to remove inactivity, social difficulties, and also create a better atmosphere in the class. But it must be remembered that the syllabus should never be so extensive as to become a burden on the child.

**4. Faster promotions to higher classes**. It has also been suggested by some psychologists that the gifted child should be promoted to higher classes more rapidly than the other children. This will give them a chance to develop their minds and also save time. But from the stand point of the child's social development, this may not prove very beneficial. He will tend to be handicapped by the fact that all the other children in his class will be older than him. It is therefore better if the gifted child is given some additional work, but without promoting him to the higher class.

**5. Individual education**. Nowadays many psychologists are of the opinion that the gifted child should be educated individually with the teacher generally acting as a guide without undue interference. The child is given a particular task to perform within a fixed period. The teacher keeps an eye on his development and provides him with fresh programmes as he goes along. This method of education has proved the most useful in the use of gifted children.

**6. Extracurricular activities**. Another way of developing the qualities of the gifted child is to engage him in extracurricular activities such as games, music, dancing, other arts, practice for debates and sports competitions.

**7. Facilities and apparatus**. Gifted children can also be given certain kinds of special facilities such as fee concessions, opportunity to do work of exceptional responsibility or importance, etc. The school should also provide many kinds of means for learning the arts, games and other activities. Very often the gifted child finds a good library as a very good aid.

It is clear from the above exposition that the teacher can play an important role in nation building by helping in the proper development of the gifted children tendered to his care. In actual fact, the proper development of the gifted child depends considerably more upon the intelligence, wisdom and the sense of responsibility of the teacher. He should try to make arrangements for developing special qualities in his more gifted children. But in this connection, the responsibility of the parents is not less than that of the teacher, because different means can be adopted for the child's development as effectively at home as in the school. The parents should also take special care of such children. If this is not done, their balanced development is retarded. Besides, they may even become very difficult problems for their parents. If a child shows some extraordinary skill at some particular work, he should be sent to a school in which he can be trained to exercise that particular skill. The government can also facilitate the development of gifted children by providing fee concessions and other kinds of monetary aid. Thus, an environment can be created in which the future leaders of the nation may develop and grow.

## QUESTIONS FOR EXERCISE

1. Write short note on Problem Children.
2. What is a backward child? What are the causes of backwardness and what remedies will you apply for them?
3. Describe the defects and abnormalities in a child's development and point out their remedies.
4. What light has educational psychology thrown on the problem of (a) stealing, (b) lying among children? Give examples.
5. What should the teacher do in the following circumstances :
   (a) A child annoys younger children without any reason.
   (b) A student does not do the homework allotted to him.
   (c) A student always absconds in the mathematics class.
   (d) A student invariably comes late to the class.
6. Write short note on Gifted Children.

# 6

# Creativity and Divergent Thinking

## DEFINITION OF CREATIVITY

**1. Guilford.** "Creativity sometimes refers to creative potential, sometimes to creative production and sometimes to creative productivity." Here creative potential means the personal disposition of the individual in which there are some more or less permanent qualities which help him in creative thinking. Creative thinking leads to new ideas. Creative production does not mean production of concrete things. It means the processes of productive thinking. Creative productivity means productivity according to socially comfortable forms of words, thoughts and phrases etc. This definition of creativity establishes creative thinking as its primary characteristic. Emphasising this element in creativity Mednik writes, "Creative thinking consists of forming new combinations of associative elements." The most important characteristic of creative thinking is the fact that in it one finds new types of associations in place of their more common varieties.

**2. Torrance.** "I have chosen to define creative thinking as the process of sensing gaps or disturbing, missing elements, forming ideas or hypotheses, and communicating the results, possibly modifying and retesting the hypotheses." According to this definition of creativity it is clear that it involves new hypotheses, their tests and constant modification. Further clarifying the process of creative thinking Torrance has pointed out that in it first of all a need is felt, then the problem is defined and clarified. After this there is a period of preparation which involves reading, writing, discussion and research and gathering possible solutions of the problems. After this the pros and cons of different solutions are evaluated. In the end of this process some new idea emerges in the form of insight.

This new solution is now examined and new researches are conducted on its basis which leads to the creation of new principles, methods, pictures, music, poems, etc. According to C.V. Good, "...the factors of creativity are tentatively described as associate and ideational fluency, originality, adaptive and spontaneous flexibility and ability to make logical evolution."

**3. James Drever.** "Producing an essentially new product; constructive (somewhat under) use of imagination where a new combination of ideas or images is constructed strictly when it is self initiated, rather than imitated, also of thought synthesis, where the mental product is not a mere summation." Sir Fredric has named creativity as bold thinking. Bold thinking means divergent thinking, breaking of old norms, having new experiences and creating new combinations. According to Simpson, creative thinking involves new forms of thinking away from the traditional forms. Thus, creativity includes curiosity, imagination, research, novelty and invention, etc. A.F. Cropley has considered divergence as the most important characteristic of creativity in his small booklet on this subject. According to him this one characteristic is sufficient to identify creative children from non-creative ones.

The above definitions of creativity point out that it means original thinking, new types of associations, divergent thinking and behaviour, new solutions of old problems, flexibility and a new approach in different fields of life. The creative person is very much aware of new problems. His thinking is dynamic, flexible, original and novel. He has more than average curiosity and is always busy in finding out new solutions of the traditional problems.

## NATURE OF CREATIVITY

Nature of creativity can be derived from its meaning. Different theories have explained the nature of creativity differently. According to psychoanalytic theory, the creative person satisfies frustrated ambitions and desires through creative processes. According to associative theory the creative person forms new associations or recognises old ones. According to Campbell, creativity involves change of central point, change of meaning, and a novel organisation. It involves insight which is the cause of sudden emergence of new ideas. Existentialists have presented a theory similar to the Gestalt theory. According to them creativity involves perception of new objects and struggle for their understanding. In the words of May, "A creative act is a process, a doing specifically, a process interrelating the person and his world." The personalists defined creativity in terms of interpersonal relationship. In the words of C.R. Roger, "Creativity is an emergence in action of novel relational product, growing out of the uniqueness of the individual on the one hand and the materials, events, people, or circumstances of his life on the other." The trait theory considers particular trait as characteristic of creativity. For example, according to Guilford, the most important traits of creativity are consciousness of the problem, continuity of thinking, continuity of words, continuity of association, continuity of expression, flexibility of thinking and accommodation, originality and redefinition, etc.

The above brief discussion of the views of different theories concerning creativity makes it clear that each theory has laid emphasis upon a particular aspect of creativity. Each theory clarifies a particular aspect of creativity better than others. Every theory is one-sided and none defines creativity from every aspect. The following characteristics of creativity summarise its nature :

**1. Commitment towards problems.** In order to be creative, a person should be very well aware of the problems in his circumstances. Without this commitment towards problems he cannot have creative thinking. A creative person is aware of the problems present in his circumstances and makes every effort to find out new solutions to these problems.

**2. Dynamic thinking.** The creative person not only thinks creatively but his thinking constantly changes according to new circumstances. He has more capacity of adjustment, but this adjustment is sought through new combinations.

**3. Divergent thinking.** The most important characteristic of creativity is divergent thinking. An average person is a convergent thinker because he thinks in terms of approved social behaviour. Convergent thinking means that in it thinking is done on the basis of traditional methods leading to traditional solutions. In it the thinker depends on old learning and mechanically fits old responses in new circumstances. It has been, therefore, rightly called closed thinking. Divergent thinking, on the other hand, is open thinking. It involves continuity, flexibility and originality. These traits can be observed in the words of great scientists, philosophers and literary thinkers. In our time tests have been devised to measure creativity. These tests have established divergent thinking as the main sign of creativity. It should be remembered here that all types of anti-traditional behaviour cannot be termed creative behaviour. In order to be creative, divergence is not a sufficient trait either in thinking or in behaviour. Young men and women wearing clothes which do not confirm to social norms are hardly creative. On the other hand, many creative persons wear socially approved dress and appear to be absolutely convergent in their normal behaviour. It may be said that opposition of traditions is one of the signs of creative process, which is not a necessary element of it. Sometimes some traits helpful in creativity have been themselves considered to be creative. For example, high I.Q., developed verbal skill have been taken as creative thought; at best these are only traits useful in creativity.

**4. Useful results.** Thus besides being divergent creativity leads to useful results. It is hence that a certain new idea gives immense pleasure to the thinker. It is hence again that creativity impresses every one. Nellar has called this trait as relevance. According to Brunor, a creative product must be impressive. It is hence that the creative person is absolutely involved in his work.

**5. Flexibility.** An important characteristic of creativity is flexibility of thinking and behaviour. Most of the people are never prepared to re-examine their attitudes, habits, ways of behaviour, etc. They utilise old solutions to solve new problems in every situation, without caring about the novelty of the present situations. The creative person, on the other hand, is always prepared to adopt new attitude, idea or behaviour. It is hence that he succeeds in finding out new solutions to problems.

**6. Originality.** Originality, therefore, is a necessary trait of creativity. A creative person is not confined to ideas or experiences, read or heard. He is always prepared to conduct new experiments. He uses new ideas, new attitudes and new methods. It is natural that sometimes he falls into great difficulties, but the result of his courage is achieved in the form of originality.

**7. Ability to go beyond the immediate circumstances.** An ordinary person is generally confined to his immediate environment and circumstances; he can not rise above it. A creative person, on the other hand, has the ability to go beyond the immediate circumstances and show novelty in thinking and behaviour. He has the capacity to behave in a way different from the general way of behaviour in a particular situation. It is hence that these are known as creative persons.

**8. Reinterpretation of the problem or its part.** In order to find out new solutions it is necessary that the problem should be looked from a new point of view. Hence reinterpretation of the problem or its part is a characteristic of creativity. Allen Nevil, J.C. Shaw and Herbert Simon have considered the following as important elements in the creative solution of a problem :

(a) The object of thinking should be novel and valuable.
(b) Thinking should be divergent.
(c) Thinking should be highly motivated and constant.
(d) The problem should be confused and undefined.

It is only in the case of the above characteristics that problem solving can be creative.

**9. Harmony of abnormal and relevant thinking.** According to Guilford, creative children are those who accommodate with relevant but abnormal thinking through creative thinking, reasoning and imagination. They accept the challenge and give a creative reply to it.

**10. Creative personality.** In the end the nature of creativity can be understood through the traits of creative personality. The most important traits in a creative personality are : capacity of original thinking, independence of judgement, curiosity, sensitivity, autonomy and humour. In his book *Creativity and Personality,* C.R. Parmesh has drawn the following conclusions on the basis of his research into the Nature of Creative Personality — (1) The High-creative individuals are neither significantly more nor less introverted than the Low-creative individuals. (2) The High-creative individuals are not significantly different from the Low-creative individuals in neuroticism and also the High-creative individuals are not significantly different from the Low-creative individuals in the level of anxiety. (3) The High-creative individuals are significantly higher in ego-strength as evidenced by body-image barrier characteristics than the Low-creative individuals. The High-creative individuals, however, are not significantly different from the Low-creative individuals in body-image penetration characteristics. (4) The High-creative individuals are significantly higher on theoretical and aesthetic values as compared to the Low-creative individuals.

In sum, the composite picture of the creative individual emerging from the present study is as follow :

"The creative individual is neither extroverted nor introverted, and is neither high nor low in neuroticism and anxiety. He is stable in personality organisation, and is characterized by high theoretical and aesthetic values."

## CREATIVITY AND PERSONALITY

Besides the studies of the relationship between creativity and intelligence, several psychologists studied the relationship between creativity and personality. In their study Getzels and Jackson have pointed out that the highly creative and highly intelligent adolescents differ not only in mental processes but also in temperament. In 1965, Wallach and Kogan clarified the interaction of personality and creativity. In 1969, Freeman concluded that creativity is not so much different from traits of intelligence as from unintelligent processes.

The first systematic idea of the relationship between creativity and personality is found in the works of Sigmund Freud. After him in 1952, Kris supported the idea of Freud that creativity is borne in mental conflict. Similar ideas were presented by Klein, Bellak and Kubie in 1958. In 1965, Berlyne pointed out that more mental conflict leads to higher creativity and a more creative person is determined to solve more difficult problems. In 1937, Allport pointed out that creativity is expressed in functional autonomy in the individual. In 1939, Goldstein maintained that there is an effective tendency to struggle with the environment. In the same year May demonstrated that the creative person seeks self-expression in the world. According to Rogers, creativity is openness to experience. According to Maslow in creativity one finds harmony between contradictory traits of personality. According to Barron, the creative person is habitually original. All these studies established the fact that personality is intimately connected with creativity. Therefore in 1963, Galton emphasised that personality variables can be used in the study of creativity. From Galton to present day many scientists have tried to point out traits of creativity and personality by the analysis of the biographies of creative persons. According to Galton the most important characteristic of famous and genius persons is the originality of their ideas. Ellis pointed out that among these persons one does not find mental symptoms more than the average.

In 1954, Terman showed by his studies that the more successful persons exhibit self-confidence, competition, leadership, sensitivity, social adaptation, mental stability, freedom, balanced temperament, etc. According to the study of Roe, a painter is better adjusted than other persons. Similar conclusions were arrived at concerning the scientists. Cattell pointed out in his studies that the scientific researchers are emotionally unstable and busy in their job. Other scientists have supported the ideas of Cattell. According to them, creative person is more introvert, thoughtful and having a dominant ego. Some other researchers have studied the personality trails of creative persons in other fields of occupations. Thus, the personalities of artists, sculptors, painters, architects, scientific researchers, industrial inventors and creative teachers have been studied. Such studies have been conducted not only in the West but also in India. All these studies establish that the creative person is more sensitive than the average and his ego is more dominant. He is more ambitious and more thoughtful. No distinction in creativity was observed on the basis of distinction of sex. Similarly no correlation was found in age and creativity.

## CONDITIONS OF CREATIVITY

What was that in the life of Rabindranath which led to make him a great poet? What are the conditions which make a person a great artist like Piccasso? How does a person become a great novelist like Prem Chand? Such questions have been often raised by thoughtful persons since society has been amply benefited by poets, artists, novelists, etc. Though science could not find out the mechanism by which creative persons can be made but psychologists have pointed out conditions favourable for the growth of creativity. Of these the most important are as follows :

**1. Detachment and commitment.** In order to do anything effectively the individual should be capable of doing some original work with determination. Thus, the capacity to be distinct from the general is a necessary condition of creativity. Trilling has referred to the detachment of poets with the society. This helps the individual to search within himself. Scientists are notorious for their unsuitability. Many great authors have been cut-off from society for very long periods during which, they were absolutely engrossed with their work. For example, Sri Aurobindo, during his 35-year stay at Pondicherry, was visible to the outside people only four lines a year. This detachment is only the other aspect of commitment. Without commitment it has no use. In fact, the scientist or the artist who is absolutely engrossed in his work has to be detached with the society for the time being. This is as much true about a creative person as about a creative group.

**2. Passion and decorum.** The creative person has the desire and ability to express his emotions and tendencies through his work. It is hence said that the artist has a passion towards art. It is due to passion that he can put in so much efforts in creative direction. No one can do much in a field with the attitude of detachment to his work. Creative work not only involves interest but also passion. Helvetius has rightly said, "...a man without passion is incapable of that degree of attention to which a superior judgement is annexed, a superiority that is perhaps less the effect of an extraordinary effort than a habitual attention." Thus it is clear that the creative person has an intense passion for his particular job. But passion or ability alone are not sufficient. Creative work involves a balance, a decorum and a respect towards things and persons. In the absence of this again no high creativity is possible.

**3. Autonomy of object.** In the beginning a creative person starts some creative process but later on this activity itself takes him further. Therefore, the creative person should have the freedom to follow the guidance of his object. Thus in the beginning what is a part of the mind of the creative person, later on, after expression, becomes an external object which has its own demand, its own freedom and norms. The creative person has now to follow the object which is autonomous though in the beginning it was created by the creative person.

**4. Deferral and immediacy.** The creative activity sometimes involves deferral of an activity and at other times immediate fulfilment of it. When should there be deferral and when should it be immediately fulfilled depends on the insight of the creative person but high creativity involves both. It is observed that an artist does nothing for a very long period and then in a passion he immediately fulfils the deferred work.

**5. The internal drama.** Creativity depends on the internal drama of the creative person. Every person has several elements in him — the ascetic element, the child, the ego, the social element, etc. The level of creativity is determined by the interaction of all these elements.

**6. Abilities.** Creativity requires several abilities such as intelligence, attention, organisation, etc. Different types of creative processes require different types of abilities.

**7. Conditions of creative thinking.** Creativity involves creative thinking. Its characteristics are factuality, novelty, freedom and harmony. Creative thinking requires several conditions. First of all there should be the capacity to grasp new ideas. Secondly, there should be the ability of involvement with the object. The creative persons can stay involved in their work for weeks, months and years. Thirdly, the creative person should be able to understand the question involved in the given problem, since only then he can arrive at the solutions. Fourthly, the creative person should learn from past failures and reform his thinking. Fifthly, he should have the capacity of detachment from the environment.

**8. Traits of creative personality.** One can be creative only if he has traits of creative personality. A creative person does not follow the tradition; he finds out his own path. He does not see the facts as average people do. His insight is deeper and divergent. It is hence that he arrives at new meanings of the given facts. He does not follow ordinary taboos, he has the capacity to take risk and he is not afraid of thinking on new formulae. In other words he is a bold thinker, his thinking is flexible and dynamic. Even the most hard job is like a play to him. He has a jolly and witty attitude and attends to funny aspects of life. Though his ego is dominant yet sometimes he is capable of extricating himself from the control of ego. As compared to others he expresses his tendencies much more and does not care about the social norms in this process. Thus he is a divergent person. Whereas he has a capacity to control his passions, he has an equal capacity of forceful expression of it. This expression again is original. Thus most of the creative persons exhibit revolt, lack of system and freedom of judgement but this does not mean that they are free from all repression. Many creative persons have shown much more repression than average persons and yet generally speaking, a creative person is independent, original, free and playful. He finds out new meanings of already known facts.

**9. Creativity and family condition.** Some particular family conditions are more favourable for the development of creativity. As a general rule if the parents possess mental and personality traits of creativity, they are likely to be inherited by the children. In families favourable to creativity children will be given freedom of self-determination. They do not emphasise much on security and social control but give them sufficient opportunity to choose according to their intellects. They do not give advice about the right and wrong but respect the opinion of the children. They do not emphasise obedience but follow the policy of *laissez-faire* in the matters concerning children. In brief, they take children as respectable human beings and provide them every opportunity to grow freely.

**10. Cultural condition.** It is clear from the above discussion that such cultures will be more favourable for the growth of creativity in which traits favourable to creativity are more easily available such as freedom, divergent thinking, emotionality, playfulness, originality, etc. On the contrary, cultures in which there is more rigid social control and less occasions for freedom and originality do not provide favourable conditions for the growth of the creativity.

Besides the above-mentioned conditions of creativity, many other conditions can be developed in the process of education and in educational institutions which may be favourable for the growth of creativity.

## IDENTIFICATION OF TALENTED AND CREATIVE STUDENTS

The future of any country depends on the identification of creativity in the new generation and effort for its growth. In every field of life such as mechanical, scientific, academic, and artistic, creative people die and new persons are required to substitute them. If this need is not fulfilled, the progress of the country in that particular field is retarded. In fact, only that society can be called an ideal society in which maximum number of members get maximum opportunity for the growth of creativity. This however requires identification of talented and creative children. Psychologists have developed some methods for this purpose. In U.S.A. Robert F. DeHann and Jack Kough published in 1956 a handbook entitled *Identifying Students with Special Needs.* In this teacher's guidance handbook characteristics for identification of talented and creative students were mentioned in details. This handbook was utilized in collaboration with more usual tests for identification. The teacher can identify talented and creative students on the basis of his observations and tests provided in this handbook. In this connection the teacher should not make haste in putting labels upon children. He should, however, closely observe their behaviour and secretly classify them in a particular group. In this connection he should remember the following principles :

1. Give each student equal consideration on each behaviour characteristic.
2. Observe each student in a variety of situations.
3. Compare each youngster with the rest of the group.
4. Be aware of your own biases.
5. Choose areas of particular concern to you.

Keeping in mind the above-mentioned principles, every teacher should observe one particular trait in a student at a particular time according to the principles of observation. He should remain free from all types of prejudices. He should keep a register about the students and note his observations in it. He should remember that talented children have specific problems, abilities and disabilities. He should constantly check his list. He will find that the number of talented children is much less than the average. While on an average 5 per cent children are backward, 15 to 20 per cent may be classified among gifted children. The sooner the process of identification of creativity among students starts, the better it is. In this process besides observations, cumulative records, standardised tests, informal tests, and observation in specific circumstances together with the opinion of the child guide in the school are helpful. Besides these data the teacher can find out facts about students from their friends and relatives. It should be remembered here that a talented student is not necessarily better than other students in every field of life. Talented students are generally divergent and therefore some of the teachers are against them. They may appear to be more lazy than others and yet they may be talented. In an average class 15 per cent to 20 per cent students may be classed as talented. It is from among this group that the future artists, musicians, writers, actors and leaders are born. The students may depict different types of abilities such as Intellectual, Scientific, Leadership, Creative, Artistic, Writing, Dramatic, Musical, Mechanical and Physical skill. The following are the important points concerning identification of students with these abilities.

**1. Identification of students with intellectual ability.** Intellectual ability depends both on heredity and environment. It cannot be developed purely by environment but without proper environment again, it cannot be properly developed. If both the heredity and environment are negative, no one can develop intellectual ability. The teacher has to gather means favourable for the growth of intellectual ability. Robert F. DeHann and Jack Kough have given lists of identifying characteristics of intellectual ability which include : (1) Learns rapidly and easily. (2) Uses a great deal of common sense and practical knowledge. (3) Reasons things out. Thinks clearly. Recognises relationships. Comprehends meanings. (4) Retains what he has heard or read without much rote drill. (5) Knows about many things of which most students are unaware. (6) Has a large vocabulary, which he uses easily and accurately. (7) Can read books that are one to two years in advance of the rest of the class. (8) Performs difficult mental tasks. (9) Asks many questions. Has a wide range of interests. (10) Does some academic work one or two years in advance of the class. (11) Is original in his thinking. Uses good but unusual methods. (12) Is alert, keenly observant and responds quickly.

Besides these characteristics the teacher can supplement his observation by the study of cumulative records, use standardised tests, etc.

**2. Identifying students with scientific ability**. Today every progressive country needs scientific ability in almost every field of life and therefore there is a constant effort for the identification of students with scientific ability. According to Robert F. DeHann and Jack Kough, the list of identifying characteristics for scientific ability include : (1) Expressing himself clearly and accurately either through writing or speaking. (2) Reads one to two years ahead of his class. (3) Is one to two years ahead of his class in mathematical ability. (4) Has greater than average ability to grasp abstract concepts and see abstract relationships. (5) Has good motor co-ordination, especially eye-hand co-ordination. Can do fine, precise manipulations. (6) Is willing to spend time beyond ordinary assignments or schedule on things that are of interest to him. (7) Is not easily discouraged by failure of experiments or projects. (8) Wants to know the causes and reasons for things. (9) Spends much of his time on special projects of his own, such as making collections, constructing a radio, making a telescope. (10) Reads a good deal of scientific literature and finds satisfaction in thinking about and discussing scientific affairs. Observations of these characteristics may be supplemented by the study of cumulative records and use of standardised tests.

**3. Identifying students with leadership ability**. Leadership is of several kinds. Qualities of leadership are required in the fields of science, industry, government, art, sports, etc. In every class some students lead others. They have leadership ability and from among them develop future leaders of society. They have some qualities which are not found among other students. These identifying characteristics are : (1) Is liked and respected by most of the members of the class. (2) Is able to influence others not to work towards undesirable goals. (3) Can take charge of the group. (4) Can judge the abilities of other students and find a place for them in the group's activities. (5) Is able to figure out what is wrong with an activity and show others how to do it better. (6) Is often asked for ideas and suggestions. (7) Is looked to by others when something must be decided. (8) Seems to sense what others want, and helps them to accomplish it. (9) Is a leader in several kinds of activities. (10) Enters into activities with contagious enthusiasm. (11) Is elected to offices. Observations of these traits may be supplemented by the study of cumulative records and sociometric tests.

**4. Identifying students with creative ability.** Though in a way all individuals are creative but 10 per cent individuals show more creative ability. These can be identified on the basis of the following characteristics : (1) Always seems to be full of new ideas pertaining to most subjects. (2) Invents things of creative original stories, plays, poetry, tunes, sketches, and so on. (3) Can use materials, words or ideas in new ways. (4) Is able to put two or more ideas together to get a new idea. (5) Sees flaws in things, including his own work, and can suggest better ways to do a job or reach an objective. (6) Is willing to experiment to get answers. (7) Asks many questions. Shows a great deal of intellectual curiosity. (8) Is flexible and open-minded. Is willing to try one method after another and to change his mind if need be. Is not afraid of new ideas and will examine them before rejecting them. Observations about these traits may be supplemented by the study of cumulative records and by giving informal tests.

**5. Identifying students with artistic talent.** In every class there are some students who show more artistic talent and whose artistic creations are better than others. These students with artistic talent can be identified on the basis of following characteristics : (1) Covers a variety of subjects in his drawings or paintings. (2) Takes art-work seriously. Seems to find much satisfaction in it. (3) Shows originality in choice of subject, technique, and composition. (4) Is willing to try out new materials and experiences. (5) Fills extra time with drawing, painting, and sculpturing activities. (6) Uses art to express his own expedience and feelings. (7) Is interested in other people's art work. Can appreciate, criticise, and learn from other's work. (8) Likes to model with clay, carve, or work with other forms of three-dimensional art. Observations of the traits may be supplemented by the study of cumulative records and by giving special art assignments and standardised tests.

**6. Identifying students with writing talent.** In every class some students exhibit better writing talents. Writing talent includes writing of different types of letters, reports, etc. besides original creative writing. Writing talent can be identified on the basis of the following characteristics : (1) Can develop a story from its beginning, through the build-up and climax, to an interesting conclusion. (2) Gives a refreshing twist, even to old ideas. (3) Uses only necessary details in telling a story. (4) Keeps the ideas organised within his story. (5) Chooses descriptive words that other youngsters miss, and still gets across the central idea. (6) Enjoys writing stories and poems. (7) Makes the characters seem life like. Captures the feelings of his characters in writing. These observations can be supplemented by study of cumulative records and by giving story-telling and writing assignments.

## QUESTIONS FOR EXERCISE

1. Define creativity and discuss its nature.
2. Explain the relationship of Creativity and Personality.
3. Write short-note on Conditions of Creativity.
4. How will you identify Talented and Creative students?

# 7

# LEARNING AND TRANSFER OF TRAINING

You are proceeding on a road and a dog follows. You give it something to eat. Now whenever you happen to traverse the road, the dog follows you. To take another example, a little girl being indisposed, is taken to the doctor. The doctor prepares the syringe while the little girl looks on with interest or indifferently, depending on her nature. The doctor injects the medicine and the girl feels pain. When the little girl is taken to the doctor the next day, her indifference is no longer there because she starts screaming the moment the doctor lays his hand on the syringe. Why this change in reaction? She did not react in this manner on the first occasion. The answer would be that she had learnt by experience that injections are painful. In this way learning brings or causes changes in her behaviour.

The following are some definitions of learning which should make it clear :

**1. Learning is change in behaviour.** In J.P. Guilford's opinion, "We may define the term very broadly by saying that learning is any change in behaviour, resulting from behaviour."[1] In this definition a distinction between change in behaviour due to maturity and change in behaviour due to learning is not clear though both these activities occur simultaneously. In the words of Woodworth, "Typically at least learning consists in doing something new, provided this something new is retained by the individual and reappears in his later activities."[2]

**2. Learning is an organisation of behaviour.** According to Garrett, "Learning is that activity by virtue of which we organise

1. Guilford, J.P., *General Psychology* (1956), p. 343.
2. Woodworth, R.S. and Marquis, D.G., *Psychology*. Methuen and Co. Ltd., London (1949), p. 491.

our response with new habits."[3] Thus the element of organisation in learning is very much important. Guilford, too, maintains that learning involves organisation of behaviour. Thus, in learning to ride a cycle we have to organise the activities of turning the pedal, balancing the handle, etc. in order to be reasonably safe with the vehicle. It is another matter that a person does not learn this organisation at the outset and that he may take much longer time to learn to balance the handle than the time he may take to learn to turn the pedal. But his learning of the activity of cycling will be complete only when he accomplishes this organisation.

**3. Learning is the reinforcement of an activity.** R.S. Woodworth maintained that the learning of a new act is an addition to the person's store of experiences. Clarifying the statement further, Woodworth says that reinforcement, too, is an indispensable element in the act of learning because it helps forming only successful responses and weeding out the unsuccessful ones. To quote Woodworth, "An activity may be called learning in so far as it develops the individual in any way, good or bad and makes his environment and experiences different from what it would otherwise have been."[4]

The psychologists who stress external behaviour consider learning to be a change of behaviour while those who lay emphasis on internal change are convinced that learning is change in the perception of the individual. Combining these two views, Murphy writes : "From this point of view it would be legitimate to regard learning as a modification both of behaviour and of the way of perceiving."[5] The following definition of learning given by Hilgard is an essence of all the foregoing definitions offered by other psychologists : "Learning is the process by which an activity originates or is changed through reacting to an encountered situation, provided that the characteristics of the change in activity cannot be explained on the basis of native response tendencies, maturity or temporary status of the organism."[6]

3. Garrett, H.E., *Great Experiments in Psychology* (Rev. ed.), New York, Appleton Century, 1941.

4. *Ibid.*, p. 532.

5. Murphy, G., *An Introduction to Psychology*, 1951, p. 248.

6. Hilgard, E.R., *Theories of Learning*, Metouen, 1958, p. 13.

## LEARNING CURVE

Learning is not always a continuous process. Sometimes there is a steady progress in learning while at other times there is hardly any progress at all. Sometimes one notices even retrogression in the process of learning. Thus, when progress of learning in the case of a student of telegraphy is shown on a graph paper, one finds a learning curve rather than a straight line. In the learning curve given in the figure on next page, the upper curve shows the speed of the words sent per minute. The rise of the curve shows the progress in sending or receiving of the words. At one end of the curve one notices a plateau of learning.

Two facts are clear from Figure 7.1 of learning curve, initial spurt and plateau. The initial spurt can be seen in the curve of all types of learning. In the learning process there is a progress in the beginning and the speed increases with the increase of practice. In the subjects where insight is possible it increases learning very much. But in other types of learning the learner sometimes reaches a stage when the curve instead of going upwards seems to be horizontal and no progress is recorded for a certain distance. This flattened surface is called *plateau of learning*. In Figure 7.1, one finds the receiving curve rising gradually till it arrives at the physiological limit after which a flattened surface is noticed. The curve again rises after the plateau of learning. The reason for this rise is the coordination of the simpler habits with the complex ones.

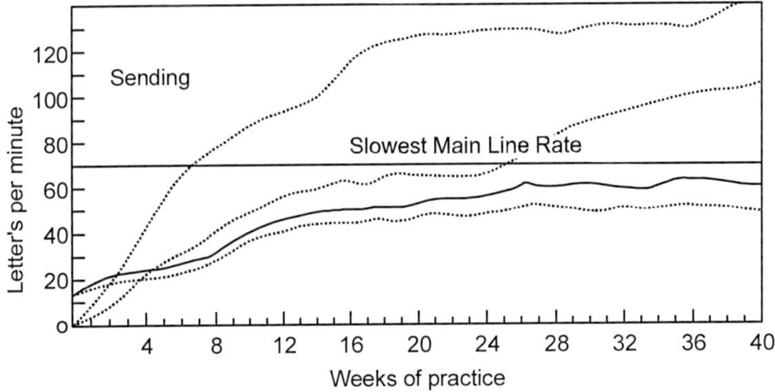


**Fig. 7.1**

There can be several reasons for the plateau of learning of which the most important are as follows :

**1. Absence of the proper motive.** The most important cause of plateau is the absence of proper and sufficient motive. In the case of factory labourers it has been observed that their speed increases after getting sufficient bonus.

**2. Insufficient coordination of the simpler habits with the more complex ones.** As it has been said earlier, learning requires coordination of the simpler habits with the complex ones. When this coordination is achieved, progress is noticed. Hence insufficient coordination between simple and complex habits is one of the causes of plateau in the learning curve. This can be seen in the habits of sending the letters and words in telegraphy.

**3. The conflict of old habits with the new ones.** Learning requires new habits. Hence there is conflict of the old habits with the new ones, e.g., a man used to a particular method of learning will find it difficult to leave it and to adopt a new though more profitable method.

But when learning by a particular method reaches the physiological limit, further progress becomes difficult. In the case of the curve of time when a man reaches a point after which he cannot progress it shows his *physiological limit.* As for example every sportsman has a physiological limit, beyond which he cannot break his records. If one finds no progress even when a certain task is done with the right process, one should suppose the existence of physiological limit. But it is very difficult to determine the right method. The daily amount of work put in by a labourer should not be taken as his physiological limit, because in the presence of new motives he shows more progress. Often one wonders as to how much more work he can put in due to some new motives. It has been seen that a young man who did not like to work for long hours, could work for 12 or 14 hours due to motivation from his beloved or wife, etc. As a matter of fact man is the most dynamic and adjusting animal and this physiological limit is not the same with all men of the same age. On the same age level some men can always work more than others. Again, in the same person also physiological limit is changing and flexible.

It is a common place experience that a man can work more while young in comparison to his old age. Again, the physiological limit in different types of learning is also different with the same learner. Hence the physiological limit for a particular man in a particular type of learning at a particular stage can be determined only by experiment. But no one can deny that such a limit does exist and that the learner cannot improve upon it appreciably.

## TRANSFER OF TRAINING

### What is Transfer of Training?

It is a matter of common observation that learning to do one thing makes it easier to perform some other action. The son of a trader is sometimes good at arithmetic in class because he is required to look after the accounts of his father's establishment. When learning for one purpose is also utilised in another situation not originally envisaged in a training, it is called transfer of training. In this manner, knowledge of mathematics helps in the study of physics and chemistry. In Figure 7.2, the difference between the learning curves of two groups as a result of transfer of training is illustrated. One of the groups has had pencil paper training for an overall twenty-four times while the other has had none.

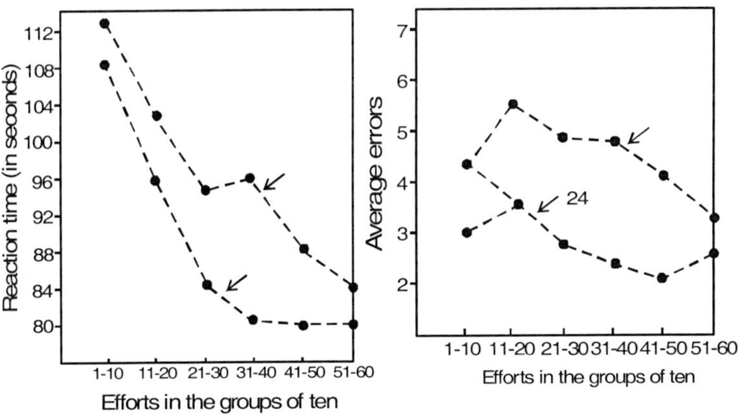


Fig. 7.2

## Kinds of Transfer

Transfer of training is normally of the following two kinds :

**1. Positive transfer of training.** In this transfer, training of one kind has positive or beneficial influence upon learning of another kind and learning is assisted thereby. For example, in an experiment, one group was taught Latin while another group was not, members of either group having common interests and similar level of intelligence. Now both the groups were put in the same class and taught by one single teacher who endeavoured to teach them English. It was found that the group knowing Latin picked up the language and acquired proficiency in it much earlier than did the other group that was ignorant of Latin. The reason for this was that the training in Latin was positively transferred to the learning of English.

**2. Negative transfer of training.** In this the training acquired in one kind of learning has a negative influence upon learning in some other connection, or in other words, it obstructs this learning. For example, individuals interested in wrestling are often found to be weak in academic pursuits because wrestling deprives them of much of their energy and they have little left to devote to any intellectual labour. In this way, wrestling proves to be obstructive to academic learning.

In certain cases, training or learning has no influence or effect at all, just as the learning of a Hindi poem has not the least effect on memorising facts of geography. In such contexts there is no transfer of training. In this way, transfer of training should involve at least some obvious influence or effect. If that effect is favourable then it is positive but if it is disadvantageous it is negative.

## Experiments Pertaining to Transfer

In the recent past, psychologists have made extensive tests and experiments concerned with the transfer of training and education, these efforts throwing considerable light on the subject under review. The major experiments in this connection have been conducted on sensorymotor transfer, transfer connecting memory, reasoning and ideation, subjects in school, problem solving, etc.

## Sensorymotor Transfer

Starch[7] made experiments concerning sensorymotor transfer with the help of mirror. In his experiment he examined the expediency that could be gained in drawing a star-shaped figure with the left hand while examining it through a mirror, it having been drawn under similar conditions with the right hand. In the experiment, the subject was asked to draw the figure with his left hand and the time taken therein was noted. This practice was continued over a period of ten days. After this, the subject was asked to use the other hand, and this too was practised for the same period of time. In this it became apparent that in the second effort the time taken was appreciably less, whereby it was deduced that the practice gained by the right hand was transferred to the left hand. In this connection, it should be mentioned that the experiments conducted by Evert,[8] Munn[9] and Bray[10] have elaborated this transference in a different sense. They came to the conclusion that progress in the above experiment is not the outcome of any transference of training from the right to the left) hand, but rather that this influence is the outcome of increase in the subject's self-confidence, improvement in his understanding of the problem, improvement of method, etc.

Webb[11] experimented with the paths of a hide-and-seek and came to the conclusion that the practice of one sensorymotor activity can be transferred to another sensorymotor activity although the extent of this transference depends upon similar elements in the two activities as well as upon their essential points of difference. In this experiment Webb tried to transfer the practice of one particular maze to the tackling of five other mazes. To begin with, the man or animal was trained in tackling one particular maze and was then led to four other mazes and the effect of previous training observed in the skill transferred to the latest tackling. After this round of activity had been completed, the subject was

7. Starch, D., in *Psychological Bulletin.*
8. Evert, P.H., *Pedagogical Memory.*
9. Munn, N.L., in *Journal of Educational Psychology.*
10. Bray, E.L., in *Journal of Experimental Psychology.*
11. Webb, L.W., *Psychological Source.* N.Y., 1917.

allowed to practise upon one maze and the influence of practices on other mazes on this one maze activity was observed. It was observed that in either condition learning in one maze definitely helped in the learning of other maze. In this experiment Webb found the extent of transference of learning varying from 20 to 77 per cent among various individuals.

**Transference Concerning Memory**

Among the experiments concerning transference in memory those of W.G. Slight are important. In his experiments he adopted the controlled group method, a group of female students being divided into four small groups. The first controlled group was not imparted any training. Another group learnt a poem for twelve days for a period of one half hour every day. The third group worked for a smaller period for an equal number of hours but instead concentrated upon population and import-export tabulated figures. The fourth group of women spent the same period of time for twelve days in trying to learn historical, scientific and literary prose tracts read out to them. It was a kind of oral learning for them. These four groups were examined before and after the following elements being examined in the process :

(1) Learning names and dates verbally.
(2) Remembering nonsensical words verbally.
(3) Remembering poetic pieces both read out by the teacher as well as read out individually.
(4) Remembering prose tracts both read out by the teacher as well as read out individually to oneself.
(5) Remembering the fundamental idea of a poetic piece verbally introduced.
(6) Remembering the order of nine numerals seen once.

The above experiments concerning the transference of memory yielded the following facts :

(1) Every group showed progress only in the matter practised upon.
(2) Learning of one kind had sometimes a favourable and sometimes an adverse influence upon learning of another kind.
(3) Learning poetry had beneficial influence upon the

learning of tables, meaningless words and prose whereas it had adverse influence upon the learning of the idea of a poetry piece or words.

Sleight came to the following conclusions :

(1) Practice does not lead to any appreciable improvement in the general memory and neither is there any evidence of working of a general memory.

(2) Related and unrelated complex memory functioning came to light in very large numbers.

Although some other experiments have discovered greater advantageous transfer of memory than Sleight has found, yet these tests do not prove that practice can help in the development of memory. The truth of the matter is that the functioning of memory is a complex process and the outcome of transfer depends upon the specific activity practised.

Memory transference was experimented upon by William James even before Sleight. James learnt by heart some 158 lines from Victor Hugo's poem *Saytr* and noted the time taken in the efforts. Then for 38 days, for a period of twenty minutes a day, he tried to commit to memory the first book of Milton's *Paradise Lost,* which contains almost 800 lines. After this effort he learnt another 158 lines from *Satyr,* and in this case he found that it took more time in obtaining the same skill as in the first case than he had taken in memorising the first 158 lines, before he had turned to Milton. Following this, James made memory experiments upon four other individuals. Three of them showed economy of time in memorising information after they had learnt one specific piece for a long time, but the fourth individual showed no appreciable progress as it took him the same time as it had taken him before the practice. James' experiments in this direction prove or at least indicate that the act of memorising cannot be improved upon through practice, although it has been observed that James' experimentation made no provision for the use of a scientific method of observation.

**Transference of Perception**

In an experiment conducted by Thorndike and Woodworth in 1901, it was observed that in estimating the area between 10 and 100 square centimetres educated or trained individuals showed an improvement of $^{1}/_{3}$rd over the estimate of an area between 150 and 300 square centimetres. But another individual was given to practise upon estimating lines between half and one and a half inches long, and it was found that he showed that no skill had been obtained when he was asked to estimate lengths between six and twelve inches.

**Transfer concerning Reasoning**

Educational psychologists have also made important experiments concerning reasoning. W.H. Winch[12] made a study of the transfer of school children's skill in solving arithmetical problems to the solution of other problems of reasoning. In this experiment, one definite group of students was put to practising the solution of arithmetical problems for ten weeks while another group of equal strength was allowed to work according to the regular curriculum with the exception of arithmetical learning. Of the two groups, the one with training in mathematics or arithmetic showed 30 per cent result. On the basis of this and other similar experiments it is believed that training in mathematics is transferred to other reasoning problems, and that such training helps in the solution of rational problems.

**Transference Concerning Ideation or Ideals**

Using some of Aesop's fables as the basis of his tests, Barrel examined the extent to which they help in the development of ideals. In this test two experimental and controlled groups of children and adults were selected. Between the first and second tests, lessons were read out to the experimental groups for periods varying between 12 and 20 minutes and the group was trained in analysis, imagination and generalization. Following examination it was observed that the experimental group made better progress than the controlled group.

**Transfer concerning Problem Solving**

Educational psychologists have also studied the question of transfer in the field of problem solving, although no distinct conclusions have been reached. In this connection S.T. Gray[13]

12. Winch, W.H., *Transfer or Improvement in Reasoning in School Children, British Journal of Psychology.*

13. Gray, S.T., A comparison of two types of learning by means of a substitution test, *Journal of Educational Psychology.*

made an experiment upon the transfer of code substitution. In this experiment the code substitution of two comparative groups was made the basis of tests. Following this, one of the two groups was taught a new code in which the logical connections were emphasised. The results of the test indicated that the group trained to observe rational relationships in its code performed its work some 20 per cent better than the other group.

Judd's[14] experiment is one of the famous ones among the many concerned with the solution of problems. In this it was required to strike a target in water. For this two groups of children were selected from the fifth and sixth grades. For the experiment one of the two groups was made aware of the occurrence of refraction in water of light rays, while the other group was allowed to proceed in ignorance of this fact. To begin with, both groups were asked to aim at and strike a target 12 inches below the surface of water. It was found that neither group showed any appreciable superiority or efficiency over the other in this practice. Now the target was raised to a height of four inches above the surface of water and again the students were required to aim at it. Now the trained group did better in their performance than did the untrained group. Judd came to the conclusion that the trained group had been able to establish a correlation between their first practice and the second, and had drawn upon their initial training as a result of which they had performed better than their untrained friends. Judd's conclusions have been supported by the experiments of others such as Ruedigear,[15] Mendrickson, Schroeder[16] and Gates, etc.

### Transfer between Educational Subjects

As a general rule it is believed that some subjects, as compared with others, help in disciplining the mind, and their study helps in the study of other subjects. Educational psychologists have made many experiments to measure this

14. Judd, C.H., *Educational Psychology*, Boston, 1939.
15. Reudigear, W.C., The indirect effect of mental function through education, *Educational Review*, 36, 1908.
16. Mendrickson and Schroeder, Transfer of training in learning to hit a submerged target, *Journal of Educational Psychology*, 32, pp. 205-13, 1951.

transference value of different subjects. Thorndike[17] conducted an experiment upon 8,000 students in 1922-33, in which the subject examined was the influence of one year's study in a high school upon intellectual activity. Tests made before the study and after it in this experiment showed that in the tests following the study, 23 extra points were gained over the score made before the study. In this experiment it was also observed that some 50 per cent of the progress made is due to the student's experience of examinations and the other 50 per cent the outcome of one year's study of the curriculum. In this study, too, some students showed better progress than others. The best students who constituted 1 per cent of the entire group improved to the extent of 20 and one-half points, while 1 per cent of the least progressive children showed improvement only to the extent of one and half points. From this it was concluded that the intelligence of children also influences their progress in the study of different subjects.

Many of the educationists believe that a study of grammar is very important for mental discipline. For an examination of this belief, in one experiment, children of average level of intelligence who belonged to the seventh grade were divided into two groups. Now the children in both groups were examined through several measuring scales. Following this one of the two groups was taught grammar for a period of three months, while the other group was taught to compare words and language. After the period was over, the groups were again rigorously examined, it being revealed thereby that the group that was taught grammar progressed in the faculty of distinguishing similarity and dissimilarity while its progress in other faculties and abilities was in no way better than that achieved by the other group.

W.H. Winch[18] conducted experiments in order to find out the extent to which a practice of adding and subtracting or problem solving in arithmetic lead to the development of a sense of logic in the subject. In the experiment, boys aged 10 and possessing similar ability in the solution of logical problems

---

17. Thorndike, E.L., Mental Discipline in High School Studies, *Journal of Educational Psychology*.
18. Winch, W.H., *Further Work in Numerical Accuracy in School Children*.

concerning arithmetic, were taken, and divided into two groups. One of the two groups was taught the solution of arithmetical problems for ten days, for a period of thirty minutes a day. The other group was given practice in drawing. Following the ten days, the two groups were examined in a manner intended to reveal reasoning ability in arithmetic, the examination yielding similar results for both groups. These results led to the conclusion that no distinct and precise relationship between the logic in arithmetic and addition- substraction or problem-solving can be established. In another experiment concerning the study of mathemetics as a source of mental development it was seen that the studying of descriptive geometry led to a 32 per cent improvement in the understanding of other subjects.[19]

In 1921-24, H. D. Rugg[20] conducted experiments to study the influence of Latin learning on the further learning of English. It became obvious from this study that children knowing Latin showed a progress in learning English of some 10 per cent over other children who were ignorant of Latin. It was concluded thereby that the knowledge of Latin helps in the speaking or learning of English. Children who had learnt Latin for one year showed that they were better in learning English than other children who had not studied Latin. The former secured better marks in the subject. This was found to be particularly true in the speaking of English. It was also found that this was true not only of English but also of Spanish and French, composition in which is facilitated by a knowledge of Latin. But this difference in the progress of those who know Latin and those who do not is not apparent over a long period of time. Experiments of Clifford Woody showed that even the knowledge of French can help in the learning of English, although French does not help in improving English sentence structure or selection of words. It was consequently concluded that the knowledge of some languages may prove to be efficacious in the learning of other languages.

---

19. Ref. *Journal of Educational Psychology*, Vol. II, No. 5, 1911.
20. Rugg, H.D., Educational Determination of Mental Discipline in School Studies, *Educational Psychology Monographs*.

Thorndike made the most extensive experiments in studying the transferability of school subjects. In one of his experiments he took some 13,500 students of the tenth, eleventh and twelfth classes. In this experiment the subject was to determine the influence upon the reasoning power of the study of different subjects. The following influence of a one-year study of ten subjects upon success or achievement in examination was evident from the experiment :

| Sl. No. | Subject group | Influence of achievement in examination |
|---|---|---|
| 1. | Algebra, geometry, trigonometry | +2.99 |
| 2. | Civics, economics, psychology, sociology | +2.89 |
| 3. | Chemistry, physics, general science | +2.71 |
| 4. | Arithmetic, accounting | +2.60 |
| 5. | Physical training | +0.83 |
| 6. | Latin, French | +0.79 |
| 7. | English, history, business, art | +0.00 |
| 8. | Shorthand, cooking, sculpture | –0.14 |
| 9. | Zoology, agriculture | –0.48 |
| 10. | Business | –0.48 |

The following conclusions are to be drawn from the above table concerning the transferability of school subjects :

(1) There is very little difference in the transference of the power of general reasoning between such academic subjects as Latin, arithmetic, etc., and such practical subjects as physical education, cooking, drawing, etc.

(2) The importance of all subjects on the power of reasoning or logical thinking is in fact equal, and there is no subject better or worse than any other.

The following summary, made by Pedro T. Oreta, is based on the various conclusions of tests concerning the transference of school subjects between 1890 and 1935 :

(1) 22% tests showed very distinct and special transferability.

(2) 48% tests showed appreciable transferability.

(3) 9% tests showed very little transference.

(4) 3.9% tests showed no transference.

(5) 7.2% tests showed transference along with obstacles.

(6) 3.9% tests showed transference in spite of obstacles.

It is evident from the above summary that it is not possible to call the study of any one subject definitive or administrative in the learning of other school subjects. While some tests have revealed some degree of transference, other tests have shown negative transference or even complete absence of it. It was only in a very small minority of tests that a transference of 92.9 per cent was recorded. And in 5.4 per cent of cases, the degree of transference that was recorded was accounted for by the difference in circumstances under which the tests were held. Hence, the following are the present conclusions regarding the transference of school subjects :

(1) Some branches of learning are positively influenced by practice in some other subjects.

(2) Study of some subjects does not help the study of other subjects in the least.

(3) Study of some subjects proves to be an obstacle in the learning of some other subjects.

(4) Of all the principles put forward concerning the phenomenon of transference, not one has proved to have any universal validity.

(5) Rote learning of any subject does not lead to its transference in any other subject.

## THEORIES CONCERNING THE TRANSFER OF TRAINING

### Ancient Theory

The principle of transfer of training took birth with the formal education system. According to this system, there are some subjects the study of which strengthens the faculties of the mind and which in turn help in the study of other subjects. It was believed, for instance, that the study of Sanskrit, Latin and Mathematics disciplined the mind which then found it easier to grasp other subjects communicated to it. These notions of the formal education system were based upon faculty psychology which conceived of the mind as a conglomerate of various powers of faculties such as observation, memory, reasoning, decision, etc. Hence it was essential that subjects should be chosen with a view to strengthening these faculties. The faculty of reasoning, for example, was believed to be strengthened by the study of mathematics, and that has helped the consequent study of law, philosophy and all such subjects that required the constant application of logical thinking.

**Modern Theory**

Modern psychology does not give any credence to the faculty psychology. Hence, modern psychologists abandoned the above elucidation of the principle of transfer of training, and replaced it with a multiplicity of explanations and principles. The following four theories are among the more important of them :

**1. Thorndike's Theory of identical elements.** According to Thorndike's opinion, identical elements are transferred from one situation to another situation, as for example, a knowledge of psychology helps in solving labour trouble and unrest.

**2. Judd's theory of generalisation.** According to this view, the recipient of one kind of training generalises the experience, knowledge and habits attained in it, and utilises this product in the new condition created in the learning of another form of training. And this transference is possible only if the recipient observes some similarity of elements between the two kinds of conditions.

**3. Sandiford's theory.** According to Sandiford, there is no essential difference between the theories of Thorndike and Judd, as both have said the same thing, *viz.*, that due to the similarity or identity of elements training in one circumstance leads to its transfer in the other. According to Sandiford, this transfer depends upon the individual's intelligence as only the perceptive individual can observe an identity of elements in two circumstances and make generalisations. It is his view that the power of generalisation is indicative of the individual's intelligence. He conducted tests to substantiate this view that the intelligent student can assimilate facts that he has gleaned from the perusal of newspapers in his paper on the languages whereas the unintelligent or backward student cannot utilise newspaper's information in his language papers. Similarly, negative transfer of training will be equally powerful in the intelligent person's case. An intelligent person adept in English will have difficulty in learning the Hindi idiom because of his practice in the other language.

**4. Skinner's view.** According to Skinner, purely oral information cannot be utilised in transfer of learning so long as the person is incapable of using that information in practical circumstances, and that the person's knowledge about using facts is not commensurate with or in proportion to his knowledge of the facts themselves. Secondly, if the individual carries a prejudicial attitude towards any learned fact, then this knowledge will not be help in the gaining of other knowledge. Thirdly, a scientific interest helps us in the accumulation of knowledge but it does not render any assistance in the transfer of knowledge. It becomes evident from these three points advanced by Skinner that only knowledge or scientific interest alone are not enough for transfer : it must also be used in practical conditions.

## Important Elements in Transfer of Training

It is evident from the above description that contemporary psychologists are desirous of discovering the conditions that help in the transfer of training. Many experiments have also been performed concerning this phenomenon. The more important facts gleaned from this extensive experimentation are the following :

**1. Subjects of learning differ in respect of their transference value.** Experiments upon the transference of subjects that are taught in school seem to indicate that these subjects have differing transfer values. As has been pointed out before, modern psychologists do not believe that any one subject can serve to discipline the mind, yet there is no denying it that the transfer value of mathematics and science is very high. Then come the languages and social sciences. History and English have no transfer value. Cooking, stitching and dancing have a negative transfer value by which is meant that a knowledge of these makes it difficult to learn other difficult subjects.

**2. Transfer is particular, not general.** From the facts used in the preceding illustrations it should not be concluded that the knowledge of language or science helps in the learning of every subject. It has further been pointed out that transfer takes place only if there is identity of circumstances or elements. Sanskrit may be of help in learning Hindi as well as Bengali, as Sanskrit words are numerously used in these languages but a knowledge of Sanskrit can be of no conceivable use in learning Urdu or Persian. It is more probable that pronunciation may be adversely influenced by such knowledge.

**3. Transfer depends much on the learner's intelligence and innate ability.** It has been clearly stated earlier that transfer is considerably influenced by the learner's intelligence. Experiments indicated that the ability of the best 1 per cent students of high school as far as transference is concerned, is something like 20 per cent more than that of the worst 1 per cent students. Similarly, an individual can make use of his knowledge only through innate ability and transfer is possible only if there is utilisation of knowledge.

**4. For achieving transference it is essential to study subjects that admit of transfer.** Accordingly, if training in Sanskrit is to be transferred, then Hindi or Bengali should be taught, while proficiency in Latin can be utilised in the teaching of English.

**5. Transfer depends upon the use of information.** It has been mentioned more than once at previous stages that no knowledge of subject that has been grasped can be transferred unless it is first utilised in practice. Moral teaching in school can only be transferred to social education if the student makes use of it in his day-to-day life.

**6. Transfer is due to similarity of material and methodology.** It, too, has been frequently pointed out earlier that the transfer of training can only be achieved in the learning of that subject which has some affinity with the first in respect of matter as well as methodology. Arithmetic can be transferred to bookkeeping.

From this description of transfer of training it is apparent that it depends upon the learner's intelligence, innate ability, knowledge, practical ability, and use of acquired information in practice. Transfer takes place in particular subjects that have similar material and similar methodology and skill in the teaching of such subjects. Transfer takes place in different quantities in different subjects. There is no transfer in some while it is negative or obstructive in others.

## QUESTIONS FOR EXERCISE

1. What is learning? How is it related to motivation and maturation?
2. What are the main methods of learning? Which of them do you like most and why?
3. Write short note on learning curve.
4. What is learning curve? How can it be of help to the school psychologist? What information does it provide for the development of efficient study method?
5. Write short note on Transfer of training.

# 8

# Psychological Testing

## Importance of Mental Tests

Psychological tests have been proved to possess great utility in many spheres. Briefly, the utility and importance of mental tests can be observed in the following spheres :

**1. Guidance.** As has been indicated earlier, psychological tests are indispensable in all forms of guidance.

**2. Appointments.** Psychological tests are nowadays resorted to for the appointment of appropriate individuals to posts in offices, factories and government services. It has the doubly beneficial effect of securing proper and desirable jobs for individuals according to their interest, inclinations, intelligence and abilities, as well as ensuring that the highest level of efficiency is achieved by the right man being in the right job. In this way, both the employee as well as the employer are benefited.

**3. Selection for training.** An individual can benefit from training for some particular job only if he is initially in possession of the requisite intelligence, abilities and qualities, besides the necessary interest in the work involved. It is evident that the individual should be tested in respect of these qualities before any training is imparted to him. Hence, in all advanced nations of the world, all kinds of training institutes make use of psychological tests for selecting the required candidates. In India, for example, the recruitment to the Police Training Colleges, the Govt. Teacher's Training College, and other technical institutions is done only on the basis of psychological tests. In public schools, the students who receive scholarships are selected on the basis of psychological tests in order to ensure that the scholarships are not wasted, as well they might be if they are provided to the wrong individuals. Psychological tests are further used for selection of candidates for the National Defence Academy in the country. Such use of psychological tests for the selection of personnel in training school is constantly on the increase.

**4. Classification according to level of intelligence.** Nowadays, all educationists agree that the success of education depends upon the student being provided education of a kind that accords with his level of intelligence. Hence, individual students are classified and stratified according to their level of intelligence, and different curricula and extacurricular programmes devised for the three categories of students, the brilliant, the average and the retarded. The classification is based on intelligence tests. It is not only in the field of education but also in various vocations, armed forces and industries that intelligence tests are used to classify individuals so that they can be given the proper kind of work that is within their capacity to perform with reasonable success.

**5. Prediction.** The term indicates the forecasting of success in the case of an individual. While guiding the individual, a psychologist can normally make fairly accurate predictions as to the degree of success that one is likely to achieve. The prediction is based upon psychological tests; the greater the capacity of a psychological test to assist in prediction, the greater is its validity and its reliability.

**6. Diagnosis.** Before giving any guidance, the directing psychologist makes a diagnosis of the problem present before him. He gives suggestions for alleviating a certain condition only after he has decided upon a diagnosis, since it is only upon diagnosing some problem that he reaches the root causes. And psychological tests are essential for diagnosis; without them a proper diagnosis cannot be achieved.

**7. Research.** Psychological tests are of use even in the field of psychological research. Intelligence tests, interest inventories, personality tests, tests of mental abilities and personality qualities help in research in these specific directions.

### What are Mental Tests?

Importance of psychological tests is fairly evident from the preceding exposition of the subject. Before proceeding to a study of the various kinds of tests, it is essential to know the kinds of psychological tests that are in use, and the principal elements active in them. Defining psychological tests, Mursell writes, "A psychological test, then, is a pattern of stimuli selected and organised to elicit responses which will reveal certain psychological characteristics in the person who takes them."[1] In this way, psychological tests are an organisation of some stimuli. These stimuli are selected with some special objectives in view. The object is to discover some psychological characteristics of the person being tested. Stimuli present in psychological tests are called test items, and they can be of several kinds — pictures, figures, wooden blocks, word groups, sentences and figures, etc. And the way in which these stimuli uncover psychological characteristics will be evident from a description of each of them.

### Psychological Tests and Experimentation

What should here be kept well in mind is that psychological tests differ from psychological experimentation although in both cases some stimuli are given, and it is the reactions to them that are examined. But the main difference between the two is one of purpose. As has been pointed out, the object of psychological tests is to ascertain the psychological characteristics of the subject, while in the case of psychological experimentation, the object is more purely academic as they aim at discovering a mental process concerned with the particular experiment. In this manner, it is evident that while psychological tests lead to the discovery of abilities or capabilities, the psychological experiments discover and confirm various mental processes. Nevertheless, the difference between the two is very subtle, since nowadays, psychological tests are also being used for discovering and identifying mental process.

## CLASSIFICATION OF PSYCHOLOGICAL TESTS

Mental tests are of various kinds. They have been classified from various different standpoints. Classifications are as follows :

**1. Classification according to method of testing.** Tests have been divided into two classes; in this case classification is based on the method involved :

1. Mursell, J.L., *Psychological Testing*, New York, Longmans Green (1953), p. I.

(a) ***Individual tests :*** These tests are administered to one individual at one time, as indicated by the term denoting them. They include performance tests. In addition to these, they also include tests that require linguistic ability. Some examples of these are Stanford Binet intelligence test, Weshler Bellevieu intelligence test, Kohez's block design test, Rorschach's ink blot test, and T.A.T. test, etc. These tests are particularly appropriate for testing of individuals, but they are not financially suitable as they are expensive, in addition to requiring more expert training than in many other cases. Secondly, they are less objective than group tests.

(b) ***Group tests :*** In this category the tests included are performed upon a large number of people simultaneously. Some examples are the group intelligence tests of the Psychological Bureau of Uttar Pradesh, interest lists, vocational lists etc. They are more objective and less expensive, requiring very little, if any, specialised training that may prove expensive. But in these tests, no real rapport between the subject and the examiner is established. Hence, they are less useful for solving problems of individuals, than are the individual tests. Nevertheless, they have proved really useful in the case of educational and vocational guidance requirements.

**2. Classification according to the medium of instruction.** In these tests, classification is based upon the medium of teaching of the subjects. The psychological tests, from this viewpoint, are divided into the following two classes :

(a) ***Verbal tests :*** This classification comprehends tests in which questions are orally asked, linguistic and concerned abilities being essentially required. One of the best examples of verbal tests is Dr. Sohan Lal's intelligence test utilised at Uttar Pradesh Bureau of Psychology. These tests are not intended for and cannot be used in the case of illiterates, only slightly educated persons and small children, since such people lack linguistic ability.

(b) ***Non-verbal tests :*** This classification includes tests that do not require the use of language, but substitute figures, pictures, blocks and other implements for it. Examples of it are Pidgon's non-verbal tests and Raven's progressive matrices. Their particular felicity lies in the fact that they can be applied to the testing of illiterates, very slightly educated individuals and very young children. This category includes all non-verbal tests.

**3. Classification according to the objectives of testing.** Division of tests on the basis of their individual objective or aim leads them to be put into the following categories :

(a) ***Intelligence tests :*** These help to test the intelligence, in the form of both verbal and non-verbal tests. They can be administered both to the individual and to a large group.

(b) ***Testing of mental abilities :*** In this are included the various tests of mental abilities such as tests of spatial ability, artistic ability, mechanical ability, etc.

(c) ***Interest tests :*** These tests help to discover the interest of the individual, some examples of which are Strong's Vocational Interest Blank, and Cudor's vocational inventory. Both of them are described in detail at a later stage. Besides these, the vocational interest list devised by the Bureau of Psychology, Uttar Pradesh, is also an effective test.

(d) ***Aptitude tests :*** These tests are devised by combining the different tests of mental abilities.

(e) ***Personality tests :*** These help to find out the individual's personality traits or characteristics. The main methods of personality testing are Rorschach's Ink Blot test and TAT.

## CHARACTERISTICS OF GOOD TESTS

Good tests of a psychological nature bear the following features :

**1. Reliability.** The higher the degree of reliability that results of a test have the greater is considered the reliability of the test itself. And the reliability of its conclusion means that if the same test is performed upon the same individual more than once, results obtained in each individual list should be the same or commensurate with the first one, if it is modified by changed circumstances.

**2. Validity.** The validity of a test is the fact that it succeeds in testing the particular quality which it is designed to test. For example, intelligence tests can be valid only if they, in fact, test correctly the intelligence level of the individual subject.

**3. Objectivity.** A test can achieve a high level of objectivity only if the answer to each of its various questions is distinct and precise and if there is no difference of opinion regarding it among the various examiners. Its efficacy lies in the fact that the conclusion or result is in no way influenced by the examiner's individual thoughts or opinions, so that the conclusions or results are obtained no matter what the number of examiners who examine the same subject.

**4. Comprehensiveness.** Another feature of a good test is its comprehensive nature. This feature involves inclusion of all features or qualities allied to the one in question. It will provide information on qualities concerned with the one quality actually being tested. In this manner, in a comprehensive test, questions cover the quality in question as well as allied qualities so that no aspect of the measured or tested ability escapes attention.

**5. Discriminating power.** This term applies to the ability which helps to distinguish between persons with greater or less ability so that they score more or less points or marks.

**6. Utility.** This feature concerns the extent to which a particular test can be used with facility. And for this it is essential that the questions asked should be simple, the method easy, the time involved less and the expenses negligible.

Of the above-mentioned characteristics, the most important are validity and reliability. Hence, both these qualities will be described in detail here :

## VALIDITY

### What is Validity?

It is apparent from the description of intelligence tests that all tests do not have a common degree of validity, it being completely dependent upon the extent to which any judgement based upon the test's result is objective. For example, validity in the case of intelligence tests can be attributed only to those tests that actually succeed in testing the individual's level of intelligence. A test can be accepted as valid only to that degree to which it can correctly gauge the intelligence of the subject. In this way, validity of a test is that quality on the basis of which the correctness or incorrectness of judgements based upon it is evaluated. For example, the validity of interest tests is less than in the case of intelligence tests. Here there is a slight difficulty. Suppose, for the moment that the intelligence of some students was measured by one particular method. Now the validity of the test will depend upon whether the students tested do in fact possess the intelligence that they are indicated as possessing. The problem that arises here is how can one ascertain whether the students do or do not possess the intelligence indicated by the above test. Evidently, there must be some independent criterion for deciding upon the validity of the particular test in question or tests in general. In this case of the intelligence level of students, the examination results can be the basis for measuring the validity of the test. Generally speaking, it can be said that if there is a correlation between marks obtained at an examination and the result of the test, then the test is valid.

**Kinds of Validity**

But as is evident from the foregoing description, validity is a relative term, as no test can have complete validity. Hence whenever a particular test is termed valid, or whenever the lack of validity of a test is in question, it is necessary to indicate the sense in which it is considered valid or invalid. Apparently, validity is of many kinds. Psychologists have roughly accepted the following kinds of validity :

**1. Face validity.** Face validity is concerned with the form of the test. Such a validity is attributed only to the test which provides an item or subject that appears valid.

**2. Content validity.** Another kind of validity is content validity in which the validity of the test is based on the validity of its contents. In order to obtain this kind of validity in a particular test, it is essential that the items of a test should achieve the objective for which they are originally designed. For example, content validity in the case of an intelligence test will be attributed only in the event of its succeeding in discovering all factors concerned with intelligence.

**3. Factorial validity.** This is inclusive of the validity of the factors in the test. And in order to judge whether a test has factorial validity, it is examined by the method of factor analysis, and a correlation between this result and the evident factor resultant of tests established.

**4. Predictive validity.** This is the most popular form of validity. In this, results are obtained on the basis of a particular criterion, and correlation between the scores and the criterion is established. In this, the choice of a criterion requires much care and attention. The coefficient obtained by this correlation between scores and criterion is called the validity coefficient. The validity coefficient varies between 0·5 and 0·8. A lower coefficient makes the test inapplicable and lacking in utility, while a higher coefficient is not normally obtained.

**5. Concurrent validity.** It resembles the predictive validity since in it, too, a correlation between the test and some definite standard is established. But, despite these common features, there are also some definite variations.

From the above analysis of the various kinds of validity, it is evident that validity exists in a particular context, or in other words, every test is valid for a particular objective and for a particular age group in individuals. It can just as well be invalid for a particular age group in individuals and in a particular context. Hence, to attribute validity to a test without qualification is completely unjustified and inaccurate. For the sentiment to have any value or meaning, it is essential to state the context and conditions in which it is applicable.

## RELIABILITY

### What is Reliability?

In addition to validity, it is essential that in every test there be a definite element of reliability. It is only then that the conclusions of the test can be considered reliable and worthy of trust. Reliability of a test consists in any quality in the test that may inspire confidence and trust. And this quality can be attributed to only that test which provides the same score every time it is performed on the same individual. Now, if some intelligence test yields one score for an individual at one time, and another if it is applied to the same individual at a different time, it is only too evident that such a test cannot be considered reliable. And this reliability of the test does not reside in any one part of it, but in its wholeness or completeness. Its reliability will considerably be weakened and decreased if even one part of it is injured in some respect. Hence it is essential that the internal parts of a test possess internal consistency and uniformity. It is only on the basis of such a reliable test that guidance can be given.

**Means of Measuring Reliability**

Reliability can be measured in the following four ways :

**1. Test re-test method.** One method of gauging reliability is to perform the same test of the same group of individuals on two different occasions, and to test the scores or results obtained. One group of individuals can be subjected to the Binet intelligence test. Then later on the same group of individuals can again be subjected to the Binet intelligence test. If the results obtained in each case do not tally, then the tests cannot be considered reliable,

**2. Parallel form method.** Another method of judging the reliability of a particular method is to prepare a method similar to the one being judged and examined. Now the same group can be examined through the basic and then through the modified or parallel methods. Finally, the results of the two can be compared to judge the reliability of the test. Gulliksen has suggested that more than one parallel method be devised for greater accuracy.

**3. Split half method.** Another method of judging the reliability of a test is to divide the components of the test into even and odd times whose results can be individually obtained. Now the results can be compared to show the reliability of the test.

**4. Inter item consistency.** In this method of measuring the reliability of a psychological test, only one method is applied at one time. The mutual relation between the scores obtained for each specific item in the test is observed. At the same time the relation between the marks obtained for one specific question and the marks obtained for the whole test is also ascertained. As this method of measuring reliability involves considerable statistical skill in correlation, psychologists Cudor and Richardson, have devised some formulae for application in this method.

As has been indicated previously, the implication and meaning of reliability also change the method of judging reliability. Hence, it is not sufficient to remark that a particular test is reliable. It is equally essential that the sense in which reliability is judged also be mentioned, or in other words mention must be made of the method by which its reliability has been established.

Of the above-mentioned methods of judging reliability of psychological tests, the third is the most prevalent and useful, since it is the most easy. In this method, the necessity of collecting the same group of individuals more than once is obviated. Reliability is known from the coefficient of reliability, and this coefficient is known as the reliability coefficient.

In this manner, both reliability and validity are important qualities of tests. Validity is related to the scale of structure of the test while reliability is an attribute of its ability of testing.

The aim and object of education are the comprehensive, overall development of the child. This development and progress are gradual. Hence, it is essential to examine the child at regular intervals to find out the extent to which he has progressed. In the school, students study a number of subjects. To test one in respect of these subjects from time to time is essential as it makes clear the success with which he is studying and understanding them. It is the examination that makes it possible for one to know the child's achievements in terms of ability in learning these subjects. Hence, in almost all schools some mode of examining the children, in respect of their attainments in learning and retaining all that is taught to them, is present.

## INTELLIGENCE TEST

### Historical Outline

As the new individual dissimilarities came to light, psychologists tried to measure the various individual differences and to this end, different tests were evolved. Among these tests, those devised to measure intelligence achieved a lot of fame. Near the close of the 19th century, Galton developed some tests to measure the function of the different organs. By these, Galton measured sensory discrimination, sensory perception and sensory acuity. Though these measures are not directly related to intelligence, they may be accepted as the forerunners of intelligence tests.

In 1880, Ebbinghaus prepared several tests to measure the differences in the intelligence of various individuals. In 1890, a famous American psychologist Cattell evolved some mental tests. On the basis of these, Cattell measured individual differences between some students of Columbia University, in respect of the speed of reactions, sensory acuity, memory and some other simple mental activities.

But in fact, the first concrete step in the direction of intelligence tests was taken by a famous French psychologist Alfred Binet. Alfred Binet was conducting some research in the mental activities of school-going children. In the course of his research he observed that in order to give any useful education to the feeble-minded children it is essential to put them in special classes. In order to investigate this subject, a committee headed by Binet was formed in 1904. The first difficulty, concerning the study of feeble-minded children, was need of a scale with which to measure the intelligence of children.

With Simon's assistance Binet developed and published a scale in 1905, known as the Binet-Simon Scale. In this scale, some 30 tasks, from the simplest to the most complex, were prescribed in a serial order. On the basis of experiments with the average and feeble-minded children carried out with the help of this scale Binet and Simon determined norms for various age levels. According to the Binet-Simon intelligence tests, if a five-year old child is capable of performing tasks which an average child of three can perform, his mental age will be rated as three years and if that child fails to perform more than the first five among the thirty tasks he will be classed as idiot.

Binet and Simon made revisions in this scale from time to time. The first revised scale was published in 1908. From the success of this revision, psychologists of other countries developed intelligence tests suitable to the environment of their own countries. Among them, Burt's London Revision and Terman's Stanford Revision are well known. The modern revised edition of the 2nd revision was published in 1937 under the name of Terman Merrill Scale.

In the Terman Merrill Scale which was a revision of the Stanford Binet Scale, some more subjects, related to intelligence tests were included. It now became useful for the age range of 2 to 18 years. In this scale, there were provisions for two types of tests, yearly and half-yearly, for children belonging to the age group of two to four years. Many other subjects were included for the adult people. For every age group there were six to eight subjects. In this scale there are tests which enable the examiner to examine the intelligence of an individual in a very short time.

In Indian conditions, Binet's test was adopted for the first time by Dr. C. Herbert Rice. But its revised form is almost completely different from the Binet tests. These tests were compiled in Urdu and Punjabi. There are two types of scale in it, one having 10 tasks, the other 35 tasks, and it was the smaller scale of tests which proved dependable. In 1927, Dr. J. Munry of Christian College started verbal group tests in Urdu, English and Hindi. In 1933, Mr. Lajja Shankar developed group tests for children from 10 to 18, which adopted a revised and studied form of Terman's group tests. Besides these, the group tests started by Dr. Jalota of Lahore, in Hindi, in Urdu and English proved very valuable. In Bihar, under the direction of Dr. S.M. Mohsin, a test battery was constructed to measure mental abilities and intelligence of participants in many group tests. In the nonverbal group tests, Menzel has created tests founded upon the ability of Indian children in drawing. Besides, Mr. I.R. Kumaria organised group tests for college students. The other importent contributions in this direction have come from Dr. Lalit Kumar Shah, C.T. Philip, H.C. Banerjee, D.H. Roy, T.P. Bhowmick and H.P. Maiti. The above description makes it quite clear that not much work has been done in the direction of non-verbal tests. There is hope of development in this direction in the future.

**Types of Intelligence Tests**

Intelligence tests are classified as follows according to the activities prescribed in them :

1. Verbal Tests,
2. Non-Verbal Tests.

As the name itself suggests, verbal tests make use of language while the non-verbal tests include such activities which do not necessitate the use of language. Both these types are suitable for individual as well as group tests. Consequently, verbal and non-verbal tests are further sub-divided into two classes — individual and group. Thus, finally there are four types of intelligence tests :

1. Verbal Individual Intelligence Tests,
2. Non-Verbal Individual Intelligence Tests,
3. Verbal Group Intelligence Tests,
4. Non-Verbal Group Intelligence Tests.

**Verbal Individual Intelligence Tests**

The very name verbal individual intelligence tests suggests that there are intelligence tests given to individuals or in other words they are meant to test the intelligence of individuals. Language finds adequate use in them. Binet-Simon tests and the various revisions are all included in this classification.

The State Manovigyanshala of Uttar Pradesh has made a Hindi version of the Terman Merrill Scale. This revision includes a variety of material, from solid objects to difficult questions. The activities in the beginning are simple like constructing a bridge or a tower of blocks or fitting in irregular wooden blocks in their proper place supplied for them. At the same time, at the end of the tests there are difficult questions which need considerable thinking. This test is divided into several age groups. The higher groups use language and its use gradually declines with the age group. For example, the two-year's group includes the following activities :

1. The form panel with three holes,
2. Recognising of objects by name,
3. Recognising the objects of the body,
4. Making a tower of blocks,
5. Naming an object from its picture,
6. Word building.

**Non-verbal Individual Intelligence Tests**

It is quite apparent from the above example that in verbal tests, the child's knowledge of language is more in demand, and therefore the use of these tests is limited to students and literate persons. But these verbal tests cannot be used in the case of illiterate individuals as these tests involve an extensive use of language which fails as a medium to measure the individual differences between the illiterates. Consequently, illiterate individuals are tested with the help of non-verbal individual intelligence tests. The name itself indicates the nature of these tests. These tests involve the least possible use of the linguistic ability and are similarly almost unaffected by knowledge derived from books. An example of these non-verbal tests is the Performance Intelligence Tests.

It would be in keeping with the context of our discussion to understand in detail the performance intelligence test as an example of the non-verbal individual intelligence tests. The word 'performance' is usually applied to tests which require a minimum use of understanding and language. Thus, these tests make use of items requiring performances and not language and these tests can be applied to children, illiterates, feeble-minded individuals as well as foreigners.

### Merrill-Palmer Block Building Tests

One of the most important of performance tests for children is Merrill-Palmer Block Building Test. Besides Seguin Form Board it includes block building test as well. Figure 8.1 a four year old boy is making a structure by means of blocks as demonstrated by the tester.

Fig. 8.1

### Pintner-Paterson Performance Scale

An example of the performance intelligence tests is the Pintner-Paterson Performance Scale. It was evolved by Pintner and Paterson in 1917. In this scale there are 15 types of tests, of which 4 are form boards, 6 picture completion, memory span and the rest picture puzzles, imitations, etc.

### Porteus Maze Test

Another example of the performance intelligence tests is the Porteus Maze Test. In it, paper and pencil mazes are used. For his tests, Porteus created mazes for children from 3 to 14 years. It gets difficult, corresponding to the increase in age. The subject is allowed two chances and if he fails in the attempts then the conclusion is that his intelligence is not of that age level. Children of 12 to 14 years are given four opportunities. These tests designed by Porteus not only measure intelligence, but they also reflect the temperament of the individual. It is distinguished from other tests in as much as that it includes some aspects ignored by such tests as the Stanford-Binet tests.

### Form Board Test

A comparatively simple example of the performance intelligence test is the form board test among which the tests of Seguin and Goddard deserve special mention. In the form board test, there are numerous blocks and a board in which there are holes corresponding to this block. The subject as shown in Fig. 8.2 has to fit the blocks in these corresponding

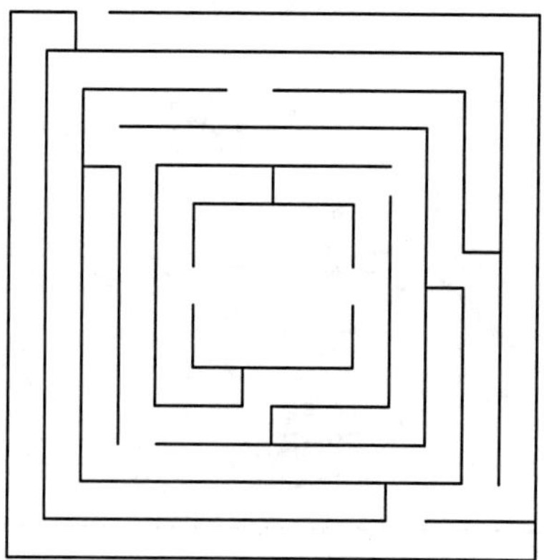

Fig. 8.2

holes in the board, the time taken and mistakes committed being noted from which the score test is calculated.

### Wechsler Bellevue Test

Another example of the performance intelligence tests is the Wechsler Bellevue test, evolved in 1939, meant for persons from 10 to 60 years of age. In a modern clinic, these tests are included in Binet class, as one of the most important. In this way it is the most apt test for measuring the intelligence of adults. In this test there are five verbal tests and five performance tests. This test affords not only an index to mental abilities but also a profile of abilities.

### Bhatia's Battery of Performance Test

Then description of performance intelligence tests is incomplete without reference to Bhatia's Battery of performance tests. It is the battery created by the former director of Uttar Pradesh Manovigyanshala Dr. Chandra Mohan Bhatia. It has the following five sub-tests :

**1. Kohez block design test.** Ten items of test out of the Kohez block design test have been included in the battery. There is one card on every subject upon which is depicted a colour design. The examinee sees this design and makes a similar one out of the blocks as shown in Fig. 8.3. These designs

Fig. 8.3

become correspondingly more and more complex, having been simple at the start.

**2. Alexander pass along test.** The Bhatia lattery also includes Alexander pass along test, in which, too, there are some designs. As shown in Fig. 8.4 the subject shifts coloured pieces in an open box and places them in similar design.

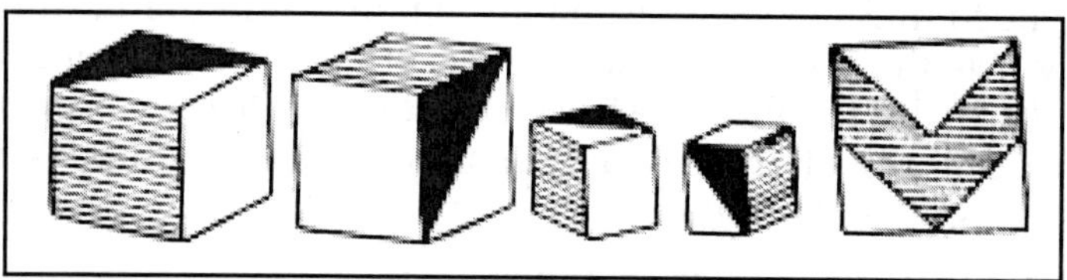

Fig. 8.4

**3. Pattern drawing test.** This test has been developed by Dr. Bhatia himself. In this there are eight cards on each of which there is a particular form. The subject draws particular figure or pattern after seeing this form.

**4. Immediate memory test.** Some digits are recited, which are immediately repeated by the subject, this activity throwing some light on the immediate memory of the subject.

Fig. 8.5

**5. Picture construction test.** In this sub-test there are five subjects in which pictures relating to the rural life are fragmented into 2, 4, 6, 8 and 12 pieces respectively. At one time pieces of a picture are placed before the subject who puts them in order and constructs the picture.

**Difficulties in the Individual Intelligence Tests**

Some difficulties are faced in both the verbal and non-verbal types of individual intelligence tests. They are roughly as follows :

**1. The difficulty of time.** The individual intelligence test takes an hour usually and only one person can be tested at one time. Obviously, at this rate it would be essential to have a very big number of trained examiners and in spite of that it would be difficult to test all the people.

**2. Need for experienced examiners.** The second obstacle in the individual intelligence tests is the need for experienced examiners because the correct result cannot be arrived at if the examiners are inexperienced. At the same time, the availability of such a large number of trained personnel is almost impossible.

Notwithstanding these difficulties, in some circumstances, the individual intelligence tests become unavoidable. This is because the level of accuracy reached by the individual intelligence tests, in the assessment of a person's intelligence, is beyond the reach of the group intelligence tests.

**Verbal Group Intelligence Tests**

The group intelligence tests owe their origin and development to the difficulties from which the individual tests suffer. As the name suggests, these tests are designed to test the intelligence of a group and not of an individual. All the people in the group are given the same directions and have to perform the same activities. Even the score of the result of group intelligence tests is calculated by machines thus dispensing with the necessity of skilled examiners, resulting in an economy of time.

**Army alpha and beta tests.** An excellent example of group intelligence tests is afforded by the Army alpha and beta tests, which were evolved during World War I in order to test the American soldiers. For example, it revealed separately the feeble-minded, men capable of becoming skilled specialists, men capable of becoming officers, men needing some training, etc.

**Naval and army general classification tests.** Due to the success which attended these tests, some group tests for classification of naval or army soldiers were evolved during the World War II. Of these two particular forms deserve mention. These two are — (1) Naval general classification tests and (2) Army general classification tests.

With the type of calculations made by Cruze, some one billion people were tested by the military general classification tests during the years 1941 to 1946. In these tests there are three subjects, *viz.*, those relating to vocabulary problems, relating to mathematics, and relating to problems of counting blocks.

From the above example, it is quite clear that these verbal group intelligence tests examine the reasoning ability, ability of comparing and contrasting, sense of directions, ability in numerals and language, of the individuals who constitute the group. It is essential that the examiner should be fully acquainted with the test and he should also understand the corresponding directions. Thus, often the examiner examines himself to start with. At the same time, it is necessary for the examiner to have some knowledge of the mechanical aspects of the conditions of examination such as the proper seating arrangement of the examinees, the distribution of test blanks and the preparation of material related to the tests, like pencils, etc.

**Difficulties in the Verbal Group Intelligence Tests**

Even after taking all the precautions, some difficulties are discernible in the verbal group intelligence tests which can be eliminated only by reverting to the individual intelligence tests. It is due to these difficulties that the individual intelligence tests are considered more realistic than the group intelligence tests. The difficulties of the verbal group tests are fundamentally as follows :

**1. Difficulties relating to co-operation in tests.** In these tests it is difficult to judge whether the examinee is extending his full co-operation or not.

**2. Difficulties related to the balance of the subject.** In these tests it is difficult to determine whether the physical and emotional balance of the examinee is even or disturbed.

**3. Difficulty related to the ease of the subject.** In the verbal group intelligence test it is difficult to ascertain if the examinee is feeling at ease and free or restrained.

**4. Possibility of cheating by the subject.** Another difficulty in these tests is that no one can testify whether the person has written the answer himself or copied it from his neighbour.

In spite of the difficulties which arise in the verbal group intelligence tests, they have their own advantages due to which they are used comprehensively. As has been said before, the advantages are the same as the difficulties of the individual intelligence tests.

### Non-verbal Group Intelligence Tests

As has been mentioned before, the verbal intelligence tests are meant only for the literates because of the requirement of linguistic ability. It is for this reason that the non-verbal group intelligence tests have been developed, the examinee making a minimum use of language but performing, instead, many activities. One example of the non-verbal intelligence test is Cattel's Culture Free test and the N.I.I.P. test. An example of the subjects given in these tests is as follows :

In Fig. 8.6 there are 3 squares with some figures drawn in the three squares. On the left various figures are shown in five squares. In the given diagram, the fourth square has to be filled with one such figure from the five squares that its relation

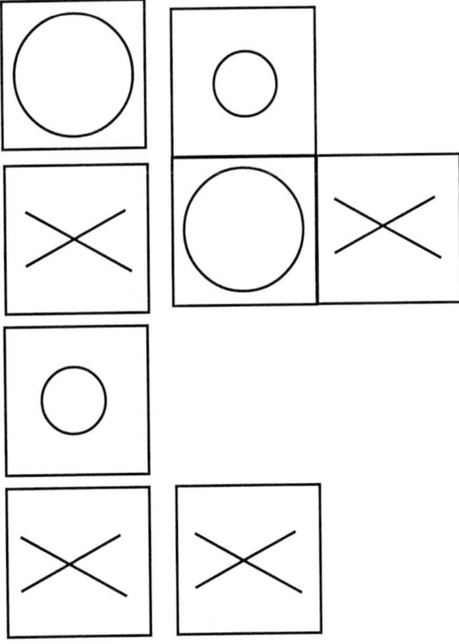

Fig. 8.6

with the third square must be the same as the relation which the figure in the first square bears to the figure in the second square.

In these non-verbal group intelligence tests, the examiners have to explain to the examinees even the simplest directions which are also demonstrated as far as possible. All this is done to make the least possible use of language. There are some performance tests in these group intelligence tests, in which the examinee draws some lines according to his abilities, fills in some empty spaces, draws some simple figures, or performs some simple activities. Some psychologists do not give credence to these non-verbal tests in their role of measuring intelligence of the subjects, while on the other hand some psychologists consider them to be better than verbal tests. For example in Alexander's opinion, "A complete performance battery will be a better measure than a complete verbal battery."

**Characteristics of the Non-verbal Group Intelligence Tests**

The truth is that even if non-verbal group intelligence tests are not more important than verbal tests, they are certainly

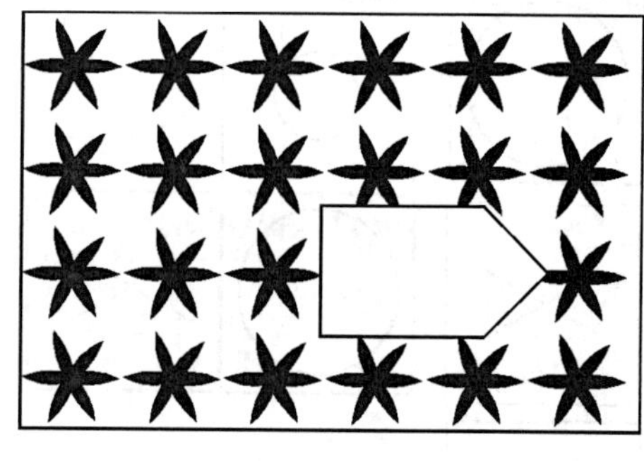

**Fig. 8.7.** Matrix similar to Raven's Progressive Matrices

not less important than these tests. Some of their characteristics are as follows :

**1. Comparison of various human groups.** The first obstacle in the comparison of human groups of various languages and cultures is the difference in their language. This obstacle can be overcome by non-verbal group intelligence tests and a comparison between different human groups is rendered possible.

**2. The testing of illiterate soldiers.** The verbal group intelligence tests are manifestly inapplicable to illiterate soldiers for the testing of their intelligence. Consequently, the abilities of illiterate soldiers are assessed by employing the non-verbal group intelligence tests and the possibilities of learning are known.

**3. Intelligence testing in children.** The linguistic ability is very low in the case of children and consequently the verbal group intelligence tests cannot be given to them.

**Reliability**

The reliability of a test depends not on any one item in the test but on the test as a whole. The reliability of the test diminishes if any one item of the test is defective. That is why there must be a uniformity and internal consistency between the various items of the test. It is only on the basis of such a reliable test that correct directions can be given.

Reliability is investigated in three ways. These ways are as follows :

1. The test is applied to the same group under two different conditions and the results thus compiled are compared. Suppose, for example, the group is tested for its intelligence using the Binet test. Now, after sometime, the same group is tested employing the Binet test. If the I.Q. resulting from both the tests is the same, the Binet tests will be accepted as reliable. If there are some differences between the I.Q. received from the two tests, they will be considered unreliable.

2. In a test in which there are many items, the results of the even and the odd items are compared, to examine its reliability.

3. Another method of examining reliability is to prepare a

test parallel to the one whose reliability is under examination. Now a group should be tested by both the original and the transformed forms of the test. This is followed by a comparison of the two results and the reliability of the test is, in this way, examined. Gulliksen has advised the preparation of more than one parallel list.

Among the three methods of examination of reliability, the second is the most popular because it is also the easiest. This method does not necessitate the collection of the group time and again. Reliability is known from the coefficient of correlation which is known as the reliability coefficient.

Thus, both validity and reliability are essential qualities of tests. While validity is related to the scale or structure of the test, reliability is related to the capacity of the test.

## MEASUREMENT OF PERSONALITY

Psychologists employ a number of methods to measure personality, *e.g.* situation test, psychoanalytic test, projective method, etc. Besides these, the case history method, interview and questionnaire and rating methods have their own importance. Briefly, the methods of measuring personality are :

1. Case history Method
2. Interview Method
3. Questionnaire Method
4. Performance Method
5. Rating Method
6. Situation Test
7. Psychoanalytic Test
8. Projection Techniques

Among the above-mentioned methods, the projection techniques are the most popular. A brief description of the other methods, before we make a detailed description of this specific one, would be quite in keeping with the context :

**1. Case history method.** In the case history method, as the name obviously indicates, the facts concerning the life of the subject are collected. This case history supplies all the facts related to man's environment and heredity. This method can be employed to study both normal and abnormal personality but it needs experienced testers.

**2. Interview method.** The interview method is the most common of all the methods for the study of personality. It is the method widely used in the selection of people for government, semi-government and private services. In this, the subject and the tester sit facing each other and the former answers questions asked by the latter'. Besides the answers which the subject offers, his personality is indicated by his expression. This method, like the case history method, needs very experienced testers who ask questions which may probe the correct thing and enable the subject to express himself without any apprehension. Thus the interview method depends as much on the tester as it does on the subject.

**3. Questionnaire method.** Questionnaires have been used extensively in the investigation of personality. The name suggests that it is a list of selected questions the answers to which throw light upon different traits of personality. 'Yes' and 'No' are written in front of these questions. The subject either strikes out the wrong answer or indicates the correct one. Questionnaires are used to gain knowledge of traits like self-confidence, sociability, introversion or extroversion, tendency to dominate or be dominated, etc.

There are some difficulties in the questionnaire method. It has the following limitations :

(a) Often the subjects conceal the facts and give wrong answers.

(b) Sometimes the framing of the questions is such that the tester takes them to mean one thing and the subject another.

(c) Usually the subjects write the answer without an adequate amount of thinking thus leaving possibility of mistakes.

In spite of these difficulties, the questionnaire method has proved to be of tremendous value. Allport, Minnesota, etc. have formed questionnaires which help in the study of some subtle traits of personality. It affords a lot of assistance to comparative study because of the various answers of the subjects to the same questions. The conclusions based on these questionnaires are comparative as well as numerical. They also facilitates wide study because a number of people can be studied simultaneously.

**4. Performance method.** The performance method was developed by May and Hartshorne. In this method the subject is given a variety of specific jobs to be performed and the particular trait of his personality is examined. For example, in order to test the honesty of children some weights with little difference between them, were presented to them. The exact weight of each was written under it and the children were told to place them in the correct order. The honest children experienced great difficulty while the dishonest read the weights under them and placed them in order promptly. A very simple method of judging the honesty of the students in the class could be something like this. Some piece should be dictated and the copies collected and examined. The mistakes of each should be secretly noted without any markings on the copy, following which the copies should be returned with the direction that the mistakes are to be noted and marks allocated. The dictation should be written on the blackboard. The honest will mark their mistakes while the dishonest will quietly correct them. The honesty of the students can be judged by comparing these with the mistakes previously noted.

**5. Rating method.** Another method of measuring personality is the rating method, in which the procedure is of two types. One, the subject is asked to answer questions related to traits of personality. The answers which the subject offers or selects exhibit his personality. Another way of applying the rating method is to place the subject in real situations and then study his behaviour and reactions. For example, in order to judge personality traits, a person is given a variety of jobs to perform.

As it is, the rating method is very simple. But it needs more skilful testers. Roughly speaking, it presents the following difficulties :

(a) Much skill and capability are essential in the tester.

(b) The possibility of prejudice is very great.

(c) It is very difficult to enumerate or evaluate the subtle traits. Mistakes are often made in this.

In spite of the above-mentioned difficulties, both social and industrial psychologists make much use of this method. As has been pointed out previously too, it can be made useful to a large extent if the tester is very skilful.

**6. Situation test.** As usual, the name suggests the nature of the method. In it, the subject is placed in some specific situations and the traits of his personality are ascertained. Actually, it resembles the performance method, the difference lying in the fact that in this case the person is placed in a situation while in the performance method he is given some work to do.

**7. Psychoanalytic method.** In the psychoanalytic method of measurement of personality, two types of tests are more popular — Free Association and Dream Analysis. Both these tests show the traits of the personality, in its unconscious aspect. In dream analysis, the subject describes his dream and without using reasoning, associates freely the dream objects and activities. Because of the absence of reasoning, the truth of the unconscious mind is expressed by this association, by which the psychoanalyst discovers many characteristics of personality. The psychoanalytic method is mostly used in discovering the personality traits and mental ailments of abnormal people. Its main condition lies in the need for a skilled and experienced psycho-analyst. Often, the psychoanalyst has to analyse his own mind in order to remove the possibility of any prejudice.

**8. Projective techniques.** The most popular of all the methods for the investigation of personality is the projective method. Its name suggests the fact that it is founded upon the element of projection. The Taj Mahal, to take an example, is a marble building many people go to see. Different people find in it different things, in keeping with the peculiarities of their personalities. An emotional person sees it in the form of a formal symbol of emotions while, to the person who gives importance to political and economic questions, it may be a symbol of exploitation. This is an example of a material object but it does make clear the fact that a human being does not see an object as it is but also projects the traits of his own personality upon it. Many peculiarities of the personality are investigated by an analysis of this projection and a comparison of it with the projections effected by others.

Two tests in the projective techniques are more widely used :

1. Rorschach ink-blot test.

2. Murry's Thematic Apperception Test, known in brief as T.A.T.

They are extensively used in the investigation of personality. These will, therefore, be described briefly here :

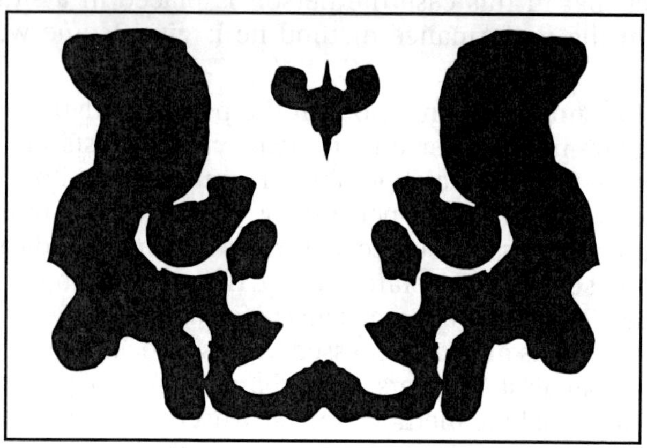

Fig. 8.8

**1. Rorschach ink-blot test.** This test was developed by the Swiss scientist Hermann Rorschach. He used 10 original ink blot cards which are still in use today. There is no picture made in these blots. Five of these are black, two black and red and the other three multicoloured. To investigate personality, they are exhibited before the subject one after the other and he is asked to describe everything he sees in the blot. These are shown for a definite interval of time. Then they are shown to the subject for

**Fig. 8.9.** An Indianised Picture from T.A.T.

a second time and he is asked to point out the location, of whatever he had seen, on the blot. In order to establish the meaning of the subject's reaction to the blots, the psychologist analyses the location, determining factors and the object. The analysis of the location serves to indicate whether the subject reacted to some particular spot on the blot or towards the blot as a whole. As a general rule, it is believed that the person who reacts more completely is more principled. The analysis of the determining factors is an attempt to find out whether the reaction of the subject is towards the share of the blot or to the colour or motion in the blot. As to the object, the analysis shows whether the subject sees in it, the figure of a man or an animal or anything else.

Besides the above analysis, facts like the time taken by the subject to react to the whole blot, the number of activities which he did and whether he did them normally or not, are also noted and observed. All these things tend to help in the analysis and investigation of the unconscious peculiarities of the subject.

The difficulty in the ink-blot test is that the description of the subject's reaction becomes quite subjective, which conceals to some extent the correct personality traits of the subject. But efforts are being made to make this test more objective.

**2. Murrey's thematic apperception test.** The founder of this test, Murrey investigated the personality traits with the help of some pictures which are still considered to be standard. Observing these pictures, the subject, by projection, identifies himself with the characters in the picture. The pictures are presented one by one to the subject who has to compose a story on each of them within some fixed time period, say five minutes. Unknowingly, the subject expresses many of the peculiarities of his personality in these stories by projection. He does not get time to think. Therefore the story expresses his natural desires, emotions, sentiments, etc. On the basis of these stories, the psychologist analyses the personality of the subject and uncovers its traits.

As in the Rorschach ink-blot test, there is some difficulty in Murrey's thematic apperception test, since the personality investigation done by it is not numerical but qualitative with possibility of mistakes. But there is no doubt that an experienced and skilful psychologist can use this method to uncover many hidden traits of the personality of the subject. This test helps in the discovery of many abnormalities of personality as well.

## MEASUREMENT OF SPECIAL ABILITIES

Such problems as the profession an individual may adopt, or the course of study a student may profitably pursue are ones that need guidance and for this guidance it is essential that in addition to measuring the individual's level of intelligence, his special abilities are investigated. Hence, efforts have been made to devise tests to discover special mental abilities, and they are being extensively used.

Before going on to a description of the testing of special mental abilities, it is necessary to know the age in which these tests can be suitably administered. This question arises for the simple reason that in childhood, these special abilities are not distinctly present and psychologists are not unanimous in their opinions regarding the age in which these abilities become distinct and separate. According to some, man's special mental abilities can be separately distinguished at the age of 11, while in the opinion of Cyril Burt, it is at 13 that these abilities become distinct. Generally, it is the former opinion that is accepted. Accordingly, all educational guidance is rendered at the age of 11 or thereabouts.

### Number of Special Mental Abilities

Having determined the age in which the special mental abilities become distinct, it is now essential that their number also be determined. In fact, it is very difficult to determine the exact number of special abilities, and there is no unanimity of opinion on this question. In 1938, Thurston and his associates fixed the number of special fundamental abilities at seven, calling them Primary Mental Abilities — verbal abilities or V, numerical ability or N, reasoning or R, memory or M, word fluency or W, and spatial ability or S, and perceptual speed or P. The Chicago primary mental abilities test has been based on these mental abilities. Another test battery formed on the same principle is used in the American Psychological Corporation. It contains the following seven tests :

(1) Verbal reasoning,

(2) Numerical ability,
(3) Abstract reasoning,
(4) Space relation,
(5) Mechanical reasoning,
(6) Clerical speed and accuracy,
(7) Language uses.

Now, we can go on to a slightly detailed account of some special abilities tests :

**1. Thurston's S.R.A. Tests of primary mental abilities.** To repeat, Thurston has discovered the presence of seven fundamental abilities through his study. This conception of primary mental abilities wrought a great change in the field of guidance and counselling. Following this discovery, in the field of guidance even more importance began to be attached to these abilities, than to intelligence, since mental abilities of different individuals with similar levels of intelligence were found to differ in the extreme. On the other hand people with the same mental abilities were found to have different levels of intelligence. In fact, the choice of a course of study to be taken Up by a student or the choice of a profession by a person requires a test of special abilities more than it requires intelligence tests since success in these fields-depends more upon innate as well as acquired ability than upon intelligence. Hence in England and America, many tests of mental abilities were evolved, and they were combined to form test batteries. Then, these test batteries were used extensively in the field of education and professions.

Thurston constructed three batteries of tests for special abilities for various children in the following three age divisions and used different test items in each of them :

**1. For children between 5 and 7.** In the test battery for this division, he included tests of verbal reasoning, spatial ability, speed of perceptual knowledge and tests of motor ability.

**2. For children between 7 and 11.** Test battery for this classification includes tests of verbal ability, numerical ability, speed of logic and perceptual knowledge.

**3. For children between 11 and 17.** Test battery for this division includes tests of verbal ability, numerical ability, word fluency, spatial ability and power of abstract reasoning.

**Tests for Individual Abilities**

Test batteries devised by Thurston reveal the main mental abilities of children of different ages, but in addition to this there are individual tests for separate mental abilities. It would be in keeping with the context to describe them also.

**1. Spatial ability tests.** This reveals the person's spatial or form ability. One example of this is the N.I.I.P. form relation test devised by the National Institute of Industrial Psychology, London. It has been described earlier. The Psychological Bureau of Uttar Pradesh has been making use of it for quite some time; besides the Bureau has also formulated its own test for measuring spatial ability. Another example of such a test is the Minnesota Paper Form Board which includes 64 test items in which one has to combine various incomplete geometrical forms to complete the figures. In the Minnesota Spatial Relation Test, there are four tests of the form board. Both these tests have proved to be of immense value.

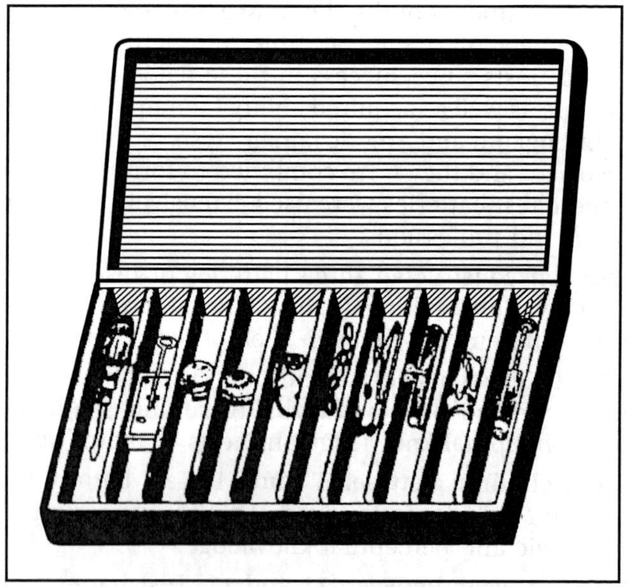

**Fig. 8.10.** Box of Minnesota Test

**2. Mechanical ability tests.** Through these tests, the person's ability of handling mechanical devices is measured. For this, some laboratories use paper and pencil while others use mechanical tools and objects. One example of this is the Minnesota Mechanical Assembly test. In this there are three boxes that contain the various parts of some common mechanical device. In the test, these parts have to be put together to form the complete objects. Other tests of mechanical ability that are famous are the Bennett Test of Mechanical Comprehension and MacQuarrie Test for Mechanical ability.

**3. Motor dexterity tests.** In these tests, the motor ability of the hands and fingers is measured. Examples of such tests are Bennett Hand Tool Dexterity Test, Purdue Peg Board Steadiness Tester and O'Conor Tweezer Dexterity Test. Only the first two will be described here :

(a) ***Steadiness tester :*** This device examines the steadiness of the hand and the fingers. In this there is a box, on one side of which there are numerous holes arranged systematically so that they proceed from the widest to the smallest. The subject takes an instrument called the stylus into his hand and inserts it completely and draws it out of these holes successively. If in doing so the stylus touches any of the walls of the hole, a bell rings. The test consists in the ability to prevent the stylus touching the wall while inserting it into the hole and drawing it out. The hole in which the bell rings is tried thrice by the subject. This test helps to discover the individual's dexterity with his hand and fingers, and the extent to which he can handle minute instruments.

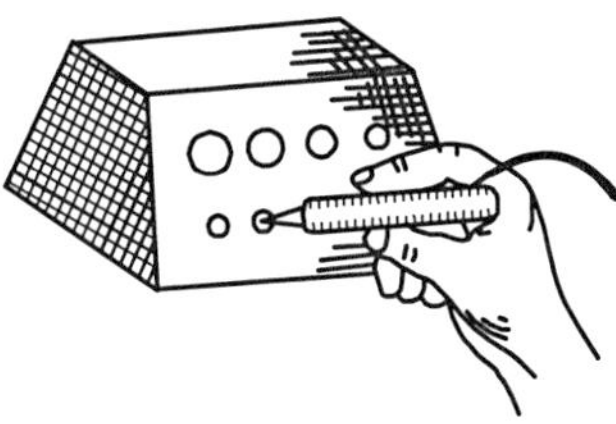

**Fig. 8.11.** Steadiness tester

(b) ***O'Conor's Tweezer Dexterity test :*** In this test, there are 100 small holes on a board, in rows of ten each. There are 100 pins placed by the side. The subject has to use a tweezer to place each of these pins in this board, one in each hole. He scores according to the short time that he takes to complete this task.

**4. Clerical tests.** These tests measure the individual's ability concerning writing and composition. It is composed of tests in arithmetic, word groups, distinct reading and good writing, tests in direct knowledge, etc. One example of the clerical test is the Minnesota Clerical test which has two parts. In one part there are pairs of numbers, the correct pair having to be marked in which both numbers are given. In the other part one has to point out pairs of names that are similar.

**5. Artistic or Aesthetic Ability test.** In these, the individual's ability concerning art is tested. One example of this is the McAdory Art Test. Sea Shore Measure of Musical Talent measures the individual's ability in respect of music. Meier Art Judgement Test is another test of artistic and aesthetic ability. In this test there are 100 pairs of pictures. In every pair there is one original and the other copy, and the student has to select the original and its copy in respect of every pair. Success in this depends upon his aesthetic ability and acuity since the original has more beauty than the copy.

## QUESTIONS FOR EXERCISE

1. Explain the importance of mental tests. Describe their classification.
2. What are the characteristics of good tests?
3. What is Validity? Describe its kinds.
4. What is Reliability? Describe its kinds.
5. Trace the history of Intelligence tests.
6. How is personality measured?
7. Explain measurement of special abilities.

# 9

# GUIDANCE

Students are perpetually perplexed with the problem of selecting suitable subjects in the course of their study. It often happens that no care is taken in making such a selection, an ill-considered selection being made. A girl decides not to study mathematics because her sister happened to fail in that subject, while another boy takes up the study of music because he is under the illusion that it is easy to pass in this subject. Another has taken up the study of science because his parents have ordered him to do so. All such methods of selection and other modifications upon them are completely unscientific. No student should turn to the study of science merely because it is an enduring passion with him to become an engineer. It is not at all essential that he may be possessed of the qualities of an engineer. Often the child endeavours to achieve that which appears glamorous or creditable to him. And on the basis of this interest or attraction nothing can be said of the success or failure with which he is likely to meet. It is totally wrong and irresponsible to select a subject either because he has been told to do so or for a variety of other equally ephemeral and meaningless reasons. The basis of the selection of subjects should be the child's individual tendencies and ability. And these tendencies and abilities cannot be understood merely by observing them. For this, a systematic and scientific testing is required. There is no student whose life is totally devoid of any problem whatsoever; whether he is rich or poor, he must face some private troubles. Most students manage to cope with these problems in some or the other manner, but there are numerous other students who fail to achieve some solution on their own effort. In this manner, some students frequently need some or the other kind of psychological guidance while others have to have recourse to it occasionally. This psychological guidance is intended to help them solve their problems. These problems are involvement of behaviour, both internal and external. Educational psychology makes use of the principles of psychology for the synthesis of this very behaviour or conduct. Evidently, guidance is required for the solution of personal problems.

## WHAT IS GUIDANCE?

The term guidance has been used in the above account of the help that psychology can render in the solution of vocational, educational and personal problems. Educational guidance is required in the field of education, vocational guidance in the field of profession and vocation, and personal guidance in the individual's personal life. Before going on to a detailed account of what these three forms entail, it would be better to understand what guidance is. Guidance may be defined as the process of helping the individual in selecting, preparing, entering and progressing in the behavioural patterns which comprise human activities in the educational, vocational, recreational field as well as in connection with community service group. This help takes the form of personal help on the psychologist's part. It is, again, in the form of advice. This does not solve problems but only helps the individual in solving his problems. Husband, in his book entitled *Applied Psychology,* has defined the term thus, "Guidance may be defined as assisting the individual to prepare for his future life, to fit him for his place in society."[1] In this way, guidance prepares the individual for his life. It informs the individual of the kind of education that he requires, the subjects that he would be advised to choose in his study, the vocation to which he should apply himself when old enough, as well as the means he should employ when faced with problems that he must solve. In society every individual has a specific status and certain roles that are concomitant with it. For example, a male member is head of his family, and from this position is derived his responsibility of providing for the needs of the family and keeping in mind the proper development of every member. But an individual does not maintain the same status throughout his life. At one and the same or at

1. Husband, *Applied Psychology*, p. 15.

different times he passes through stages where he occupies the status of son, father, husband, teacher or advocate, a citizen of the nation, etc. In each of these different statuses he has distinct and definite roles to play. The person who has ability or sense enough to work as befits his status in society is the one who wins the acclaim of society and its approval as well. It is in the performance of these various roles and duties, which conform to his differing statuses, that he needs guidance. In this way, the psychologist's guidance helps the individual fit into his role and status in society. Every individual is not fit to take up any and every position in society. Teaching, doctoring, advocacy and a variety of other professions are not jobs that require the same individual qualities from the person occupied in doing them. Introducing fitness in an individual to occupy some position is a matter that has two aspects. The first is that his ability should be commensurate with the requirements of the job and the second that he should try to become qualified to occupy that position. The second of these aspects has some limitations. Whatever the effort expended every person cannot become an artist or author, because every individual does not have the ability or quality to adopt any and every profession. Even every individual cannot become a successful trader as that requires a definite shrewd and calculating mentality that is not possessed by everyone. Hence, in order to prove able for some particular position, a person should choose the position that concurs with his capabilities and qualities. Educational psychology helps the individual in his choice. In this way, guidance helps the individual to settle down into positions that are, or are not of his own choosing. As has been said in the preceding definition, guidance helps to prepare the individual for this future life. Preparation for the future life implies creating ability in the individual to bear responsibilities that fall to his lot. These future responsibilities can take a variety of forms. Normally, for example, every boy and girl gets married when he and she grows up, creates a family and indulges in prolific procreation. In this manner, every individual is to face in the future responsibilities concerning his children, responsibilities concerning the partner he has chosen for life as well as further responsibilities of the family in general. And in the normal circumstances, again, most young men and some young women have also to adopt some or the other profession, whether to their liking or not. A child grows up to be not only a man but also a citizen of his country and in this position certain rights devolve upon him that bring with them some additional responsibilities. Consequently, when we talk of preparing an individual for the future we mean to prepare him for bearing his responsibilities ably and sufficiently whether he be called upon to do so in the field of family relations, the economic sphere, the political field or any other situation in life. For this every individual boy and girl should turn to a profession that conforms to the education they have had so that they may be in positions for which they have been prepared and act with skill and confidence. They should decide upon the profession that they would like to adopt. They should have the capacity to face and solve their own problems as well as the problems that are likely to arise in their relation with others. Guidance helps the individual in all these kinds of efforts.

It should be quite apparent from the above detailed discussion on the meaning of the term that guidance helps in determining the objective of life, in establishing a synthesis in life and in solving various kinds of problems. In the words of Jones, "Guidance is the personal help that is given by one person to another in developing life goals, in making adjustment and in solving problems that confront him in the attainment of goals."[2] In this manner guidance is personal assistance. Although guidance is sometimes offered at the group level, yet even in these matters every member of the group is also individually given advice. Applied psychology is based on the conception of individual differences. General experience and scientific research have both established that every single individual has certain abilities, problems and difficulties that are distinctly his own, as distinct from those of others. Evidently, if any advice or guidance is to be rendered, it must be rendered individually and personally. This personal help is forthcoming from one individual to another. One of these two individuals is a psychologist, or one who knows psychology and the other a person who is in need of psychological guidance. Guidance,

---

2. Jones, A.J., *Principles of Guidance*, McGraw-Hill Book Co., New York (1951), p. 85.

then, is the help rendered to an individual by the psychologist. In its more extensive sense, the term may be taken to comprehend the advice rendered by any individual who is in the know concerning psychology to another who is in need of it. For example, if a father guides his son in solving a problem, this, too, amounts to guidance, irrespective of the fact that it may or may not be based on the most incorrect notion of psychological principles. But this extensive meaning of the term is its general meaning and implication. In a scientific analysis it is not taken in its general meaning but reduced to more definite and precise terms whereby its meaning becomes limited. That is why it is first defined. Guidance in psychology means a particular thing. It is the personal advice or service rendered by a psychologist, and not by any Tom, Dick and Harry, to another person. The guidance takes the form of advice which helps the guided individual to adjust to various conditions and circumstances. If one would only look at it that way, it would become evident that adjustment is the basic problem of human life. The person who fails to adjust to his circumstances becomes a failure, suffers himself and inflicts it upon others, and is branded an abnormal being. In this way, educational psychology, through its helping the individual in adjusting himself, helps to spread happiness, peace and organisation in society. Problems in human life do not come to an end, because new ones keep on arising. There is no end to trouble. A child, for example, is faced by very few problems, much of his anxiety being centred around the work forced upon him by the teacher, or the means of dealing with the more recalcitrant of his friends and such minor things. He has not to worry about keeping the home fires burning. But these are problems that gradually engulf every individual as he grows older. As a general rule, most people marry and have children who must go to school and with equal inevitability fall ill and be treated for it, only to grow up and get married themselves and keep the almost eternal circle moving forward. Thus, one trouble grows out of another, and never lets the individual being sit back contented and unworried. Human psychology is much like this. One desire arises and destroys the being's peace till it is satisfied. Hence he immediately busies himself in searching for the means to satisfy this desire and achieves this after more or less trouble. But the story does not end here, it is followed by the arising of another desire, and the inevitable circle of objective, search for objective, obstacles in search for means of solving the desire, overcoming of the obstacles, possession of the satisfying object, satisfaction of the desire, and the arising of another desire. It is evident that every individual is continually faced with new objective the achievement of which entails the facing of many other difficulties. As Jones has stated in his definition, guidance helps the overcoming of these difficulties that beset the achievement of an objective.

**Kinds of Guidance**

As has been pointed out, an individual has to run to the psychologist, in the latter's role of a specialist, for personal advice when he fails to solve the problems that confront him. This personal advice is guidance. How this guidance can take effect depends on the fact that it be given in the context of some problem the solution of which is being sought. As a matter of fact, it is no easy matter to recount all the possible problems that arise in various spheres of human life, but some psychologists have attempted a classification of them. For example, Jones has divided the problems of life into eight spheres on the basis of their nature :

(1) Related to health and psychological development, (2) Related to house and family, (3) Related to time for recreation, (4) Concerned with personality, (5) Religious, (6) Educational, (7) Social and (8) Vocational or occupational. Having achieved the classification of problems it becomes possible to classify the kinds or forms of guidance that is to be given correspondingly. For example, vocational guidance is required in connection with profession and educational guidance in the field of education. Psychologists have professed many and various kinds of guidance. For example, Myers has mentioned the following eight kinds of guidance :

(1) Vocational Guidance,

(2) Educational Guidance,

(3) Recreational Guidance,

(4) Civic Guidance.

(5) Community Service Guidance,

(6) Social and Moral Guidance,

(7) Health Guidance,

(8) Leadership Guidance.

The present chapter makes a study of three kinds of guidance. The Bureau of Psychology, Uttar Pradesh, has also put guidance in these three categories, and much the same classification of guidance kinds has been followed in the other Indian states as well. These three kinds are : (1) Educational guidance, (2) Vocational guidance and (3) Personal guidance.

If the matter is looked at closely it will be seen that the above three classes in fact include all kinds of classification. If child guidance is considered, for example, and this guidance requires the opening of clinics in various places, it will be found that problems concerning the children are either concerned with education or are of a personal nature. Hence, child guidance is jointly comprehended under educational and personal guidance. Similarly, the various forms of guidance, such as health guidance, recreational guidance, civic guidance, social and moral guidance, community service guidance and leadership guidance are all comprehended in personal guidance.

Dividing of the various spheres of guidance does not imply that these spheres are completely separated and uncounted. In fact, guidance is a dynamic and progressive concept in which advice given on every aspect of human life is comprehended, but nevertheless, with a view to convenience in discussion, its aspects and spheres have been differentiated. Educational guidance and vocational guidance are closely related, and both of them are very intimately concerned with personal guidance. The basis of this correlation between the various spheres is that all problems of human beings are connected with each other. For example, when a person experiences difficulty in selecting a particular curriculum or a definite profession, his indecision may stem from certain personal difficulties. It happens quite often that young men become so engrossed in their love affairs that they are not able to devote any serious thought to their careers and future. Death of a close and loved relative may be another reason why he may be at a loss and groping in the dark. The fundamental problem here is of a personal nature, with the result that all educational or vocational guidance to such an individual will be modified by the personal guidance given to him. On the other hand, many personal problems may be the consequence of certain deficiencies of education and the lack of educational guidance. If a child runs away from school and becomes vagrant, finds no interest in study but chooses to pursue a life of crime or one of antisocial conduct, then it is evident that there is something wrong somewhere and as likely as not it may be that his choice of curriculum may have been undesirable. In much the same manner certain individual and personal problems may be the outcome of an absence of vocational guidance. A young man, for example, in his school days may have been a very fine sportsman, and by its virtue he would naturally not appreciate a job that ties him down, offers no opportunity of leadership, and does not allow the development of any of his sportsman-like qualities like motivation, patience, adventure and courage. If he is forced to take on such a job for a variety of reasons, it would be natural for him to become irritable and lose his mental balance and calm to some extent. This may lead to further complications in the form of personal problems. Here the personal problems have been caused by lack of proper vocational guidance. Similarly, educational, vocational and personal guidance are mutually related.

**Classification according to Mode**

The above classification that we have been viewing is made on the basis of problems for which such guidance is required. If the mode of guidance is taken into consideration, guidance can be classified in the following manner :

(1) Individual guidance,

(2) Group guidance.

Before going on to a detailed description of educational, vocational and personal guidance, it would be advisable to comprehend this classification of guidance made on the basis of its modes.

**1. Individual guidance method.** In the individual guidance method the person to be guided and his guide, the Psychologist, are in direct and personal contact with each other. He invades the ill person's house and makes a study of his family conditions, and for this purpose he interviews the various members of the individual's household. Besides the family background, the individual's social, financial and cultural background is also investigated so that no possible source of information is left untapped. And for this it becomes essential to study his neighbourhood and to collect as many facts of his life as are possible so as to build up a fairly complete case history. The schools and colleges that he has attended are contacted in order to gain information concerning his behaviour and scholastic attainments there. His teachers, too, are consulted on the matter.

Study of this type and the collection of all possible information concerning the individual is followed by testing of the individual himself. He is made to take tests of intelligence, specific mental abilities, interest, attitudes, and personality. Interview is another weapon that is used to uncover much information and, incidentally to learn the patient's opinion of himself. Accordingly, then in individual guidance, the following information concerning the individual is gathered :

(1) Information concerning his intelligence, mental abilities, interests, attitudes and personality.

(2) Information concerning family conditions.

(3) Information concerning the social, financial and cultural background.

(4) Other relevant information.

Having gathered all this information it is subjected to close and intelligent scrutiny, and then curative measures are introduced to remove the problems which have made this guidance necessary. Among these efforts are logical arguments, suggestions, psychoanalysis.

The individual guidance method has the following qualities :

(1) It renders almost complete information concerning the individual. Hence, a proper cure can be effected.

(2) Cures in this method are simpler and more effective.

Despite these advantages, the method suffers from the following drawbacks :

(1) It consumes much time, with the result that a very large number of psychologists are required if there is a big number of patients.

(2) Accordingly, this method is extremely expensive also.

(3) It needs highly trained and specialist psychologists.

**2. Group guidance method.** The shortcomings of the individual guidance method are not found in group method because in this a number of people are guided simultaneously. Group guidance should not be interpreted to imply that it involves guiding the group. Actually, the guidance is aimed at the individual because it consists of the personal assistance rendered by a psychologist. In the group guidance technique, a complete group is guided. But this guidance is intended to help the individual members of the group to solve their own problems, the sole difference being that the group is comprises individuals facing more or less the same problems. Evidently, then, there is no need to waste money and time in giving individual guidance to individuals who are facing similar problems and the advice given is likely to be similar. Hence, there can be no questioning of the importance of the group guidance technique. It economises upon time and money.

Nevertheless, group guidance technique lacks all the advantage that accrues from an application of the individual guidance method. Due to the smaller degree of personal contact between the psychologist and his subjects, the cures are not quite so effective as in the case of individual guidance. When group guidance is administered it is also not possible to gather the same amount of authentic information concerning the subject as is feasible in the individual guidance method. Hence it may be tentatively concluded that group guidance method can be of value only in circumstances in which the problems faced are similar to a degree without wide individual differences and are also not particularly complex.

## EDUCATIONAL GUIDANCE

Defining educational guidance, Jones has written, "Educational guidance, in so far as it can be distinguished from other aspects of guidance, is concerned with the assistance given to pupils in their choices and adjustments with relation to schools, curriculums, courses and school life."[3] This definition of guidance reveals the following facts concerning its nature :

3. *Ibid.*, p. 357.

**1. Educational guidance is administered to students.** Out of the many problems that the student is often faced with, there are some that he fails to solve of his own accord, and these do not even admit of any fruitful assistance from the teachers or the parents. Solution of these problems calls for the intervention of the specialist, and this specialist is none other than the psychologist.

**2. Intended for educational selection.** One part of the student's education consists in making a variety of selections, the first of them being the kind of college or school in which he would like to be educated. Then he has to follow this in the selection of the curriculum that he imagines will be suitable for him. Another problem that confronts him is the choice of the subjects that he wishes to study. It must also be remembered in this connection that normal kind of curriculum is not suitable for either morons, brilliant children or for the backward children. The child himself has normally no way of telling whether he is a moron, a brilliant chap or a backward person. This is something that the psychologist alone can discover through his psychological examination. Hence, the need of guidance in this respect.

**3. Rendered for adjustment in education.** A student finds a peculiar atmosphere in the college, the like of which he cannot find outside, and he has to adjust himself to this atmosphere. This atmosphere is a composite of his friends, teachers, daily routine of the institution, method of teaching, curriculum, subjects taught, extracurricular programmes, etc. This environment is the same for every individual student, whatever his personal capability or drawback. Evidently, and as a result, problems of adjustment arise. One student finds the teaching terribly dull while his more enterprising partner runs away from school. Another child might find himself tired most of the time while another is constantly bored stuff. Some of them indulge in systematically destroying discipline while others turn to crime and delinquency. Educational guidance is rendered for the solution of such problems that arise in the educative process.

### Individual Guidance

The following information concerning the individual is required in the individual educational guidance method :

**1. Scholastic attainments.** As a general rule, if one is to discover these holistic achievements of the students all that is necessary is to secure the results obtained in the various tests or examinations taken by him. But sometimes attainment tests are also given to secure more reliable information on this point.

**2. Personality characteristics.** Problems of adjustment and selection concerning education are influenced in an important way by personality characteristics. Hence, the psychologist gathers facts of this through astute testing.

**3. Interest.** Selection in connection with many important elements in education such as curriculum, subjects, extracurricular programmes, etc., depends upon the individual's interests. Hence, in educational guidance, interests of the individual are determined through tests and lists of interests.

**4. Level of intelligence.** Different subjects require differing levels of intelligence for successful study. Hence, intelligence tests are given to the student to discover his level of intelligence.

**5. Special mental abilities.** Selection of curricular subjects requires that attention be paid not only to the level of intelligence but also to special mental abilities. For example, literal subjects require verbal felicity, memory, mathematical ability, logic, flow of thought, etc., while creative subjects require speed in perception, spatial ability, artistic ability etc. Different tests have been devised to discover different mental abilities.

**6. Aptitude.** Educational guidance requires that the student's aptitude also be known.

**7. Health and physical development.** Many of the problems of adjustment that arise, in fact, originate in problematic health and physical development. Hence, it is essential that the selection of curriculum, subjects and extracurricular activities for the student should take into account his health and physical development. For example, students taking up the study of agriculture should be sturdy of body and strong of will.

**8. Family background and economic condition.** Many of the problems of adjustment that appear in the college are in fact born in the family. Hence, guidance concerning them requires knowledge of the family background. Similarly, many of the educational problems that arise have an intimate relation with the student's economic condition. It is within the pale of possibility that a student may not have been able to select a desirable and suitable curriculum only because of his economic condition. In such conditions, a scholarship should be provided, if the student be deserving,

Having gathered the above-mentioned variety and quantity of information concerning the student, the next step in educational guidance is to collect useful information about the curriculum, subjects taught, the college and other allied matters. A psychologist keeps fairly extensive information concerning these things at his disposal. Nowadays colleges specialise in the teaching of specific subject. Agricultural colleges impart knowledge of agricultural techniques and all that there is to know on the subject while technical institutions or colleges impart technical training. Engineering and medical colleges teach their respective subjects. Besides these there are some multipurpose colleges that take up the simultaneous teaching of technical subjects along with the sciences as well as humanities. The psychologist keeps extensive information concerning all such colleges, their individual curriculum, their subjects and atmosphere, etc. In educational guidance his function is to help the student to make a choice of curriculum, subjects to be studied and a college, according to his abilities and aptitudes.

### Group Educational Guidance Method

Besides individual guidance, educational guidance is also rendered in the form of group guidance. Following are the steps in group guidance :

**1. Orientation talks.** These talks or lectures, as is apparent from the term, establish a proper orientation for guidance. Before turning to actual group guidance, the psychologist first lectures the group on the importance of guidance and encourages them to collect information on the various adjuncts of educational guidance to be rendered.

**2. Psychological testing.** Following the lacture, the members of the group are then subjected to psychological testing in order to gain some data on their general and individual intelligence, mental abilities, interest, aptitudes and personality.

**3. Collection of data from the school.** A considerable fund of useful information concerning the child is normally available from his school. His scholarly achievement is usually epitomised in the marks that he obtains in the various regular tests held in the class, while interview with the teachers reveals much of the child's general behaviour, interest, personality, etc. And, in most cases, teacher is the only reliable source of such information. The small confined circle that the child has in school is a mine and treasure of information for the psychologist.

**4. Collection of data from the family.** The next step is consolidation of information by applying to the child's family. Parents and other members of the family have usually been with the child ever since his birth, and are thereby in a position to reveal many very interesting and unique facts to the psychologist, he being able to make much of them. And for them it is a personal matter as they are anxious to solve the child's difficulties. In addition to the report of the child's nature given to him by the parents and relatives, the psychologist also tries to discover the family's economic, cultural and educational status. And, in fact, many of the child's problems have their origin in his relations with his parents. Hence, it is very necessary for the psychologist to have adequate knowledge of this relationship.

**5. Interview with the child.** Finally, the psychologist personally interviews the child occasionally and finds out his views on his past, present and the future that he looks forward to. Self-inventory can be of much help in this respect.

**6. Formation of profile.** Consolidating and integrating all the above information that the psychologist has compiled, a profile of the child is now constructed which supplies a good view of all aspects of the child. Educational guidance can now be rendered on the basis of this profile.

**7. Follow-up studies.** Educational guidance does not end with the actual giving of advice but proceeds one step further to the follow-up study of the child. Having provided the guidance and advice, the psychologist keeps an eye on the child to make sure that the child is, in fact, benefiting from his labour. If the child fails to show any appreciable progress then he is given more tests and the necessary changes in guidance are effected.

In this manner, what educational guidance amounts to is the personal advice given by the psychologist to the child for solving various problems connected with the process of education. Educational guidance forms the basis of vocational guidance, since, the vocation that the child will ultimately select depends much upon, the subjects that he chose in his period of education. Now, a person who has never studied science has the worst possible prospect for an engineer or overseer. But the process being one of reciprocity, educational guidance also depends upon vocational guidance since, once, the matriculation level of education has been attained through a more or less general pattern, choice of subjects at the intermediate and university level is determined by the profession to be followed later by the student. Thus, educational and vocational guidance are interdependent.

### Functions of Educational Guidance

The objective of guidance in respect of education is the solution of educational problems, helping the student select his curriculum, and to impart to him the ability to adjust to school surroundings and conditions. Mainly, the following can be said to be the objectives of educational guidance :

(1) Selection of curriculum according to ability and capability,

(2) Improvement in the method of study,

(3) Arrangement of a special method of education for the backward child,

(4) Creation of special education programmes for the gifted children,

(5) Consideration and solution of failures at examinations,

(6) Encouraging the child's inspiration to study,

(7) Removing weakness in particular subjects.

In order to clarify the outlines of educational guidance, it would be useful to go into a detailed description of the above-mentioned problems.

**1. Selection of curriculum according to ability and capability.** Researches in psychology have established that success in education depends upon the student's judicious choice of a study curriculum that suits his capability and aptitude. In this, two factors are at work and have to be established. The first is that the student's abilities should be tested and evaluated and the second that the subjects conforming to those abilities determined. To take a simple example, it is essential that the qualities required for the study of mathematics should be known and found to exist in the student before any educational guidance can be rendered. Some definite and reliable knowledge of the various mental abilities required for the study of different distinct subjects has been established through psychological research. Now, the main thing that is to be done is to test the student and find the mental abilities that he happens to possess. This test of the student is designed to reveal his memory, intelligence, power of reasoning, imagination, skill in manual work, special interests and his personality. All these various tests have been described at adequate length in the preceding chapters. In this examination while some tests are resorted to, study of the student's living environment is also undertaken. In this manner, the psychologist tests each individual case, and then advises the young student as to the educational course he should profitably pursue. Experiments have shown that advice of this nature, concerning the selection of curriculum, has not only resulted in marked improvement in examination results but has also had the effect of appreciably improving the child's or student's chances of gaining a real ability in his sphere. Educational guidance is normally required at the 8th or 10th class level. The high school or school leaving stage is divided into four courses, one in sciences, the others in the arts, agriculture and commerce. The particular course that a student is to take up has to be determined by the 8th class, by reason of which this class has been called the Delta class. As a general rule the subject that a student chooses in the 10th class is also continued late, but renewed guidance is required at this stage. In India, in particular, this is all the more necessary since at this stage the student has to decide the profession that he intends to follow and to choose a course to suit that profession. In giving educational guidance at this level, the psychologist has to keep in mind the guidance that he rendered to the same student when the latter was in the 8th class.

In rendering advice besides paying attention to the results of various tests performed upon the student, it is essential to pay attention to his progress in school as well. Much information concerning school progress takes the form of annual, bi-annual and monthly test scores, educational habits regarding general discussion and play, and the teacher's evaluation of the student's personality and ability. All this information is collected in the cumulative record, which is prepared either by the teacher or by the school psychologist.

Besides the cumulative record, another source of valuable information is the guardian's schedule in which the parents of the students record important facts concerning the student. Besides, the student himself is required to furnish information regarding himself and the subjects that he would prefer to study at a higher level. In this manner, the student prepares a self-inventory in which he includes mention of the subjects that he prefers and others that he does not and besides mentions the profession that he finds attractive and suitable. Generally, subjects are chosen from among the following classification of a general nature :

(1) Literary,
(2) Scientific,
(3) Agricultural,
(4) Commercial,
(5) Technical,
(6) Constructive and
(7) Aesthetic.

Making use of the cumulative record, the guardian's schedule and the self-inventory, the psychologist prepares an information record, following which he interviews the student. In this interview the psychologist may also invite the parent or guardian. Following this interview the guide or psychologist offers his advice to the student. Educational guidance at the Delta class level is available to almost all students in the Western countries, but, unfortunately, in India at present only a few students are in a position to benefit by this scheme of things. And the paucity of such advice is evident from the fact that a state of the size and population of Uttar Pradesh has only 25 schools that provide facilities for such guidance.

One major difference between the guidance at the 8th class level and the 10th class level is that in the former case the guidance is limited solely to the concerns of curriculum selection while in the latter stage it must also be concerned with the need for future selection of profession and career. In this manner, the educational guidance after the 10th is more of an educational, vocational nature, and hence it naturally requires more information. In this, in addition to the student's educational career records such as the cumulative record, guardian's schedule and self-inventory, the teacher's rating is also solicited, and finally the student is again interviewed. What usually happens is that confronted with all this information in the form of a profile, the student is himself able to choose a suitable profession and curriculum, but if for some reasons he is unable to sort out his way, the psychologist has to intervene and offer his assistance.

**2. Improvement in the method of study.** The other important aspect is the improvement in the study method of the individual. The study method comprises such factors as mode of taking notes, mode of reading, ability to summarise, method of memorising, proper division of time, arrangements for rest, etc. It would be useful to go into a slightly detailed account of these factors :

(i) ***Mode of taking notes :*** Charles Bird has sagaciously observed that study improves if notes are taken, but taking notes is an art that is not given equally to all men. Taking notes does not involve taking down all that the teacher says or in omitting the important points. In fact, taking notes implies taking down in brief all that is said. Signs can be used as in the case of shorthand. Notes should not be so brief as to be incomprehensible on a second reading and neither should they be so extensive as to be difficult to memorising. Notes should be so designed that all important facts mentioned should be noted and all extraneous or detailed explanatory matter excluded.

(ii) ***Mode of reading :*** Considerable research has been made in psychology concerning the mode of reading. For example, the various conditions under which and the degree to which either the whole or the part method is useful have been discovered. Reading quietly or reading aloud have their own qualities and these too have been discovered. When reading it is essential that sufficient light be available and that least disturbance be present. Speed of reading can be improved by practice and effort.

(iii) ***Method of memorising :*** Considerable research on the memorising of facts having been made, the following conclusions concerning the various method of memorising are recommended :

(a) *Recitation :* Recitation does not mean reading a piece of matter over and over again but its repetition. This has advantages over rote learning and over numerous readings. But this does not mean that making more than one reading has no advantage. In fact, recitation and repetition should go on side by side.

(b) *Part and whole methods :* In the part method, the matter to be learned is divided into suitable pieces while in the whole method it is learnt as one piece. And the method that is to be used in a particular case depends upon the quantity, kind and nature of the matter as well, upon the capability of the learner. A small poem can be learnt whole but if the poem is long it is best to use the part method. Similarly, the whole method is advisable when the matter is difficult as this helps in the understanding of the various individual parts of the matter. But it is perhaps best to use both methods. In practical life, a student has to decide for himself but in choosing between the two methods he must be aware of his own capacity to learn and remember. Individuals who tire of the whole method should use the part method while others who only warm up after a short period of study would probably benefit by using the whole method.

(c) *Spaced and unspaced methods :* In the spaced method, as is evident from the name, memorising is done with intervals introduced between pieces. Contrary to this, in the unspaced method, the entire subject is tackled in a single sitting. As to which method will prove more efficacious depends upon the learner's ability and the extent and nature of the subject being tackled, A small poem with no more than ten or fifteen lines can conveniently be memorised in a single sitting, but if the poem has something like 200 lines it is usually found more practicable to distribute the burden over more than one sitting. And, there is no definite rule as to the space or time period that should be provided between two successive sittings. Roughly speaking, the only thing that can definitely be said is that the second meeting should commence only when the exhaustion of the first is completely removed, and memory impressions of it have had a chance to become permanent. In fact, the spaced method has many advantages. It not only provides opportunity for removing fatigue and creates chance for mental consideration of what has been memorised, it also reduces monotony and helps to concentrate attention upon the work in hand.

(d) *Active and passive methods :* Memorising by reading out aloud is called the active method while learning quietly without any external aid is known as the passive method. Experiments have indicated that in the active method, as compared with the passive method, attention is disturbed much less, a pattern of the subject is formed in the mind, and the various parts of it establish relations with each other. The learner is aware of all that he has in fact learned and the desire and effort of learning are retained. Yet, it may sometimes be more convenient and profitable to precede the loud reading with a quiet reading of the subject matter.

(e) *Rote and intelligent methods :* In the rote or mechanical method the learner memorises without understanding what he is learning, whereas in the intelligent method the learner understands its meaning and comprehends it along with memorising it. Experiments and tests have shown almost conclusively that the intelligent method of learning is almost invariably better than the rote method. In it thoughts form definite associations, the subject matter sinks into the brain, and the memorising is more permanent and longer lasting. When the above methods of learning and memorising are supplemented with grouping, association and rhythmic learning it becomes possible to be much more expensive when writing on the subject. The importance of learning poetry by rhyming is known to one and all. Association helps the newly memorised subject matter to be related to that which is already in the mind and hence improves its retention. Besides, self-confidence is another important factor in memorising. Memory is further helped by mental set. The objective in learning a piece also helps its successful retention in the mind. Attention is quite essential as without it memorising is impossible. Mental commentary also helps memory. In this process the subject matter learnt is repeated in the mind. Finally, apperception, or mixing newly learnt with that which is present in the mind, helps the process of memorising.

(f) *Method of summary :* Another aspect of learning that is very important is the method of summarising. The main thing in this is perception of the heart of the matter, and selection of terms that succinctly sum up all that has been said in the minimum possible number of words.

(g) *Division of time :* As has been pointed out, much benefit is to be derived by reading over divided periods of time rather than continuously. Division is also twofold — division between periods of study and rest, and division of study period according to the subject to be studied. Division of both kinds is essential.

(h) *Provision of rest :* If one rests after having read for sometime the fatigue caused thereby is relieved, boredom is obviated, and all that has been read gets a chance to sink into the mind. Experiments have shown that if one sleeps after reading, all that is read in that period is retained for far greater time than any other material read under differing circumstances. This occurs because sleep provides complete rest to the brain. The extent of rest required after reading a book depends not only upon the capacity of the student himself, but also upon the material read because if the subject is abstruse and difficult rest will be needed only after a short reading, whereas in the case of a simple or light subject much reading can be done before fatigue sets in.

From the above analysis of the results of psychological investigation in study methods, students can discover the faults and advantages of their own methods and can also effect improvements in them. Students who cannot do this stand in need of a psychologist's guidance. And in giving such guidance and advice the psychologist should find out the complete capacity and capability of the student, as this is intimately related to the method of study.

**3. Provision of a special method of education for the backward child.** One specific aspect of educational guidance is the guidance concerning backward children. This category includes children who usually fail at examinations, or show signs of indiscipline, running away from school, juvenile delinquency, or other defects of such nature. Backwardness in education can be caused by personal causes as well as by the method of teaching or external factors. The advisor must be able to gather all possible relevant information regarding the backward child whom he is called upon to guide. In this besides getting hold of the cumulative record and guardian's schedule, or the self-inventory it is necessary to gather information from the parents and teachers. It is only on the basis of such information that any advice for the solution of educational problems can be given. In case a child is intellectually of a lower level or suffers from some mental defect, then he requires a special curriculum and a special method of teaching to suit his needs. Psychologists can advise on this matter also. If it is observed that the backward child fails to show any progress despite persistent effort then he would be best advised to go into some technical profession requiring training rather than mental acumen. If the child's backwardness is due to family conditions or the school environment then the psychologist should advise his parents and teachers. Sometimes backwardness can be the result of some mental disease. In such a case the child stands in need of medical treatment rather than guidance. Briefly, the psychologist and the advisor must individually consider the case of each child and give private and separate advice to each patient.

**4. Provision of special educational programmes for the gifted children.** While backward children require guidance and care, the unusually gifted children require a special educational arrangement as otherwise there is fear of their falling into bad activities. A gifted child does not find the ordinary programme that satisfies and invigorates the average child, satisfying and helpful. The psychologist discovers such exceptional children, gathers all available information regarding them and guides their parents and teachers as to the manner in which the child should be treated. Guidance of such cases more usually concerns suggestion for some special extracurricular programmes that can help the child develop properly and in accordance with his special gifts. Putting in briefly, it can be said that the psychologist arranges a curriculum that suits well with the child's gifts.

**5. Consideration and failures at examinations.** In the intermediate and high school examinations held every year by the U.P. Board of High School and Intermediate education, the results are almost invariably below 50 per cent. More than half the students that appear for the examinations fail to pass. And while one hears a few odd cases of suicide that are the result of this failure there are many more individuals who become discouraged and give up their educational career when it has just begun. Some of the more enterprising turn to antisocial activity, others lose their mental balance, while a major portion of them become morose and frustrated. Almost all educationists are of the view that as a result of this very high rate of failures, the nation's wealth and strength are being greatly undermined. On the face of it, it is a national problem or at best the fault of the state's faulty educational methods and educational organisation that admits of almost no interference on the psychologist's part, but he can nevertheless resolve the factors that lead children to failure in examinations through his guidance.

**6. Encouragement to the child's inspiration to study.** Another problem that makes itself felt to the psychologist is when a particular child evinces lack of inspiration and enthusiasm to study. Causes of this lack of motivation may both be personal as well as related to the total environment whether social, family or school. Among the personal reasons can be physical factors such as a weak constitution or mental reasons such as anxiety and irritation. Environmental factors are concerned either with the home or the school. As far as the school is concerned it may produce a variety of causes such as uninteresting curriculum and routine, the method of education or teaching being anything but psychological, absence of extra-curricular programmes, etc. The psychologist sifts all these factors and causes, and then advises the child to create motivation in him. In fact, this can be achieved more by removing causes that destroy motivation than by any guidance. For this the psychologist guides either the teacher or the parents. The parents, teachers and the psychologist can jointly exert themselves to create a condition in which the student will take an interest in his education of his own volition. Then, and only then, can the child be inspired to take an interest in the study of his subjects.

**7. Removal of weakness in particular subjects.** Yet another problem confronts the psychologist when a student shows signs of being weak in some particular subject or subjects. English, for example, is one subject in which most students in Uttar Pradesh are lamentably weak. A major portion of college students failing is of those who fail in the English language papers. Some students evade some subjects as if they were running for the safety of their very lives. Mathematics, for example, is another subject that is something of a burden for many people, equalled perhaps only by grammar for the dread it causes. Weakness in a particular subject is not due to lack of the required ability in the student, but more often because the student fails to take a keen interest in the subject. Through tests and observation the psychologist can locate the individual cause that is responsible for the weakness. If it is the study of that subject as soon as possible, or if some ability can possibly be injected into the students, effort should be made to create it in him. If the cause of weakness is something else, then in that case teachers, parents, the psychologist and the student can cooperate to put an end to the meaningless weakness threatening student's progress.

From the above brief outline of the various aspects of educational guidance, it becomes evident that it is concerned with the various problems of education. All the problems that have been mentioned in the process are only the major problems, and there can be, besides them, many other problems that may require the intervention of the psychologist.

## VOCATIONAL GUIDANCE

### Historical Outline

Vocational guidance was defined by the 1954 Committee of the International Labour Organisation in its suggestions concerning vocational guidance, as assistance rendered by an individual to another in the latter's solving of problems related to his progress and vocational selection, keeping in mind the individual's peculiarities or special abilities and their relations with his occupational opportunity. In this manner, the objective of vocational guidance is the proper and complete utilisation of a nation's man power through helping the individual to achieve his development and satisfaction in his profession. An individual should choose a profession that suits his abilities in order that both he and the nation may profit. It is not possible for any one individual to be capable of doing every job. Special kinds of job require particular kinds of skill and special know-how. It is possible that it may be asked why guidance thereby becomes necessary since every individual can tell the kind of skill he has and choose a profession accordingly. But if the situation is objectively viewed it will be found that it is not precisely of this nature, as only few people are able to gauge their own abilities and capabilities. A large majority of persons are wrong in their estimate of their own capabilities, many of them overestimating while a fair number denigrating themselves. It is not possible for the proverbial human eye to see the very grit that is in it, it being implied that the human eye rarely lights upon the individual's own defects. If one were to go to any student doing post-graduate work in the university and ask him as to what he proposes to do after obtaining the degree, the most likely reply would be that he would take one of the competitive examinations, preferably the administrative service, and if not fortunate enough to be selected, carry on to do research and finally become a teacher. The audacity and over-weaning self-confidence of the student is stupendous. If you were to ask him as to what he will do if neither of these contingencies comes about, then it will only be a regard for your social standing that will prevent him from denouncing you on the spot. The implication is that very few of the students who fail in these and other competitive examinations realise that they do not possess the requisite qualities. When they fail, they turn their wrath upon the examiner while the more charitable abuse only their bad luck. There will hardly be one student who will acquiesce in the knowledge that it was he himself who was lacking in the qualities required in the job. Again, to prevent unnecessary meanings being read into these statements it must be pointed out that the competitive examinations held in the present era can hardly be considered sufficient to gauge an individual's inherent merit. The sole intention of introducing this example is to point out the fact that young men and women do not think rationally and scientifically when faced with the choice of a profession. Vocational guidance helps in the solution of no other than this problem. Scientific testing reveals all that there is to know of the individual to the guide, who then advises the former as to the profession most suitable for him. Experiments have succeeded in pointing out roughly the qualities that a particular kind of profession requires of the individual. For example, efforts were made to establish the intelligence level required for various kinds of jobs. The following table states the intelligence quotient that a person should possess in order to go in for one or the other profession :

| *Sl.No.* | *Professional Class* | *I.Q.* |
|---|---|---|
| 1. | Administrative work and high level professional work | 150 or more |
| 2. | Low level professional and technical work | 130 to 153 |
| 3. | Clerical or high level skilled labour | 115 to 130 |
| 4. | Skilled work | 100 to 115 |
| 5. | Semi-skilled work | 85 to 100 |
| 6. | Work not requiring intelligence | 70 to 85 |
| 7. | Labour work | 50 to 70 |

Similarly, other tests and experiments have been conducted to establish some relation between vocation and other mental abilities. For example, engineering and other industrial work requires mechanical skill in the individual, with the result that persons who possess it in a slight degree cannot in the normal course be expected to become successful engineers or skilled technicians. Some kinds of work, for example the repair of chronometers and surgery, require the ability to do minute accurate work skilfully. Lacking this quality, no individual can become a good surgeon, watch repairer or experimenter or research worker. In much the same manner other industries and professions require different kinds of expertise and skill.

The above description makes evident the importance inherent in vocational guidance. But this hardly means that the guide pays no attention to the person's aptitude. Aptitude is one of the bases of guidance, but one thing that is beyond question is that no individual can attain much success on the sole basis of aptitude. Accordingly, the guide has to collect elaborate and detailed information concerning the individual's aptitudes and capabilities, and give guidance on the basis of such information. Vocational guidance does not involve categorical declarations that one shall be doctor while such another shall be a clerk or an engineer. It is only a hypothesis and a suggestion that has its own limitations. What the guide says is simply that such and such a person possesses certain qualities in abundance that fit him for such a profession, and there is much greater possibility of success in that profession than in any other for that individual.

**Personnel Selection**

It was the National Institute of Industrial Psychology that commenced research on matters concerning vocational guidance, and its results have been used much by all the big industries. Every productive unit has a large variety of functions which can best be performed by individuals having different kinds of ability and training. Now, the selection of separate individuals for each of these jobs is what is called personnel selection. And this personnel selection is based upon vocational guidance. Here, it is essential that the distinction between personnel selection and vocational guidance be well marked and known. In both it is essential that the qualities fit for different jobs be present in the person being considered for selection or guidance, as the case may be. But, in personnel selection, the quality required for some particular function is marked, and one person out of many applicants is selected to perform that function, of course care being taken that the best of the applicants is thereby selected. In vocational guidance, the qualities of a person are gauged and he is accordingly advised to take up some vocational training or adopt a particular profession that suits him and is likely to bring him satisfaction. Vocational guidance and personnel selection are two branches of vocational psychology. Both these branches are interdependent since the provision of the right man for the right job and right job for the right man requires, on the one hand, analysis of the individual, and an analysis of the job on the other.

## PROGRESS OF VOCATIONAL GUIDANCE

The Western nations have done much work concerning vocational guidance, particularly in the United States of America personnel selection is itself a specialised job now. Considerable moderation and improvement work is being carried on there to improve the collection of information regarding the professions and the methods of selection. A Dictionary of Occupational Titles has been prepared to search for and thereby provide information concerning vocations that are open to individuals. Then, an Occupational Code has been prepared by classifying the vocations according to the qualities that they require in the man as well as according to their different levels. Detailed information regarding every profession is collected. Job description, which is an important organ of the information concerning every profession, provides a detailed and exhaustive account of the various factors such as conditions of work, wages, responsibility, etc. that are operative in the industry or vocation. The first dictionary included details of 75 per cent vocations and occupations, and it comprehended some 90 per cent of working population of that country. This dictionary went through additional and improved editions in 1942, 1944 and 1945 while in its 1959 revised version some 40,40,023 professions were detailed. And job analysis in 1942 have been confined to 16 professions.

### Vocational Guidance in India

In India, vocational guidance is not easily available, as are few other technical and specialised services. In 1945, the Training and Employment Service Organisation Committee headed by Shri B. Shivarao suggested that occupational information be selected and published. As a result, during the Second Five Year Plan period a project was prepared to set up 50 vocational guidance centres to supplement the efforts of the employment exchanges in their personnel selection. There have been certain appointments in this connection but the actual achievement is not very noticeable. And the books on occupations that have been published are no scientific research material but merely constitute a description. Besides the efforts of the Government of India, the state governments have also opened some centres, while this in turn has been supplemented by certain non-governmental agencies. Among them the

Y.M.C.A. and the Rotary Club have achieved things that deserve mention. As is apparent from the above rather short account, the progress in the direction of vocational guidance for a large country like India, is not worthy of praise. It need hardly be pointed out that much of this failure is to be attributed to the lack of organisation.

**List of Abilities and Traits**

Much important research and modification work has been carried on in connection with finding out the qualities and traits required for different professions. The National Institute of Industrial Psychology of England has prepared a list of approximately 20 psychological abilities and traits. On the basis of this list, an industrial survey was undertaken. In this survey, the specialists and senior officers working in the different occupations were requested to supply information as to the qualities and traits required of their respective functions. Specialists of different occupations effected a rating from three standpoints — average, high level, and very high level. Now the specialists of National Institute took the average of the rating made available from some 80 occupations. This average was categorised in the form of a table. And on the basis of this table it is possible to determine whether a particular individual is suitable for a specific profession or not. For example, this table clarifies the qualities that are requisites for the medical and the legal professions and the qualities that are quite desirable.

Another bit of important research work in connection with various professions and mental abilities was carried on by R.B. Cattell.[4] Cattell tested some 100 adult persons and found out their average intelligence level. This average indicates the approximate level of intelligence required by a person wishing to join some particular profession. This is made apparent in the table shown on next page.

**Tests by Dvorak and Dodge**

Dvorak and Dodge also conducted tests upon employees of different professions, of persons successful and unsuccessful

4. Cattell, R.B., *Occupational Norms of Intelligence and Standardisation of Adult Intelligence Test, British Journal of Psychology,* Vol. XXV, July 1954.

| *Sl. No.* | *Profession* | *No. of trained people* | *Average I.Q.* |
|---|---|---|---|
| 1. | Teachers of universities and inter-colleges | 30 | 151 |
| 2. | Doctors and surgeons | 25 | 146.5 |
| 3. | Teachers of government schools | 50 | 145 |
| 4. | Civil engineers | 20 | 142 |
| 5. | Mechanical engineers | 18 | 140 |
| 6. | Teachers of primary schools | 90 | 137 |
| 7. | Managers of industry | 20 | 137 |
| 8. | Stenographers | 57 | 129 |
| 9. | Clerks | 54 | 127 |
| 10. | Travelling representatives | 24 | 123 |
| 11. | Nurses | 250 | 122 |
| 12. | Telephone department employees | 52 | 115 |
| 13. | Workers doing minute work | 19 | 114 |
| 14. | Workers doing gross work | — | 106 to 78 |

within one profession, of people working in the same profession but in differing capacities. This testing was based upon a wide variety of authentic psychological testing techniques. These tests revealed considerable difference between the abilities of motor mechanics, successful or unsuccessful clerks, and other people. But these tests were neither extensive and comprehensive to be applied to a majority of professions nor concentrated enough to have completely distinguished one profession from another. In this manner, it is essential to exercise the greatest care in applying the conclusions in these tests. Dodge himself has acknowledged this fact.

**Minnesota Occupational Rating Scales**

In Minnesota University six mental abilities and their extent were determined for 430 professions and occupations. And even in this the ability was individually divided into four categories — a, b, c, d. These six mental abilities were Verbal, Mechanical, Sociability, Clerical, Musical and Artistic. And, these six abilities were divided into four classes each for different professions. For example, the Minnesota occupational rating scale concerning the ability of verbal efficacy can be understood from the following table :

| *Class Level of Intelligence* | *Necessary Ability* | *Example* |
|---|---|---|
| (a) High level | Highest university education, creative ability and power of argument. | Professors, authors, scientists, advocates, etc. |
| (b) Higher than average | High school and college level of education. | Clerks, photographers, foremen, etc. |
| (c) Average level | High school level of education. | Typists, Mechanics, etc. |
| (d) Below average | Junior high school or eighth grade education. | Labourers, porters, etc. |

## PROCESS OF VOCATIONAL GUIDANCE

The preceding description of vocational guidance must have made it apparent that it requires two kinds of information or subject matter to be collected, the first concerning indispensable information about the individual, and the second pertaining to knowledge of the industrial or occupational aspect. In this manner, vocational guidance has two aspects :

(1) Study of the individual.

(2) Study of the occupational or professional sphere.

### Study of the Individual

Before any vocational guidance can be rendered to an individual, it is essential that adequate information concerning his education, level of intelligence, mental abilities, aptitudes, interests, physical development, health, nature, personality characteristics and economic status be gathered, because variations in any of them will necessarily require change in guidance.

**1. Education.** Individuals need differing levels of education in order to enter into and succeed in different professions, as for example, the highest education is required for advocates, professors, engineers, doctors, and other such professions, whereas a general and lower level of education can serve the purpose if the profession is clerk, overseer, mechanic, compounder, teacher, etc. Besides these there are certain other occupations in which the medium level of education suffices *e.g.* business salesmanship. In such professions only the basic necessities of literacy must be fulfilled, as much else depends upon practice. It is only because of this importance of various levels of education being relative and relevant to different professions that most advertisements for applications for job contain specific instructions regarding the educational qualifications. For example, a person teaching students at the high school and intermediate level need only be a graduate while no mere graduate can teach the college or graduate level. Doctors require medical degrees while in order to qualify as an engineer it is essential that one passes an engineering examination.

**2. Training.** Education does not merely imply the degree obtained at the end of a session by passing a prescribed examination. Nowadays, most occupational units make it obligatory on all new entrants to be trained in addition to being educated, and this is being carried to the extent that only a trained individual is allowed to fill the post of a high school teacher. Certain occupations need training inevitably, for example, the occupations of an electrician, stenographer, chemist, compounder, etc. As it is, the tendency to train personnel in industry and other occupations is catching on. In certain professions, the individual after having entered it is oriented for a period of few weeks, and only then is he allowed to handle work on his own responsibility.

**3. Level of intelligence.** Besides difference in education, different professions require differing levels of intelligence. For example, the medical, technical, legal, teaching and administrative professions require the highest intelligence level, while on the other hand, the peon and the domestic worker can be selected from people with a much lower level of intelligence. Other professions require only the average level of intelligence, so that evidently, before a person can be told of the profession that suits his natural endowments, it is essential to know the level of intelligence to which he belongs.

**4. Special mental abilities.** Individuals differ not only in respect of their intelligence but also in respect of their special mental abilities. For example, all people do not possess mechanical ability, to the same degree and neither is verbal felicity shared by all in equal degree. Different professions require differing mental abilities, verbal ability being required by advocates and teachers, etc., mechanical ability by doctors and engineers, etc. Hence, prior to the selection of a profession it is essential for the individual to be aware of his mental abilities.

**5. Aptitudes.** Success in a particular profession seems to depend to some extent upon one's aptitude for it. If a person lacks artistic and creative aptitude, there is not much likelihood of his succeeding in the role of an artist, and one need not expect it. As a general rule, it is advisable for every person to join the profession for which he has any natural aptitude. Hence, knowledge of a person's aptitude is also essential before he can be given any vocational guidance.

**6. Interest.** Interest helps to increase the possibility of success in a profession. Interesting work is done enthusiastically and patiently while uninteresting work tends to fall upon most men, and requires very conscious application to be carried through. Success in work requires that serious interest be taken in the work, or that interest in that kind of work be created, and this is possible. Interests are mutable, and it is possible to create interest in work that was once repugnant. But if the individual is originally endowed with interest for a particular occupation and is also possessed of the requisite mental abilities, then he would be best advised to adopt it. It need hardly be repeated, as a slogan is, that a knowledge of the person's interest is essential before any vocational guidance can be rendered.

**7. Health and physical development.** As a general rule, proper health and physical development is necessarily taken into consideration in every profession, but in certain other occupations success depends almost solely upon these factors. For success in the armed forces or in the police department, health and good physical development are quite indispensable. In the absence of these factors, the presence of no other quantities of ability will bring success to the individual. Hence, physical development, constitution and health are additional factors that must be taken into consideration when the question of vocational guidance comes up for consideration.

**8. Nature.** Different people show very pertinent and obvious difference in their nature, some being introverted while others more extroverted. And, different kinds of people can successfully settle down only in some specific professions that suit their nature. An extroverted personality, for example, is essential if one wants to succeed as a salesman, agent, administrator or even as a leader, while on the other hand gifted introverts make great artist, authors, scholars, scientists, specialists, etc.

If choice of profession is contrary to one's natural inclination, it goes against the grain and deprives the individual's life of happiness and contentment, and the profession becomes a burden. While if the profession conforms to one's nature, then one is happy and enthusiastic in his work, and these conditions are conducive to progress and success. Hence, before vocational guidance can be ventured upon, it is necessary to judge a person's nature also.

**9. Personality characteristics.** It is a fact generally known that different qualities of the personality are required in such widely separated professions as teaching, artistic creation, selling, labour work etc. Hence choice of profession should also be made with a due regard for the qualities of the person's personality.

**10. Financial status.** As a general rule, it is improper and unnecessary to take into consideration a person's financial status before making a choice of profession, but in a country like India here scholarships are hard to come by, the economic status of the student also plays an important part in his choice of the future that he wants to shape for himself. Now a person with middle class status is in no position to afford a technical or medical education for his child because either of these two special courses involve the expenditure of a considerable amount of money. And it is unnecessary and improper to advise a poor and needy person to go in for higher education when he cannot afford it. It is equally useless to advise such a person to choose a profession in which high education and specialised qualifications are desired. Hence, a person should be recommended only to that profession for which he can afford to gain education and any training that may be essential. He must have the means to gain such training. It must also be remembered that economic or financial status can be a bar to earning some profession only under certain circumstances. There are many examples of people who came from poor families having gained very high education and improved their lot in life. The truth or crux of the matter is that instead of discouraging a student from entertaining thoughts of a profession for which he apparently has not the economic means, the psychologist should expend his effort in arranging scholarships or other facilities whereby he may be able to attain the goal for which the former is striving, as he stands great chances of success. In India, these things are still unexplored, and many individuals fail to gain satisfying and rewarding positions in life that conform to their abilities, interests and aptitudes, for no reason other than that they were born in poor families.

**11. Other important factors.** In addition to all these elements pointed out above, it is necessary to keep in mind certain other factors concerning the individual before giving vocational guidance. Age of the person, for example, is another factor that must be taken into account since many jobs and occupations set the maximum and minimum age limits on all applicants, so that people not qualifying for them in this respect cannot enter these services. Hence, there is hardly any point in advising them to take up such a profession. Sex of the person is another consideration in vocational guidance upon which much depends because some occupations are more suitable to the male individual while others are within the capacities of the female, and for these she is eminently suitable. Nursing and caring for the diseased in hospitals is one function that can safely and even desirably be allocated to women, while in the armed forces and the police, most of the jobs, with very few exceptions, are suitable only for the male.

### Study of Professional World

Having collected all the necessary and desired information regarding the individual under consideration, it is necessary to turn to another aspect of vocational guidance, that of studying the professional world. While the psychologist must necessarily have enough information concerning the person to whom he is imparting vocational guidance, it is equally important that he be well informed on its professional and occupational aspect. Only then can he provide proper and effective assistance. It is enough for the psychologist to be knowing the number and kinds of professions but also the kind of education, training, intelligence, mental abilities, interests, aptitudes, personality, qualities, etc., that are desired as well as the conditions of work that prevail therein.

### Classification of Occupations

Occupations have been classified in different ways,

according to the viewpoint adopted in doing so. Classification is beneficial because the individual comes to know all the professions from one point of view and can select from among them. This has the twofold advantage of narrowing down the range from which the selection is to be made while at the same time it provides a number of alternatives. It will be advantageous now to glance at these various professions :

(a) ***Classification according to interest :*** Professions have been divided into the following classes on the basis of interest :

(1) Occupation concerned with child life,
(2) Mechanical occupations,
(3) Computational occupations,
(4) Scientific occupations,
(5) Occupations concerned with change,
(6) Artistic occupations,
(7) Literary occupations,
(8) Musical occupations,
(9) Occupations concerned with social service,
(10) Clerical occupations.

In each of these classes there are professions belonging to five levels, depicted in the following classification :

(b) ***Classification on the basis of educational level, mental ability or skill, training, age and social respect :*** This classification of the professions which is the work of Beckman,[5] is as follows :

1. *Executive, managerial and professional :* This class includes the following three kinds of occupations :

(i) Verbal — such as advocate, judge, editor, auditor, professor, etc.
(ii) Scientific — such as doctor, engineer, scientist, accountant, etc.
(iii) Executive or managerial — such as the various kinds of managers and executives, etc.

5. Beckman, R.O., *A New Scale for Gauging Occupational Rank, Personnel Journal* (1954), pp. 223-35.

2. *Business and sub-professional :* This class includes the following two kind :

(i) Business — such as trader, salesman, agent, etc.

(ii) Sub-professional — such as actor, photographer, designer, etc.

3. *Skilled occupation :* This class includes the following two kinds of occupations :

(i) Physical labour such as electrician, dyer, machineman and press mechanics, etc.

(ii) Intellectual such as clerk, supervisor, stenographer, cashier, etc.

4. *Semi-skilled occupation :* Such as policeman, bus conductor, driver, guard, etc.

5. *Unskilled occupation :* Such as labourer, peon, night-watchman, etc.

(c) ***Classification according to the form of work :*** Professions have been divided into the following four classes according to the nature of work done by them :

1. Social occupations. These professions require that the person be possessed of social qualities and a high degree of sociability because he comes into contact with very many individuals. Examples of such professions are advocate, leader, salesman, agent, administrator, manager, teacher, etc.

2. Occupations of mental skill. In these professions, tools are used for work that requires a high degree of manual skill, examples being carpenter, mechanic, mason, binder, overseer, engineer, etc.

3. Occupations concerned with offices. This class includes all people concerned with office organisations such as clerks, cashiers, peons, etc.

4. Intellectual and scholarly occupation. In this class come the professions that require intellectual acumen and love of academic work of the individual, examples of which are philosopher, author, inventor, poet, scientist, etc.

**Job Families**

From the above classification of occupations it becomes evident that there are many professions that are similar in respect of their nature of work done, conditions of work, desired skill, interest, mental abilities, and personality qualities, etc. When such similar families are put together, a job family is constituted. In one job family, the work can be carried on different levels such as high, medium or low. Evidently, then, the individual will first have to select a job family, and then the level of that family on which he is capable of functioning.

**Sources of Information regarding Occupations**

The question that may justifiably intrigue the beginner is the source of all this comprehensive information regarding a profession. The following are the sources from which such information is forthcoming and can be gathered :

(1) Through papers and magazines.
(2) Through information published by government organisations.
(3) Through radio discussions.
(4) From employment exchanges.
(5) From information broadcast by industrial and commercial institutions.
(6) Through lectures delivered by specialists.
(7) Through examination of factories and people working in them.
(8) By working on any particular profession.
(9) From guidance psychologist and vocational adviser.

**Significant Facts in Vocational Selection**

After gathering information regarding the profession from one or more of the above-mentioned sources it is possible to select one's profession, but before committing oneself finally, as has been pointed out before, the following things must be taken into consideration and made a note of :

(1) Nature of work which includes the kind of work, charge, responsibility, duty, interest, etc.
(2) Working conditions, which include both psychological and physical needs.
(3) Necessary personality traits such as nature, adaptation in behaviour, power of leadership, etc.
(4) Level of intelligence.

(5) Mental abilities.

(6) Interest and aptitudes.

(7) Necessary education and training.

(8) Income, chances of promotion and permanency of work.

(9) Procedure of entrance.

(10) Necessary physical development and health.

(11) Social prestige.

(12) Demand of the job.

In this manner, a profession is chosen after analysing the individual on the one hand, and the various occupations upon the other. Analysis of the individual reveals the abilities and qualities present in him while analysis of the job or profession reveals the desired qualities and abilities. Now, all that remains to be done is that the person who possesses abilities and qualities requisite for a particular profession should be prompted to join it.

**Steps of the Vocational Guidance Method**

Vocational guidance, as in the case of all other forms of guidance, can be given by two methods — the individual method and the collective method. And, in these methods, the steps are the same as were described in the case of educational guidance. In this manner, vocational guidance will involve the following steps :

(1) Orientation talks.

(2) Psychological testing.

(3) Collection of data from the school.

(4) Collection of data from the family.

(5) Interview.

(6) Formation of profile.

(7) Achievement besides the above important steps in vocational guidance, which means that the psychologist, along with providing vocational guidance, also helps the individual to attain to the desired profession. For this he keeps in contact with employment exchange offices and social workers.

(8) Follow-up studies.

## PERSONAL GUIDANCE

An important part of guidance is personal guidance, and it constitutes the personal and individual advice offered by a guide to an individual for the solution of latter's personal problems. This helps the person to adjust to circumstances in his life. As a general rule, problems are a part and parcel of human life, but not everyone is the able to solve the problems that arise in his life and ruffle the calm of existence. People who find no way out of the morass of problems need the guidance and expert. And, a opinions of a specialist and psychologist is the only one who can provide advice concerning the solving of personal psychological problems.

### Need for Personal Guidance

There cannot be exact prescription of the number and kind of problems that can be called essentially personal, because while the same person may be faced with a wide variety of problems at different stages of his life, the same problems may assume a different shape when they plague another individual. In this manner, personal problems are so numerous and have so many incongruous and varying forms that it is well nigh impossible to indulge in a description of them, and yet, the main personal problems that beset the human animal can be distinguished. Roughly speaking, human problems of a personal nature can be of two kinds — (1) Personal or individual. (2) Social. Individual problems can also be divided into two classes : (1) Physiological problems such as health, disease, development and concerned problems, (2) Psychological problems such as sex problems, problems concerning the satisfaction of instinctive needs. Among the psychological problems those of emotional adjustment are very' important because inability to solve them has very great debilitating influence upon the entire personality of the individual. And social more than the personal problems cause anxiety to the person. If the truth be required, it may be declared that human life, from the moment of birth to the time of death, is a continuous and ceaseless process of adjustment with social circumstances. These social conditions keep on changing and being transmuted, with the result that new problems are constantly presented to the person for solution. Now, as to which of these problems is likely to cause disorganisation in his personality, it is not easy to say with any degree of certitude. It is the opinion of psychologists that most men need personal guidance at some or the other occasion in life when the cross that they have to bear becomes a mite too heavy for them. That life continues on its desultory path even without guidance is a mundane truth. Life continues even in strife, poverty, unemployment, disease and trial. But man wants to improve his lot in life with the help of science. The psychologist's guidance helps the individual to solve certain personal problems, the failure to attain which only increases the burden of life, stops all development and progress in the person, even though he may continue to exist and outwardly appear to be hale and hearty. There are many aspects of social adjustment and adaptation because there are more than one dimensions to man's social circumstances. Social problems are generally interpreted to include family problems of school and college if the individual is a student, vocational problems if he is an earning individual, moral and ideal problems. Of these, the family problems are the most prominent and varied, comprehending problems of relations between the child and his parents, relations between husband and wife, conjugal problems, relations between brothers and sisters, financial status of the family, mutual adaptations of the individuals and others. And, any one of these problems is herculean enough to destroy the peace and calm of an individual. Problems of conjugal love, for example, compel an infinity of couples to spend their life in utter misery and misunderstanding.

Very often the individual makes some-slap dash trial and error efforts to solve his personal problems or turns to good friends for personal advice, or instead turns to the older family members or teachers. Though this advice may have some practical validity, yet scientifically it is difficult to find any justification for it. If we take up for consideration the problem of conjugal love and bliss, then, it will be seen that the advice rendered by the best friends and sages of the family is all based upon their personal experience, and cannot provide any real guidance for a person. The crux of the matter is that the conjugal relations between no two pairs are identical. The conjugal problem of one specific pair is a personal and particular problem. Examples from other persons and solutions can only provide some general suggestions but it is dangerous to emulate others without paying attention to the particular merits of one specific case, for which the solution is being sought. Evidently, then, the individual can tackle his own problem after making a comprehensive study and gathering considerable psychological knowledge, but if this psychological knowledge is present in him, then why should that problem arise in the first place? Naturally, it is essential for the person to turn to the psychologist for expert advice. But it must be kept in mind that guidance and advice cannot solve the problem in its entirety. This advice is more of the nature of suggestions, is scientific, and has no qualities of hit and miss about it. If the individual is to profit from such suggestions, he must be possessed of understanding, sympathy and skill.

**Process of Personal Guidance**

The first condition of personal guidance is that the person to be guided be fully and completely understood. It is desirable that the individual should himself come forward with all relevant information in the form of life history, present conditions, feelings, thoughts, activities and all main facts concerning his life, and pass it on to the psychologist. He should not try to conceal anything, irrespective of the inhibitions that may urge him to do so, for it has often been found that the root of the problems to be solved existed in things from which the person wanted to escape, that he not only did not want to reveal to others but of which he did not even want to think himself. Briefly stated, in personal guidance, the psychologist should, with the cooperation of the person himself as well as with the help of various tests, gather all relevant and necessary information concerning the person. Roughly, personal guidance has the following five steps :

(1) Gathering the facts.
(2) Diagnosis of the problem.
(3) Prognosis.
(4) Therapy.
(5) Follow-up studies.

**1. Gathering the facts.** Gathering of factual information is the first and most important step in personal guidance. These facts can be of two kinds — those connected with the particular problem, and those concerned with the general life history of the person. And, the facts concerned merely with the problem also can be of two kinds — the first concerned with the individual and his characteristic qualities, the second concerned with the external circumstances of the problem. And the need for knowing these facts compels the psychologist to turn to observation, interview and various tests that yield it. The person himself is not the only one interviewed, as much valuable information is forthcoming from the interviews of people nearest to him, such as friends and relatives. In an interview it is essential that the psychologist ventures to speak as little as possible, that he asks questions that elicit the correct and desired responses by allowing the interviewed person to carry on the bulk of the talking. As in the case of educational and vocational guidance, in personal guidance, too, the opportunity for interview arrives only after a profile has been formed from the available information. And for this profile, the school, family, and other sources are ransacked for information. This necessitates the use of the cumulative record, the guardian's schedule, the self inventory and the teacher's ratings, besides which a number of tests are also performed. The outline of the profile is something like what is described below :

(a) ***Physical description :*** Physical description includes the person's age, sex and physical health.

(b) ***Family description :*** In family description are included facts concerning the family background and hereditary relationships, parents (whether real or step, living; or dead), brothers and sisters (their mutual relationships), economic status of the family, social standard of the family, mutual relations between all the members of the family, etc.

(c) ***History of social development*** : This class includes the student's relations with other members of his class, and with other friends outside the class. If the person requiring guidance is not a student, then his relations with his neighbours and relatives outside the family will be studied.

(d) ***History of college life :*** This classification includes the student's history in his progress through the primary, secondary and college educational stages which is constituted by results of examination and record of part taken in extracurricular programmes. If the person being studied and guided is not a student, then his life outside the sphere of his family should be studied to provide equivalent information. If he is engaged in some professional pursuit, it is necessary that the information regarding level of income, conditions of work, relations with other members of the profession or institution, etc. is collected.

(e) ***Mental abilities :*** By means of various tests and examinations intended for the purpose, the psychologist gathers information concerning the individual's level of intelligence, mental abilities and aptitudes, etc.

(f) ***Qualities of Personality :*** Qualities of the personality have an important part in the personal problems, hence the psychologist finds it incumbent to secure information concerning the person's interests, emotional maturity, motives, ambitions, objectives and ideals, etc.

One very important part of gathering such information is the keeping of proper records so that the information be available in future. Even in interview it is desirable for the psychologist not to depend upon his memory too much but to take adequate notes so that the information revealed is permanently available to him when it is required. But this requires an attitude of cooperation on the subject's part and a reassuring approach on the psychologist's part so that the subject should not become suspicious. If a person finds any objection to his statements being recorded, then modern tape recording machines can be used without the person being informed of them. Facts which do not qualify for this kind can be recorded after the person has been informed of their importance. For example, the psychologist should encourage and praise the subject and lead him into believing that all that he says deserves to be recorded.

**2. Diagnosis of the problem.** Having gathered all the facts that he wanted to collect the psychologist is now ready to start his own work. He has to search and analyse this information in order to see some system in it as well as any pattern that will help to reveal the cause of the problem under consideration. Such a discovery of patterns is the diagnosis of the problem.

And this diagnosis is the basis on which the problem is to be solved and the trouble cured. The better and more accurate the diagnosis, the better will be the cure ultimately effected. And it would be no misnomer to state that with a proper and accurate diagnosis half the psychologist's work is over.

**3. Prognosis.** Prognosis consists in estimating the benefit or result of the guidance. A psychologist tries to visualise the extent to which he will be able to solve the person's problem, or, in other words, to what extent is there hope of the problem being solved. For example, by seeing a person's past performance in mathematics and by measuring his mental abilities, it becomes possible to make some tentative estimate of what he will be able to achieve after the guidance is rendered.

**4. Therapy.** Now the time for therapy or cure has arrived, or, in other words, it is the time for the psychologist to come forward with a satisfactory solution of the problem. Seeing the profile of the problem from all the information gathered about it as well as from the interviews with the psychologist, the counselee himself gains insight into the problem and sometimes even comes up with some sensible and practicable solution. The truth of the matter is that this in fact should be the aim of the psychologist, for he should try to make the counselee see his problem and its patterns, and even to think up a solution for it. If this happens, he will on the one hand gain considerable pleasure from having solved the problem of his own accord, while on the other he will have considerable enthusiasm in solving the problem, and he will exert himself to the maximum limit. Freud, who used to cure mental diseases by the psychoanalytic method, used this method very effectively. When his patients became aware of the unconscious cause of their trouble, much of the problem was solved, whereas if the psychologist insists on giving his own suggestions and advice, then it becomes possible that due to certain tendencies and motives the subject may choose to ignore it. But if the counselee fails to understand the therapeutic measures implied by the psychologists, then the latter has to take positive steps. And, in the event of such a condition being precipitated it is always best for the advice not to seem to be authoritative or sermon-like, and neither should any of the person's shortcomings be mentioned. The counselee should be given some hope that his problem will be solved, and it should be so expressed that it may appear to have come from the counselee instead of the psychologist.

**5. Follow-up studies.** Personal guidance does not come to an end with therapeutic measures being introduced because the psychologist's job is not only to provide guidance, but also to see the actual success of his advice. Hence, even after the therapy he has to keep up contact with the subject, and to make inquiries to find out the success that he has had in solving the problem originally entrusted to his care. This not only furthers the help rendered to the counselee but also adds to the experience and knowledge of the psychologist, because much of what is learnt in guidance is through trial and error. Human psychology is so complex that it cannot be tied down by any laws. Success in guidance depends upon the psychologist's own experience and insight, and as has been said before, he is assisted in acquiring these through follow-up studies. It need hardly be emphasised at this stage that personal guidance is more or less incomplete without a follow-up study.

### Methods of Follow-up Studies

The following methods are utilized in follow-up studies :

**1. Follow-up through letters.** As is evident from the term applied to this method, in this method the counselee is contacted through the medium of letters. Letters reveal only a small quantity of information, but they do contribute something positively to the study. And, if need be, these letters can be used to transmit further guidance to the person or even meet him.

**2. Questionnaire method.** In the questionnaire method, the counselee is sent a questionnaire, and he is asked to answer it, and return it to the psychologist. Most questions selected for the purpose have the quality of requiring short, simple, concise and precise answer, most of them being in terms of positives and negatives. This questionnaire is concerned with various aspects of the progress of a problem concerning which the advice was given. Psychologist tries to find the extent to which he has succeeded in curing the person, and if not, why. The questionnaire method has the advantage of soliciting more varied and comprehensive information than mere letters, but the main disadvantage lies in the small number of questionnaires returned to the psychologists.

**3. Card file method.** In this method, details of an interview, in terms of the name of counselee, age, address, purpose of interview and details of the problem are inscribed. This is kept in the central office of the guidance centre, so that the counselee can contact his guide at any time that he wishes. The file method also makes use of the tickler file, in which the psychologist keeps an open file of the counselee within easy reach, which keeps details of the further contacts than have to be made. The file is so named because it tickles the guide into contacting the person guided.

The above three methods are prevalent and have beneficial results. There are some other methods also, in addition to these main ones, by means of which the contact between the psychologist and the counselee can be kept alive. Telephone, for example, is another instrument that is frequently used in U.S.A. for renewing such contacts and gathering fresh information from the subject.

It would be very useful to present a realistic example of personal guidance before winding up a description of it. This will improve realisation of the actual causes that are confronted and the extent to which our state provides facilities for dealing with them.

A professor in a local college at Allahabad went to take a look at the central jail there, where he saw a young boy undergoing sentence for breaking in or effecting an entry and thieving, the term being six months. The professor had the boy released on probation and took him into his own household. The boy maltreated the professor and continued on his path of theft and crime. He was also often absent for a couple of days from home. Finally, the professor handed the boy over to the parents who were living within the college campus. The boy was sent to school where he was admitted to the sixth class, but his progress was not satisfactory by any standards. Psychological tests revealed that he was definitely below the average in mental traits and capacities. But his practical skill and ability was somewhat better than the average. His other faculties were definitely weak. He naturally did not pay any attention to his study, and took no interest in social activities. At times he was filled with feelings of guilt and remorse, but at other times he showed to be very aggressive and antisocial. This boy was brought to the bureau of psychology for personal guidance, where it was advised that the boy needed a change of environment. It was opined that an understanding and sympathetic person might help to improve his adjustment to life, and that there was no benefit to be derived from further study. He should turn to acquiring training in a mechanical trade. Psychologists also felt that the boy required regular mental treatment, but as the bureau was not able to provide this assistance not much could be done in this direction. Even then, the boy did benefit somewhat from the guidance of the psychologists. He learned to understand some of his problems and this helped him in his adjustment.

## QUESTIONS FOR EXERCISE

1. What is guidance? What are its principal types?
2. Describe the process of educational guidance.
3. What are the constituents of vocational guidance? Describe its procedure.
4. What is the need of personal guidance? Give examples.

# 10

# GUIDANCE SERVICE IN SCHOOLS

At present there is an urgent need of organising guidance services in schools. Hence, guidance should be part of every school activity. It is not something which may be separated from the general life of the school. Thus, it must be an organised service of the school. It has to be adopted as a school policy. It should be recognised as an integrating and uniting force in the school.

## MEANING OF GUIDANCE SERVICE IN SCHOOLS

Organisation of guidance service in schools means supervision, planning and co-ordination on the part of the head of the institution. Moreover it means active co-operation of the parents, the staff, the guidance experts and the pupils. Thus, organisation of guidance work in school implies the following :

1. Laying down objectives in clear terms.
2. Mustering resources and utilising them in the possible manner.
3. Systematic planning of guidance work.
4. Co-ordination and conduct of certain activities within administrative framework.
5. Allocation of duties and responsibilities.
6. Provision of minimum essentials.
7. An able leadership to co-ordinate, supervise and direct activities.
8. Working of various guidance personnel as a team.

## PRINCIPLES OF ORGANISATION OF GUIDANCE SERVICES

The following are the general principles underlying organisation of guidance services in schools :

**1. Child-centredness.** Guidance services should be organised while keeping in view the needs, interests and purposes of the students in the school.

**2. Continuity.** Guidance services should be continuous because individuals face problems through out their lives. Guidance services should be meant for all and not merely for the maladjusted.

**3. Wholeness.** Guidance services should be concerned with the whole individual in his total environment and with specific needs and principles.

**4. Prevention as well as cure.** Guidance should be organised to deal not only with serious problems after they arise, but also with causes of such problems, in order to prevent them from arising or to prepare better for their solution.

**5. Specialisation.** Guidance is a specialised service. It should be provided by specialists like school counsellor, school psychologist, school psychiatrist, school social worker, school physician, curriculum expert, placement worker and co-ordinator of school activities. Services of these specialists should be organised and administered in such a way so that they may constantly strengthen all other members of the school personnel and help in their problems.

**6. Self-knowledge and self-direction.** All guidance should be directed towards improvement and opportunities through tests and other devices.

**7. Securing and recording adequate information.** Guidance services should provide for securing and recording adequate information regarding educational and occupational requirement and opportunities through tests and other devices.

**8. Leadership and co-ordination.** Guidance service should provide for leadership and co-ordination of all the agencies of school and community for long term guidance of youth.

**9. Co-operation.** Guidance service should enlist the active co-operation of parents so that better organisation may be arrived at. It should also enlist the interest and effort of every member of the school staff.

**10. Simplicity.** Guidance service should be as simple as possible.

**11. Collection and analysis of data.** Up-to-date data of the student should be obtained, properly recorded and cautiously analysed.

**12. Latest ways and means.** Some definite ways and means should be selected so as the latest "technical know-how" can be imparted to the concerned workers.

**13. Budgetary provision.** The organisation of guidance services should be according to the budgetary provision, which should be made before hand.

## ROLE OF GUIDANCE PERSONNEL IN SCHOOL

Since guidance is a specialised job in schools, it requires specialised personnel which may include the headmaster, school counsellor, school psychologist, school social worker, child welfare worker, school physician, school psychiatrist, curriculum expert, placement worker and co-ordinator of school activities. The following are the role of various specialised personnels :

**1. Role of the headmaster.** The headmaster occupies an important place in the school. He is the leader, director and co-ordinator of guidance programme in the school. Some of his functions are the following :

(i) Recommending to the authorities for the employing of competent counsellor.

(ii) Appointing a guidance committee to study the school's guidance needs.

(iii) Providing necessary facilities to the guidance worker and staff connected with guidance.

(iv) Providing assistance in planning guidance programme in the school.

(v) Assigning of definite tasks to each member of the committee according to his interests and potentialities.

(vi) Encouraging teacher to attend special guidance courses and seminars.

(vii) Keeping the parents informed about the guidance activities available in the school.

(viii) Formulating plans and policies regarding organisation of guidance programme.

(ix) Interpreting the programme of guidance services to the school and the community.

**2. Role of the teacher.** The following are the role of the teacher in organising guidance services in school :

(i) Collecting information and maintaining cumulative record.

(ii) Observing the pupils in various situations — in the classroom, in the library, in the playground, etc.

(iii) Detecting maladjustments of pupils.

(iv) Preparing case histories of problem children.

(v) Helping the pupils to secure better educational, personal and social adjustments.

(vi) Sending information about the pupils to the parents and the headmaster and taking an active part in the Parent-Teacher Associations.

(vii) Helping the pupils in evaluating their own growth.

(viii) Providing opportunities for the maximum development of the pupils.

(ix) To take the help of experts.

**3. Role of the counsellor.** The role of the counsellor has been explained in counselling,

**4. Role of the school psychologist.** The functions of the psychologist in organising guidance services in schools may be summed up as follows :

(i) To know the individual *i.e.* his abilities, potentialities, interests and aptitudes with the help of psychological tests and other sources.

(ii) To help the individual in solving emotional and other problems and making maximum adjustments.

(iii) To conduct research.

**5. Role of the health specialist.** In organising Guidance Services in Schools, the role of the health specialist are as follows :

(i) To make arrangement for medical examination of each child after a suitable interval.

(ii) To report physical handicaps of students to parents, teachers and headmaster.

(iii) To maintain complete record pertaining to the health of children.

(iv) To develop a programme of improving physical health of the pupils.

(v) To take up follow-up work.

## TYPE OF GUIDANCE SERVICES IN SCHOOL

A systematic and comprehensive programme of guidance in a school is concerned with following different types of guidance services :

**1. Data collection service.** This service collects identifying data, psychological data such as data regarding pupil's interests, abilities, aptitudes and personality traits, family background or social environment data, school data and data concerning educational and vocational plans. These data are collected with the help of various psychological tests such as intelligence tests, aptitude tests, personality tests and interest inventories : questionnaire, interview, observation, rating scales, case history and cumulative record card. These data help the guidance worker in understanding the pupil and also in imparting educational, vocational and psychological guidance.

**2. Occupational information service.** This relates to supply of information concerning occupations to pupils according to their abilities, aptitudes and interests. The information includes importance of occupation, nature of work, opportunities for advancement, remunerations, advantages and disadvantages, industrial information, training information, educational information, social, economic and cultural information. Occupational information may be supplied through : (i) School subjects, (ii) Field trips and visits, (iii) career conferences, (iv) films, (v) radio and television, (vi) charts, (vii) Library, (viii) co-curricular activities and (ix) talks on occupation by teacher-counsellor or any other specialist.

**3. Self-inventory service.** This enables the individual to obtain information about his assets, liabilities, aptitudes, interests, limitations and personality traits without which he cannot make a wise selection of an occupation.

**4. Counselling service.** This enables the individual to solve educational, vocational and psychological problems through personal interviews. Counselling interviews are conducted in privacy and friendly atmosphere.

**5. Vocational preparatory service.** This is the service which is designed to help the individual to make preparation through pre-service training, in-service training or apprenticeship. Vocational education helps the individual in such preparation. Success in occupations mostly depends upon how this service is performed.

**6. Placement service.** This is concerned with assisting the pupils to get admission in suitable schools, colleges or training institutions and to get suitable jobs.

**7. Follow-up service.** The main purpose of follow-up service is to find out the progress and achievements made by the students in the educational or professional career. Counselling is incomplete without such service.

**8. Research service.** The main function of research services is to bring about improvement in the effectiveness of the other services by conducting research regarding new techniques.

## ESSENTIAL REQUISITES OF GUIDANCE PROGRAMME

Guidance is not a celestial plan that may take root in any soil. The ground conducive to its growth has to be provided. Accepted that it is not possible to start with all the above-mentioned services in the schools, yet a beginning may be made with the modest effort to have some minimum programme of guidance. The following points may be mentioned in this connection.

**1. Minimum Services.** The minimum services which must be started in every school are data collection service, occupational information service and counselling service.

**2. Provision in time table.** There must be a provision for guidance programme in the school time table as well as in the school budget.

**3. Co-operation.** There must be active co-operation between the staff and the counsellor. A committee for guidance may be set up to enlist the co-operation of the staff. The headmaster or principal should be the administrative head. The counsellor should be the advisory head of the committee.

**4. Trained counsellors.** There must be trained counsellors, one for every 200 students in every school.

**5. Facilities to teachers.** Facilities to the teachers should be provided so that they may become increasingly efficient in guidance work. These include orientation courses and seminars in guidance for as many teachers as possible to enable them to assess and evaluate pupils' needs and the ways to meet them.

**6. Guidance bureau.** In every school, there should be a guidance Bureau in the charge of an expert psychologist or under a teacher having a sound knowledge of psychology and guidance techniques. He should be holder of the responsibility of developing information, knowledge, skills, attitudes, interests, co-curricular activities like debates, dramas, self-government, social service programmes, sports and games, manual work of different types. He should acquaint himself with the environment and orient the pupils accordingly in educational, vocational and psychological or personal areas.

## NEED, IMPORTANCE AND ADVANTAGES

Organization of guidance services is needed due to the following advantages which prove its importance :

**1. Advantages for the students.** Guidance services have the following advantages for the students :

(i) Understanding of themselves *i.e.,* their abilities, aptitudes, interests, personality patterns, their strengths and weaknesses.

(ii) Developing their potentialities in the right manner.

(iii) Selection of subjects, books, hobbies, co-curricular activities and preparing from the examination point of view.

(iv) Selection of occupation, preparing for it, entering in it and to make suitable progress in it.

(v) Solving personal, sexual and social problems.

(vi) Making educational, vocational and psychological adjustment.

**2. Advantages for the teachers.** Guidance services have the following advantages for the teachers :

(i) Understanding their students *i.e.,* their abilities, aptitudes, interests, personality patterns, their strengths and weakness, their emotional and social characteristics, affection, self-recognition, rest, their physical condition, family history and achievements through intelligence tests, aptitude tests, personality tests, interest inventories, and various other data collection techniques such as questionnaire, interview, rating scale, case history, cumulative record, anecdotal record, autobiography and sociometry.

(ii) Developing their potentialities by detecting maladjustments and solving their problems.

(iii) Improving class-room relationships and emotional climate through emphasis upon democratic procedures.

(iv) Providing educational, vocational and psychological guidance.

**3. Advantages for the parents.** The parents have the following advantages from guidance services :

(i) Understanding the abilities, aptitudes, interests, personality patterns, good and weak points of their children.

(ii) Improving parent-child relationships.

(iii) Improving parent, school and community relationships.

(iv) Improving study habits of children.

(v) Helping the parents in solving the problems of their children and assisting them in making adjustments.

**4. Advantages for the community.** Guidance services have the following advantages for the community :

(i) Preventing crimes and problems which may lead to mental illness.

(ii) Identifying and developing the talents of gifted children.

(iii) Producing better adjusted citizens.

(iv) Utilising the staff, energy, money and other resources of the community in more efficient way.

**5. Advantages for the administration.** Guidance services have the following advantages for the administration :

(i) Selecting candidates at the time of admission.

(ii) Selecting or recruiting staff members or employees.

(iii) Using appropriate techniques of evaluating the educational programme of the school.

(iv) Using guidance data in promotional policy and practice.

(v) Setting up and maintaining an effective cumulative record system.

(vi) Decreasing the number of failures and increasing the achievements of the school.

(vii) Collecting, organising and using occupational information.

(viii) Planning placement and follow-up procedures.

(ix) Knowing the areas of the school where improvement is needed.

(x) Increasing the over all efficiency of the school programme by providing more information through contacts between school and employer concerning educational institutions, courses and jobs.

## QUESTIONS FOR EXERCISE

1. Explain the meaning of guidance services in schools. What are the general principles of its organisation?
2. Discuss the role of guidance personnel in school.
3. Explain types of guidance services in school.
4. What are the essential requirements of a guidance programme? Discuss its need, importance and advantage.

# 11

# COUNSELLING

Counselling is called the crux, heart, essence, pivot or core of all guidance programmes. The proper functioning and growth of the body depend upon the proper functioning of the heart. Similarly, the success or failure of the guidance programme is determined by counselling service.

**What is Counselling?**

Some of the definitions of counselling by various experts are the following :

**1. Webster's Dictionary.** "Consultation, mutual interchange of opinion; deliberating together."

**2. Strong.** "Face to face relationship in which growth takes place in the counsellor as well as the counsel."

**3. Robinson.** "The term counselling covers all types of two-person situations in which one person, the client is helped to adjust more effectively to himself and his environment."

**4. Wren.** "Counselling is a personal and dynamic relationship between two individuals — an older, more experienced and wiser (counsellor) and a younger, less wise (counsel). The latter has a problem for which he seeks the help of the former. The two work together so that the problem may be more clearly defined and the counsel may be helped to a self-determined solution."

Thus, counselling is a process in which the pupil is approached on an individual level. He is helped in educational, vocational or psychological field only at problem points. In counselling, the subject matter is pupil's needs, abilities, aims, aspirations, plans, decisions, actions and limitations. It is a sort of specialised, personalised and individualised service which makes effective use of information gathered about any individual. This information leads to self-insight, self-analysis and self-direction. This self-direction helps the individual in making maximum educational, vocational and psychological adjustment.

### Characteristics of Counselling

From the above discussion it is clear that the following are major characteristics of counselling :

1. Counselling is a person to person relationship.
2. It involves two individuals — one seeking help and the other, a professionally trained person who can help the first.
3. The objective is to help the counsel to discover and solve his personal problems independently.
4. In order to help and assist properly, the counsellor must establish a relationship of mutual respect, cooperation and friendliness between the two individuals.
5. The counsellor discovers the problems of the client and helps him to set up goals and guide him through difficulties and problems.
6. In the whole of counselling process, the main emphasis is on the counsellor's self-direction and self-acceptance.
7. Counselling is democratic. It sets up a democratic pattern and allows the counsel to do freely whatever he likes while with the consultant and not under the consultant.

## DISTINCTION FROM RELATED CONCEPTS

Counselling differs from other related terms or activities as follows :

**1. Counselling and guidance.** Counselling is a part of guidance, not all of it. It is a specialised or individualised part which deals with the individual at problem points. Thus all counselling is guidance but all guidance is not counselling.

**2. Counselling and interview.** While counselling is a part of guidance, interview is only a technique used in the process of counselling. Counselling is a wider and comprehensive term.

**3. Counselling and advising.** Counselling is not synonymous with giving advice. A wise counsellor never gives advice until it is absolutely essential. Counselling is a process in which the counsellor assumes the responsibility for the quality of the decisions made. In counselling, the counsel arrives at the decision as a result of process and not because of the advice of the counsellor.

**4. Counselling and teaching.** Counselling is not teaching. The following are some of the points of difference between counselling and teaching :

(i) Whereas counselling is one to one relationship, teaching is done in group.

(ii) Whereas counsellor is concerned with social and emotional problems, the teacher is concerned with academic and intellectual problems.

(iii) Counsellor uses many techniques like diagnostic tools, occupational information and several types of tests to understand the psychological make-up of the counsel. Teacher uses various techniques like lecturing and audio-visual aids to make the teaching interesting and effective.

(iv) In counselling, the counsellor does not know the subject-matter of the counselling interview. On the other hand, in teaching, the teacher knows the subject-matter of teaching.

**5. Counselling and psychotherapy.** Counselling is not psychotherapy although it is used by psychotherapists as one of the techniques of treatment. The following are some of the points of difference between counselling and psychotherapy :

(i) Counselling is concerned mostly with normal individuals having normal anxieties whereas psychotherapy is concerned with individuals whose behaviours are neurotic.

(ii) Counsellor works in educational setting whereas psychotherapists works in medical setting.

(iii) Counsellor uses techniques and tools that can be used in schools whereas psychotherapist uses tools and techniques that are applicable in any situation such as play-therapy, psychodrama, sociodrama, etc.

(iv) In counselling, psychology is not the only basis for studying the individual. In psychotherapy, psychology is the only basis for studying the individual.

(v) Counselling is broader in scope as it touches all the problems of the individual, but does not go deep in them. Psychotherapy is deeper rather than broader in scope. It deals with fewer problems but goes very deep in studying the personality of individuals.

## BASIC PRINCIPLES OF COUNSELLING

The following are the basic principles of counselling :

**1. Acceptance.** All schools of counselling agree that the client must be accepted as a whole person, as a human being.

**2. Respect for the individual.** All schools of counselling attach importance to respect for individual.

**3. Permissiveness.** All schools of counselling accept relative permissiveness of counselling relationship.

**4. Learning.** All schools of counselling accept the learning element in counselling.

**5. Thinking with client.** Thinking with rather than for the client is another basic principle of counselling.

## DUTIES AND FUNCTIONS OF COUNSELLOR

According to Myer, the following are the primary functions of counsellor :

1. Scheduling the interview.
2. Setting the interview.
3. Preparing the interview.
4. Conducting the interview.
5. Recording the interview.

The following are four more functions of a counsellor :

6. Group guidance.
7. Meeting the staff and getting their cooperation.
8. Meeting employment bureaus and collecting information.
9. Meeting social agencies.

According to Stewart, there are the following eight functions of counsellor :

1. Helping the pupil to evaluate his experiences.
2. Data collection about the individual.
3. Understanding the needs and problems of the individual.
4. Interview.
5. Providing liaison between school and home, school and community.
6. Co-ordination of school activity.
7. Remedial work in academic progress and social adjustment.
8. Group guidance.

On the basis of the above discussion, the following functions of a counsellor may be deduced :

1. Programme of guidance and its organisation. It includes all the services such as vocational information service, self-inventory service, personal data collection service, counselling service, vocational preparatory service, placement or employment service, follow-up or adjustment service and research service.

2. Orientation a sort of preparation, including collecting the data about sources and jobs, disseminating information to pupils and planning the activities.

3. Data Collection about the individual, administering the test and analysing the same.

4. Interview and individual counselling.

5. Contacting outside agencies like parents, guidance bureaus and employment exchanges.

6. Placement and follow-up work.

## QUALIFICATIONS OF COUNSELLOR

Qualifications of a counsellor may be studied in the following three major headings :

**(A) Personality Traits.** According to Walter B. Jones, the counsellor should have the following five personality traits :

1. ***Breadth of interest :*** The counsellor should be interested in various types of people, jobs and organisations.

2. ***Cooperation :*** The counsellor should cooperate with all the staff in a cheerful manner.

3. ***Refinement*** : The counsellor should not be over confident but on the other hand he should be modest and humble towards the pupils.

4. ***Magnetism*** : The counsellor should inspire confidence in others and put others at ease.

5. ***Considerateness*** : The counsellor should appreciate the difficulties of teachers, exhibit human understanding and possess real love for fellow beings.

**(B) Mental traits and Training.** Myer says that the counsellor must have the following mental traits :

1. Good liberal education including knowledge of humanities such as sociology, psychology, economics, history and geography, etc.
2. Knowledge of objectives, curriculum and methods of secondary schools.
3. Knowledge of principles of guidance.
4. Knowledge of vocational activities.
5. Knowledge of methods of imparting occupational information.
6. Knowledge of psychological tests and guidance services.
7. Knowledge of organisation of guidance services.

A seminar of headmasters held in Delhi recommended the following qualifications for counsellor :

(i) M.A. in Psychology or B.A., B.Ed., (with guidance) or B.A., M.Ed. (with guidance).

(ii) Diploma Course in Guidance.

(iii) Counsellor must have knowledge about personality problems, testing mental hygiene and counselling techniques.

**(C) Experiences.** Smith requires the following six types of experiences in a counsellor :

1. Competence as a leader in guidance programme.

2. Competence as a counsellor. This includes competence in the following three directions :

(i) Understanding the problem of the child.

(ii) Establishing a rapport with the child.

(iii) Helping the child to solve the problem.

3. Competence in interpreting and using information.
4. Competence in placement and follow-up service.
5. Competence in evaluating the counselling service itself.

## THEORIES OF COUNSELLING

### Directive Counselling

Directive counselling is also known as prescriptive or counsellor-centred counselling. It is problem-centred and not paedo-centred. In it the counsellor prepares entire plans and sees through the process. According to the leading exponent of this school of thought, E.G. Williams, the following are the assumptions of directive counselling :

(i) Efforts should be focused on the problem of the counsel.

(ii) The counsellor is more competent than the counsellee. Therefore he plays a more active role than the client. He is the pivot, the centre or the leader of the situation.

(iii) As counselling is primarily an intellectual rather than emotional process, therefore, the intellectual aspect is given more weightage than emotional aspect.

### Steps in Directive Counselling

According to E.G. Williams, the following steps are involved in directive counselling :

**1. Analysis.** Collection of data from a variety of sources by using a variety of tools and techniques. The data are needed for an adequate understanding of the client.

**2. Synthesis.** Summarising and organising the data so as to reveal the client's assets, liabilities, adjustments and maladjustments.

**3. Diagnosis.** Finding out the root cause of the problems exhibited by the client.

**4. Prognosis.** Prediction of the future development of the client's problems.

**5. Treatment of counselling.** This may include some or all of the following procedures :

(i) Establishing rapport with the student.

(ii) Interpreting the collected data to the student.

(iii) Advising or planning a programme of action with the student.

(iv) Assisting the student in carrying out the plan of action.

(v) Referring to other counsellors for assistance in diagnosing or counselling.

In short, at this stage, the counsellor takes steps with the student or client to bring adjustment and readjustment for him.

**6. Follow-up.** In follow-up, the counsellor helps the client with new problems or with recurrences of the original problem. He determines the effectiveness of counselling provided to him.

**Advantages of Directive Counselling.** The following are the chief advantages of directive counselling :

(i) Counselling is economical in time.

(ii) It emphasises the problem and not the individual. The counsellor can see the client more objectively than the client himself.

(iii) Directive counselling lays more emphasis upon the intellectual rather than the emotional aspects of the personality of the individual. The counsel is helped to solve the problem at the intellectual and not at the emotional level.

(iv) In directive counselling, the methods used are direct, persuasive and explanatory.

**Limitations of Directive Counselling.** The following are the chief limitations of counselling :

1. The client or counsel does not gain any ability of self-analysis or solving new problems of adjustment by counselling.
2. Counselling serves to make the counsel over-dependent on the counsellor. He never becomes independent of the counsellor. Counselling kills his initiative.
3. Problems regarding emotional maladjustment may be better solved by non-directive counselling and not by directive counselling.
4. Sometimes counselling lacks information regarding

the counsel. This lack of information causes wrong counselling.

5. Directive counselling does not guarantee that the counsel will not make mistakes in future.

## NON-DIRECTIVE COUNSELLING

Non-directive counselling is also called Permissive Counselling or Client-centred Counselling. The chief exponent of this school of thought is Carl Roger. The client — the counsel — is the pivot or the centre in this type of counselling. He plays the primary role. He actively participates in the process, gains insight into his problem with the help of the counsellor and takes decisions as to the action to be taken. The following are the assumptions underlying non-directive counselling:

1. Direction and integration of the client are important than the client.
2. Emotional aspects are more significant than the intellectual aspects.
3. Creation of an atmosphere in which the client can work out his understanding is more important than cultivating self-understanding in the client.
4. Counselling leads to a voluntary choice of goals and a conscious selection of courses of action.

Rogers suggested the following steps in non-directive counselling :

1. The counsel recognises the need of counselling and comes for help. Thus help is sought and not given.
2. The counsellor defines the situation and creates congenial atmosphere.
3. The attitude of the counsellor is of friendship, sympathy and affection in the counselling. He feels interested in the child and encourages free expression of feeling regarding the problem of individual.
4. The counsellor tries to understand the feeling of the individual.
5. The counsellor accepts and recognises the positive as well as negative feelings.
6. The counsellor pays attention to negative self-feelings of counselee or child. He leads him from negative

self-feelings to positive self-feelings, from emotional release to gradual insight.

7. The counsellor helps the counselee to translate his insight into action.
8. Positive steps are taken towards the solution of the problem situation.
9. Gradually, a decreased need for help is felt and the counsel is the one who decides to end the contact.

**Advantages of Non-Directive Counselling.** The following are the advantages of Non-Directive Counselling :

(i) It is a sure process to make the individual capable of making adjustment.

(ii) No tests are used in it and thus one avoids all that is laborious and difficult.

(iii) It removes the emotional block and helps the individual to bring the repressed thoughts on conscious level thereby reducing the tension.

**Limitations of Non-Directive Counselling.** The following are the chief limitations of Non-Directive Counselling :

(i) It is a slow and time consuming process. It is not possible because a counsellor has to attend many students in school.

(ii) As the child, the client, the student or the counselee is immature to make the decisions himself, therefore, one cannot rely upon one's resources, judgement and wisdom.

(iii) The counsellor's passive attitude might irritate the counsel so much that he may hesitate to express his feelings.

## DIRECTIVE *VS.* NON-DIRECTIVE COUNSELLING

The following are the distinctions between Directive and Non-Directive Counselling :

**1. Different centres of interest.** While in directive technique, the problem itself is the centre of interest, in non-directive technique, it is the counselee which is the centre of interest and the problem is incidental. While directive counselling is problem-centred, counsellor-centred, active, prescriptive;

non-directive technique is counsellee- centred, client-centred or permissive.

**2. Different needs for assistance.** In directive technique, assistance is offered by the counsellor himself as he can see the problem and the solution better than the counselee. In non-directive technique it is assumed that the counselee has within himself the power to solve his own problem, therefore the counselee may see the problem and the solution better than the counsellor.

**3. Different uses of records.** Indirective technique tests, records and past history are very important in finding the origin of the problem. In non-directive technique, tests, records and past history may be eliminated altogether, as they often interfere with the solution of the problem.

**4. Difference in intellectual and emotional aspects.** In directive technique, the intellectual aspect is given more weightage; on the other hand, in non-directive technique the solution is given more weightage.

**5. Difference in type of interview.** In directive technique rapport is not essential but in non-directive technique rapport is very essential.

**6. Difference in post-contact.** In directive counselling post-contact is counsellor-initiated follow-up while in non-directive technique, post-contact is on counsellee's initiative.

**7. Difference in counsellor's role.** While in directive technique counsellor's role is active in non-directive counselling, counsellor's, role is one of intent listening or passive.

## ECLECTIC COUNSELLING

Eclectic counselling is defined as the synthesis and combination of directive and non-directive counselling. It represents a middle status between the two extremes represented by the 'non-directive' technique on the one hand and the directive technique on the other. In eclectic counselling, the counsellor is neither too active as in the directive counselling, nor too passive as in non-directive counselling. He just follows the middle path between these two extremes.

In eclectic counselling, the counsellor first takes into consideration the personality and needs of the counselee. He selects the directive or non-directive technique that seems to serve the purpose best. The counsellor may start with the directive technique. When the situation demands, he may switch over to the non-directive counselling and *vice versa*. An attempt is made to adjust the techniques to the requirements of the situation and the individual.

### Steps in Eclectic Counselling

The leading exponent of eclectic counselling, Thorne, suggested the following in the process :

1. Diagnosis of the cause.
2. Analysis of the problem.
3. Preparation of a tentative plan for modifying factors.
4. Securing effective conditions for counselling.
5. Interviewing and stimulating the client to develop his own resources and to assume its responsibility for trying new modes of adjustment.
6. Proper handling of any related problems which may contribute to adjustment.

### Assumptions of Eclectic Counselling

Eclectic counselling is based on the following assumptions :

1. In general, passive methods should be used whenever possible.
2. Active methods may be used with specific indications.
3. In the early stages when the client is telling his story, passive techniques are usually the methods of choice. This permits emotional release.
4. Until simpler methods have failed, complicated methods should not be attempted.
5. All counselling should be client-centred.
6. Every client should be given an opportunity to resolve his problems non-directly. Inability of the client to progress therapeutically as using passive methods alone, is an indication for utilising more directive methods.
7. Directive methods are usually indicated in situational maladjustment where a solution cannot be achieved without co-operation from other persons.

8. Even in reaching the decision to use passive methods, some degree of directiveness is inevitable in all counselling.

**Limitations of Eclectic Counselling**

The following are the chief limitations of eclectic counselling :

(i) Eclecticism is not possible because directive and non-directive concepts cannot be merged together.

(ii) Eclecticism is vague, superficial and opportunistic.

To conclude one may say that in spite of the above-mentioned limitations, the eclectic counselling proves to be of much practical value in the methodology of counselling.

## QUESTIONS FOR EXERCISE

1. What is counselling? Discuss its characteristics.
2. Distinguish counselling from related concepts.
3. Explain the basic principles of counselling. Discuss the functions and qualifications of a counsellor.
4. Explain important theories of counselling.

# PART III

# PSYCHOLOGY APPLIED TO HUMAN DEVELOPMENT

# 12

# DEVELOPMENTAL PSYCHOLOGY

## WHAT IS DEVELOPMENTAL PSYCHOLOGY

Psychology is the investigation of behaviour in an environment. It studies the various aspects of human behaviour. However, the behaviour of man is not constant; it is ever changing. Man is a developing and growing animal. Therefore, any study of human behaviour will be the study of human behaviour at a particular stage of development. As we pass from one stage of development to another, our behaviour undergoes change. In appreciation of and response to this feature of human behaviour, there has come into being the branch of developmental psychology in the field of psychology. As will be apparent from the nomenclature, in developmental psychology we study the human behaviour as it passes from one stage to another. The search and pursuit of happiness is the goal of all — be he a child, adult or old.

According to an eminent psychologist, Elizabeth B. Hurlock, "Developmental psychology is the branch of psychology that studies the development of the human being from conception to death. Its major emphasis has been on finding out what are the common and characteristic age changes in appearance, in behaviour, in interests and the goals from one development period to another; when these changes occur; what cause them; and whether they are individual or universal." Thus, the developmental psychology studies the attitudes, the interests and goals of individuals at the various stages of their development and tries to analyse and explain their differentia and causes.

### Historical Background

With the coming into being of developmental psychology,

the experimental psychology has got a new direction. Initially, the experimental psychology was confined to a particular level of age of the individual. The experiments made in psychology did not take into account the whole of life. For example, certain studies on the development of children in school were made; but it was later on found out that the development is a continuous process and that we cannot break it into parts. After the First World War, the experiments in developmental psychology were started but till the Second World War these were confined to the specific problems of the adults. Till 1933 only a few experiments were made about the middle and old aged persons but later on there was a phenomenal increase in these experiments. Earlier, the psychologists were primarily interested in the first two decades of life. This was so because they believed that the personality of man is formed in the first two decades only and then by the second decade it is completely chiselled out with no scope of modification. No doubt, the early years are most important from the point of view of personality development. But it is also seen that the lazy and apathetic lasses bloom into wistful and energetic maids. They surprise others by this phenomenal change. Some over-active and domineering boys, on the other hand, are known to grow into docile adults. The main reason for this phenomenon is that though the main features of human personality are well laid out in the early stages of life, the man is ever facing the challenges by modifying his reactions and exerting his incipient capacities. Thus a series of new adjustments give rise to changes in his personality, accentuation of some and blowing out of other features. The life is like a race in which the early fast runners may tire midway and fall out whereas the early slow runners may pick up speed as they reach the target. Nothing can be said definitely in this regard.

## DIFFICULTIES IN DEVELOPMENTAL STUDIES

The fact that there has not been much work in the developmental studies is due to the reason that there are serious difficulties in this regard. Following are the main difficulties :

**1. Difficulty in representative samples.** It is not very difficult to find a representative sample in the case of school children; but it is very difficult to collect such a sample in case of adults and aged persons.

**2. Opposition by parents.** Some parents are opposed to the idea that their children may be subject of study by the psychologists. They entertain the wrong notion that this will harm their children.

**3. Difficulties in interview.** The psychological experiments carried on adults make use of the method of interview. However, many people are not prepared to give interviews, either on account of their shyness or their lack of confidence in the experiment.

**4. Lack of appropriate method.** The biggest drawback in the developmental studies is the lack of appropriate method or technique. In the beginning, all experiments made in developmental psychology utilised the cross-sectional comparison technique but the studies in the psychology of culture have revealed the insufficiency of this technique. Of late, the longitudinal method is being used in the developmental studies. Though there are some difficulties in this method also, it is still in use. The chief drawback of this method is the establishment of facts. It is found that the parents usually exaggerate the good qualities of their children and tend to overlook their defects. Even if their attention is drawn towards these, they are not prepared to admit them. Moreover, in establishing certain facts, introspection is needed, while in others, retrospection is required. In both cases, however, satisfactory answers are not available. In the longitudinal method it is possible to make a continuous study, but an effective use of this method requires well-educated subjects.

## MEANING OF DEVELOPMENT

According to Elizabeth B. Hurlock, "Development means a progressive series of changes in an orderly coherent pattern. It is a process in which the internal physiological changes and the psychological processes stimulated by them are integrated in a way which enables the individual to master further and anew, environmental stimulations." It is clear from this definition that the development is a progressive and continuous process. According to Elizabeth B. Hurlock, "Development means a progressive series of changes in an orderly coherent pattern. It is a process in which the internal physiological changes and the psychological processes stimulated by them are integrated in a way which enables the individual to master further and anew, environmental stimulation." It is clear from this definition that the development is a progressive and continuous process. According to Anderson, "Changes occur in almost every relation within and without the human being. For our present purpose, we may call attention to the increased range of objects and experiences to which the growing person responds, to his increased strength, speed and motor skill, to his growing intellectual and problem solving capacity : to his greater ease in using language and communicating with others : to his enriched social life with its web of interrelation : and to his changed interests, activities and values. From the dependence of infancy the person moves to the maturity and responsibility of adult life." This long passage makes clear the dimensions of development. There are a number of dimensions of development. By means of the developmental process, a helpless infant becomes a responsible and able individual. In the developmental process, however, there is progress and retrogression, zeal and depression, acceleration and slow movement — these cycles go on from cradle to death. In infancy and childhood the development is very fast and it slows down a little bit in adolescence and further comes down in adulthood. After middle age the development stops and a slow decline begins. Whether positive or negative, the development never stands still in man. He keeps undergoing change and from a tiny thing becomes a grown up person of 5 to 6 feet height and 60 to 100 kg in weight. In early life the development is fast.

However, physical development is not confined to shape and size only. For example, in infancy the nerves, glands and muscles grow and add to the weight but later on, the addition to weight is primarily due to deposition of fat. With the physical changes there are corresponding mental changes also. In the first part of life the capacities grow while in the later half these decline. A curve of human development exhibits a positive acceleration in the beginning followed by plateau and then by a negative acceleration. The changes in man are so gradual as to be imperceptible. It is only during adolescence and senescence that these are felt internally.

## STAGES OF HUMAN DEVELOPMENT

According to S. Feldman, "Human life proceeds by stages. The life periods of the individual are no less real and significant than the geographical ages of the earth or the evolutionary stages of life. Each stage is distinguished by a dominant feature, a leading characteristic which gives the period its coherence, its unity, and its uniqueness." And Lawton has observed very correctly that "each period in the life-span has its own problems of adjustment. These age periods are related, not in surface story, since problems change; it is the method of attacking these problems which is likely to remain the same. Throughout the lifespan, people develop techniques of handling each of their difficulties. Some of these techniques are suitable and efficient, others are inappropriate and wasteful, or a method may be suitable for one age period and not another." As to the question what is permanent and what is transitory in human behaviour it can be said that while problems are transitory because these keep changing, the techniques to tackle the problems remain same throughout and are, therefore, permanent. For example, some persons are in the habit of facing each and every problem squarely and boldly while others initially try to escape them and face them hesitatingly when forced to do so. The human lifespan can be divided into eleven distinct stages. These are :

1. **Pre-natal.** From conception to birth.
2. **Infancy.** Two weeks from birth.
3. **Babyhood.** From two weeks to two years.
4. **Early childhood.** From two years to six years.
5. **Late childhood.** From six years to ten years.
6. **Puberty or Pre-Adolescence.** From ten to thirteen or fourteen years.
7. **Early Adolescence.** From thirteen or fourteen to seventeen years.
8. **Late Adolescence.** From seventeen to twenty-one years.
9. **Early Adulthood.** From forty to sixty years.
10. **Middle Age.** From forty to sixty years.
11. **Old Age or Senescence.** From sixty years till death.

## ESSENTIAL DEVELOPMENTAL TASKS

The story of human life, according to Developmental Psychology, is the story of developments necessary at the various stages of life. At every stage man needs new abilities to meet the fresh problems of life. As it is recorded by experience if a man is unable to acquire fresh abilities and give up old habits to meet the ever new exigencies of life he cannot survive long. Whether you will know or not, organism is continuously developing. It can never be static. A man who is able to shed old and useless habits and acquire instead new and effective ones will succeed in life; and a man unable to do so will be overwhelmed by life forces. For example, an adult must go out in the world, seek job, get married and adult who hangs on to his parents cannot grow properly. No escapism by taking to intoxicants, debauchery or dependency on parents will be of any avail in man's struggle in life. Man must face the challenge by himself; there can be no proxy in this matter. Developmental Psychology defines the tasks essential at each stage of life. According to R.J. Havighurst, "A developmental task is a task which arises at or about a certain period in the life of the individual, successful achievement of which leads to his happiness and difficulty with later tasks." Therefore, to perform the developmental tasks successfully is the key to happiness. At certain stages in life, the need for developmental task is particularly great. This may be described as a critical or dangerous age. For example, adolescence is a critical period because special developmental tasks are essential at this stage. Havighurst has enumerated the developmental tasks essential at various stages of life. A summary of these will be helpful :

**1. Tasks essential in infancy and early childhood.** Learning is the essential characteristic of tasks at this stage such as walking, talking, lifting heavy things, learning excretory tasks and to experience sex organs, to gain physical balance, to form concepts about the physical world and to develop emotional relationships with parents, brothers and sisters.

**2. Tasks essential to middle childhood.** Following tasks are essential at this stage-proper behaviour with children of same age, skill for reading and counting, concept formation about the objects of daily life.

**3. Tasks essential to adolescence.** Following tasks are essential at this stage — recognition of one's identity as a male or female, to behave properly with persons of both sexes. Independence from parents in emotional matters, an attempt to gain economic independence, choice of profession, adequate mental development for civic and social responsibilities, preparedness for marriage and family life.

**4. Tasks essential to early adulthood.** Following tasks are essential at this stage — choice of marriage partner, bearing the responsibilities incidental to marriage, preparedness to assume responsibilities of parenthood and also consciousness of social and political obligations.

**5. Tasks essential to middle age.** Following tasks are essential at this stage-assuming social and cultural responsibilities, striving to maintain and improve one's social and economic status, to develop suitable hobbies and recreations, etc.

**6. Tasks essential to old age.** Putting up without emotional loss with the psychical and mental decline incidental to this age. To reconcile oneself with slowing down of activity and develop a spirit of tolerance and understanding towards younger generation. Ability to mixup with other old persons.

## REASONS FOR FAILURE IN DEVELOPMENTAL TASKS

By performing tasks essential to one's age and by developing new capacities to meet new challenges, one gets success and feels happy in life. There are, of course, persons who fail to make up and fail in the tasks. They feel depressed and unhappy. Following are the main causes of this failure :

**1. Lack of learning opportunities.** A man can perform tasks for which he has had an opportunity to learn. Without learning man can achieve little. If in a family all the things are done by the servants and the child has nothing to do himself, it will be small surprise if he is found unfit for many tasks. Again, if the father takes all the decisions, the boy will not be able to decide for himself later in life. Therefore, in the absence of adequate opportunities for learning, nobody will learn the tasks essential for his development.

**2. Lack of motivation.** Some persons have the opportunity for learning but they still do not learn because they lack the motivation. The motivation may come from self, society or some divine agency. Only self-motivation is not all. There are societies in which old persons are not respected. Therefore, the child will not learn to respect old people. In some societies there is little restriction on sexual expression. As a consequence, the members of such a society will have little motivation to be restrained in sexual behaviour.

## IMPORTANCE OF DEVELOPMENTAL TASKS

The above discussion makes quite clear the importance of developmental tasks in the life of man. Briefly, their significance is as follows :

**1. Direction to individual.** The list of tasks appropriate to various stages of life given earlier clearly shows to an individual what the society expects from him at various stages of life.

**2. Prediction about future.** The knowledge of the developmental tasks tells a person in advance as to what physical and mental changes to expect in future. For example, the middle-aged person who knows what will be his state of affairs after retirement, he can prepare in advance for all exigencies. He can save more or start some side-business to be taken up fully later on. It is always difficult to make adjustments with new situations and this gives rise to a great deal of tension. However, if one is mentally prepared for the change, difficulty will be less.

The developmental psychologists have found out certain facts which would help a man to make better adjustment. Following are significant facts in this regard :

(i) ***Childhood is the foundation of life :*** It is well said that the coming events send their shadows before. A strong foundation laid in the childhood will surely ensure happy and prosperous adulthood. It is generally found that the physical and mental characteristics observed in the childhood persist throughout. An honest child is likely to grow an honest adult. A study of fat adults has revealed that in childhood they were over-protected. As Adler has shown, a lone child displays specific characteristics throughout his life. Similarly it also matters whether the child is first or last. The roles children play in their family later on determine their basic personality traits. If the experiences in childhood are positive and favourable, the child grows into a healthy, normal and happy adult; but if these experiences are negative the child tends to develop abnormalities. The causes of a number of mental diseases are to be found in childhood experiences. The most important influence upon the child is that of his parents. If the child is taught to be tardy and clean, it develops in him a habit of cleanliness. Besides if there are some inborn defects in the children they can be best rectified in childhood. The child is a tender creeper. He must be zealously cared for and good habits inculcated in him. This will help him to become a healthy and moral adult.

(ii) ***Development is dependent upon maturity and learning :*** In the past there was a controversy among the psychologists as to what is more crucial in the development — maturity or learning. Some opted for maturity and the others regarded learning to be the crucial factor. Now it is settled beyond doubt that there is an interaction between the two. It is also proved that in the absence of certain level of maturity there can be no learning. The interaction between maturity and learning can be seen in three ways. It tells us about individual differences. It tells us why some individuals cannot learn beyond a certain point. Thirdly, we know what age is most appropriate for a particular type of learning. Educational psychologists have made special investigation in this regard. Upon the basis of these studies individual differences have been noted. No two persons are equal and same. Individuals therefore differ *inter se* in their reaction. A situation which may be ridiculous for some may be serious for others. Briefly, people differ in their level of maturity and learning and they therefore behave in different ways.

## ORDER OF DEVELOPMENT

The study of developmental psychology shows that there are special characteristics for every stage. These may be described briefly :

**1. Infancy.** Infancy is the smallest span in the life of a person. It is barely for two weeks. In these two weeks the infant tries to make adjustment with physical environment. This adjustment consists of getting used to the outside temperature and learning to suck the teats or nipples. At times there are difficulties in such adjustment and mother's help is needed by the infant.

**2. Babyhood.** The stage of babyhood is a critical period. It is also dangerous. The baby is prey to so many foreign microbes which can cause diseases for which it may have little resistance. These diseases often prove fatal. However, now improved medical facilities have reduced the danger quite a bit. This is of course a period requiring maximum care and protection.

**3. Early childhood.** The period of babyhood is an age of helplessness, but in early childhood there is a certain amount of independence. A child wants to do all the work by himself. Now not only home but the school also contributes to his development. A child tries to discover many things. As many opportunities he gets for learning better would he be. He should be encouraged to learn various skills. There is also development of speech at this age. The development of speech and language is the foundation of mental development. There is emotional development also at this stage. The socialisation also begins now. Play has an important role at this age. The child also shows interest in his body. He makes a distinction between male and female. The presence of other siblings and the serial order of his birth also affect development.

**4. Late childhood.** The child is now a boy. He now grows tall and his sex organ is developed. Now the child develops self-reliance and the environment of school and playground affect him. There is development of language and also mental development. In mental development home and school both contribute. In emotional development home plays the crucial role. The boy likes many games and also develops many interests.

**5. Adolescence.** The adolescence is best known for sexual development. The sex organs develop remarkably and there is as if onslaught of sexual impulse. The adolescence is split up for psychological studies in two parts — Early adolescence and late adolescence :

(i) ***Early adolescence :*** Adolescence literally means rapidity in maturation. Thus adolescence is a stepping stone to adulthood. This is a crucial period marked by quick changes in physical and emotional development. There are so many problems to be forced at this stage. It is a stage of twilight. The young man fools himself at crossroad with no body to guide him. There is a welling of feeling which he cannot easily express.

(ii) ***Late adolescence :*** In late adolescence things settle down and there is relative stability. The technique of attacking problems is now perfected.

**6. Early adulthood.** Adult means fully grown and mature. This is an age when the power of reproduction is fully developed. At this stage the individual enters upon life and creates place for himself in the world. There are of course other problems at this stage.

**7. Middle age.** Middle age is between 40 and 60. At this stage the problems of individual and social adjustments predominate. There are great changes and they require adjustment. This is an age of achievement as well as frustration. It is here that man works hardest and tries to ensure a smooth transition to old age. At this age the professional and family responsibilities also become enormous. At this stage there is marked difference in the role of men and women.

**8. Old age.** This is the ultimate stage in man's development. Here the development comes to a halt. In fact, this is a period of decline and degeneration. Generally in old age people feel useless. They can do little constructive work. However, the problems of old age are not insurmountable and the old age need not be dreaded. The modern psychological researches have revealed that there are vast individual differences among the old regarding their outlook — physical and mental characteristics. The interest in sex generally becomes less and the interest in religion increases. In India moksha is considered an ideal of life and the old age is a stepping-stone. By adopting realistic outlook man can solve most of his problems. The best preparation for old age is made early in life. If old age is faced gracefully it can be a period of great spiritual development.

**What is Heredity?**

Heredity involves all those physiological and psychological peculiarities which a person inherits from his parents. These peculiarities are transmitted to use through the gene. In this way, the children of white parents are fair while those of dark parents are generally dark. Negro children exhibit all physiological peculiarities of their Negro parents. If one of the parents is fair while the other is dark, the child may be either fair or dark complexioned. It is heredity which determines the structure and colour of the skin, the colour of the hair, structure, height, facial features, nasal index, cephalic index, etc.

**How does Heredity Work?**

Before there was any scientific investigation, it was believed that the effect of heredity arises from the mixing of the bloods of parents. But nearly one hundred years ago, priest Mendal proved the fallacy of this theory by his experiments on the seeds of peas. Mendal's experiments and the investigations of other scientists proved that the effect of heredity is transferred from one generation to the next through the gene. By the intercourse between male and female, the sperm cell of the male meets the egg cell of the female and the child is conceived. These cells are made of protoplasm, and they have chromosomes in their nucleus. There are genes inside these chromosomes. The heredity of the child worked from these genes, determining his physiological traits and some psychological trait has a definite gene corresponding to it. This gene is never found in other because both the parents contribute one gene each. Thus the person gets a part of gene from his parents for every physiological trait. This is heredity. If these two genes are similar, the child inherits that quality, but if the two are dissimilar it is the dominant of the two genes which gives its qualities to the child. Take an example, if both mother and father are fair, and their genes are of fair colour, the children too will be, in all probability, fair. If the gene of one parent is fair while that of the other is dark, the colour that the child will inherit will come from the more prominent of the two, though it is not inevitable that the child will be fair if the parents are both fair. The importance is that of the genes. If the child of fair parents is dark, it means that one of the two was carrying a dark gene from his previous generations which became dominant at that time. Sometimes one gene lies dormant for generations but flares up or becomes extremely active in one generation. Sometimes there is a change in the power of transmission of the gene. The mutation causes a sudden change in the gene. No one gene can, however, produce some physiological trait by staying away from the other genes. In reality different genes create a condition in which all the physiological traits are determined for thc child.

### Controversy between Heredity and Environment

Scholars are not unanimous about the relation between heredity and environment. Some psychologists opine that all physiological and psychological characteristics of the individual find their determinants in heredity. Galton, the eminent author of *Hereditary Genius*, says that genius is an innate quality immune to the environment. On the other hand, some psychologists think that environment alone is responsible for moulding the character of a person so much so that heredity does not in any way effect the individual. Dr. Watson said, "Give me a child and I will make him anything." Thus, the supporters of heredity and those of environment theories have been engaged in an extreme controversy.

### Relation between Heredity and Environment

In reality, both heredity and environment share the importance. MacIver and Page have said very correctly, "Every phenomenon of life is the product of both. Both determine the character of the individual. Neither can ever be eliminated nor can ever be isolated." Experiments relating to heredity have proved that it is not the sole factor which determines development of the personality of human beings. And similarly, experiments conducted in the field of environment also indicate that it is not the only factor influencing personality. In Altenberg's words, "Each trait requires both heredity and environment for its development."

### Heredity and Environment are Complementary

Actually, heredity and environment are the two aspects of the same phenomenon. Davis writes, and very correctly, "Terms like heredity or environment do not refer to anything tangible but to an abstraction." In relation to human development heredity cannot be imagined apart from environment and neither can environment be imagined apart from heredity. Lysenco has taken an example from Nature to explain it. Only wheat will sprout from a seed of wheat and the same applies to mustard. But when the farmer decides to sow wheat he has in mind all those things which he needs to make that seed sprout and the extent to which he can lay his hands on them. Obviously, the sprouting of the wheat-seed and its development depend on both environment and heredity. David Abrahamson writes, "What the individual can do is decided by heredity and what he does is determined by the environment." The energies to the individual are in the heredity but it is up to the environment to extract these energies. Lumley has beautifully described this relation between heredity and environment. He wrote, "It is not heredity or environment, but heredity and environment."

## EFFECT OF HEREDITY

### Effect of Heredity on Physiological Appearance

To study the effects of heredity on physical appearances, children of many varied races were compared with their parents. From these experiments it was concluded that it is the heredity which determines physical appearance. But other scientists pointed out that the effects of food and environment are by no means negligible. Franz Boaz collected examples in which Japanese and Jews residing in U.S.A. had increased in height and the shapes of their heads had also changed.

### Effects of Heredity on Intelligence

Having experienced upon Negroes and white soldiers in connection with their intelligence, Yerkes concluded that due to heredity, there is a difference of intelligence between the two. Clark experimented in New York and Los Angeles and contradicted Yerkes in his conclusion that the difference in intelligence between Negroes and the Whites is insubstantial. In an imposing school in New York, 10 per cent of the selected 500 students were Negroes, equivalent numerically to the ratio of the Negro population of New York. Besides this, a 9-year old Negro girl registered an intelligence quotient of 200, twice the intelligence of a normal child. Even among the Negroes Klineberg found a disparity between those of the North and those of the South, the former being the more intelligent because of better developed education and environment. Then, again scientists have pointed out that the Negroes are always at a disadvantage in these tests designed specifically for the Whites. Intelligence tests developed for one group do not suit other groups.

J. Mackeen Cattell, in his book *American Men of Science* wrote that if the generations of 885 American scientists are studied it is seen that 1/5th of them come from the trade people, another 1/5th from the agriculturists, notwithstanding the fact that the agriculturists comprise 40 per cent of the population while the handful of trades people, represent only 3 per cent of the population. From this study, attempts have been made to prove that due to effects of heredity, some specific groups or classes show a greater propensity or ability for trade than those belonging to other groups. But Cooley, in his essay 'Genius, Fame and Comparison of Races' disproved this opinion by recounting the examples of 71 scientists of Europe.

**Effect of Heredity on Personality**

It is indisputable that heredity determines and the difference of sex and on this basis some scientists contend that heredity determines personality because it is the difference of sex which determines the personality of men and women. People, in general, believe in a fundamental difference in the personality of men and women due to the difference in sex. Thus the qualities of patience and emotion are attributed to a woman and she is called the very picture of love and affection. It is generally believed that their main function is to give birth, to look after their offspring and to work in the house. Every literature holds such typical thoughts that woman is like a creeper which lives entwined about man. Her personality is considerably influenced by man's personality. On the other hand, man by nature is hard, persistent, intelligent, independent and self-supporter. While women take an interest in art and literature, men take an interest in science, mathematics and war and other difficult works.

**Effect of Heredity on Temperament**

Besides difference in sex, difference in temperament is also an important part of personality. The nature of an individual depends very much on the environment. Temperaments develop according to the environment in which the child grows. Thus the difference in environment affects temperament. Family relations, social circle of friendship and working conditions all hare an effect upon the temperament of an individual. In poverty, temperament becomes hard, irritable, overbearing etc.

Even though it may not be accepted as a law, no man of experience will deny that the financial status, occupation, nature of life partner and living conditions all have a profound effect on temperament and all these collectively consisted the environment. But the effect of heredity on temperament is more profound than the effect of environment. Temperament depends, to a large extent, upon internal drives which are deeply affected by endocrine glands. In modern times extensive research has been carried out to find out the effect of endocrine glands that glands determine personality. People have been classified on the basis of the effects of glands. Scientific discoveries have proved beyond dispute that the effects on temperament once attributed to the environment are actually the effect of glands. The change which occurs in the temperament of boys and girls caused by the increased activity of the sex glands with the coming of youth is inevitable. Besides as the secretion of the thyroid increases, an individual becomes restless and active and if it decreases he becomes slow and lazy. If the para-thyroid secretes more, a person remains calm but he becomes excited with every fall in the secretion. Research on the effects of the glands located in various parts of the body is in progress. Attempts are being made to bring about artificial increase or decrease in the glandular secretions. Undoubtedly, many ways of improving human personality will be evolved but to conclude from this, that temperament is determined by glandular secretions or that heredity determines everything in the subject, would be completely one-sided. These secretions have tremendous but unperceived effects. A big change in these secretions is affected by cultural and social environments. For example, the mental disturbance through which adolescents in our societies pass when they attain youth is absent in many tribes because in those tribes there are no restrictions upon sex relations. Obviously, the change is not exclusively due to the activity of sex glands, but it is also due to social customs. Heredity then does not mould the personality. The above description of the effects of heredity on personality can be beautifully summed up in the words of Biesanz and Biesanz, "Personality is the organisation of a person's habits, attitudes and traits and arises from the interplay of biological, social and cultural factors."

The above exposition of the effects of heredity upon physical appearance, intelligence and personality makes it quite obvious that its effects are not similar and equal in all cases. We know from experience that heredity has its most pronounced effect upon physical appearance, somewhat less on intelligence and least of all upon personality. This conclusion is supported by scientific research.

## ENVIRONMENT

Environment has a very significant effect on man. Its effect starts from his birth and continues almost till his very death. The status of the child, youth and old man in the family and society is not the same and as a result of this difference a man's personality, roles, temperament, ways of thinking, tendencies, inclinations, and character are affected. In the same way, the status, of the person in places like school, office, occupation, etc., affects his role to a great extent.

Environment can be roughly divided into two parts — controlled and uncontrolled environment and social and geographical environment. In both the social and geographical environment of man, a part of them is controlled and the other part is not controlled. Both these types of social and geographical environments have a profound effect upon the individual.

### Effect of Social Environment

The various parts of society like the family, school, occupation, social customs and primitive concepts all affect the individual. In this context one example from family life will suffice. In the opinion of the famous psychoanalyst Sigmund Freud, the personality of a person is fashioned in the first seven years, the rest of the life being an expression of those tendencies. Whether all thinkers agree with Freud's opinion or not, all have agreed with regard to the effect of the environment on the family, upon the character, nature, mental tendencies, habits and behaviour of the individual, and there are enough existing causes which justify family's influence upon the individual. This special knowledge can be gained by comparing children brought up in families and those bred in government institutions. Havelock Ellis in his essay, *The Problem of Race Regeneration,* says, "The advantages of a mother suckling her baby are more than merely physical, it is a stimulus to her affection for their child and a guarantee that the child will receive in other respect the loving care it needs." In childhood parental love affects stability of the emotions for the child. It is inevitable that excessive love and care spoil the children and lack of affection leaves their feelings undeveloped, which are then unnaturally expressed. The famous psychologist Alfred Adler said that even the birth order of the child in the family affects personality. This may be expressed or clarified better thus in the family. Mother, father, husband, wife, elder brother, younger brother, elder sister, younger sister, beloved child, unwanted offspring all have their respective, dissimilar status which affect their personality.

## PRENATAL DEVELOPMENT

Child psychology studies child development, the study starting not with the infant's birth but before it, while it is in embryonic form within its mother's womb. The child's development within the womb is a very important phase of his entire development. Hence, there have been detailed studies of the human embryonic state. The human being originates in the form of a fertilised ovum. Gradually, and continually, the fertilised ovum shows signs of structural and functional development. In the structural development, the ovum cells multiply in number and increase in size. These cells are of two kinds, the germ cells and the somatic cells. The germ cells help the germ plasm to develop from one stage to the next higher level. The somatic cells are concerned with the development of various physiological parts such as bones, muscles, nerves, etc. Besides changes in structure, the functions of the embryo also take on a variety and complexity. Functional development occurs with the addition of new activities. While the human being is in the embryo, the structural and functional developments take place in the nature of two mutually supplementary aspects of total development. Psychologists have divided the embryonic development of the being into several states. These stages and a brief mention of them are given below :

**1. Germinal period.** The period beginning with the conception of the child and lasting for a period of two weeks is called the germinal period, the being's development. During this period the being exists in the form of a fertilised ovum; not being given any external nutrition it does not develop. The form of the fertilised ovum is that of an egg, and its cells are equally divided.

**2. Embryonic period.** The period from the third to the eighteenth week of pregnancy is called the embryonic period, during which the embryo gets nutrition from its parent. As a result, its form undergoes rapid change. In this change there is a hive related to the ovum and it is situated between the cells that lie in between the Omni-otic sac and the Yolk sac. In this hive, the cells those lying next to the omni-otic sac are called the endoderm cells, while those lying next to the omni-otic sac are called the ectoderm cells. The cells of the first kind prove of help in the development of the digestive and the respiratory systems, while the latter or second kind of cells lead to the development of the nervous system and the skin or epidermis. The mixing of the two kinds of cells leads to the development of a new layer called the mesoderm. Development of the two kinds of cells leads to the creation of muscles and bones. The cellular structure which is originally flat and convex, gradually spreads out. Every cell has its own peculiar position, and if it is changed its characteristic feature will also undergo some change. For example, if it would originally have developed into skin, it will develop into the muscles of the eye on changing the cells. Certain chemical substances are also of importance in the separate and individual development of the cells. These chemicals are called organisers. Besides these, the development of the embryo is influenced by the use of light, electrical field, X-rays, and other chemical rays.

**3. Fetal period.** In the development of the being, this state begins with the eighth week, and in it the number of cells increase, following which their size improves. Change in this stage is very rapid.

## LAWS OF HUMAN DEVELOPMENT

The child's development during pregnancy is characterised by two types of development, the structural and functional. The following two laws are accepted in respect of structural development :

(a) **Law of cephalocaudal development.** According to this

law, in the development of the embryo, the development starts with the cephalic portion or the head and gradually proceeds to the tail portion. In this way, law of development shows the direction of the bodily development. This law applies to growth as well as differentiation.

(b) **Law of proximo development.** According to this law, the progress in development is more rapid in peripheral parts than in the part situated in the centre.

In structural development, the structure of the nervous system is a very important one. In this development, the first layer of the ectoderm cells turns inwards to form the neural tube, the major portion of which, the spinal cord and the upper part, develop into the brain. In the fifth week of development, the medulla, cerebellum and the mid-brain become distinctly visible. The nervous system develops very rapidly during the fetal period. Muscles begin to be formed even before the nervous and sensory organs. Almost all the sensory parts develop in the child before delivery or actual birth. The development of vision starts with the second week, and continues even after birth. Receptors concerned with olfactory sensations reach maturity in the womb in the case of some children. Taste cells develop in the third month, that is, during the fetal period. Besides this, during pregnancy the child attains the power of feeling sensations of pressure on the skin.

## PRENATAL FUNCTIONAL DEVELOPMENT

Functional development during pregnancy is divided into two parts, those of motor development and sensory development. Their description is as follows :

1. **Motor development.** During pregnancy, the embryo shows constant activity before birth. During this period, this movement is also felt by the pregnant woman carrying the child. At the age of three weeks, the heart starts beating, and after 18 weeks this heart beating becomes audible. In this period, some motion is also evident in the chest. In the seventh week, the organs of digestion evince some movement while there is sometimes some tension of the urinary bladder. Children born in the sixth month of pregnancy produce certain sounds. Research experts have made study of the embryonic movement in rats, cats, pigs, etc., and compared it with the movement in

human animals. This research has shown that till a certain stage of development is achieved, the embryo does not show any reaction to any stimuli. In the beginning, the tail section does not show any reaction, but it is evident when maturity of this part sets in. The movement starts with the leg, continues to the knee and can then be successively in the foot and the ankle. Minkowski and Hooker have conducted important research in connection with motor development. The two laws concerning structural development are also applicable to motor development. According to Toghill's principle, in the functional development there is a movement from the general to particular. Putting it more explicitly, it can be said that at first general activities appear, and then through gradual development these general activities are divided into particular activities that become distinct.

**2. Sensory Development.** The second important aspect of motor development is that of sensory development. In the eighth week, the embryo becomes susceptible to epidermic sensations. Later on, it reacts to pressure and temperature sensations. According to the law of cephalocaudal development, in sensory development, epidermic reaction is the first to appear, while sensibility of the rest of the body follows later. Reactions to the sensations present within the body are also in evidence, but the sensation of pain does not develop during pregnancy, while the ability to recognise and react to direct smell and taste is engendered during pregnancy. Some experiments have shown that the child can react to strong sensations one month before it is born.

The bodily parts develop gradually in the child during its pregnancy. After birth during the 4th, 16th, 28th and 40th weeks, the eyes, hands, back and fingers attain expertise respectively. In the ninth month movements of the legs and feet are evident. At the age of one year and half, babbling sounds are produced, which are the rudiments of speech. At two, the intestines and the bladder are brought under control. At the age of three years, he develops the capacity for thought and reasoning. And when he attains five, he shows the tendency to socialisation.

## ROLE OF MATURATION AND LEARNING

Learning changes behaviour and for the matter of that, so

does maturation. Thus sometimes it becomes difficult for any one to say definitely as to which of the subject's activities are the result of learning and which are the consequences of maturation. Automatic activity, random acts, reflexes and unexpected expressions of pain and emotion can be accepted as unlearned actions and the result of maturation, but in most of the activities of human beings it is difficult to decide whether these activities result from maturation or learning. In reality, these activities develop from the complex of learning and maturation. Take the example of learning. It is true, of course, that a child is manifestly incapable of learning language until he reaches a certain stage or age in maturation, but it is also equally true that he does not learn the language just because he attains that stage. The language is taught to him.

**Example of co-twins.** An experiment on co-twins indicates the extent of the changes in behaviour caused by maturation and the extent to which changes may be affected by learning. The experiment has been extracted from an essay "Maturation of Behaviour" by M.B. McGraw published in Carmichael's book *A Manual of Child Psychology.* The purpose of the experiment was to measure the extent of advantageous of application of learning to such activities as climbing the stairs. Two twins were chosen for the experiment because due to the similarity in heredity, the speed of maturation is the same and any changes which may occur may be attributed to learning. One of the twins 'S' was not given the opportunity of climbing stairs for 53 weeks while the other twin 'T' was taught to climb the stairs from her forty-sixth week. On examination, this twin 'T' failed to climb at all at the age of 46 weeks and had to be aided up all the five stairs. In the space of four weeks she climbed all the stairs in 26 seconds.

When 'S' was placed on the stairs at the age of 53 weeks, she climbed all the five stairs unaided but it took her some 45 seconds. After two weeks of practice 'S', at the age of 55 weeks, traversed the distance in 10 seconds. In this way, at this age 'S' was ahead of 'T' who, at a younger age had practised there times as much 'S' was three weeks older than T. Thus, in spite of all kinds of learning, 'T' was left behind, due to a lack of maturity.

This experiment proves that maturation plays an insignificant part in reflex activities and other psychological activities peculiar to one's race. Those activities which appear in all human beings at a certain age, as a universal rule, are due to maturity. Those activities which do not inevitably appear in every person are affected by maturation to the extent that they can be learnt with ease such as swimming, horse-riding, climbing trees, etc. The learning of these activities is made facile by motor, sensory and neural maturation.

The above exposition on the relation of learning and maturation provides some very practical suggestions for learning and training. It is not useful to make an attempt to teach a child forcibly before he matures. Many parents try to precipitate their children into higher classes with the help of coaching, at a young age. This type of coaching cannot have a lasting or permanent effect and the children become weak in senior classes. The teaching of the proper job at a specific age depends on many factors two of which are the child's brain and psychological development. But a general age for the beginning of the teaching of various subjects can be established. For example, it is comparatively easier to study Algebra at 15 or 16 than it is at 11 or 12. This relation between maturation and training is an initial cause of the suggestion for the fixing of a minimum age limit for admission to universities.

## QUESTIONS FOR EXERCISE

1. What is developmental psychology? What difficulties have to be faced in developmental studies?
2. What is development? What are its changes?
3. Explain developmental tasks and the order of human development.
4. What is heredity? Bring out the relative importance of heredity and environment in the development of child.
5. Discuss the effect of heredity on physiological appearance, intelligence, personality and temperament.
6. Describe the importance of environmental factors in child development. Give experimental evidence.
7. State the different periods in prenatal development. What are the factors influencing prenatal development?

8. Describe the important laws of human development.
9. Elucidate the role of maturation and learning in human development by citing experiment on maturation and learning.

# 13

# Psychological Problems of Adolescence

## WHAT IS ADOLESCENCE?

The English word adolescence is derivative of the Latin 'adolescence' which means to grow to maturity. The age begins from twelve and continues till the age of twenty. In the words of Jersild, "Adolescence is the period through which a growing person makes transition from childhood to maturity." Adolescence, in the opinion of most educational psychologists, begins between the age of 12 and 14 years. Compared to boys, girls enter the period of adolescence a couple of years earlier. According to Dr. Jones, adolescence is the recollection of infancy. It parallels the states in infancy and childhood in being patterned into two conditions, the first of growth and the second of maturation.

**1. State of growth.** In this state, the adolescent is seen to be very active and unstable as well as disturbed. He gives the impression of being somewhat lost, and is subject to rapidly varying moods of dejection undulation, enthusiasm and deep lethargy, etc. The main thing concerning this period in life is that adolescent is no longer a child but an adult, though the society in which he lives continues to treat him as a child. Secondly, he climbs down from the dizzy heights of imagination that he reached in his infancy and childhood and steps firmly into the real world. Both these factors engender in him a constant fear of reproof and criticism at the hands of others. He often becomes selfless and far for the real world, but that he tries to modify it according to his own notions. In efforts of this kind, elation and dejection are only natural, and it is not this reason that the adolescent is often seen wearing a look of anxiety.

**2. State of maturation.** By the time he enters this stage, he has calmed down a bit and showing signs of stability. He carves a niche for himself in his society, and gradually his tendencies, habits and activities become stable and regular.

## MENTAL CHARACTERISTICS OF ADOLESCENCE

In adolescence the individual is so transformed that he wears a new and unrecognised look. Mental changes in his this period of life find their best expression in the works of poets as they depict the mental states of young men and women. Adolescence exhibits the following mental characteristics generally :

**1. Development of mental abilities.** In adolescence the individual's nervous system becomes more strong with the result that his mental activities show greater tenacity and system. Ability to think, to solve problems, to differentiate and evaluate are some of the more prominent characteristics and abilities that he exhibits.

**2. Sexual development.** From the psychological viewpoint, the most significant characteristic of the period of adolescence is sexual development. According to Dr. Jones, the repressed sexual force of infancy, that continued latent through the period of childhood, once again awakens and the individual passes through various stages of sexual development. The truth of the matter is, that even if it is not the only tendency, sexual tendency is undoubtedly the most prominent and stable tendency to be found in adolescence. Hence, to disregard it is to make a fatal mistake as it is most harmful form of negligence conceivable. The development in this sphere is so rapid that his entire personality appears to be coloured by it. Sexual development in adolescence finds its expression in attraction towards strangers, rather than towards parents as in the case of infancy. It announces its presence even in such small activities as the young boy's anxiety and nervousness, biting of fingernails, putting a pencil in one's mouth, tying knots in handkerchiefs, etc. Both physical and mental teaching in this age can use the sexual tendency as an important force. Normally, the development of the sexual tendency passes through the following three stages :

(a) ***Auto-eroticism :*** In the beginning of adolescence, sexual tendency manifests itself in self-love, but this self-love differs from the infant's self-love. In infancy, the child finds physical pleasure in exploring and touching various parts of his own body. But in the adolescent self-love, the individual dresses himself well and meticulously, observes his face continuously in the mirror, and does his very best to make himself as presentable as possible. Many young men and women passing through this stage can be seen humming as they look at themselves in the mirror. They are content to be with themselves and love only themselves. As yet they have no time to observe and appreciate others. Freud calls this the state of narcissism. Narcissus was a Greek prince of almost unparalleled beauty, who could not find anyone more handsome than himself : he loved himself, probably justifiably. A flower is called narcissus, and it grows by the side of lake in such a manner that its image is visible in the water. Young men and women in their teens behave in a similar manner as they love to look upon themselves, to preen themselves and beautify themselves. One of the most prominent and common malpractices in which the adolescents indulge is masturbation. The American psychologist Kinsey, in his famous report, has mentioned the various ways in which young men and women derive pleasure from their sexual experiences. Sometimes the feelings of guilt that arise as a result of indulgence in these activities lead to the formation of complexes that are very harmful to the mental development of individuals. The one and only means of escaping such consequences is proper sex education. In order to impart the right attitude towards the sexual tendency in young people, it is essential that teachers and parents tell them things frankly so that they may adopt this healthy attitude.

(b) ***Homosexuality :*** Progressing from the stage of self-love, young boys and girls are attracted to members of their own sex, either older or younger than themselves. Homosexual love of this age is accompanied by great anxiety and deep affection but later on it turns into heterosexual love. Persons of this age can often be seen caressing each other, romancing together, preferring only each other's company, sleeping together, praising each other and finding other modes of expressing their mutual attraction. Similar aberration is present in boys in the form of sodomy, which leads to feelings of guilt and crime if the person is reproved for these activities. Such bad habits can be got rid of only through the medium of sensible guidance and sex education of the children by the parents and teachers. It is always desirable that adolescents passing through this phase should be controlled sensibly but it is equally essential that all control exercised over them should be in the form of loving advice rather than punishment.

(c) ***Heterosexuality :*** The state of homosexuality in adolescents is succeeded by sexual maturity, a state of normal heterosexual reactions between man and woman. Young men and women who have attained this age can often be seen being attracted to members of the other sex, meeting each other, talking incessantly for hours, putting their best foot forward to appear the more attractive, going for walks together, visiting picture houses together, caressing each other and sometimes even going to the extent of actual sexual intercourse, though this often has disastrous results as the girls become mothers even before they are married. The strength of this sexual tendency can neither be curbed nor can any strict control upon it prove efficacious even if it is considered desirable. Excessive restrictions on meetings between boys and girls in colleges and universities only leads to greater indiscipline and misconduct. Hence, many educational psychologists have advised that instead of restricting communication between them, relations should be encouraged. On the other hand, the traditions that have continued in our culture stress the complete segregation of the sexes during this period. In the modern context any effort at emulating these traditions can only prove foolhardy in the future, and in any case such efforts are not likely to prove efficacious. Uncontrolled and detestable consequences lead to suicides, unmarried mothers, social corruption, etc. Hence it is essential that the youth of today be provided with proper sex education and encouraged to develop a healthy attitude towards sex. This will have the desirable effect of preparing them for responsible parenthood when they ultimately get married.

Another method of solving problems of the sexual impulse, besides sex education, is inspiring the young men and women to develop interest in various kinds of games and sports, dances, singing, art, painting, etc. It is a matter of universal regret, particularly among the enlightened population of the nation, that nearly 90 per cent of teachers and guardians find it embarrassing to discuss any sexual matter with their young charges. The consequences are undesirable as the young inexperienced adolescent learns the same things from bad and uncouth companions who convey to him all the aberrant forms of sexual information. Such a situation is true of many civilised societies, and all the more of India. When the adolescent observes that his teachers and guardians prefer to keep all sex information secret and concealed from him, he forms a guilt complex regarding sex. Due to the normal stage of development, he can do nothing to abate the force or strength of the urge, and he is helpless as no assistance from his teacher is forthcoming. Thus, he either indulges all his energies in trying to control the instinct, losing all interest in studies, in which he cannot concentrate or from obnoxious and deforming habits, or as an alternative contracts serious mental diseases through excessive repression. Hence, teachers and parents should assist adolescent males and females to organise, control and sublimate the sexual impulse through adequate sex education.

**3. Hero worship.** Generally speaking, adolescents evince a strong tendency towards hero worship, though the criterion of heroism is not the same in all children. Possession of any quality that attracts an individual child the most is sufficient qualification for a man or woman to become its ideal. While one child may regard a wrestler as hero, another may profess allegiance to a scientist, yet another may be devoted to a dim personality or a political leader. In schools some teachers impress their students considerably with the result that they come to be tenderly and affectionately regarded by them, also being imitated by the tender children. Sometimes this hero worship turns to love. It is not till considerably later that the young man turns his thoughts to his own heroic qualities, when he begins praising them. The tendency to hero worship can be turned to good account by inculcating a proper character and personality in the child's mind. For this it is essential that the teacher himself should represent the highest ideals, as he is the best example that the child can facilely imitate.

**4. Religious feeling.** Many adolescents become positively and deeply religious in this period of their lives. One can often observe them loving God in some one image, talking to him, sacrificing themselves to him and praying to him. India is particularly productive of such specimens since, for one, the religious tendency is deeply ingrained in the people's mind, and for another, in Indian society young boys and girls meet great leaders and famous personalities on very rare occasions. While religious tendency protects the young inexperienced child from many bad habits, it sometimes helps in making him somewhat impractical. Teachers can help to create a healthy attitude towards religion.

**5. Gregarious instinct.** Adolescents are always acutely desirous of praising them and of improving their relations with them. Often, they form definite groups in which each adolescent has his specific status and a role to suit it. This status and role play an important part in determining his status and role in adult life.

**6. Extroversion.** In this period, the child once again regains his extrovert flamboyancy, taking deep interest in his surroundings and other individuals, their activities and conflicts. In school, too, he likes to take part in all kinds of activities and conflicts. And it is a matter of joy with him if he can spend the larger part of his time in the company of his friends. Various individuals become engaged in programmes of social service and welfare. In this manner does the adolescent announce the interest that he takes in the real world. This interest can be usefully exploited to ingrain in him such useful qualities as self-dependence, self-determination, cooperation, discipline, honesty and the quality of maintaining good relations with others or develop the social instinct. This is the age in which foundations of good citizenship can be deeply laid.

**7. Lack of stability and adjustment.** It has been pointed out earlier, too, that in his adolescence, the growing individual is at the threshold of his life, although he is rarely if ever considered an adult by his seniors. From the psychological point of view, he takes himself seriously enough not to consider himself a child, and likes to be treated as an adult. Evidently, he shows considerable instability and lack of adjustment. His adaptation to his environment is upset by such small considerations as the growth of pimples on his face or the presence of other small physical deformities. In fact, it is a stage in which he learns to lead adult life in every sphere and direction, hence, the presence and continual development of problems is only natural. And these problems are susceptible to ready solutions if the seniors are prepared to extend their sympathetic cooperation and guidance.

**8. Excessive sentimentality.** The adolescent is very sentimental and emotionally unstable, although at this age his mind is fairly well developed. Of the many feelings that drive him, the strongest are the desire to win praise and self respect, any injury to or repression of them leading to serious malformations and even open rebellion. Sentimentality can be turned to good use in developing culture qualities in the adolescent. Participation in programmes of dancing, acting, music, painting, etc. makes the emotional life more stable.

**9. Excessive imagination.** Although the adolescent is as much in this world as any other living being, yet he is prone to much imaginary flights into the world of fancy. The smallest thing can persuade him to temporarily abandon the world of reality and turn to the imaginary world. Such excessive imagination manifests itself in the strong tendency towards daydreaming, but some gifted children express their creative and aesthetic imagination through literature, music and painting, besides other arts.

**10. Particular interests.** In adolescence, as the individual develops both in mind and body, his interests vary. Progressively the boys and girls develop the interests of their adult counterparts. Girls show this development in such interests as the use of various cosmetics, efforts at appearing very beautiful, reading or taking interest in romantic novels, love stories, dramas or poems, participating in music, art and acting programmes, etc. Boys manifest their approaching adulthood in the form of various active games, running around, doing acts of valour, developing a vocation that they are to pursue in their adult life. Both boys and girls take constant interest in developing friendship with members of the other sex and maturing it to fruition through conversation, intimacy, letters and romance.

**11. Development of the mind.** In adolescence, the mind develops rapidly. The cells of the nervous system increase rapidly, and the chemical composition of the nerves also undergoes a change. In this way, the mind and the nervous system rapidly mature. In this period along with physical and mental development, practice helps to develop mental abilities. Linguistic ability also registers improvement during this period. In his adolescence the child develops the vocabulary that he possesses. His vocabulary reveals general intelligence. Mental development, too, reaches its apex in adolescence. Despite the inevitable individual differences that are invariably present, mental maturity achieves its completion normally by the age of twenty. Practice or experience contributes considerably to this maturation. Normally, the individual's intelligence continues on the same level, or, in other words, even in different ages the intelligence quotient of an individual remains more or less the same. Many detailed studies have revealed that during the first five years of life, the mental development is greater than that achieved during the following five. In this manner, the mental development during the age of 10 and 15 is greater than that during 15 and 20, in respect of rapidity. At the age of ten, the mental development of a child is at its fastest. Following this, as the child approaches the stage of adolescence, the speed of mental development slows down. In his infancy, the child only acknowledges and indicates the feeling of sensations, while at the age of three he is in a position to distinguish between objects, animals and human beings. At six, he is capable of describing a picture that he has seen, but in his adolescence he rises above description to the level of interpretation of pictures that he sees. In this manner, one can see constant development and improvement in the mind's reactions to stimuli. Generally, an individual's memory is tested by the number of digits he can remember after they have once been announced to him. In adolescence, the ability to remember digits improves with age, and reaches its highest peak at the age of twenty.

## EDUCATION IN ADOLESCENCE

The sensible teacher can make his teaching psychological if he has knowledge of an adolescent's mental development. The intensity and proper use of imagination can help to make an individual a poet, painter, sculptor or a psychologist. Intelligence, observation, reasoning, and thinking having reached the required state of development in adolescence, the school and college curriculum can be fairly diversified and made comprehensive. The truth of the matter is that actual education begins only in adolescence since at this stage the young boys and girls treat themselves as adults and they come to entertain a serious and responsible attitude to their education. What is needed is that the teacher should inspire them to work hard in their studies through self inspiration.

1. Physical development is rapid during adolescence. The bodily structure develops at a rapid pace. This age is the time of revolutionary physical development as in this age young boys and girls attain to their maximum heights and specific bodily developments, conforming to their respective sexes, take place. Hence, they should be trained in games and beneficial exercises. In educational institutions, they should be specially trained in health and bodily development since, if they do not pay attention in health and bodily development at this stage they are not likely to appear beautiful later on in life.

2. The extreme sentimentality of adolescence can be used to induce the girls and boys to learn literature, music, art and science. This age is propitious for the teaching of all subjects. Transfer of learning during this period is also considerable.

3. Good conduct, proper interest and good habits of living can be developed in boys and girls by making adequate use of the strong sexual tendency that is a strong motivating force. In adolescence, the sexual organs of the boys and girls undergo startling development. In girls, the menstrual cycle starts while the boys are subject to nightly emissions. The sexual organs are covered by hair. Persistent development in the girl's breasts sometimes leads to pain. Lacking knowledge of the basics and cause of all these physiological changes, boys and girls are often subject to much perplexity. Many of the girls are not even aware that the blood emitted during the menstrual cycle does not happen to them alone but to every other girl passing the same stage of development. This leads to much anxiety and sometimes even results in the creation of guilty feelings. Not knowing the manner in which they should dress hygienically during the menstrual cycle they are sometimes put in very embarrassing situations that are very painful to them. They are even rendered ridiculous. It is a matter of no little sorrow and pain that much changes are inevitable in the lives of every

young man and woman, but almost all of them have to get over them through trial and error. The parents, who have themselves been through these conditions, are content to leave the helpless children on their own resources and wit. This is not a desirable practice. In this connection it is for the parents to inform the children of all necessary details and methods, without making secret of anything. It is never a good practice to hate or scold or deliver moral lectures if one sees an adolescent developing bad habits. It is a matter of physiology and psychology, and it should be treated accordingly. It is for the teacher to inform the growing boy and girl of the complete formation of the male and female body, and to train them adequately in all forms of hygiene.

4. Hero worship and idealisation are two very useful tendencies with which the adolescent is endowed. This stage in his development is particularly efficacious for laying the foundations for a good character. The lives of great idealists should be revealed to him and he can think in terms of great characters as opposed to the imaginative pictures of heroes that he has been sketching to himself. The adolescent should be persuaded to read extensively in hygiene. It is never desirable to prevent him from reading stories and novels. All that is needed is that he should be intelligently guided in forming his taste by being taught to read interesting works of great novelists and psychologists so that his knowledge of human nature increases and his sexual tendency reduces its hold upon him.

5. The adolescent is by nature a rebel against the traditions and customs prevailing in his society. His rebellious instinct can be channelled to good use by the teacher who can help to develop a generation which hates all the bad traditions and rids society of them. Adolescents can be taught to rise above their narrow interests and comprehend the spirit of nationality, internationality and cosmic love.

6. It is no less important to impart ethical, moral and religious education to the child. Although all educational psychologists fail to see eye to eye on this subject, moral and religious education can benefit the recipient only if it is psychological and volitional or simple.

7. In adolescence, the individual should be given vocational

guidance after his mental capacities, inclinations and interests have been examined. His education should conform to the vocation that he is going to pursue in the future so that he may not be a misfit in any occupation but should rather be able to earn a comfortable living, establish a household and contribute actively to national development.

## CHARACTERISTICS OF ADOLESCENCE

The second stage when the child develops very rapidly is the period of adolescence, after the first stage in his infancy. The same pattern of three years of growth and three following years of maturation can be assumed to exist in this period of the individual's life also. Maximum physical development takes place in first three years. Normally, adolescence appears at the age of 11 and 12 in girls and at 12 and 13 in boys. Commonly, boys are taller and heavier than girls, but in adolescence between 12 and 14 it is the female who is both taller and heavier as she develops earlier than the male child. It is for the same reason that in these years girls consider boys of the same age as younger and prefer to be with boys a couple of years older than themselves. Another characteristic is the desire for mixing between boys and girls. In adolescence, boys and girls attain 90 per cent of the height that they are going to have in later years. In other words, by the time a young boy is 14 he has developed to 90 per cent of his ultimate or final stature. But it takes him another six years to cover the remaining 10 per cent. On the other hand, the weight of the adolescent is only two-thirds of what is going to be. Even after the adolescent has stopped growing upwards, his weight continues to increase at a rapid pace. Compared to boys, girls gain both height and weight faster but the development in these directions also stops earlier. Consequently, the adolescent girl looks more developed than her male counterpart of equal age. Muscles, in particular, develop mainly only after adolescence is over. In this age, physical education is most important and very meaningful. Sex education is equally important as it is in this age that boys and girls develop the characteristic features of their respective sexes. Girls develop lady like features. Of the many changes in the girl, the most perceptible is the roundness of the breasts and hips while among the boys their faces become adorned with beard and moustache. While the girl's voice becomes sweet, the boy's sound takes on a deeper and more thrilling note. Within a year or two of adolescence, both men and women attain the capability of procreation.

## NOTABLE FACTS CONCERNING ADOLESCENCE

Physical exercise and games are important for physical development in adolescence. The well-balanced body shows apt proportion between length and weight. Much of this proportionate development depends upon the exercise taken. But neither height nor weight is in fact indicative of the healthy state of an individual's body. Physical health finds adequate expression and recognition in the enthusiasm, energy, swiftness and interest with which he performs his functions. Although it is always desirable for youth to be active and vibrant in adolescence, yet one should guard against excessive exercise that completely tires the body, as such exhaustion has adverse effects on the body's development. Nutritive food is as important for getting rid of exhaustion as rest is. Exercise, too, should be balanced. It should be remembered that the physical development of a player's body is sometimes impaired by his playing a particular game in which only some of the bodily organs are exercised and strained. Excessive indulgence in such a game can have only the least desirable effect. But even if regular practice of the game benefits these parts, other organs of the body are not benefited. Hence, generally speaking, it would be more efficacious to induce adolescents to take interest in physical education rather than spending long and weary hours in the pursuit of perfection in the various competitive games. Schools should divert their expenditure on coaching scheme to the physical education of their students. This measure will help to improve the level of health among adolescents. Proper exercise steps up blood circulation with the result that many waste materials are thrown out of the body, while other parts of the body such as lungs also develop better and faster. Physical capacities are also developed besides the progress of the body itself. Ignoring the exceptions, one could draw up a chart of the various physical capacities, as correlated to the various stages in physical development at this period of life is proper food and adequate exercise without excess in either of the two. Of course, there can be no common level of food and exercise for everyone. The amount of food, rest, sleep and exercise that an individual requires can be found out from his friends or teachers. Provision of sex education can help the young boys and girls to form the proper attitude towards bodily development concerning sex. Suppression of any feeling on account of fear will only have adverse effects on them. Their clothing should be such as not to restrict the growth of their bodies. Just as at any other stage in life, it is not advisable to wear very tight clothes, as they will harm the body even if they do appear temporarily attractive and smart. And, particularly among the young girls, it is essential for the development of the breasts and hips that they wear slightly lose and comfortable clothes. Any female child who aspires after beauty can begin practising her wiles from this age. Hence, in this respect some intelligence is the adolescent's best companion.

## MORAL DEVELOPMENT DURING ADOLESCENCE

An adolescent's moral development, during the most crucial stage in an individual's development, is peculiarly susceptible to the effects of his mental and social development. Detailed study and analysis have revealed that in this age the sexual urge of both male and female adolescents is particularly intense. Hence, it is only natural for the notions of good and bad to become associated with sexual behaviour. Since the laws pertaining to sexual behaviour differ considerably in various cultures, the moral concepts and conduct of adolescents do not exhibit any universal conformity but differ according to their culture. Sex education has the best and most profitable influence upon the adolescent's moral development at this stage. Actually, in this age, it is best to utilise the techniques of sublimation and modification of manifestation rather than that of suppression. Many educational psychologists also advocate moral and ethical teaching in schools. But it is commonly and generally accepted that moral education is best imparted through practical representation of best ideals and values rather than through academic teaching and preaching of them. It is equally important for both teachers and parents to do their best to set the best example to their wards. Another factor that is equally important in respect of its influence upon the moral development of the students is the atmosphere prevailing in the school.

**Influence of Society and Culture**

Besides the school and family, the general social atmosphere also affects the moral development of individuals. It is for this reason that moral behaviour and conduct of individuals belonging to cultured and uncivilised societies show such marked differences that they appear almost incompatible. It is in society that an individual's axiological concepts are formed. Although the contemplative among society's members do not blindly conform to the social morality, the greater majority of them do follow, more or less unthinkingly, the general morality prevailing in society. Hence all individuals who set examples to the multitude, individuals such as leaders, great personalities, saints, scientists, actors, etc., influence the moral development of the individuals. In addition to this, more indirect matters such as employment or unemployment, inability to secure the desired profession, economic status of the family, practical adjustment, peace in the family, intellectual and educational status, morals of friends and intimates, presence of immoral institutions such as prostitution in society, etc., also cast a serious influence upon the moral development of the individual.

Moral development normally exhibits individual variations within very wide limits. There can be no saying what the actual moral implications of a particular instance will be for an individual, though, generally speaking, good situations normally have a desirable influence.

## QUESTIONS FOR EXERCISE

1. What is Adolescence? Explain the characteristics of mental development during adolescent period.
2. Of what value is education for the mental development of adolescence? Discuss.
3. Describe the physical and emotional characteristics of Adolescence, mentioning notable facts.
4. Discuss moral problems in Adolescence.

# 14

# Psychological Problems at Middle and Old Age

In the development of man, the age group from forty to sixty is considered the middle-age. As in every other stage of development, the middle-age has also got its peculiar characteristics, developmental problems and tasks, characteristic syndromes, changes in interest, problems of social adjustment and conditions conducive to good functioning.

## CHARACTERISTICS OF MIDDLE AGE

According to Elizabeth B. Hurlock, "Middle-age is generally considered to extend from age forty to age sixty. The onset is marked by physical and mental changes, as is the end. At sixty, there is usually a decline in physical vigour, often accompanied by a lessening of mental alertness. Although many adults experience these changes later now than in the past, the traditional boundary lines are still recognised. The increasing trend toward voluntary or involuntary retirement at age sixty rather than age sixty-five also justifies considering sixty to be boundary line between middle and old age." The following are the most important characteristics of the middle-age :

**1. A dreaded period.** According to Desmond, "Americans slump into middle-age grudgingly, sadly and with a tinge of fear." This is also generally true about Indians. The most important reason for this fear is the belief that physical and mental energies deteriorate with the onset of middle-age. This fear influences attitudes and philosophy of life.

**2. Transitional period.** In middle-age men and women enter a period of life in which there are important physical changes. Men undergo a change in virility and women find a change in fertility. This transition requires new adjustment. There are role changes, crises and consequent problems. The main crises are concerning parenthood, dealing with ageing parents and the crisis of the untimely death of a spouse.

**3. Age of stress.** According to Hurlock, the following are the main categories of stress in middle-age :

(a) ***Somatic stress :*** Which is due to physical evidence of ageing.

(b) ***Cultural stress :*** Stemming from the high value placed on youth, vigour and success by the cultural group.

(c) ***Economic stress :*** Resulting from the financial burden of educating children and proving status symbols for all family members.

(d) ***Psychological stress :*** Which may be the result of the death of spouse, the departure of children from the home, boredom with marriage, or a sense of lost youth and approaching death.

**4. Dangerous age.** This age is characterised by increase of sexuality in the male, physical breakdown due to overwork, overworry or careless living, mental illness and finally tendencies of suicides, alcoholism and drug addiction, etc. These dangers, of course, are not compulsory but differ from person to person.

**5. Awkward age.** The middle-aged men and women are neither young nor old. Therefore they feel awkward and one notices the desire to be as much inconspicuous as possible.

**6. Period of achievement.** During this period, one notices the peak of earnings in a person's life. Those who are very ambitions reach their maximum success and start reaping the benefits of their hard work. It is not only the period of achievement in income and social success but also in authority and prestige.

**7. Period of evaluation.** Peaks of achievements naturally lead to self evaluation. As a result, there is a more realistic appraisal of one's ambitions, imaginations and realities.

**8. Double standards.** However, the standard of evaluation in this period is different for men and women. This double standard is apparent in the approval of ways for members of both the sexes. Women are more likely to adopt rock chair philosophy.

**9. Period of empty nest.** As the sons join their jobs and the daughters are married, there is empty nest in the house. This creates its own problems such as loneliness needing readjustments.

**10. Period of boredom.** In the words of Archer, "By the time you are 40 everyone — including you — knows that you can do whatever you are doing. And at that point some men get bored. Some begin looking for new territory. In most men, however, this impulse is checked by the sense that one has passed the last chance to change directions to choose new goals."

## DEVELOPMENTAL TASKS OF MIDDLE AGE

According to Hurlock, the following are the most important developmental tasks of the middle-age :

**1. Tasks relating to physical changes.** These include the acceptance of and adjustment to the physical changes that normally occur during middle-age.

**2. Tasks relating to changed interests.** The middle-aged person often assumes civic and social responsibilities and develops an interest in adult oriented leisure-time activities in place of family-oriented activities, which prevailed during early adulthood.

**3. Tasks relating to vocational adjustments.** These tasks revolve around establishing and maintaining a relatively stable standard of living.

**4. Tasks relating to family life.** The important tasks in this category include relating oneself to one's spouse as a person, adjusting to ageing parents, and assisting teenage children to become responsible and happy adults.

## CHANGES IN MIDDLE AGE

The following changes may be noticed during the period of middle-age :

**1. Physical changes.** This involves changes in appearance such as gain in weight, loss and greying of hair, skin changes, sagging of the body, sagging of the muscles, pain in the joints, yellowing of the teeth and less brightness in the eyes, etc. There are changes in physiological functioning of almost all the internal organs and glands. This result in changes in health. The physical fitness declines and general deterioration occurs. Some common physical problems are : the tendency to fatigue easily; buzzing or ringing in the ears; muscular pains; skin sensitivity; general aches and pains; gastro-intestinal complaints, such as constipation, acid stomach, and belching, loss of appetite; and insomnia. There are sexual changes due to male's climacteric and the females menopausal. The menopausal syndrome involves the following changes : Cessation of Menstruation, Generalised Atrophy of the Reproductive System, Deline in Feminine Appearance, Physical Discomforts, Weight Gain, Knobbiness and Personality Changes such as self-criticism, Depression, Hostility, Lack of balance, etc. The male climacteric syndrome involves : Decline in Functioning of the Sex Organs, Decline in Sexual Desire, Decline in Masculine Appearance, Anixety about Virility, Physical Discomforts, Decline in Strength and Endurance, Personality Change such as concern about loss of virility, Desire of extramarital affairs, Carelessness about business, etc. All these problems require new adjustments. The male and female have to adjust to physical and mental changes.

**2. Changes in interests.** Elizabeth B. Hurlock has summarised the characteristic changes in interests in middle-age as follows :

1. Interests are more commonly narrowed down than expanded with advancing age.

2. There is a shift in emphasis on already-present interests as when interest in the fashionable quality of clothes shifts to interests in clothes that make the wearer look younger.

3. There is a shift toward interests that are more solitary in nature, such as hobbies, reading and television watching.

4. Many middle-aged people develop increased interests in cultural pursuits such as reading, painting and attending lectures and concerts.

5. There is a lessening of sex differences in interests with men showing more interest in so-called women's activities, such as reading for pleasure, than in so-called men's activities, such as engaging in sports or watching sports contests.

6. There is a tendency for men and women to engage in shared interests, such as hobbies and cultural pursuits, instead of engaging in interests with members of their own sex.

7. There is an increased interest in activities leading to self-improvement, such as attending lectures and concerts and taking courses, and a decreased interest in activities that are purely for enjoyment, such as going to the movies or playing cards. This applies more to the lower classes.

Thus, one finds changes in interests in appearance, clothes, money, status, religion, community affairs and recreation. In all these changes of interests, differences may be noted between males and females. This difference may be noted in recreational activities such as sports, reading, movies, radio and television, trips, hobbies and courses for vocational advancement, etc.

**3. Social changes.** So many middle-aged men and women exhibit decrease in social adjustment due to the following reasons : The "Rocking-Chair" Philosophy, Unattractive Appearance, Lack of Social Skills, Preference for family contacts, Financial Problems, Family pressures, Desire for popularity, Social Mobility. Adjustment problems in society are some time due to personal hazards, acceptance of traditional beliefs, idealisation of youth, rebellion against social taboos, changing and more difficult roles, change in interests due to physical decline and increased interests in status symbols, and finally unrealistic aspirations. Social adjustments are most seriously influenced by such traditional beliefs as you cannot teach an old dog new tricks or once leader always a leader, etc. The following conditions have been laid down by E.B. Hurlock for good social functioning in middle-age :

1. Reasonably good health to enable participation in group activities.
2. A strong liking for social activities to motivate putting forth the effort needed to take part in these activities.
3. Previous requisition of social skills to ensure self-confidence and to be feel-at-ease in social situations.
4. Absence of circumstances such as family responsibilities or insufficient financial resources, that limit the ability to function as the social group expects.
5. A social status that is compatible with peers in desired social groups and that allows affiliation with community organisations.
6. A willingness to play follower roles graciously even

though leadership roles were customary in adolescence and early adulthood.

## ADJUSTMENTS IN MIDDLE AGE

**1. Vocational adjustments.** An important problem in middle-age is the adjustment to vocational changes. The changed working conditions are the main cause of the problems of adjustment. One notices sex differences in vocational adjustments though most of the vocational problems are common for men and women. According to psychological researches, the following working conditions affect middle-aged workers : Unfavourable social attitudes, Hiring policies, Increased use of automation, Group work, Role of the wife, Compulsory retirement, Dominance of big Business, Relocation. The conditions influencing vocational adjustment in middle-age include : Satisfaction with work, Opportunities for promotion, Vocational Expectations, Increased use of Automation, Attitudes toward Co-workers, Relocation. The peak of vocational success is generally reached by men during the forties and early fifties. This is the peak of status as well as income. However, some middle-aged men are not satisfied by their success and constantly look for better jobs and even better work. The factors influencing vocational adjustment in middle-age include : Assessment of vocational achievements such as income, authority, autonomy, training experience, etc. and the job satisfaction. Job satisfaction wanes with the progress of middle-age because the pressure of work appears to be more than their declining capacity can tolerate. Middle-aged women appear to be even more frustrated during the middle-age and they welcome compulsory retirement.

According to E.B. Hurlock, the following conditions contribute to vocational satisfaction in middle-age :

1. Achievement or near achievement of a vocational goal set earlier.
2. Satisfaction on the part of family members, especially the spouse, with the worker's vocational achievements.
3. Opportunities for self-actualisation on the job.
4. Congenial relationships with co-workers.
5. Satisfaction with treatment from management and direct superiors.

6. Satisfaction with the provisions made by management for illness, vocations, disability, retirement, and other fringe benefits.
7. Feelings of security about the job.
8. Not being forced to relocate to hold a job, advance in it, or get a new job.

**2. Adjustment to changes in family.** According to Cavan, "The most obvious thing is the withdrawal of children of the family, leaving husband and wife as the family unit." This shrinking circle stage is more difficult for the women than men. This is further complicated by other changes peculiar to family patterns in middle-age such as : Physical changes, Loss of parental role, Lack of preparation, Feeling of failure, Feelings of uselessness, Disenchantment with Marriage, Care of elderly relatives.

The most difficult problem concerns sexual adjustment and adjustment with spouse. This requires a closer relationship between the husband and wife as they had during the early years of marriage. The causes of poor sexual adjustment during the middle-age have been enumerated as follows :

1. One of the major causes of poor sexual adjustment in middle-age is differences in the sex drive at this time.
2. Poor sexual adjustments often result when men become concerned with the loss of their sexual vigour.
3. During the forties and early fifties, many women lose their earlier inhibitions and develop more interest in sex.
4. Some middle-aged women who derive little satisfaction from intercourse or who feel that they are no longer interesting to their husband or a necessary part of their marriage may take the initiative in stopping it.

The effects of good sexual adjustments may be seen in increasing satisfaction of the male and female.

**3. Adjustments to in-laws.** The adjustments to in-laws include adjustment to mother in-law and father-in-law as well as adjustment to children's spouses. While the former is quite important, the latter are even more important in Indian conditions. The conditions contributing to difficulties in adjusting to children's spouses have been ably summarised by E.B. Hurlock as follows :

1. Short courtships that give parents little time to know their future in-laws or their families.
2. Spouses from other communities, states, or even countries. This deprives both sets of parents of opportunities to get to know their future in-laws before marriage.
3. Few parents of today are consulted about their children's choice of spouse; they often consider the choice "unsuitable".
4. The expectation on the part of the middle-aged couple that they will continue to have the same relationship with their children that existed before marriage and that their relationship with a son or daughter-in-law will be the same as their relationship with their own children.
5. The necessity for married children to live with their parents or in-laws.
6. The tendency of the middle-aged couple of often too much advice to a son or daughter-in-law.
7. Dissimilarity of sociocultural background of in-laws, leading to criticisms and strained relationships.
8. Elopement, which leads to parental embarrassment and resentment.
9. Disapproval of spouse because of willingness to cohabit for a year or more before marriage.
10. Residential propinquity, which encourages frequent contacts and parental over-protectiveness and interference.
11. Psychological dependency of a married daughter on her parents, which may make her husband resent them.
12. A lack of grandchildren, which may be a disappointment to the middle-aged parents and which may also give the married children more independence and thus cause them to neglect their parents, which adds to parental resentment.

13. Disapproval of son-in-law's occupation or that daughter-in-law works after marriage.

As has been pointed out earlier, the above-mentioned points are particularly important in Indian conditions specially in the context of the increasing problem of dowry deaths. Among the above mentioned conditions, the most important conditions are no. 4, 5, 6, 7, and 12.

One finds a difference between the conditions affecting adjustment to care of aged parents in India and the West. This adjustment is definitely better in Indian conditions. The most important conditions affecting adjustment to care of aged parents include : Role reversal, Place of residence, Degree of Responsibility, Relationship of Aging parent to Middle-aged person, Role played by Elderly parents, Sex of Elderly parents, Earlier Experiences with elderly parents, Attitudes toward elderly parents. Of these the last point is the most important for a successful adjustment to aged parents. On the other hand, the adjustment also very much requires initiative from the parents as well. They should always perform the functions of inspiration and patting the back and never the functions of interference and even sometimes guidance. Adjustment to the older generation also includes adjustment between grandparents and grand sons and daughters. The roles played by today's grandparents include : The formal role, The fun-seeking role, The surrogate-parent role, The "Reservoir of family wisdom" role. The distant-figure role. All these roles are useful in successful adjustment. It is good to adopt a "hands of" policy. It is good to be fun seeking providing special knowledge when sought after. Those who maintain the distant figure roles and visit the grandchildren only occasionally sometimes receive more respects. However, as has been said earlier, the most important element is the person attitude towards grandparents. It is this attitude which sets the pattern of grandchildren's behaviour towards the grandparents.

**4. Adjustment to singlehood.** An important problem in family adjustment is concerned with adjustment to singlehood. While the problems of single men and single women are peculiar, the most important problems concern widowhood in the middle-age. These include economic, social, familiar, sexual, residential and practical problems. Some of these are solved by remarriage if the widow is comparatively young. This is also the case in singlehood due to divorce by the spouse. However, singlehood due to loss of spouse by death in the middle-age may not be always solved by remarriage.

**5. Adjustment to approaching retirement.** For most of the persons, particularly those whose economic condition is not very good, it is difficult to adjust to the approaching retirement. This adjustment however has to be made. It is successfully done by intelligent economic planning and planning for work and leisure after retirement. This is also true about adjustment to approaching old age. The most important thing in this connection is to shed of all fear and worry as well as unrealistic ideas concerning old age. One should always take it in good humour and prepare for it in the middle-age; one will not feel the bite of the old age. E.B. Hurlock has very ably summarised the areas of preparation for old age as follows :

1. ***Health :*** Preparation for old age should include health measures that will prevent or mitigate the effects of the chronic or debilitating diseases of old age. These include diet, exercise and regular medical check-ups.

2. ***Retirement :*** Middle-aged people who have prepared for vocational retirement, or for termination of the parental role by acquiring new interests and engaging in new activities, adjust better to old age than those who have made no such preparation.

3. ***Use of leisure time :*** In preparation for old age, middle-aged people should pursue hobbies and acquire interests that will be satisfactory in old age when they must give up more strenuous leisure-time activities.

4. ***Financial independence :*** Middle-aged people should learn to live on incomes equivalent to what their social security and pension incomes will be when they retire. In addition, they should try to set aside a nest egg for emergencies even if it means foregoing some of the expenditures for symbols and pleasures their friends enjoy.

5. ***Social contacts :*** Because social contact with contemporaries becomes increasingly difficult in old age middle-aged, men and women should form friendships with neighbours

and members of community organisations who are younger than they to avoid becoming socially isolated, thus assuring themselves of a continuation of social contacts in old age.

6. ***Role changes :*** Middle-aged men and women must prepare for the role changes that are inevitable in old age, whether in business, in the home, or in community activities. It is especially important that they learn gradually to follow, and to adapt to this change.

7. ***Life patterns :*** Middle-aged people should recognise that circumstances in old age, such as poor health or reduced income, may force them to move from their homes and to change their life patterns. Those who are unprepared to make such changes will have difficulty in adjusting to a new pattern of life and will be unhappy.

## MIDDLE AGE HAZARDS

**1. Vocational hazards.** Middle-age has to face many vocational hazards such as failure to reach earlier goals, decline in creativity, boredom, bigness, feelings of being trapped, unemployment, unfavourable attitudes towards jobs and the problems concerning geographical mobility. These hazards must be faced for successfully passing the middle-age.

**2. Marital hazards.** In middle-age one also faces marital hazards involving role changes, boredom, opposition to child marriage, inability to establish satisfactory relationships with the spouse as a person, sexual adjustment, caring for an elderly parent, loss of spouse and remarriage. E.B. Hurlock has pointed out the following husband's attitudes militating against the establishment of good relationships with the wife :

1. Dissatisfaction with sexual adjustments.
2. If he is successful vocationally, the feeling that his wife has not kept pace with him in his upward climb.
3. If he is unsuccessful vocationally, the feeling that his wife has been of no help and may even have handicapped him.
4. The feeling that he and his wife have little in common because she has refused to be interested in the things that are important to him.
5. A critical attitude toward his wife's management of

the home and the family finances and a belief that her child-training methods have been too permissive.

6. Dissatisfaction with his wife's appearance.
7. The feeling that his wife dominates him and treats him like a child.

The following attitudes have been mentioned by Hurlock as militating against the establishment of good relationships of the wife with the husband :

1. Dissatisfaction with sexual adjustment.
2. Disillusionment with her husband because of his lack of vocational success.
3. The feeling of being a slave to the home or to an elderly relative.
4. The belief that her husband is stingy about money for clothes and recreation.
5. The belief that her husband does not appreciate the time and effort she has devoted to homemaking.
6. The feeling that her husband is more interested in his career than in her.
7. The feeling that her husband spends too much time and money on members of his own family.
8. The suspicions that he is involved with another woman.

## ASSESSMENT OF MIDDLE-AGE ADJUSTMENTS

The middle-age adjustments have been assessed by four criteria : achievements, emotional states, effects of their adjustments on their personality and happiness.

**1. Achievements.** Unless the assessment of achievements is realistic, one feels dejected about his success. Therefore, success should be judged only in the light of one's capacity.

**2. Emotional states.** Middle-age brings anxiety, insecurity and stress. Middle-aged persons have more worries. They however generally become adjusted by mid-fifties when the person adjusts to his new roles, interests and activities.

**3. Effects on personality.** Positive and negative effects on personality show the results of adjustment. Lack of adjustment leads to personality disorganisation. On the other hand, those who are well adjusted show even more confidence, stability and maturity than was seen in their youth.

**4. Happiness.** Happiness is the most sure criterion of successful adjustment. It comes when the individual's needs and desires are satisfied. It shows good adjustment. It may be the result of success in chosen vocation, prestige, financial regards, improved social status, etc. For women it may be the result of success in homemaking. According to E.B. Hurlock, "To be happy in middle-age, as at all ages, the person must be realistic and realise that life has its problems as well as its rewards. If the rewards are adequate to compensate for the problems, the scale will be balanced in favour of happiness."

Pointing out such compensations peculiar to middle-age, Levine writes, "What the mind loses in alertness, it makes up for it in the assurance of reflective thinking. If the muscles grow sensitive to fatigue, they learn to respond more selectively to stimuli. If the bodily functions show signs of impairment, they flash intermittently the amber lights of caution. And if the fires of passion are being dampened, one comes to prize the release from their tyrannical domination."

## CHARACTERISTICS OF OLD AGE

After sixty-men and women become old. Sixty has been recognised as marking age of the beginning of old age. Old age may be recognised by the following characteristics :

1. Old age is a period of decline, physical, mental and psychological.
2. There are individual differences in the effects of ageing, some showing more and some showing less symptoms.
3. Old age is judged by different criteria in the case of different persons and also as regards male and female and members of different cultures.
4. There are many stereotypes of old people such as physical deterioration, deterioration of mental capacities and intelligence.
5. Unfavourable social attitudes towards the old age.
6. The elderly have a minority-group status and therefore treated as second class citizens.

7. Ageing requires role changes in home, in society, in state and almost everywhere.
8. Poor adjustment is characteristic of old age, particularly due to unfavourable social attitudes of the comparatively younger persons shown in their behaviour.
9. The desire for rejuvenation is widespread in old age.

## DEVELOPMENTAL TASKS OF OLD AGE

The developmental tasks of old age concern adjustments to physical and mental changes. These may be understood separately.

**1. Adjustment to physical changes.** E.B. Hurlock has summarised the common physical changes in appearance during old age as follows :

### A. Head Region

1. The nose elongates.

2. The mouth changes shape as a result of tooth loss or necessity of wearing dentures.

3. The eyes are seen dull and lustreless and often have watery look.

4. A double or triple chin develops.

5. The cheeks become pendulous, wrinkled and baggy.

6. The skin becomes wrinkled and dry and dark spots, moles, or wats may appear.

7. The hair on the head become thin and turn gray or white, and tough, bristly hair appear in the nose, ears and eyebrows.

### B. Trunk Region

1. The shoulders stoop and thus seem smaller.

2. The abdomen bulges and droops.

3. The hips seem flabbier and broader than they did earlier.

4. The waistline broadens, giving the trunk a sack-like appearance.

5. The women's breasts become flabby and droop.

### C. Limbs

1. The upper arm becomes flabby and heavy, while the lower arm seems to shrink in diameter.

2. The legs become flabby and thc veins prominent, especially around the ankles.

3. The hands become scrawny, and the veins on the back of the hand are prominent.

4. The feet become larger as result of sagging muscles, and corns, bunions, and calluses often appear.

5. The nails of the hands and feet become thick, tough, and brittle.

Besides these changes in appearance, there are certain internal changes, sensory, sexual and concerning the digestive system, glandular secretions, strength and ability of muscles and the functioning of lungs, heart and other internal organs. In sensory functioning, one finds marked changes in the acuteness of sensations and perceptions. There is a general decline of the sensory functioning of vision, hearing, taste, smell and touch. There are also changes in motor abilities showing decline in strength, speed and learning of new skills.

**2. Adjustment to mental changes.** Mental changes characteristic of old age are found with individual variations. These changes show a general decline of the various mental processes such as learning, reasoning, creativity, memory, recall, reminiscing, sense of humour, vocabulary. Mental rigidity is a sign of old age though it is not universal. Some old people exhibit admirable flexibility and the will to learn new ways. Along with changes in mental processes, there are changes in personal interests such as interest in self, interest in appearance, interest in clothes and interest in money. Most of the old people become self-centred. Most of them become more interested in money though there may be some exceptions. Recreational interests also change due to these physical and mental changes. Common recreational activities of older people include reading, writing letters, listening to the radio, watching television, visiting friends and relatives, sewing, embroidering, gardening, travelling, playing cards, going to the theatre or movies, and taking part in the activities of civic, political or religious organisations. These changes in interests are very much influenced by the health, economic status, education, marital status, living conditions and interest in sex. Social interests also show a change leading to disengagements, voluntary and involuntary. The sources of social contact affected by ageing include personal friendships, friendship cliches and formal groups of clubs. Generally, social participation declines. However, among elderly people, religious interests definitely show a sign of increase. Some common effects of religious changes during old age are religious tolerance, religious beliefs and religious observances. One notices more interest in death, about its reality, its future date, reason, etc. One finds old people worrying whether they will have a good death or not.

## PROBLEMS OF OLD AGE

According to E.B. Hurlock, the following are some common problems unique to old age :

1. Physical helplessness, which necessitates dependency on others.
2. Economic insecurity severe enough to necessitate a complete change in pattern of living.
3. Establishing living conditions in accordance with changes in economic or physical conditions.
4. Making new friends to replace those who have died or moved away or who are invalid.
5. Developing new activities to occupy increased leisure time.
6. Learning to treat grown-up children as adults.
7. Becoming involved in community activities planned for the elderly.
8. Deriving enjoyment from activities suited to the elderly and willingness to substitute them for activities formerly enjoyed but now too strenuous.
9. Being "victimised" or taken advantage of by sales persons, hoodlums and criminals because they are unable to defend themselves.

**1. Common physical hazards.** The most important hazards of old age are undoubtedly physical. Physical disability increases with age. The disabled percentage of population among age 85 and over is 10 per cent in America. The percentage of impaired is as much as 70. This percentage gradually grows with age. The disability starts in middle-age and proceeds fast after 60. The most common physical hazards are diseases and physical handicaps such as circulatory disturbance, metabolic disorders, involutional mental disorders, disorders of the joints, tumors (both benign and malignant), heart diseases, rheumatism, arthritis, visual and hearing impairments, hypertension, gait disorder and mental and nervous conditions. An important cause of physical hazards is malnutrition. However, even among those who get sufficient nutrition, the failure of endocrine system and digestive system is common to old age. Sooner or later most elderly persons lose some or all their teeth. Sexual deprivation or unfavourable attitudes towards sex in old age harm the people as much as in middle-age. Older people are generally more accident prone than younger ones. The frequent activities associated with burns among the elderly, aged sixty-five and older include smoking (including falling asleep while smoking) 25.3 per cent cooking, 22.0 per cent using matches, lighter 19.9 per cent, other or unknown activity 32.8%. Some of the physical hazards may be sometimes imaginary.

**2. Psychological hazards.** Some of the most common psychological hazards of old age are as follows :

1. Acceptance of cultural stereotypes of the elderly. For example, elderly people who believe that they are too old to learn new skills, because "you cannot teach an old dog new tricks", will be at a disadvantage.
2. Effects of physical changes of ageing such as the loss of an attractive sex appropriate appearance.
3. Changes in life patterns such as empty nest.
4. Tendency to slip mentally.
5. Feelings of guilt about idleness while other people are still working.
6. Reduced income due to retirement, absence of leisure time activities and financial drains.
7. Social disengagement due to impairment of social contacts and voluntary or involuntary social isolation.

## OLD AGE ADJUSTMENTS

**1. Vocational adjustments.** Old age is marked by retirement from job. This creates the most important problems of adjustment. The conditions limiting employment opportunities for older workers include : Compulsory Retirement, Hiring Policies, Pension Plans, Social Attitudes, Fluctuations in Business Cycles, Kind of work, Sex. Women more than men find it difficult to hold their jobs in old age. For some people retirement may be termination of a pattern of life or transition to a new pattern of life which is marked by : Not setting an alarm clock; reactivating your public library card; starting a second career if anyone wants you; wondering how long you can keep going if inflation does too; dispensing with dress-up clothes; taking the grandchildren to places on weekdays; wondering why your former colleagues don't phone once in a while; waiting for the postman to bring some excitement into your day; taking a course you want instead of have to reading a book all the way through at one sitting; getting special low rates on the bus, at the movies, in the hotels, trying to keep out of your loved one's way; going to matinees; travelling in the off season; taking a coffee break at odd time and frequently; receiving all sorts of invitations to serve as a volunteer; replaying the past, playing in the present, preparing for the future; looking at the obituary column and being gratified at not finding your name there; reading the newspaper all the way through; getting better acquainted with your neighbours; making the best out of the rest of your life; anticipation followed by deprivation, stagnation, institutionalisation, or anticipation followed by participation, recreation, exultation.

**2. Adjustment to retirement.** Retirement may be voluntary or compulsory, regular or early. For most workers, forced retirement is a source of much dejection and loss of face. E.B. Hurlock has mentioned the following conditions affecting adjustment to retirement :

1. Workers who retire voluntarily adjust better than those who are forced to retire, especially if they want to continue to work.

2. Poor health at the time of retirement facilitates adjustment while good health is likely to militate against it.

3. Most workers find that tapering off is better than abruptly ending patterns of work and living established many years earlier.

4. Pre-retirement counselling and planning age adjustment.

5. Workers who develop interests in substitute activities that are meaningful to them and which provide many to the satisfactions they formerly derived from work will not find adjustment to retirement as emotionally disturbing as those who fail to develop substitute interests.

6. Social contacts like those provided in many homes for the aged, aid in adjusting to retirement. Remaining in their own homes or in the homes of relatives usually cuts retired people off from social contacts.

7. The less change in the pattern of living retirement necessitates, the better the adjustment will be.

8. A good economic status, which makes it possible to live comfortably and enjoy meaningful recreations, is essential to good adjustment to retirement.

9. A happy marital status aids adjustment to retirement while a frictional one militates against it.

10. The more the workers like their work, the poorer their adjustment to retirement. There is an inverse relationship between work satisfaction and retirement satisfaction.

11. Place of residence affects adjustments to retirement. The more the community offers for companionship and activities for the elderly, the better they will adjust to retirement.

12. The attitudes of family members towards retirement have a profound effect on worker's attitudes. This is especially true of the attitudes of spouses.

**3. Adjustments to changes in family life.** Adjustments to changes in family life in old age include relationships with spouse, changes in sexual behaviour, relationships with children, parental dependency and relationships with grandchildren. Among the common factors affecting sexual behaviour in old age, the following are the most important, according to E.B. Hurlock :

***1. Pattern of earlier sexual behaviour :*** People who derived enjoyment from sexual behaviour and were sexually active during the earlier years of their marriage continue to be sexually more active in old age than those who were less active earlier.

***2. Compatibility of spouses :*** When there is a close bond between husband and wife built on mutual interests and respect, the desire for intercourse is much stronger than when a frictional relationship exists.

***3. Social attitudes :*** Unfavourable social attitudes towards sex in old age make many elderly men and women feel that interest in sexual matters not only is "not nice" but may even be perverted.

***4. Marital status :*** Married people are likely to continue sexual activity into old age. Those who are single or divorced or whose spouses have died usually do not have a strong enough sex drive to make them seek new sex partners.

***5. Preoccupation with outside problems :*** When either or both spouses are preoccupied with financial, family, or other problems, it tends to weaken sexual desire. If they eat or drink excessively in order to escape from these problems, the sexual desires are further weakened.

***6. Over-familiarity :*** Being together too much over a long period of time tends to deaden a couple's sexual desire in old age.

***7. Impotence :*** Many men who find themselves impotent on one occasion, regardless of the condition that gave rise to it, withdraw from further sexual activity to avoid the ego-shattering experience of repeated episodes of sexual inadequacy.

A major adjustment in old age is to the loss of a spouse. This is particularly important because of loneliness characteristic of old age. The major adjustment problem faced by widows in old age is loss of income which results in lower social status, lower standard of living and other problems. As a general rule, loss of spouse in old age is more unfortunate for female than male. In West remarriage in old age is now becoming more frequent and more socially acceptable than it formerly was. The following conditions contribute to adjustment in such marriages :

1. A happy first marriage.

2. Knowing what traits and behaviour patterns to look for in a potential mate.

3. A desire to marry because of love and a need for companionship, rather than for reasons of convenience of financial support.

4. An interest in continuing sexual behaviour.

5. A similarity of educational and social backgrounds.

6. Adequate income.

7. Approval of the marriage by offspring and friends.

8. Reasonably good health and a lack of disabling physical condition on the part of both spouses.

9. Avoidance of uprooting from area where grown-up children, relatives and friends live.

Some older people however try to solve these problems by living together without marriage. This is called cohabitation. The needs and wants of elderly people for living arrangements differ from person to person. However the most important conditions influencing the choice of living arrangements for the elderly people include economic status, marital status, ease of caring for, sex, children, desire for companionship and climate. E. B. Hurlock has mentioned the following physical and psychological needs in living arrangements for the elderly :

**A. Physical Needs**

1. The house temperature should be comparatively even from floor to ceiling because poor circulation makes the elderly especially sensitive to chilling.

2. Elderly people need large windows to ensure plenty of light because of the gradual impairment of vision.

3. Provisions should be made for safety. The elderly people should have to climb few steps, floors should be unwaxed or covered with wall-to-wall carpeting and danger areas should be lighted at all times.

4. There should be adequate space for indoor and outdoor recreation, a condition best met in multiple housing developments or in institutions.

5. Noise should be controlled, especially during the night. This can be done by locating sleeping quarters in a quiet part of a house or an apartment.

6. Elderly people should have labour-saving devices, especially for cooking, dishwashing and cleaning.

7. The living quarters should be on one floor to avoid possible falls on steps.

**B. Psychological Needs**

1. Elderly people should have at least one small room of their own so that they can have some privacy.

2. Living arrangements should include space for sedentary recreation, such as reading and television watching.

3. There should be provision for storage of cherished possessions.

4. Elderly people should live close to stores and community organizations so that they can be independent in their activities.

5. Elderly people should be near relatives and friends so that frequent contacts are possible.

6. Provisions should be made for recreation and amusements, especially during the winter months when going outdoors is difficult and being housebound becomes monotonous and boring.

7. Provision should be made for transportation to shopping areas, places of amusement, hairdressers and churches.

In West institutional living for the elderly people is more common. As a general rule, its advantages include provisions for maintenance, meals, recreations, contacts, companionship, holiday celebrations and opportunity for social accomplishment. Its disadvantages include expensiveness, lower quality of food, uncongenial contacts and distance from family and friends. The geographical mobility is considerably lower in old age. It has been found that those elderly people who voluntarily enter old age institutions are likely to make better adjustment than those who are forced to do so.

Like middle-age, old age also has its own vocational and family life hazards. The conditions contributing to the seriousness of unemployment in old age, include : of work, new job versus job shift, necessity for retraining, minority group status. Retirement itself is the most serious vocational hazard. The family life hazards include sexual deprivation, loneliness, living arrangements and role changes. The common substitute sources of sexual satisfaction in old age include masturbation, erotic dreams and daydreams, thinking about sex and sexual attraction to younger persons.

## ASSESSMENT OF OLD AGE ADJUSTMENT

Factors influencing adjustment to old age include : Preparation for Old Age, Earlier Experiences, Satisfaction of Needs, Retention of Old Friendships, Grown-up Children, Social Attitudes, Personal Attitudes, Methods of adjustment, Health conditions, Living conditions, Economic conditions. According to E.B. Hurlock, the common characteristics of good and poor adjustment in old age are as follows :

**Good Adjustment**

1. Strong and varied interests.
2. Economic independence, which makes independence in living possible.
3. Many social contacts with people of all ages, not just the elderly.
4. The enjoyment of work which is pleasant and useful but not overtaxing.
5. Participation in community organization.
6. The ability to maintain comfortable home without exerting too much physical effort.
7. The ability to enjoy present activities without regretting the past.
8. A minimum of worry about self or others.
9. Enjoyment of day-to-day activities regardless of how repetitious they may be.
10. Avoidance of criticism of others, especially members of the younger generation.
11. Avoidance of fault-finding especially about living conditions and treatment from others.

**Poor Adjustment**

1. Little interest in the world of today or the individual's role in it.
2. Withdrawal into the world of fantasy.
3. Constant reminiscing.
4. Constant worry, encouraged by idleness.
5. A lack of drive, leading to low productivity in all areas.

6. The attitude that the only activities available are "make work", activities and, therefore, a "waste of time".

7. Loneliness due to poor family relationships and lack of interest in contemporaries.

8. Involuntary geographic isolation.

9. Involuntary residence in an institution or with a grown-up child.

10. Constant complaining and criticizing of anything and everything.

11. Refusal to take part in activities for the elderly on the grounds that they are "boring".

The quality of behaviour of elderly people generally declines with the old age. There are changes in emotional behaviour, it being less varied and less appropriate to the occasion. Then, there are personality changes due to physical, psychological and self-concept changes. A radical change in the self-concept is likely to lead to a breakdown in the personality structure.

**Conditions of Happiness**

The most important criterion of good adjustment in old age is the degree of self-satisfaction or happiness. Happiness in old age, as in any other age, depends upon acceptance, affection and achievement which E.B. Hurlock appropriately calls "There is happiness." Variations are also an important factor for happiness in old age, as they are in any other age. E.B. Hurlock has mentioned the following among the important conditions contributing to happiness in old age :

1. A favourable attitude towards old age developed as a result of earlier pleasurable contacts with elderly people.

2. Happy memories of childhood and adulthood.

3. Freedom to pursue a desired lifestyle without outside interference.

4. A realistic attitude toward, and acceptance of the physical and psychological changes that ageing inevitably brings.

5. Acceptance of self and present living conditions even if these fall below expectations.

6. An opportunity to establish a satisfying socially acceptable pattern of life.

7. Continued participation in interesting and meaningful activities.

8. A feeling of satisfaction with present status and past achievements.

9. Satisfaction with marital status and sex life.

10. Reasonably good health without chronic health problems.

11. Enjoyment of recreational activities planned for the elderly.

12. Enjoyment of social activities with relatives and friends.

13. Productive activities whether in housework or volunteer services.

14. A financial situation adequate to meet needs and wants.

The above conditions prove that happiness in old age is characterised by continued activity, while unhappiness is influenced by disengagement, either voluntary or involuntary. In the words of Havighurst, "Persons with an active, achieving and outward directed life style will be best satisfied with a continuation of this style into old age with only slight diminution. Other persons with a passive, dependent, home-centered lifestyle will be best satisfied with disengagement.... Undoubtedly there is a disengaging force operating on and within people as they pass 70 and 80. But they will still retain the personality lifestyle characteristics of their middle years."

It may be remembered here that the above analysis drawn upon the Western conditions is not applicable in Indian society as such. It may be accepted a general rule that an active life is necessary for happiness in old age but disengagement is not necessarily linked to unhappiness. In Hindu society there had been a long tradition of renunciation partly after 50 years of age and fully after 75 years of age. This renunciation of the family does not lead to inactivity but concentration to spiritual activities such as meditation and yoga, etc.

## QUESTIONS FOR EXERCISE

1. Explain the characteristics of middle-age. Discuss its developmental tasks and characteristic changes.

2. Discuss various types of adjustments required in middle-age.
3. Explain various hazards faced in middle-age. What are the criteria of assessment of middle-age adjustments.
4. Explain characteristics and developmental tasks of old age. What are its problems?
5. Explain various adjustments required in old age. What are the criteria of adjustments in this age?

# Part IV
# Clinical Psychology

# 15

# Psychology in the Diagnosis of Mental Disorders

## PSYCHIATRIC INTERVIEW

The psychiatric interview is of paramount importance as it is the basis of all treatment and investigation. The psychiatrist, in his conduct of the interview, can demonstrate the art of psychiatry at its best. Interviews can be fact-finding, therapeutic or both. In either type the interview enables rapport to be developed between the patient and the doctor.

### Setting of Interview

The setting of the interview room is important. The patient should not be made to feel inferior or small by the presence of a huge desk by which he is separated from the physician.

The physician must allow adequate time for the interview and have freedom from interruption. Both physician and patient should be comfortable and relaxed.

Patients are usually anxious and frightened when coming for a psychiatric interview and they must be put at their ease. If necessary, the physician should get up from his chair, go to meet the patient and a handshake is usually very helpful in welcoming and reassuring the patient.

The physician places the chair comfortably for the patient and then himself sits down. He should adopt a listening attitude and should avoid interrupting the patient, at least in the early stages.

The interviewer must not only feel interested but should make it clearly manifest to the patient and be friendly and accepting in manner. Note-taking is generally better left till afterward as it often puts the patient off and may interfere with the establishment of a good doctor-patient relationship.

The physician must never give the impression that he is in a hurry. He must be flexible in taking the history and incurring out the interview. It is necessary to have a scheme in mind in order to ensure that important aspects are not overlooked but the course the interview takes will largely depend on what emerges initially and subsequently the physician should let things come gently and naturally.

**Asking Questions**

Questions which can be answered 'yes' or 'no' should be avoided. Questions containing a lead must not, of course, be given. The wider the question the better, as this will give the patient a chance to reply as he wishes, will not restrict or impede him in so doing and will give the best opportunity of obtaining relevant and important data.

The interview is a two-way process and the physician must convey his interest by nodding the head and by making remarks such as 'surely', 'naturally', 'of course', 'I see', etc. A friendly attitude and demeanour are much more important than the particular words chosen. If there are silences, the physician should show greater interest; leaning forward, repeating the last word or phrase and urging the patient to carry on will often overcome the silence. Emotional expression should be encouraged. The interview should be channelled and encouraged by increasing one's interest and uttering suitable remarks. Unimportant or irrelevant topics can be discouraged by showing less interest.

**Noting Down**

Careful note should be made of the patient's facial expression, change of colour, halting evasion of a topic, sudden silences, increased rapidity of speech, pleading or laughing. Points made by the patient should be emphasised to let him know that you understand his feeling. Repeat the patient's statement or reformulate what he has said in order to reinforce the understanding and rapport.

**General Rules for Interviews**

1. Make no promises. Questions can be countered with other questions for further information.

2. Reassurance must only be given after careful enquiry and investigation. Interpretation is very dangerous unless done appropriately and at the right time.

3. Don't take sides with the patient.

4. Don't egg the patient on to action.

5. Don't give advice.

**Historical Review**

Ascertain the patient's complaints or difficulties or, if he has no complaints, enquire the reason for his referral. Following this it is usually convenient to start with the history of the present illness.

In recording this, facts should be included rather than technical terms. It is important that the present mental state and the history should not be mixed up.

Whilst the history is being taken, the patient's behaviour, his reactions should be observed and should later be recorded under 'general behaviour'.

It is also important that objective and subjective data should not be mixed up. It is undesirable to make the greater part of the record a mere transcript of what the patient has said. The examiner's observations, summaries and conclusions should be recorded as well.

**1. Family history.** One usually starts with questions about the patient's parents, enquiring if they are alive and, if so, are they in good health; if not, what is wrong or, if dead, what they died from.

It is important to assess the social position and general efficiency of the family, as well as the occurrence of familial diseases and, also a note made of the home atmosphere, particularly any significant happenings among parents and siblings during the patient's early years and the patient's relationship to parents, siblings and others.

It is always wise to obtain a history from a second person as well as the patient, as important additional information may be acquired, and, in any event, any discrepancies may be valuable in the assessment and understanding of the patient.

**2. Personal history.** Ascertain the date and place of birth, whether the birth was normal or prolonged, instrumental or premature, the mother's health during pregnancy and after birth, whether the patient was breast-or bottle-fed, brought up by the mother or, if someone else, the reasons for this.

**3. Infancy and childhood.** Note the age of which the patient passed the milestones of development such as feeling, talking, walking, achievement of bowel and bladder control. Note general health.

Note the occurrence of neurotic traits in childhood such as night terrors, somnambulism, tantrums, enuresis, nail-biting, stammering, fear states, school phobia, model child, chorea, convulsions, etc.

**4. School.** Age of starting and finishing, standard reached, attitude to teachers, attitude to school-work and success achieved, attitude to school-mates, whether he played games, mixed well, was bullied, able to stand up for himself or not.

**5. Work.** Age when started work and the jobs held, listed in chronological order with dates, reasons for changes; (poor work record with unduly frequent changes of employment is often an indicator of personality instability).

**6. Menstrual functions.** Note the age of menarche, reactions to menarche regularity and duration of menses, length of cycle, amount of loss, dysmenorrhoea, premenstrual tension, date of last period, climacteric symptoms.

**7. Sexual inclinations and practice.** Note how sexual information was gained and received, whether prudery, worries about masturbation, homosexuality, heterosexual experiences apart from marriage are frequent.

**8. Marital history.** Note if marriage partner was known before marriage and engagement, compatibility, sex relations — whether satisfactory or not, contraceptive measures used, any financial, domestic or temperamental difficulties.

**9. Children.** Give chronological list of children, miscarriages, with ages, names, etc.

**10. Personal habits.** Note amount of alcohol, tobacco, drugs taken recently and previously.

**11. Medical history.** Note details of illnesses, operations and accidents, in chronological order.

**12. Previous mental health.** Note history of any previous psychiatric illnesses, whether medical attention sought and treatment given by GP, as an out-patient or inpatient, duration and description of such illnesses.

**13. Personality.** Describe the personality before the onset of the present illness and aim to present a picture of an individual and not a type, give illustrative anecdotes and detailed statements rather than relying on a series of adjectives.

**Conditions of Examination**

**1. General appearance and behaviour.** When taking the history, a great deal of information about the patient's appearance and behaviour will already have been obtained.

The first thing to observe is whether the patient looks ill, whether he looks his age or looks much older or younger. Note his general posture and facial expression. The tense, anxious patient sits on the edge of the chair, jumps at sudden noises. The depressed patient lacks muscular tone, has a dejected posture.

Is he in touch with the situation? Does he behave appropriately to it? Does he respond to the requirements of the examination? Does he show any oddities or eccentricities in speech, dress or manner?

Motor activity may be diminished, the patient being slow in his movements and slow in his replies. Marked reduction of activity, with the patient showing no spontaneous activity and little response to stimuli is termed stupor.

Over activity may be manifestation of general pressure of activity found in the hypomanic patient, in which there is general psychomotor activity, restlessness, circumstantiality in speech, or it may be in the form of the agitated movements found in agitated melancholia, the patient continually fidgeting, picking his clothes, wringing his hands and walking to and fro.

Are there tics, mannerisms or stereotyped movements? Is the activity abrupt, fitful, erratic or constant?

In catatonic schizophrenics the following phenomena may be found : Automatic obedience, Echolalia (repetition by the patient of what is said to him), Echopraxia (imitation of actions), Waxy flexibility with maintenance of postures even in uncomfortable positions, Negativism in which the patient does the opposite of what is required or resists attempts to help him (*e.g.* if when you offer to shake hands with him he moves his hand away, when you withdraw your hand his hand will come forward).

Finally, a note should be made of his eating and sleeping habits, whether he is clean and how he spends his time.

**2. Form of talk.** Observe whether he says a great deal or is uncommunicative or retarded in speech, whether he talks spontaneously or only in answer to questions, whether he is hesitant, slow, fast, discursive, disconnected; sudden silences, changes of topic, going off at a tangent; whether he uses rhymes, puns or strange words.

Perseveration in speech and in action is found in organic mental state; the patient, when asked to do a certain thing, will continue doing this action even though he is asked to do other things. This is case of momentum and inertia carrying on and interfering with following events.

**3. Mood of the patient.** The patient's mood will already have been reflected in his general behaviour, in speech and manner. He should be asked : How do you feel in yourself? What are your spirits like? What is your mood? Note the constancy of mood, whether it changes rapidly or whether it is constant, the factors which change the mood and, also, whether the patient's behaviour, facial expression agree with what he says about his mood.

**4. Mental content.** Enquire about the patient's attitude to himself, to the people around him and to the various things in his environment; does he feel a special reference made to him, does he feel that people shun him or admire him, does he tend to depreciate himself regarding his past behaviour, morals, possessions and health or, conversely, is he expansive and grandiose about his possessions and personal abilities? Enquire about the predominant thoughts or preoccupations that the patient has; in depressive states these are characteristically painful and unhappy, full of regrets, dwelling on the past, the present or the future in a hopeless and gloomy way.

**5. Disorders of perception.** It will be necessary to know whether the patient has auditory, visual, olfactory, gustatory, tactile or other hallucinations. It is usually convenient to broach this by asking the patient if he ever hears noises, later communications and then definitely voices. It is important to note at what time the hallucinations occur, whether by night or by day, their complexity, their vividness and how received by the patient. If they occur when falling asleep, it is usually of little significance. In severely depressed patients, they report that there are unusual sensations, lack of sensations or lack of organs.

**6. Consciousness (Sensorium).** It is important to note whether the patient is alert, dull, self-absorbed, confused or delirious. Try to discover his grasp of the environment and his judgement. Enquire into his orientation to time and with regard to place and to persons.

**7. Orientation.** General orientation can be assessed by questions such as "Where are you now?", "What is the name of this place?", "Where is it situated?", "What day of the week is it today?", "What month are we in?", "What day of the month is it?" and "What is the year?"

If he is in hospital one can ascertain his orientation in the ward, such as "Show me the nearest lavatory", "Where is the bathroom?", "Where is the main entrance?", "Are there any other ways out?", "Where is the television?", and "Where is the nurses' office?", etc.

**8. Compulsive phenomena**. Does he get any recurrent thoughts which distress him, which are unwanted and which he finds difficult to dismiss? Does he feel them to be a part of his own mind or to come from without? Does he regard them as inappropriate or irrational? Are they related to his emotional state, *e.g.*, a state of depression or anxiety? Does he tend to repeat actions with compulsion and a tendency to resist such as touching things, washing his hands unduly frequently?

**9. Memory**. The patient's memory functions are assessed by comparing his account of his life with that given by others. It is important to test also for recent events when he was admitted, whether he had seen another doctor and, if so, whom and where the doctor saw him and when.

The patient may be given a name and address to remember and then asked to recall it three or five minutes later. He can be given a series of digits to repeat forwards, then ordered to repeat backwards.

**10. Grasp of general information.** Questions regarding general information should be varied according to the patient's educational level, his experience and interests. He should be asked the name of the monarch and the immediate predecessors, the Prime Minister and the capitals of France, Italy, Spain and the United States. He should be asked to name six large cities in India. He should be asked to carry out the serial 7 test *i.e.*, subtraction of 7 from 100, and note the answer given and the time taken.

The purpose of these tests is to give a general idea whether there has been any falling off in a person's former presumptive level of knowledge and intellectual capacity.

**11. Insight and judgement.** What is his attitude to his present state? Are his attitude and assessment of it reasonable for his intelligence and experience? Does he regard himself as being ill or as suffering from a nervous or mental illness or needing treatment? How does he regard his present difficulties or deficits? What is his opinion regarding his previous attacks of mental illness if any?

### Examination of Non-cooperative Patients

The difficulties of getting information from non-cooperative or stuporous patients should not discourage the physician from making and recording observations, which can be made of great importance in presenting a record of the clinical state at the time in case the patient's clinical condition should change suddenly. Observations can be made under the following headings :

**1. Posture and general reactions.** Note whether his posture is natural or awkward; whether he maintains his limbs when they are placed in awkward positions; whether his behaviour is negativistic, evasive, irritable, apathetic or obedient; whether he exhibits any spontaneous actions; his behaviour with regard to dressing, eating and personal hygiene. Describe his facial expression whether it was vacant, placid, perplexed, depressed, distressed, any tears, flushing, etc., whether the eyes are open or closed; if the eyes are closed whether they resist attempts to having the lid raised; reaction to sudden approach or threat to touch the eye.

**2. Reactions to commands.** The patient should be asked to show his tongue, close his eyes, open his eyes, move limbs, shake hands. Notice whether there is negativism, echopraxia, echolalia or automatic obedience.

**3. Muscular functions.** Note whether muscles are tensed, rigid or show waxy flexibility.

Test how the patient reacts to passive movements, of the head and neck and of the limbs, and whether it is possible to influence these reactions by commands or distractions.

### Physical Examination

It may cause surprise to include physical examination as an important part of treatment. Physical examination and any additional investigations that may be necessary must be carried out thoroughly, not only to detect, assess or exclude the presence of organic disease but, also, to give weight and conviction to the reassurance and explanation given by the physician at the appropriate time to the patient concerning his illness. The patient will be impressed by a thorough physical examination and, thus, more likely to accept the physician's opinion about his physical state.

It will only antagonise a patient to tell him there is nothing wrong with him. He may be told that there is nothing physically wrong but this must be followed by an explanation of his symptoms, in terms suitable to his intelligence and his personality.

### Special Investigation

Similarly, when special investigations are necessary, the reasons and nature of the investigations should be explained to the patient beforehand. Wherever possible, he should be told about the outcome of these results, otherwise feelings of anxiety and apprehension will be fostered.

Once a physician is reasonably satisfied with a patient's physical state, he should avoid repeating the physical examination unless this is dictated by the patient's medical condition. Repeated examination usually has a harmful effect on the patient, suggesting to him that the doctor is not sure of his case and reinforcing his fears that there may be something seriously, physically wrong with him. Prolonged and exhaustive clinical and laboratory investigations also may make the patient very apprehensive. Special investigations, when necessary, should be reduced to the minimum and always given with adequate explanation and, when possible, strong reassurance.

## CASE HISTORY METHOD

Psychiatric examination comprises the following stages :

1. History-taking;

2. Examination of physical state and special investigations which are indicated and

3. Examination of the patient's mental state.

The taking of the patient's history is of fundamental importance, both for investigation and for treatment. The history, when completed, gives a picture of the patient's development and adjustment during his life. It contains relevant information on possible genetic and family influences on his personality and his illness. It portrays his development from childhood to adult life. It provides evidence of adjustment to school, work, marriage, society, together with a record of his physical and mental health and previous personality.

### What is Case History Method?

The parents and teachers seek the guidance of the psychologist in their dealings with the children and students. They complain of the abnormality of the child or student, to the psychologist who with their help finds out the causes and tries to remove them. In the Western countries, the frequency of nervous diseases is gradually growing as the rush of life is increasing with industrialisation and urbanisation. This has increased the necessity of guidance. The psychologists use a certain method known as case history in their study of abnormal cases. As is clear by the name of the method, in this method the psychologist traces the whole history of case. The tracing of the history requires not only the statement of his story by the patient, but also whatever can be gathered from his relatives. The psychologist interviews the near relatives of the patient and also his friends. By this interview much is known about the habits, routine, thinking, nature, etc., besides the various incidents of the life of the patient. This interview also makes the psychologist know the various types of relation which the patient has with different persons. Again, the patient is asked to relate his life history so far as he can prove. He is also asked to relate his dreams, etc., and they are interpreted by the psychologist to get an idea about the infantile life of the patient. All the data gathered through the patient as well as those related to him in some way give an outline of the history of his case. By the analysis of this history, the psychologist tries to find out the causes of abnormality. Suppose a child is taken to the psychologist whose behaviour is not normal, or who has run away from the school several times. The child is ill-mannered and bad tempered. He does not bother about punishment or dictates of the elders. The psychologist interviews the parents and other relatives of the child and tries to know his case history. He takes the child with him into a room and sympathetically tries to know various things about his life. He enquires about the child's relations with his parents, teachers and relatives. He enquires about his conditions in school and about his friends. In short, he enquires about everything concerning the child and his relations with others. An analysis of all this data gives an idea about the cases of abnormality, truancy or bad manners. If the causes are discovered, the parents and teachers are guided accordingly and the malady is removed.

### Example of a Case History

An example from the report by Katherine, M. Mourer known as a 'Behaviour Problem in a Young Child' will give an idea as to how the clinical psychologist uses the case history method :

Loucy was 3 years and 9 months old. She was very obstinate and short tempered. From an interview with her parents it was learnt that the father and mother held each other responsible for bringing up the child as emotional and unbalanced. Then they were interviewed separately. An aunt of Loucy and a nursery teacher were also interviewed. In the interview, Loucy's mother described her family background. She told that Loucy was not normal and that her mother-in-law did not take part in the household work but remained with Loucy for hours. Loucy had acute constipation. She had occasional fits in which she lay down on the ground, cried and attacked others. Loucy's mother did not want to disclose her marital adjustment. Her mother-in-law severely criticised her friends, her household management and her behaviour towards Loucy.

Loucy's problem began at the age of 2. At the age of 3 she liked to hear stories instead of playing with the children of her age. While among other children, she quarrelled with them. She liked to live with her father and go for a walk with him, though when angry she did not hear him; she bit him in the leg.

An interview with her father disclosed that he was proud of Loucy. He thought her to be very intelligent and described how Loucy paid attention to him and worked like an adult woman. He expressed doubt in Loucy's happiness and that perhaps she never felt secure.

A physical examination of Loucy disclosed that except some weight she had no physical abnormality. According to the doctor, constipation was due to wrong habits of diet. Sucking the thumb, biting off the nails and turning the hair, was clearly observed. When her father brought her to the psychiatrist, she appeared to be attractive, modest and feminine. When her mother brought her she appeared to be obstinate and unmanageable. Sometimes she struggled and quarrelled and lay down on the ground and cried, when requested by the mother to wear the coat. Psychological tests showed that she commanded a vocabulary found in a child of eight years of age and that she was more intelligent than the average. The powers of language were far more developed than the physical powers.

The clinical psychologist came to the following conclusions about Loucy's abnormal behaviour :

She was a very well developed and brilliant child with an attractive personality. She was used to close attention and company of the adults, and her daily routine was extremely unsystematic, resulting in fatigue. This resulted in absence of harmony in the parent-child relationship. She did not get opportunity of adjustment with the children of her age. Her intellect was too much developed because of absence of variety in experience. Her capacity did not develop harmoniously and her word powers were excessively developed beyond motor capacity. She understood her weakness which made her adjustment on child's level still more difficult. She appeared to be extremely fatigued, small child tyrant who did not get emotional contentment from her mother and was emotional, introvert and dependent on her father.

The psychologist mainly recommended the following things for her :

Friendly relations with mother should be established and her life at home should be reorganised. She must get more sleep, balanced diet and should play with children of her age. In the evening she must be attended by some members of the family, mother, father, or grandmother. The mother should feel that she is responsible for the progress of the child. But father and mother-in-law were also told that they should change their routine in order to make the relations of mother and Loucy better. The child was admitted into a nursery school and arrangements were made between the school and clinic so that she might not be turned out of the school before she could be reformed. In the beginning, Loucy felt it difficult to adjust herself to the nursery school. But after some years, it was found that Loucy was far more brilliant than the children of her age in studies as well as in scouting, etc. But she could not overcome her early weakness which lay in the lack of attention for the mother and excessive attachment to daddy. At 15 years of age, she was a beautiful girl who appeared to be very able and behaved with a balance. She had no nervous habits. According to her own report, her greatest happiness was to work with daddy. The man whom she dreamt to marry was exactly like daddy.

The example cited above shows very well the problem, the procedure and the work of the clinical psychologists with the aid of the case history method.

**Limitations of Case-history Method**

Like other methods in psychology, case history method has also its own difficulties and limitations. One of the limitations is that it is very difficult to know the whole history of any patient and to observe it objectively. It is possible that while relatives are interviewed, they may be prejudiced in their answers or try to hide something unpleasant. In the case of the children, it is difficult to know their history through them, because their memory is neither strong nor reliable and the psychologist has to depend upon the reports of the relatives. It is possible that the parents do not observe something about the history of the child which is very important, for the case. These and other limitations make it difficult for the clinical psychologist to arrive at a proper diagnosis. In the case of the adult abnormals, however, the psychologist gets the data of their dreams, analysis them and finds out some unconscious causes. He may also ask the patient to explain things about his childhood and tell the psychologist his history. The psychologist may question him from time to time and can get much out of his statement. Thus in the case of the adult abnormals, the difficulties are less than those in the case of the child. This, however, does not mean absence of difficulties and limitations which are always there. But in the ultimate analysis, the case history method has proved to be very valuable for the diagnosis of mental abnormalities. As a matter of fact it all depends upon the experience and ability of the psychologist as to how far he is able to gather a history and analyse it to find the causes. A psychologist like Sigmund Freud can very well make use of a case history to discover the cause of the most complex type of abnormality.

## QUESTIONS FOR EXERCISE

1. Write short note on psychiatric interview.
2. What is the case history method? What is its special value? What are its defects and limitations?

# 16

# Minor Mental Disorders

### What is a Complex?

Every individual human being lives within some particular environment; in the manifestation of his various tendencies and drives he comes into contact with the various objects of the environment, many of which satisfy his desires while many cause him frustration. In this continuing process gradually, his tendencies become attached to, associated with or conditioned to these objects and individuals, effectively. If these objects and persons that are part of the environment, are also the natural aim and object of their correlated drives, then in becoming conditioned to them these drives give rise to normal and healthy feelings, but if these objects are not natural to the respective drives and forces, then in becoming conditioned to them the drives give rise to complexes. Such complexes compel the person harbouring them to behave abnormally, and this leads to the emergence of various mental symptoms.

### Influence of a Complex upon Human Behaviour

The very term complex implies that in this condition a certain obsession concerning some object or person is created in the human mind, with the result that the individual's behaviour towards that objects or person becomes abnormal. Thus, complexes give rise to abnormal behaviour and in order to maintain a condition of mental health it is best to avoid them. But from this one should not conclude that mental complexes invariably give rise to antisocial tendencies; instead, much of the greatest achievements of the greatest social workers and great people had their origin in some or the other complex. Hence, if normal considerations must be worked out, even if complexes are abnormal, they are not necessarily bad.

### Why are Complexes Formed?

Complexes are formed in the mind because objects and persons present within the environment in some way or other frustrate some drive or need of the individual. We form an inhibiting complex towards every individual or object that in any way frustrates one or other of our drives and needs, and causes us disappointment or frustration. Secondly, sometimes we find satisfaction for a particular drive or motive in us in some object or person that is not the natural aim, object or supplement of the motive, and because that aim is not natural the affective unification formed with it cannot be called sentiment : it takes the form of a complex. To take a simple example, the natural aim and end of an adult person's sexual drive is copulation or intercourse with a person of the opposite sex. Now, if a person tries to satisfy the sexual instinct through love-making with a person of his or her own sex then it is possible for him or her to form a complex concerning the sex drive.

### Superiority Complex

It would be very appropriate to provide an example of superiority complex in order to elucidate the working of a complex in the human mind. Generally speaking, every individual finds within himself some special quality in respect of which he is superior to every other, but in some people this sense of superiority is so disproportionate, when compared to their actual level, and so abnormal that the only appropriate term for describing it is complex. Such individuals give the impression of being obstinate, uncultured and vain, and falsely they believe themselves to be possessed of various virtues. A complex of this kind leads to the creation of abnormal symptoms and gradually the individual becomes a mental patient.

## FIXATION

In the opinion of Freud, the famous psychoanalyst, an individual's infant drives and tendencies remain with him throughout his life, in repressed but unmodified form, and due to frustration these repressed drives and desires of infancy once again rear their head in his adult life. The comparatively early development of psychological and physiological desires in infancy, and simultaneously the desire or tendency to maintain them intact and alive is called fixation. This fixation takes place at some or other level of libido in the child. When in adulthood, the repressed desires of infancy come to life again they normally include those desires most of which have become fixed. Frued has explained regression as a tendency in man to return to those desires of infancy which have become fixed. What this implies is that the patient, instead of behaving in a manner, gives expression to fixed ideas of infancy. During the period of fixation, the patient's behaviour towards the doctor is similar to that of a child's towards the parents. Fixed ideas are those upon which the child's libido has become fixed, and due to this fixation such desires have the tendency to seek expression repeatedly. A person suffering from fixation repeats the actions of childhood over and over again.

In order to cure a person of fixation what is necessary is that the patient should be compelled to understand the reason why he is behaving in a childish manner, because all such causes are unconscious, but when they become conscious they may be eliminated. Fixation finds expression in the form of regression, so that the presence of regression indicates the presence of fixation.

## ORGANIC INFERIORITY

Although even now the exact correlation between physical and psychological process has not been determined, psychologists hold the belief that both are mutually interrelated activities. Changes in the physical condition of the body can be seen leading to changes in behaviour while change in behaviour can be observed causing change in physical condition. Modern science looks upon a creature's physical and psychological structure as a unit, the two being anything but separate. And between these two, instead of difference, there exists correlation, and it is only with a view to convenience the mental and physical activities are distinguished for study.

If follows, therefore, that physical or organic defects contribute very much to mental abnormality. Such organic defects or deficiency can take various forms, such as ugliness, some or the other handicap, weakness of some particular organs, etc. Because of inferiority, and in order to get rid of it he tries to compensate for his physical weakness by excelling in some other sphere. Socrates, for example, was a very ugly man, but a very great philosopher. Other people, however, do not really compensate for their organic shortcoming, instead they only pretend to do so. Some weak people, for example, can be seen walking with a definite swagger merely in order to indicate that they have no shortcoming in their make-up. Another type of individual is so much susceptible to his shortcomings that he becomes prey to them and develops an inferiority complex, as a result of which he manifests various abnormal mental symptoms. In fact, all kinds of organic defects cannot be overcome through effort, so that the only sensible solution is to realise one's shortcoming, and develop a healthy attitude towards them and reach a definite understanding.

## FETISHISM

In the case of sexual deviation of fetishism, as is evident from the phrase, the end of a person's sexual drive is some peculiar object such as shoe, sock, hair, etc. At the root of this is the fear of insult or degradation at the hands of a member of the other sex. The peculiar object or the fetish cannot show disrespect, disregard or disinclination towards the person loving it, a love that has been inspired by the sexual impulse. Thus the fetish object is completely in the possession of the person, and the latter can behave towards it in any manner that he wants to. Sometimes fetishism also has at its root the tendency towards self-denigration, and is to be seen particularly in sexual attraction towards the shoe.

In a fetishistic attraction, some particular part of the body or object is chosen as an object of love because it supplants the sex organs. One example of this would be the person who can be satisfied with the shoe of the person he loves. Such people derive the same love and satisfaction from such fetishistic objects that the normal person derives from intercourse with the other sex. And, among all people taken with fetishism, which particular individual will choose which object for his love depends upon the individual life history of the individual patient. When a person develops a very strong sexual attraction for some particular object, he chooses that object, be it a shoe, sock, hair or what else. Fetishism is a sexual deviation due to which the individual fails to develop normal sexual relationships.

Hence, if it is not cured the person cannot establish healthy relations.

## INFERIORITY COMPLEX

As a general rule almost every individual has, at one time or the other during his life, to face a situation in which he finds himself backward, weak and inferior to other people. For example, people find themselves inferior to other on account of their poverty, their lack of education, or some physical shortcoming. Normally, the individual manages to adjust himself to such conditions, realises his position, accepts the other but without forming any detrimental complexes in his mind. In this form, the sense of inferiority is very useful since it inspires the individual to remove that inferiority the classic example of which is Demosthenes, the famous Greek orator. This prodigy used to stutter as a child, but in order to get rid of this shortcoming he made it a habit to go to the seashore and practise speaking to the waves with pebbles in his mouth. In this manner he succeeded in removing his defect, and in time rose to become one of the greatest orator his city ever produced. Another example is that of Theodore Roosevelt who started horse riding in order to avoid developing a complex with regard to physical weakness. He succeeded in strengthening his body.

But, on the other hand, there are some other individuals who did not manage to remove their cause of inferiority by direct means and their sense of inferiority became a complex. Individuals of this kind develop many symptoms of mental imbalance because of this sense of inferiority, they become mentally diseased and their social balance is destroyed. Because of sense of inferiority, people are seen indulging in antisocial activity. Many criminals who are very ugly and consequently fail to attract members of the other sex try to compensate by influencing such members through cruelty and crime, so that their inferiority is compensated for. When the adolescent is constantly heckled by the teacher in college and rebuked by his parents at home, he feels neglected and therefore inferior; he then turns to crime and hooliganism. When he finds that he cannot preserve his self-respect through normal channels he has recourse to antisocial means.

If people with inferiority complexes are to be cured, it is necessary that the cause of their inferiority be first eliminated.

## AUTISTIC THINKING

In the present-day world one often comes across young men and women who, under the influence of cinema and modern fiction, live in an unique world of their own, far removed from the real one. Their ways of thinking and their thoughts are unique in that their thought has no reference to any accepted standard, custom, tradition and school. Standards of society seem to fill them with loathing. Thinking of this kind is called autistic thinking.

As is evident from the above example, in autistic thinking, no attention is paid to any criticism or standard. It is the thought which is complete and sufficient in itself, since it does not bother about reality or social necessity. Autistic thinking is found in abnormal individuals, introverts and insane people. And a person who is too much taken up with daydreams also tends towards autistic thinking.

Austistic thinking in fact is an obstacle in the person's adjustment with his environment, and when present in excess it can make the person abnormal. In other words, when it is present in excess, it is indicative of abnormality.

## GENIUS

All psychologists do not agree as to the intelligence quotient a person must possess in order to be classed a genius. Some people accept I.Q. of 120 as genius level while other psychologists contend that it must be no less than 140. As a general rule, only individuals with intelligence quotients above 140 are classed geniuses. According to an estimate, one out of every four hundred children is genius. An intelligence rating between 140 and/or 190 can only result in the person being regarded as some kind of super-genius, but an intelligence rating above 170 is extremely rare. A genius is above the average man not only in respect of intelligence but also in respect of physique as well as weight and other qualities of the body. Besides, physical defects in the genius are less than in the normal or average person. But many studies and enquiries have indicated that geniuses, in comparison with the average person, have less emotional balance and social adjustability.

Lombroso believed that genius is akin to insanity, and undoubtedly it is certainly true that many geniuses give the impression of being unbalanced persons. But studies seem to indicate that a statement which claims that the rate of insanity is more in geniuses than among ordinary persons is not true or accurate. Havelock Ellis published in his book *A Study of British Genius* a report of his study of 1,030 geniuses belonging to Britain. He proved that the rate of mental disease among these geniuses was only 4 per cent and among them none could definitely be classed as insane. Besides, it was found that people in whom symptoms of mental illness were present for a long period in their lives had less genius than the ones who exhibited such symptoms only in the later stages of their lives or those who did not become a prey to mental illness at all. Distorted geniuses are to be found mainly among poets and authors, rarely among scientists.

It is apparent, from the above statistics that the common view that genius is akin to insanity is erroneous. On the other hand, statistics further reveal that insanity is the very antithesis of genius implying therein that insanity reduces genius or destroys it. Although some poets created their greatest poems and achieved their greatest triumphs in a condition of mental imbalance, but the majority of geniuses have rarely managed to attain their greatest heights in such moments. In fact, it would be no fallacy to assert that the relation between insanity and genius is based purely on flight of the imagination.

## KRAEPELIN'S CLASSIFICATION OF MENTAL DISORDERS

Among the many famous names concerned with propounding the organic theory of mental disease, the name of Emile Kraepelin is very famous. His justly famous book appeared in 1883, and it emphasized the importance of mental deformity in mental disease. In his book on psychotherapy, Kraepelin put forward his classification of mental disorders. Kraepelin observed that similar to such specific physical ailments as smallpox, there were certain mental characteristics so distinct and permanent that they could be treated as special kind of mental disorder. From this standpoint Kraepelin described the various mental disorders and showed distinctions.

Kraepelin believed each mental disease to be distinct and separate from every other, and he believed its development and progress to be as predetermined as any psychological ailment is. From Kraepelin started the tradition of determining, describing and classifying various mental disorders in the field of psychotherapy. It came to be believed that by observing characteristics and symptoms, a mental disease can be identified. Hence Kraepelin is a very important figure in the history of classification of mental disorders.

## DISSOCIATION

### What is Dissociation?

Dissociation is believed to be a special kind of hysteria in which the characteristic symptoms of amnesia, fugue, multiple personality and somnambulism are evident. In each one of these, the patient excludes some portion of his life from the sphere of his consciousness.

### Forms of Dissociation

Dissociation takes the following forms mainly :

**1. Amnesia fugue.** In this past experience is either totally or partially forgotten, and this can occur in psychosis, psychoneurosis, insanity or in any diseased condition. If amnesia is due to an injury to the brain there can be no cure for it, but among its causes various kinds of conflicts and repressions are particularly important and in order to remove them amnesia can be treated.

**2. Multiple personality.** Another form of dissociation is that in which the personality is divided into two or more persons, but there are very few examples of this disorder. Erickson has illustrated the disorder with the case of Miss Brown in whom there were two conscious personalities, one of which knew the other but the latter was not aware of the former. In the case of Beauchamp there were five distinct personalities. Multiple split personality also has its origin in repression and mental conflict, which can be removed by hypnosis and other methods.

**3. Somnambulism.** In the condition of somnambulism, the patient goes through a variety of actions while asleep. According to the report prepared by Jargenson and Janice, 5 per cent of 1,808 college students walked in their sleep. The cause of this mental disease is some very stern injurious experience which conjoins to the feeling of insecurity, lack of self-confidence, crime and conflict.

Concerning the causes of dissociation it has been remarked that repression arising of mental conflict causes dissociation. When a sensitive individual passes through a set of circumstances that force him to suffer tremendous mental conflict, his first step is to actively solve this conflict, but when he fails to resolve it, meaning thereby that he fails to distinguish between the relative importance of the various alternatives open to him, the conflict assumes an even more radical shape and in order to evade it the patient resorts to repression. Because of the process of repression, the conflict passes out of the sphere of conscious thought and realisation but it strikes strong roots in the unconscious mind. From there it emerges through unconscious means of which the person is not aware. Dissociation activity consists in the expression and manifestation of the repressed conflicts.

There is a clear-cut and precise difference between repression and dissociation. Repression refers to the forcible eviction of some thought, desire or tendency from the conscious mind and its relation to the unconscious sphere. Dissociation occurs when a person's mind is divided in two or more personalities that can be distinctly viewed. Dissociation is the outcome of repression and repression is the cause of dissociation. Hence, each has its own significance.

Repression and conflict are also intimately connected. The normal course of facing a situation of mental conflict is to solve that conflict, but when this normal course cannot be pursued, then the person has recourse to repression, which is an abnormal means.

Repression and dissociation are different kinds of disorders. Examples of the first kinds of disorders can be seen in various psychoses, while example of the second kind are amnesia, multiple personality, etc. Both these kinds of mental disorders are intimately connected.

## MENTAL DISORDERS AND THE REPRESSION OF SEX

Sigmund Freud, the originator of psychoanalysis, believed that one major cause of mental disorders was repression of the sex drive. According to Freud, normal development of his personality in man is essential for the normal development of the sex instinct rendered abnormal or influenced in any undesirable way. Sex adjustment is very important during the period of adolescence and sex education is desirable. Sex instinct can lead to four kinds of frustrations, oral, anal, phallic and general. In different cultures, the form of these different frustrations change somewhat. The extent to which a particular culture allows the normal development of the human personality depends upon the limits within which free expression of human instinct is permitted in that cultural complex.

This above view of causation of mental disease has come in for considerable criticism. Modern psychologists accept that repression of the sex instinct is one important factor in causing mental disorders, but they do not accept it as the exclusive cause. Adler, Jung and other prominent psychologists have indicated certain other causes of mental disorder. Adler opines that the inferiority complex is also a very important element in the causing of mental deformity, because normally every person makes an effort to compensate in some manner any deficiency that may exist within him, but with some people the normal compensation fails so that they are oppressed with the sense of inferiority, so much so that they lose their mental balance. People of this kind can be observed indulging in antisocial behaviour and criminality or generally destructive activity.

Repression of the sex drive and the inferiority complex are both important factors in mental disorders and diseases, but there are certain other factors also that are no less important. Such factors can be related to one's own personality or his environment.

## MELANCHOLIA

### Symptoms of Melancholia

The chief symptoms of melancholia are anxiety, delusion or extreme worry, self-denigration, etc. In this disorder the patient is oppressed with deep sorrow which normally occurs around middle age when the physical energies of both men and women are on the decline. In this condition a person's mind is full of doubts, insecurity, fear and anxiety, and he gets the feeling that in the near future he will not be able to do anything really valuable. Among women this disease occurs between 40 and 65 years of age.

Melancholia progresses very gradually, and it has its origin in some painful incident such as loss of job, death of a family member, economic loss or some other accident. The patient begins to lose weight, and he manifests such symptoms as headache, lack of interest, insomnia, anxiety, wandering of attention, lack of enthusiasm, etc. He appears very anxious and afraid. Many such patients come to believe that their past life has been one of sin and degradation, with the result that even the smallest lapses from very high standards of conduct are looked upon with very great loathing. They are also inclined to feel that they will now have their retribution for the sinful life they have led or that he even commits suicide. Hence it is essential that the patient be carefully looked after.

Melancholia also leads to the manifestation of various delusions and patients have been known to complain of very strange anxiety delusions. They sometimes feel that they have no stomach or that their brain has turned to stone or water. Such delusions are seen to be accompanied by tensions in various parts of the body, disorder in the functioning of intestines and general physical weakness or debility, but the patient's mental powers are more or less unimpaired.

### Causes of Melancholia

Roughly, the causes of melancholia are divided into two classes : physical and psychological.

**1. Physical causes.** In this age menstruation in women ceases and men lose to some extent their sexual ability. Hence, some people believe that these factors cause melancholia, but in actual fact physical cause of melancholia consists, not in these localised changes, but in the general debility that sets in with advancing age.

**2. Psychological causes.** Every individual does not suffer from melancholia after middle age, hence it is obvious that this disorder is psychological rather than physiological. In fact, melancholia happens normally to people who manifest excessive tenacity, sense of responsibility, of duty, morality, shame or obstinacy. Often the number of their friends is very small, and they do not pay any attention towards their recreation.

Their sexual adjustment is not satisfactory. While the energy and exuberance of youth lasts, they maintain their social adjustment but when this energy begins to decline they are assailed by doubt and fear. Women begin to feel that their energy for physical, social and economic work is declining, and men experience the feeling that the golden period of their lives is well nigh past. The world around them looks dark and uncompromising, with the result that they become self-centred, wishing for the restful case of death.

**Cures of Melancholia**

If the patient is endowed with sufficient wealth, his melancholia can be treated at home, otherwise it is best to get him admitted to some hospital because in this disease the patient requires constant attention in order to prevent him from committing suicide. Very often the patient refuses to take food so that nutrition has to be forced upon him through a tube, for he needs nutritious food and adequate rest. He should be made to live in a healthy and well ventilated place. Different patients are administered different kinds of medicines, according to their requirements. Occupational therapy proves very useful in this disorder, and as the patient succeeds with his work his self-confidence and satisfaction return. Hydro-therapy does not have any really good effect. In the normal cases some good can come by discussing the patient's troubles with him, but if his symptoms are acute he will only suffer if the subject is forced upon him. If the patient also suffers from physical diseases he should be carefully treated. His general health should be regarded with close attention. Modern doctors find that shock therapy can be used to good effect on patients suffering from melancholia.

## HOMOSEXUALITY

**Definition**

According to W.L. Linford Rees, "The term homosexual is applied to sexual relationship whether overt or psychic between individuals of the same sex. It is derived from the Greek 'homo' meaning the same, rather than the Latin for man. It denotes the sameness of the two individuals involved in the sexual relationship and is the antithesis of the word heterosexual."

It has been shown that there is a continuous gradation among members of the general population between exclusively heterosexual and exclusively homosexual behaviour.

Kinsey (1948) proposed a very useful heterosexual-homosexual rating scale :

1. Exclusively heterosexual with no homosexual tendencies.
2. Predominantly heterosexual and only incidentally homosexual.
3. Predominantly heterosexual but with more than incidental homosexuality.
4. Equally heterosexual and homosexual.
5. Predominantly homosexual but more than incidentally heterosexual.
6. Predominantly homosexual but incidentally heterosexual.
7. Exclusively homosexual.

It is difficult to estimate the prevalence of homosexuality for obvious reasons. Kinsey considered that 4 per cent of American men were exclusively homosexual.

It must be remembered that homosexuality can occur in apparently normal, stable persons free from psychiatric symptoms and who are otherwise socially well-adjusted. It can also occur in unstable personalities, persons with neurosis, psychopathy, mental subnormality, psychosis and organic mental states.

**Aetiology**

Different authorities emphasise the importance of one or more of the following :

1. Genetic factors;
2. Constitutional predisposition;
3. Conditioning factors;
4. Psychodynamic mechanisms;
5. The influence of physiological and hormonal factors.

Twin studies provide some evidence that homosexuality may be genetically determined, but only in a proportion of patients. Studies of endocrine factors have been, on the whole, inconclusive.

With regard to personality, it must be remembered that masculinity and femininity are not an 'all or nothing' affair, because persons of each sex may show varying proportions of both. One may get extremely masculine females and extremely feminine males.

Surveys reveal that homosexuals who have come to psychiatric care or who have come to the notice of Courts of Law tend to have a higher incidence of neurotic or schizoid types of personality but, on the whole, only showed minor differences from moral.

**Classification**

The following classes of homosexual may be described.

1. Adolescents and emotionally immature adults, who go through a phase in which they are uncomfortably aware of their attraction to both sexes and are in a quandary which they cannot solve. They usually respond well to supportive psychiatric treatment.

2. Markedly abnormal personalities with marked effeminacy who often solicit and not infrequently become homosexual prostitutes, preferring the chase to the actual sexual contact.

3. The inadequate, dull person who has never experienced loving relationships with anyone, and who is usually very socially isolated.

4. The resentful, antisocial person who often has a long record of court appearances.

5. Homosexuality in relatively normal, intact personalities.

6. Latent, well-compensated homosexual. These may be intelligent, married and have children.

7. Homosexuality occurring along with serious mental disability such as psychopathy, psychosis or organic brain damage. These patients are apt to injure victims in a way that none of the others would contemplate, nor do they take only predisposed victims.

Some, authorities believe that parental influences may play an important role in the causation of homosexuality. Some implicate a maternal attitude of excessive strictness and perfectionism; others implicate father-deprivation at a time when awareness of homosexual attraction is not abnormal as a phase of development.

**Treatment**

Treatment may be by psychotherapy or by behaviour therapy.

Psychotherapy can help some homosexuals who are burdened by guilt, neurotic difficulties or intolerable sexual tension, and also those persons who request help in order to fortify them in restraining overt behaviour likely to involve them in trouble with the law.

It is the view of most practising psychiatrists that no cure can be offered to complete homosexuals with a Kinsey rating of 6. A great deal can be done to make the homosexual a more happy, well-adjusted and effective person.

Aversion therapy may be applied, either using apomorphine injections to produce vomiting or an electrical current to produce a painful stimulus. Whenever nausea, vomiting or pain are felt, the patients are confronted with photographs of nude or near nude men whom they find attractive. This is repeated until a marked aversion develops. Sometimes a substitution of photographs of sexually attractive women are presented, accompanied by injections of testosterone propitiate.

It is difficult to evaluate the role of aversion therapy. It is important to realise that in many patients the goal of treatment has to be realistic and must be limited. Many patients cannot and have no wish to change their homosexuality. If they can be helped to be relieved of psychiatric symptoms and to adjust reasonably well in work and society a worthwhile result is achieved.

Behaviour therapy, consisting of systematic desensitisation of fears relating to approaching females, is also effective and sometimes more acceptable in some forms of male homosexuality.

## EXPOSURE AND EXHIBITIONISM

Exhibitionism is one of the commonest sexual deviations. It consists of the exposure of the external genitalia in public, usually to persons of the opposite sex for sexual arousal and satisfaction. Genital exposure is normal in children, as part of sexual exploration. In adults the condition is almost exclusively confined to men and complete relief does not usually occur by the act of exposure, but is achieved by masturbation.

The age of onset of exhibition is usually at puberty, but is variable. Patients are usually inadequate in personality. Supportive psychotherapy and behaviour therapy have proved helpful when the patient is willing to accept treatment.

## TRANSVESTISM AND TRANSEXUALISM

Transvestism is the impulse to wear the clothing of the opposite sex. Transexualism is the term given to describe the wish to change the anatomical sex.

Transvestites proper were defined as those men who obtained sexual gratification from dressing as women. In transvestism the clothes or the wearing of them may provide an end in itself, as they are usually endowed with sexual significance and the act of wearing them may provide the sole form of sexual expression. Many transvestites lack sexual drives and state that they feel more contented and more comfortable while wearing female attire. The onset of transvestism and transexualism is usually before 12 years of age. It occurs in all social classes and in men and women.

Aversion therapy has proved effective in treating transvestism and may need to be supplemented by vocational, social and psycho-therapeutic guidance to help readjustment.

Transexualism is more difficult to treat and the result of surgical treatment attempting to make person appear more like the opposite sex has, on the whole, been disappointing. Its legality is doubtful.

### General Principles in the Management of Psychosexual Disorders

The first requirement is a physical examination and a full psychiatric history with an assessment of the patient's personality and present mental state.

Masters and Johnson have elaborated very effective techniques for dealing with psychosexual problems. They point out that psychosexual problems frequently reflect other areas of disharmony or misunderstanding in the marriage. The marital relationship is treated as a whole with the emphasis that sexual function is a part of this relationship. The couple, together with a male and female therapist, meet at a round table session to clarify, discuss and work through problems. Specific exercises are prescribed for the couple to help them with their particular sexual difficulty. Experience has revealed that most forms of sexual inadequacy involve a lack of information, or misinformation, and fear of performance. Couples are specifically prohibited from any sexual play other than that prescribed by the therapist. In the beginning, exercises are usually devoted to increasing sensual awareness to touch, sight, sound and smell, and the couples learn to give and receive bodily pleasure without the pressure of performance. A very important element is that they simultaneously learn to communicate bodily in a mutually satisfactory way and that sexual foreplay is as important as intercourse. Genital stimulation is later added to general bodily stimulation.

## SEXUAL DEVIATION

### What is Sexual Deviation?

Among the most important types of abnormalities are the sexual deviations. They are important because they are so much common and also because they play very important role in causing mental diseases. Now, sex impulse and the consequent behaviour are normal in male and female. Then what are the characteristics that make it abnormal? Dr. Benjamin Morse has laid down the following five important rules to distinguish sexual deviations from normal sex behaviour :

1. An act is perverted if it causes physical harm or severe pain to either participant.

2. An act is perverted if either party finds it personally abhorrent.

3. An act is perverted if not specifically limited to husband and wife.

4. An act (other than coitus) is perverted if it is the sole or chief sexual outlet of the couple involved.

5. An act is perverted when it is the *sine qua non* of a sexual relationship.

The above-mentioned rules make it clear that sexual perversions are relative to persons involved, culture of the particular society and purpose of the sexual act. Most of the acts which are categorised as sexual perversions can be so called only when occasionally indulged. A new type of sex play indulged just for change between wife and husband, with mutual consent, and without causing any injury to any one is definitely not sexual perversion however it may deviate from the normal pattern of sex behaviour. Such an act should not cause guilt sense and if it does, it must be abandoned because it is perverse.

**Types of Sexual Deviations**

Among the more important types of sexual deviations are : voyeurism, masturbation, sadism, masochism, mate swapping, exhibitionism, necrophilia, vicarious participation, the orgies, satyriasis, the nymphomania, the bestiality and fetishism.

## QUESTIONS FOR EXERCISE

1. Write a short note on Complexes and their formation.
2. Examine critically the concept of fixation.
3. Write short note on Organic inferiority.
4. Write a short note on Fetishism.
5. Write a short note on Inferiority Complex.
6. Write a short note on Autistic thinking.
7. What is genius? Examine the view that genius is akin to insanity.
8. State and illustrate Kraepelin's classification of mental disorders.
9. "Conflict followed by repression brings about Dissociation." Explain fully.
10. Would you agree with Freud's theory that neuroses arise invariably from sexual repression?
11. Describe the causes and symptoms of melancholia. Give illustrations.
12. Write short note on Homosexuality.
13. Write short note on Exposure and Exhibitionism.
14. Explain Transvestism and Transexualism. Lay down general principles in the management of psychosexual disorders.
15. Write short note on Sexual Deviation.

# 17

# Personality and its Disorders : Psychopathic Personality

## PSYCHOPATHIC PERSONALITY

Criminals, and more often habitual criminals, possess a particular kind of personality known as the psychopathic personality. Such a person being essentially at variance with the society, is not adjusted to it. Individuals of this kind are neither psychotic nor neurotic, but a class by themselves, a class that is hard to define objectively.

### Definition

The term psychopathic personality is emotionally charged and has been overworked, abused and ill-used. It is sometimes employed as a term of abuse for one's political or religious opponents and the term tends to engender hostile attitudes on the part of society.

Although many definitions have been given, the consensus of opinion is that the psychopath's behaviour shows a lack of social responsibility, of consideration for others and of prudence and foresight.

The psychopath's persistent antisocial mode of conduct ranges from inefficiency, lack of interest in any form of occupation to pathological lying, swindling, slandering, alcoholism, drug addiction, sexual offences and violent actions with little motivation and an entire absence of self-restraint. If the term is to have any real value, it should be applied to antisocial or criminal behaviour only after the strict exclusion of intellectual defect, psychosis, neurosis, cerebral injury or diseases.

The characteristics of psychopathy are immaturity, self-centredness, little or no regard for the rights or convenience of others; the immediate satisfaction of desires is imperative, acting violently if frustrated, associated with lack of conscience or sense of guilt.

The definitions of psychopathic disorder are as follows :

**1. The Mental Health Act (1959) of England.** Describes "psychopathic disorder as persistent disorder of personality, whether or not accompanied by subnormality of intelligence, which results in abnormally aggressive or seriously irresponsible conduct on the part of the patient and requires, or is susceptible to, medical treatment."

**2. W.L. Linford Rees.** "A convenient definition is that a psychopath is a person who, from an early age, shows abnormality of character marked by episodes of antisocial behaviour and tendencies to act on impulse to satisfy the need of the moment, without giving due regard to the consequences of such action."

**3. J.D. Prichard.** "In case of this nature the moral and active principles of the mind are strongly prevented or depraved, the power of self-government is lost or greatly impaired and the individual is found to be incapable, not of talking or reasoning upon any subject proposed to him, for this he will often do with shrewdness and volubility, but of conducting himself with shrewdness and propriety in the business of life."

**4. Landis and Bolles.** "Psychopathic personality is a category of those, whose behaviour is socially disturbing and destructive but who are not psychoneurotic, psychotic or mentally defective."

The various definitions applied to psychopathic personality have four common features :

1. Excluding cause, *viz.*, the condition does not amount to mental defect, he is not insane or psychoneurotic; whether or not the person is of low intelligence it is independent of subnormality and mental illness.

2. Time factor. The abnormality exists throughout life or from a comparatively early age and is usually recurrent, episodic or persistent.

3. Description of behaviour, *viz.* antisocial, unable to accept social requirements on account of peculiarities of impulse, temperament or character; conduct is abnormally aggressive or irresponsible.

4. Personality characteristics which have been described as part of psychopathy are marked egocentricity, lack of sincerity, lack of feeling and lack of guilt. In practice, one sees many psychopaths who possess these attributes quite clearly in certain circumstances.

The differentiation between aggressive and inadequate psychopaths is not satisfactory, as one form may turn into the other.

**Classification of Psychopaths**

Scott classifies psychopaths as follows :

**1. Persons trained in antisocial standards.** These are persons who behave as they were taught to behave and do what is normal in their families or districts. The offender has learned this behaviour consistently and will not feel guilt about doing what he was taught to do. His family or circle will not be critical. The offence is strictly goal motivated, intended as a means to material gain or the acquisition of prestige. The observer can easily find sympathy and find it possible to identify himself with the offender and his setting.

**2. Reparative behaviour.** Here the offence is part of an intelligently, laboriously and often consciously worked out policy, aimed at the adjustment of the individual to difficulties in his environment and to personal handicaps which that environment has produced in him, *e.g.* compensations for feelings of inadequacy and inferiority.

The offender is identified with his pattern of misbehaviour and is even proud of it. The offence is goal-motivated.

**3. The untrained offender.** Here there are no steady standards of behaviour provided in early life. The adult is, therefore, without standards and weak in character. Conduct difficulties show themselves diffusely and from early childhood.

**4. Rigid fixations.** Here learning has broken down and has been replaced by a fixed, maladaptive pattern of response. The crime is stereotyped, non-adaptive and non-goal directed, which persists unaltered despite long periods in a controlled environment and is utterly improved by severe punishment. The offender dissociates himself from his behaviour but may be genuinely remorseful and anxious about it. He is bewildered about it. The offence is stereotyped. It brings nothing but relief from immediate tension. The observer cannot feel sympathy with the offender. Punishment is useless.

## CHARACTERISTICS OF PSYCHOPATHIC PERSONALITY

**1. All levels of intelligence.** In a personality of this kind, the intelligence of the individual is not influenced, since cases of this personality include individuals belonging to all intelligence levels.

**2. Lacking direction of means.** Such individuals do not hesitate to adopt any means for gaining pleasure that come to hand at the moment, any means that may even be illegal or harmful to another individual, even if that individual be a relative or friend. From this point of view they are almost like spoilt children who care only for the fulfilment of their own desire without any care of the pain inflicted on any other person.

**3. Inability to profit from insight or experience.** These people do not benefit from their experience and their functioning does not improve. They repay the obligations with indecency and pain. Any sense of respect or propriety is completely lacking in their mental make-up. Remorse does not invade their mental fortress so that they never suffer pain for their activity.

**4. Found at all levels of intelligence.** In a personality of this kind intelligence of the individual is not influenced, since cases of this personality include individuals belonging to all intelligence levels.

**5. Lacking discretion of means.** Such individuals do not hesitate to adopt any means for gaining pleasure that comes to hand at the moment, any means that may even be illegal or harmful to another individual, even if that individual be relative or friend. From this point of view they are almost like spoilt children who care only for the fulfilment of their own desire without any care of the pain inflicted on any other person.

**6. Inability to profit from insight or experience.** These people do not benefit from their experience and their functioning has no clement of insight or determination since they do not think positively of results but act merely to satisfy a temporary but strong impulse.

**7. Emotional distortion.** Individuals of such kind exhibit emotional distortions of various kinds; they are of a crude, cruel, escapist, cold and violent temperament, they do not seem to learn control of their emotions and they are very unpredictable in their movements and activities. Very profound emotional disturbance comes to them over occurrences that the normal man would dismiss as trivial, with the result that they appear, exhilarated at one time and depressed at another, peaceful at one time and like a seething volcano at another.

**8. Changeable and temporary activities.** Activities of such individuals do not exhibit any sign of permanence in respect of objective or direction, and their ambitions are continuously changing. They even keep on changing their profession while many of them even lead a nomadic sort of life. Briefly, their life has no stability.

**9. Sexual deviations.** Their sexual development is retarded and abnormal. They show all kinds of sexual deviations and they do not show any signs of remorse or pain at them. Their efforts at marriage are temporary and unsuccessful.

**10. Various kinds of personality.** But finally as has been said earlier, it must be kept in mind that the class as a whole contains an astonishing variety of personality types, and it is difficult to discover any prominent element of equality among them. Some of them, for example, are so well mannered and highly cultured that they have a positively beneficial influence upon others, while on the other hand many of them are very weak, negative, inactive and inadequate. Despite these more obvious differences, fundamentally they are all very selfish, self- centred and hard and they all exhibit all the characteristics recounted earlier.

### Incidence of Psychopathy

In the opinion of L.G. Rowntree, K.H.M. Gilt and T.D. Edwards, there are approximately 1 per cent psychopaths in the male population, but among the females the percentage is less. A large majority of psychopaths normally evade jails and hospitals, since of all the mental cases registered in hospitals only 2 per cent have been found to be psychopathic while 16 to 20 per cent of the cruel prisoners jailed are psychopathic cases. From the psychological viewpoint such individuals are not susceptible to threats or prison sentences, and are almost incurable. They have the capacity to distinguish between the right and the wrong, though they never use it. The class of psychopathic individuals includes people who are victims of mental deformities such as lying, sexual deviation, eccentricity, wavering, antisociality, etc.

It is evident from the above description that a psychopathic personality differs from a psychotic or neurotic individual, since it has neither the anxiety and worry of the neurotic personality, nor the delusions, mental deformities and hallucinations of the psychotic personality. On the contrary, a large number of psychopathic individuals are quite intelligent and they possess attractive personalities. As has been mentioned earlier, their main abnormal feature is inhibition of every kind as well as a complete indifference to all moral and social laws or restrictions. Not being bothered of their future life they are not able to make any really accurate judgement concerning it. They revolt against society and are constantly in conflict with the social environment. And the root cause of this conflict is not the lack of intelligence but absence of the desire to improve. It is for this reason that Prichard, an English psychologist, has called them moral imbeciles. In his words, "In cases of this nature, the moral and active principles of the mind are strongly perverted or depraved; the power of self-government is lost or greatly impaired, and the individual is found to be incapable, not of talking or reasoning upon any subject proposed to him, for this he will often do with shrewdness and volubility, but of conducting himself with decency and propriety in the business of life." It will be easier to understand the tendency of a psychopathic individual through the following example.

One psychopathic individual pretended to be a visiting psychologist from another state in order to gain acquaintance of a thirty-year old teacher and went through a one-week whirlwind courtship with her and married her. He issued cheques amounting to a few thousand dollars for defraying expenses of the honeymoon and some medicines, but lack of money in the bank account led to the cheques being returned.

These cheques had been guaranteed by his wife and father-in-law. He then presented certain obviously plausible excuses to his wife : she agreed to them and paid the money on those cheques from her own resources. But his doings aroused the suspicions of his father-in-law who investigated his antecedents and found that the person was not a physician that he posed to be and also that he had a previous wife and a child by her, both of whom he had abandoned before coming to his daughter. When this evidence was presented to the psychopathic individual, he immediately accepted the validity of all evidence against him, but said that he had deceived and married the school teacher because he loved her and wanted to make her happy. He had evidently successfully deceived his second bride for she now gave him a large sum of money to arrange for a divorce with his first wife so that they could be legally united. This psychopathic individual accepted the money for that purpose but never put in an appearance again.

It is evident from the above example of a psychopathic individual that he is otherwise a very eligible, attractive and intelligent individual, but the only quality that compels one to call him psychopathic is his irresistible urge to cheat another person and to continue to cheat him, without any thought to his feelings, and thus to satisfy his own ends.

**Aetiology**

Studies of the degree of concordance of criminality in pairs of uni-ovular and bin-ovular twins show that personality is dependent, to some extent, upon hereditary factors but that the environment may largely control the expression of the personality disposition.

Neuroses and psychopathic states are multifactorially determined. Studies of the relationships between rates of juvenile crime and social disturbances conclude that there appears to be something particularly significant in social disturbances occurring in the fourth and fifth year of a child's life.

Constitutional attributes found in psychopaths also favour genetic factors, such as mesomorphic body build and abnormalities in the electroencephalogram which are correlated with aggressiveness.

The evidence regarding aetiology is conflicting and we are not yet in a position to make dogmatic statements as to the relative importance of inherited and environmental factors, except to say that it is the interaction of both rather than either one or the other which is important.

**Management and Treatment of Psychopathy**

**1. Individual psychotherapy.** Psychopaths notoriously lack persistence and determination and, even when they present themselves for treatment, they often want a magical cure and are prepared to do very little themselves to help. Very often they only seek treatment when they are in difficulties with the law or with their families.

Individual psychotherapy over a period of years, if the patient cooperates, may occasionally help to achieve a better adjustment.

**2. Drug treatment.** In some aggressive psychopaths with marked aggressive outbursts, amphetamines given with phenytoin sodium have been found to be helpful, particularly if there is evidence of cerebral dysrhythmia.

Major tranquillisers and tranquillo-sedatives are of limited value in psychopathy itself and although one of the phenothiazines (Pericyazine) has been claimed to be helpful in the management of behaviour disturbances in psychopaths, these claims have yet to be substantiated.

**3. Group therapy.** Group therapy is often a preferable method of dealing with psychopaths and group therapy in a special hospital such as that at Belmont, is particularly promising.

It is generally agreed that psychopaths admitted to psychiatric hospitals are probably better treated as a group in separate wards or units because of their tendency to act out their behaviour. It is interesting that patients with psychiatric illnesses such as depression or schizopaths, in turn, very often manipulate people and situations and create a great many difficulties in the running of the ward or hospital.

In a proportional psychopaths there is tendency for a greater maturity with greater normality and better adjustment to occur in middle life, but this is not invariably so.

## PERSONALITY INTEGRATION

Personality is the dynamic organisation of the psycho-physical traits, exhibited in its adjustment with the environment. If the organisation of psycho-physical qualities in personality is not orderly or strong, difficulties will arise in the adjustment to the environment. Such a personality will be called disintegrated.

The integration of personality is necessary in order to effect adjustment with the environment. Adjustment will be natural and easy if this integration is strong. The integration of personality is the integration of the psycho-physical traits of personality. There is an absence of conflicts in it. In it, mind and emotion, desire and determination, and all mental activities are in no way disorganised but all of them work in an organised way. An integrated personality is flexible, strong and organised as well as balanced. In it there is a compromise of mind and emotions. McDougall has called it the organisation of character and intellect.

The integration of personality is found in everyone to a lesser or greater degree. If this integration is less than is essential, then problems of adjusting of the environment arise. Freud believed in three elements in personality — Id, Ego and Super-Ego. Id includes the person's desires, instincts, suppressed desires, etc. Super-ego is the representative of social control, the result of the person's socialisation. It exercises social control over the person while the id demands the fulfilment of animal desires. Ego includes the tendencies which revolt for the existence of life. Thus, often the super-ego conflicts with the id or ego. The problems of personality are the problems of the mental adjustment of these three.

The weakness of the ego is fundamental in personality problems in the person. Either the person's ego cannot control his desires and instincts or it cannot adjust with the super ego. For the integration of personality, it is necessary that the person maintains a balanced and realistic outlook. Some failures and frustrations cross everyone's path, and the person should pursue his life task without being extraordinarily disturbed by happiness or sorrow. Balance is the golden path of life. It is only the balance of emotions, demands, needs and imagination and thinking which can keep the personality integrated.

The definition of the integration of personality must have made it clear that it needs socialisation essentially without which the person finds it difficult to adjust to the environment. The social environment is not the total environment of the person and neither is sociability by itself the sufficient quality for one's adaptation to society, but in spite of this it can be said that sociability is an essential quality in the adaptation to society. Sociability, as the name suggests, is the tendency by which a person mixes with the other people of the society and lives with them. An unsocial person is introspective and likes to live alone. He experiences difficulty in meeting other people and having relations with them or behaving towards them. In daily life, the problems which arise in his meeting with other people assume alarming proportions while the social man solves them with ease. For example, the unsocial person feels lonely when he is alone, and bored and restless upon the advent of new people while the social person mixes with them easily and occupies his correct position.

### Effect of the Deficiency of Integration

The most glaring example of a deficiency of integration is seen in the absence of adjustment with the environment, which also exhibits the effects of deficiency. The reason is that in the absence of integration the personality is unbalanced, there being no proper blending of psycho-physical qualities. It is not essential that deficiency of integration will render him incapable of work. Many of the greatest persons suffered from grave deficiencies in the integration of their personalities, but though this did not hinder or restrict their greatness, their personalities were incomplete and one-sided. With people of average capabilities any such deficiency will affect even their skill in behaviour. It may be generally said that in the case of deficiency in integration of personality, the person can neither be skilled in his behaviour nor get success in his life's works. He not only makes his own life disturbed but also disturbs the peace in the lives of others. Thus, psychologists help in the integration of their personalities by giving suggestions.

## PERSONALITY DISINTEGRATION

As an individual, man is a dynamic organisation of psycho-physical traits. His individuality finds expression through his personality, and forms of behaviour, interests, attitudes, capacities and abilities. This personality remains integrated till the individual maintains adjustment with his social environment. A state of personality disintegration sets in when this adjustment breaks down and the individual becomes involved in following mutually contradictory and opposed paths. Personality disintegration of the individual increases when social disintegration is on the increase, but the reverse is no less true. In this manner, in a condition of personality disintegration the individual's social relationships lose their organised character, he fails to perform his roles at all adequately and becomes tendentious towards crime, drink, prostitution, suicide, etc. A very wide gap between his individual values and points of view and the socially accepted values and attitudes is precipitated. But there is no unbridgeable gulf between the organised and disorganised personality, the two having a continuity. In fact, no one individual is either completely organised or completely disorganised as some degree of disorganisation is evident in every individual. As Ralph Linton has said, "We all fail in one way or another, to play exactly the role set up by the group." Hence, personality disintegration is a dynamic and relative concept.

**Definitions**

The following definitions of personality disorganisation will further serve to clarify the concept's nature :

**1. Eliott and Merrill.** "The disorganised individual is unable to play his roles properly in relation to other's and hence sets up reaction for social disorganisation." Every individual has a specific role or roles in society, and he has certain specific relationships with other members of society. The more efficiently the individual's role is performed and the stronger a person's ties in society, the greater will his organisation and integration be. As Ralph Kramer has written, "The individuals are actors in the drama of society and their relationships are the ties that bind them together. Each person is only as strong as his social relationships, for no man lives unto himself alone. Hence although social disorganisation properly refers only to the failure and dissolution of the relationship between individuals, the actors themselves are inevitably involved in the process." In this manner the disorganised individual achieves his own disintegration but at the same time he precipitates social disintegration.

**2. Mowrer.** "All personal disorganisation represents behaviour upon the part of the individual which deviates from culturally approved norms to such an extent as arouses social disapproval." In this manner, the chief feature of personality disintegration is the socially disapproved manner of behaviour, or antisocial activity, such as begging, prostitution, corruption, crime, delinquency, suicide, etc.

**3. Lamert.** "Personal disorganisation is a condition or process in which the person has not stabilised his behaviour around major role. There is conflict and confusion over his choice of roles. Such disorganisation may be transitional or it may be continuous." Definite roles are allotted to individual persons in society so that one single individual can be father, son and some sort of professional simultaneously. If a person succeeds in ordering his behaviour patterns according to the required role, then his mind is constantly in a state of conflict. Gradually, his conflict results in the origin of defects in the mind with the result that the individual engages in antisocial conduct that not only eventually leads to his disorganisation but also seriously imperils the structure of society.

**4. Jansen.** "Thus deviation from accepted norms and standards in attitudes or behaviour may be seen in the maladjusted persons." Personality disorganisation is a condition of maladjustment. Personality is a pattern of adjustment with circumstances, and when this adjustment loses its harmony or becomes defective, the disorganisation of personality occurs. When this happens signs of personality disintegration become prominent and obvious.

### Personality Disintegration and Social Structure

As has been pointed out earlier, the connection between individual and social disorganisation is an intimate one. Cooley rightly remarked, "Social disorganisation is both cause and effect, but the same can be said for personal disorganisation." Personal disorganisation does give rise to social disorganisation, but it at the same time also is consequence. Social disorganisation weakens the controls and influences of society, and the individual conduct becomes uncontrolled and lax when the control exercised by social associations, institutions, communities, groups and traditions becomes weak. For example, if all social restrictions are removed then men and women, in control of the strongest sex drive would be found behaving like animals. As Freud has pointed out after analysis in his book *Civilisation and its Discontents,* human culture is a mode of retaining social control over the individual, and when social control is removed individuals become uncultured. Individual conduct suffers when such institutions as marriage, family, etc., lose their organisation. In this manner personal disorganisation and the social structure are closely related. If the social structure maintains its organisation then individuals will also be organised and integrated, but if it is disorganised the individual's personality will also be disorganised. As the social structure undergoes normal change and development, individual's roles, functions and duties within it also vary. According to Ralph Linton, "The individual finds himself frequently confronted by situations in which he is uncertain both of his own status and roles and those of others." Due to this indecision and lack of certainty people do the wrong things or fail to do what it is their duty to perform. They make demands for rights that are not properly theirs and they forget the duties that are. And the distinction between right and wrong is also lost to them. In such conditions signs of personality disintegration of the individual can be seen writ large.

**Personal Disorganisation and Social Values**

It is only too readily apparent that personal disorganisation and social values are related. In every society every individual is faced with certain values which he constantly tries to achieve, these values being his objectives or aims. And it is their achievement which is the ultimate goal of all his activities. For example, the normal majority of individuals want to win respect in society, and to this end they fashion their conduct so that their objective may be attained. If in a society it is customary that the good man wins, regard then the aim of all those who want to be respected is quite clear, and they can tune their activities accordingly. But if a society tends to respect a person for his wealth even if he be a patently unlikable individual, then all others are not sure of themselves because they do not know whether they should try to be good or they should try to amass wealth by every means at their disposal. In this manner the conflict of values originates, then all others are not sure of themselves because they do not know whether they should try to be good or they should try to amass wealth by every means at their disposal. In this manner the conflict of values originates, as a consequence of which people find it hard to distinguish between the good and the bad. Often they indulge in the very activity that is discarded and roundly rated by their own inner conscience. As a result they develop a guilt consciousness, lose their self-confidence and start on the path to degradation and downfall. Wherever it may start, in wine, prostitution, corruption, crime, all the signs of disintegration slowly manifest themselves.

**Process of Personal Disorganisation**

It is apparent from the above treatment that personal disorganisation is not fixed or continuing state but a continuous process in which there are many stages. Among the many stages, the following are the main ones in personal disorganisation :

**1. Mild disapproval.** The very first phase in personal disorganisation is that of mild disapproval in which the individual indulges in activities which draw a mild rebuff from society. These also win him some slight ill-fame but no positive objection on hindrance is created.

**2. Violent disapproval.** If some of the individual's activities inflict heavy blows on some social values then society objects to it violently and unequivocally. In Indian society, for example, premarital and extra-marital sexual relationships are strongly condemned so that when such relationships come to light they are not only censured but the people involved also face much unpalatable remarks. Violent disapproval also results when one indulges in wine, women, prostitution, etc.

**3. Subjective Social Disapproval.** As has already been remarked, the final result of personality disintegration is that the individual's own mental balance is disturbed. When the society registers violent disapproval of some of his activities, his social emotions are violently injured, since man is naturally a social animal and it is a normal instinct in him to desire social approbation and approval. When this approbation is not forthcoming he is definitely disturbed even if he maintains an outward appearance of indifference. If this respect does not accrue to him even later on, then he loses his self-confidence, and, as a protest, engages in further antisocial activity. But this only serves to accentuate the conflict within him between his social and antisocial instincts. Gradually his personality is disintegrated and when he finds no working solution for this conflict, he becomes tendentious towards suicide as the only solution available.

### Forms of Personal Disintegration

In the foregoing description of the nature and conditions of personal disintegration, there have been occasional references to its various forms : the main ones are the following :

**1. Sex crimes.** Signs of personality disintegration are various such as rape, unnatural sexual intercourse, bestiality, masturbation, etc. Incest and other sexual deviations are also classed as indicative or symptomatic of personality disintegration.

**2. Prostitution.** Another quite prevalent form of personal disintegration is prostituting oneself or indulging in prostitution, the main causes of which are economic conditions, family disintegration or other environmental factors. According to the preface writer of *Women of the Street,* its main cause is a broken family. Other causes of prostitution are industrialisation and hypersexuality. Both forms of prostitution lead to a disintegration of the family, both are unsocial, and both lead to disorganisation of the individual.

**3. Alcoholism and drug addiction.** Another form of personal disintegration is alcoholism and the use of narcotic drugs particularly when an individual cannot live without them, and cannot avoid them even when he so desires. Early drinking, escape drinking and extreme alcoholism are indicative of personal disintegration and these tend to further precipitate this disorganisation.

**4. Suicide.** But the most dangerous form of personal disintegration is suicide. Durkheim, in his *Le Suicide,* has mentioned three kinds of individuals who tend to commit suicide — the altruistic, egoistic and the anomic or those who commit suicide because of inspired social disorganisation.

**5. Crime.** Another major form of personal disorganisation is crime, since the criminal, in the fulfilment of his wishes, chooses the undesirable path instead of desirable one. But the guild consciousness undermines his balance and tends him towards disorganisation which further increases his propensity towards crime.

**6. Juvenile delinquency.** Juvenile delinquency is another cause of personal disintegration and among such delinquents one finds a high percentage of young men and women who suffer from some psychological deficiency or deformation.

**Causes of Personal Disintegration**

There maybe many possible causes of personal disintegration of which the main ones are the following :

**1. Conflict between personal viewpoint and social values.** Individual viewpoints vary as the social conditions of persons change. It is on the basis of these individual viewpoints that the individual develops certain social values. Consequently, the individual standpoints and social values of individuals differ considerably, but normally two forms are adjusted and adapted to each other. Yet there is no necessity for these two sets of values to continue in adjustment or to change correspondingly. And quite often the individual himself is not aware of his own actual viewpoint. Hence, social values and individual viewpoints come into conflict, with the result that the individual is driven to drink, prostitution, crime, etc., even if he does not want it. Ultimately, he finds himself unable to get out of the morass into which he has got himself.

**2. Abnormalities of personality.** Quite the most important source of personal disintegration is an abnormality of the personality. An individual who has it, cannot achieve any adjustment with his circumstances and finds himself unable to fulfil the roles allotted to him by his circumstances and environment. Both these factors combine to develop his guilt and criminal consciousness as also his mental complexes. When these complexes are formed, he tends towards un-natural and improper sexual relationships and other undesirable activities.

**3. Personal disabilities.** Physical as well as mental disabilities prevent the individual from adjusting with his environment efficiently or performing his allotted role, thus improving his chances of becoming disorganised. Normal fulfilment of his desires is made improbable by the very disability, with the result that he is forced to turn to un-natural and improper means of seeking such satisfaction, and in moments of utter dejection or imbalance he even commits suicide.

**4. Conflict between various roles.** Another reason for disintegration is the person's inability to conform his various roles to his different positions in society, by reason of which, for example, he cannot attain any balance between his role as a judge and as a human being.

**5. Social crisis.** Conditions are created by cumulative as well as precipitate crisis in which the individual fails to adjust adequately to changed circumstances. For example, when the one earning member in the family is precipitated into a condition in which his or her disintegration is possible.

**6. Conflict between old and new social values.** There is invariably some difference between old and new social values, that change from generation to generation. But when the gulf between them widens to such an extent that conflict occurs, then men and women lose their guiding light since they are unable to ascertain right and wrong in chaotic conditions of value.

According to Woodworth, "An integrated personality is one of which the several traits, interests and desires are combined in an effective harmonious unity." It is absence of this unity that causes this disintegration. Continued conflict between the individual's various desires and traits over a long period, and the continued inability to find some balance or synthesis is another cause of personality disintegration. This lack of synthesis can be the outcome of many such causes as abnormalities of personality, prolonged conflict, multiple personality, hysteria and other mental diseases, various phobias, weakness of will, abnormal manifestation of instincts and drives, insanity, excessive daydreaming, and many shortcomings of behaviour, such as lack of sociability, irritability, suspicious or quarrelsome nature, etc. The organisation of personality also breaks down when the individual develops mutually contradictory habits. Another cause of this may be the continued and strong opposition between intellect and instincts. Morons and imbeciles find it impossible to adjust between their various interests, desires and tendencies. Hence their personality is normally disorganised. Another cause of personality disintegration can be through physical pain suffered over a long time through disease or suffering from an incurable disease. Organisation of personality is also rendered difficult if desires are continuously expressed or denied satisfaction for a long time. A painful, hard and tenuous life can also lead to such disintegration. According to Freud, sex repression leads to personality disintegration : it is, in fact, the most potent cause of it. The tendency towards self-assertion is a strong one, and when this becomes difficult, the person tends to lose his organised condition of mind and personality. Putting it briefly, excessive repression of natural tendencies, an unhealthy environment, defects of nature and character, mental disease and mental abnormality, weakness of volition or intelligence any of these may cause personal disintegration.

**Cure of Personality Disintegration**

The initial step towards curing a disintegrating personality is the preparation of a case history of the individual so that the causes of this disintegration may be indicated. Hence, the cure and treatment of individual cases of personality disintegration are done on definite lines indicated in the study. Evidently, then there can be no one general method which can cure all cases of personality disintegration, but, nevertheless, the following methods may be used in cure of a majority of cases of disintegration :

1. Suggestion
2. Hypnosis
3. Psychoanalysis.

**1. Suggestion.** Suggestion is an important method in psychotherapy for which it is essential that the patients have full faith, in the doctor and his method of curing. Evidently, what is required for this is a psychologist who can create love and respect in the individual patient for him, and the greater is this love and faith the greater will be the efficacy of the cure. Many mental and neural diseases are cured merely due to his faith and confidence. Auto-suggestion is also sometimes helpful in curing the individual. In this the individual makes suggestions to himself. Counter-suggestion may also prove quite useful and effective, particularly in cases in which simple suggestion does not succeed. In common and simple matters, the psychologist has to explain the causes of his cure to the patient in order to win his confidence. This is called rational suggestion. Briefly, in suggestion, the psychologist first wins the confidence of his patient, and when some intimacy has developed between the two, he cures the patient by suggestion.

**2. Hypnosis.** Suggestion in connection with hypnosis is particularly effective in the cure of personality disintegration. In a hypnotic state, the individual is in a condition of inactivity and sleep, and he, more or less, surrenders, to the psychologist. He accepts suggestions of the psychologist with alacrity, without any criticism or questioning. Hence, in the hypnotic condition, the patient may be suggested cures for mental diseases, relinquishing of bad habits and physical defects that are not organic. Use of suggestion in conjunction with hypnosis has succeeded in the curing of many dangerous mental diseases. But all mental diseases cannot be cured by this method. Yet it is an important method in the cure of many defects of personality.

**3. Psychoanalysis.** By far the best method of curing certain diseases and defects of personality is psychoanalysis. In psychoanalysis the causes of disease are known through free association. The patient is required to relax in a sitting or reclining position and freely express his thoughts and feelings. Gradually, the fundamental causes of his defects and problems come to light, since these normally originate in the repression of instincts. When these tendencies have been discovered, their more harmful aspects are pointed out and then their sublimation, synthesis or substitution is attempted.

However, the christian science of healing is based on faith cure, and even though it is not scientific yet it has shown surprising results. Indian religious texts have also laid much stress on the importance of faith as an element in cure and healing. In this the individual is led to believe that day-by-day, in every way, he is getting better and better. And his difficulties are removed.

Finally, for the cure of personality disintegration, it is essential that the individual learns to face his circumstances, develops a good degree of self-confidence, improves his power of volition, understands his environment and that he learns to sublimate his instincts instead of repressing them. For this it is essential that the individual leads as normal a life as is possible for him. A change of environment often does no good to a person, but sometimes physical treatment is directly needed.

## QUESTIONS FOR EXERCISE

1. What is psychopathic personality? Discuss its aetiology and prognosis.
2. What do you understand by personality integration? Discuss with reference to Multiple Personality.
3. Write an essay on Personality Disintegration.

# 18

# ADJUSTMENT, FRUSTRATION AND STRESS

## MEANING OF ADJUSTMENT

In the words of Laurence F. Shaffer, "Adjustment is the process by which a living organism maintains a balance between its needs and the circumstances that influence the satisfaction of these needs." Accordingly, the process of adjustment has two primary or main elements : one, the needs of the living organism, and two, the conditions or circumstances that influence those needs. These needs can be bio-genic, originating in society, personal or communal, or arising from any other conceivable source. On the other hand, the circumstances influencing these needs also can either be inside the individual or outside him. Factors within the individual that influence these needs are his physical and mental states, capacity, attitudes, interests, etc. For example, most weakly constituted individuals cannot fulfil their own psychological motives, and thus their needs are definitely affected by their lack of strength. Factors arising within the environment are usually geographic conditions, social conditions, political and cultural influences. And, these conditions and circumstances can help as well as deter the fulfilment of the individual's requirements. In this manner, the nature of influences upon the person's needs can be of two kinds — favourable and unfavourable. Positive or favourable influences help in the fulfilment of needs while unfavourable influences hinder their satisfaction.

## THREE ELEMENTS OF ADJUSTMENT

An analysis of the process of adjustment will reveal the presence of three main elements :

**1. Motive.** The very process of adjustment in the living being is set in motion by the presence within him of some motive or need or requirement.

**2. Thwarting conditions.** When the environment does not present any features that tend to become obstacles in the fulfilment of these needs, then the adjustment is natural, tactile and effortless, and no problem results. But if circumstances create obstacles in the path of such fulfilment then the process of adjustment progresses further.

**3. Varied responses.** Once the fulfilment of a need has been obstructed, the individual indulges in various actions which are a reaction to the obstacle. Such a reaction can be normal just as much as it can be abnormal

As a result of these reactions and responses, an individual achieves a degree of adjustment with the circumstances. The problem of adjustment is thereby solved.

### Example of Adjustment

All these various component elements of adjustment can be well understood with the aid of a concrete example. A student is actuated by a strong desire to stand first in his class, and to do so by scoring very well. He works extremely hard but fails to achieve his objective because he has not the necessary mental equipment. Lack of the requisite intelligence forms an obstacle to the satisfaction of this motive, and hence, as a result, the student condescends to lower his aim somewhat by aiming at securing a second division. In order to accommodate this change of objective, the student changes his mode of study. A change of response, a suitable modification of the objective, and the objective is achieved with satisfaction. The adjustment problem is also solved. Such a process of adjustment is an universal phenomenon, and is to be seen at every level of life, at various times and under most conditions.

## MOTIVES AND ADJUSTMENT

Generally speaking, the process of adjustment can be set at motion by any motive; for example, our physical needs are constantly being manifested in the form of adjustive behaviour patterns. But from our point of view these needs do not have much importance, for on the one hand they are easily satisfied, and, on the other, in the event of their dissatisfaction, life itself ceases in the organs, thus obviating all further adjustment activity. Hence, social motives and requirements have greater importance for the adjustment process. Social motives are developed within a cultural environment. Individuals of different cultures have different motives, and different cultures do not generate identical motives. For example, our society requires the development and encouragement of such motives as self-respect, self-realisation, acceptance, security, love, sympathy, etc. and these social motives naturally have definite influences upon sex and other biological needs. Just as social motives have greater importance than physiological needs, in the same manner the processes of adjustment place greater emphasis upon motives that are stronger than others. Strong motives, once they have been excited, can only be satisfied. Inability to satisfy them only leads to further dissatisfaction and this tension is not ended till the objective has been attained.

### Thwarting in Adjustment

It has been remarked earlier that one important element in the process of adjustment is the presence of conditions that thwart the satisfaction of motives. Many are the forms that this thwarting can take, and is known to take. One form is frustration. If, for example, a person fails to catch a train and reach his destination because his wrist-watch was not functioning properly, then he has to face frustration that arises out of the environment. This frustration can also be present in the individual himself. Another form of thwarting of obstacles is conflict. A state of conflict is precipitated when the individual is actuated by more than one motive arising simultaneously. And in the throes of these various motives he cannot decide upon the direction of action that he should adopt. Among the classical examples of a state of conflict and indecision is the state of the mind of Arjuna, described in the *Gita,* when he is divided between war and peace, between indecision and attraction. If similarly, a student wants to continue his interest in games while at the same time he does not want to neglect his academic pursuit, then his mind will be a battlefield of contention between these two desires. The state of conflict and tension will continue till the individual decides upon one particular motive and rejects the other. When conflict extends over a very long period of time, the individual shows signs of mental illness and other abnormalities of behaviour and conduct.

Frustration and conflict, the two forms of thwarting mentioned earlier, are closely related. Normally, when frustration results from some obstruction, the organism involved is seen adopting aggressive and violent behaviour towards the obstacle. Such aggressive behaviour can be direct as well as indirect. In children and unintelligent people, it takes a direct form while in the case of most adults and intelligent people it takes a more indirect manifestation. Now, if the child's normal expression of aggression and violence resulting from some form of frustration is curbed and restricted, then it is actually prevented, but at the same time it becomes repressed and gives rise to feelings of fear and insecurity. Thus, some people become violent on being faced with some frustrating feelings of fear and insecurity as a result of the curb on their aggressive behaviour. As to the mode of behaviour that should be adopted in dealing with obstacles that cause frustration, an individual learns through trial and error. Different situations and circumstances find him behaving differently, and the behaviour patterns of adjustment that satisfy him are repeated while the patterns that cause him displeasure are discarded and replaced. And, the various reactions concerning the adjustment to different frustrations gradually take on the form of habits. Hence, adult individuals display permanent individual differences in the patterns of adjustment.

**Maladjusted Reactions**

Any state that contradicts that of adjustment is called maladjustment. In this condition contradicting that of adjustment, the individual organism fails to maintain a balance between his needs and the circumstances that influence the satisfaction of them. And, in this condition one observes reactions that are tendentious towards further imbalance. Reactions of this kind include all those behaviour patterns which can be called abnormal. For example, all kinds of mental illness will be cited as maladjusted reactions. Maladjustment will be the term to be applied to criminal, delinquent and antisocial behaviour. The maladjusted individual fails to attain to a state of adjustment with his circumstances, and, instead of trying to face up to the situation, tries to turn away from it. Abnormal fears and mental formations are to be seen in the individual. Even his mistakes are construed as no mistakes, and he rationalises upon them. Instead of working to achieve something of his own accord, he identifies himself to achievement of others and thereby satisfies himself. He has very little capacity to cooperate with others, and he finds it difficult to live with them. He prefers solitude and loves to wander in an imaginary world. Extreme daydreaming is a maladjusted reaction. Another example of it is the projection of one's faults upon another and holding him responsible for one's own frustrations. Similarly, many apparently adult individuals are seen behaving in markedly childish manner : this too is a form of maladjusted reaction. Briefly, maladjusted reactions include all such reactions which prove obstacles to adjustment.

## CRITERIA OF PERSONALITY ADJUSTMENT

The implication of adjustment is the balance between an individual's needs and the circumstances that satisfy these needs. Hence, other evaluation of the adjustment achieved by a person will require the knowledge of two things : The first is the requirement of this person and second the conditions and circumstances that influence the satisfaction of his need. Once these two are known it will be necessary to find the balance that is struck between them. If the balance is good and desirable, then the individual can be said to be properly adjusted, but if the balance is disturbed then the person will be considered maladjusted. Evidently, this adjustment will differ from individual to individual, since their needs and the conditions that satisfy them need not be common. In this manner, the criterion of personality adjustment is relative to the individual's requirements and the cultural and social complex of circumstances in which he lives. In other words, the criterion changes when these conditions change. For example, in a culture that encourages the combative and aggressive spirit, men have greater need for their adjustment. On the other hand, in a culture that places very great stress upon ability, the adjustment of personality will depend upon this motive, and it will have great influence upon the criterion of adjustment. Adjustment itself is relative to the individual and his circumstances. Thus, the qualities that are required for adjustment to a particular society and culture cannot be considered efficacious in every society and culture.

Despite the fact that the above limitations are operative everywhere, certain tentative and general criteria of adjustment can be established. Main criteria would be the following :

**1. Integration of personality.** One criterion of adjustment is the integration of personality. Personality system is a complex of all psycho-physical traits. In this the various mental reactions and processes of intelligence and sentiment, desire and determination, etc., do not subsist in any disorder but rather in a proper organised system of functioning. Conflict is quite absent from them. Evidently, the proper integration of the personality is an ideal at which one and all should aim. It is only in such a state that personality is flexible, determined and organised. McDougall calls it the organisation of character and intelligence. The higher the degree of organisation in an individual's personality, the better will be the degree of his adjustment, since in the absence of adjustment personality cannot be integrated and organised. On the other hand, permanent adjustment is not possible in the absence of personality integration. The individual with an adjusted and organised personality maintains a balanced and practical outlook on life. Failures and frustrations do not disturb him unduly and he persists in looking calm and master of the situation. His emotions, needs, thinking and other mental activities are adequately balanced and systematic. On the other hand, the personality of a maladjusted person is disintegrated. His life is disturbed, without any peace and he also tends to disturb peace of everyone else.

**2. Reduction in tension.** Another criterion of personality adjustment is the reduction or decrease in tension, a decrease that is consequent upon the fulfilment of his needs, irrespective of whether the fulfilment is achieved through socially acceptable or objectionable modes. It is a psychological fact that whenever some one or the other need of a person remains dissatisfied it creates a state of tension. And this tension is removed only when the object satisfying that need is obtained. Absence of adjustment results in the increase of tension while its increase helps in reducing tension. In other words, a person's adjustment can be evaluated in terms of tension existing in his mind.

**3. Harmony between needs and environment.** As has been mentioned earlier, the adjusted personality can be recognised from a harmony between his needs and his environment. Greater the degree of such harmony, the better will be his adjustment, while on the other hand his personality will be considered less adjusted if this harmony is not of a high order. An adjusted individual has the capacity and energy to accommodate his needs and motives according to his environment, as also to mould this environment to suit his own needs and motives. In this manner, maximum satisfaction and pleasure are to be had in the mutual adjustment and harmony of both environment and requirement. Persons who fail to make an adjustment of their motives and needs to the environment in which they are placed cannot be happy even in the best of circumstances, and are always to be found complaining of the adversity of conditions. Failure of this kind also meets the individual who has not within him the power and capacity to mould conditions according to his own requirements; his usual condition is one of frustration and maladjustment. Problems are a part of everyone's life, but they also add spice to its otherwise dull fare. There is hardly any, if any at all, individual who is never in his life called upon to face a situation that promises conflict, promises him frustration and anger. If such conditions are present then the enterprising individual bends himself to varying conditions and modify them to suit his own requirements and thus achieves adjustment or otherwise makes changes in his own requirements and needs. For example, it is commonly noticed that some people succeed in making their ends meet very lankly even on a low income, and they give the very appearance of being happy and contented. Contrary to such are people who are incessantly complaining of the paucity of their means even when they have a reasonable income. Theirs is a condition of unhappiness, since there is a wide gap between their income and expenditure; their needs are never even temporarily completely fulfilled. In such a condition, the adjustment of personality is liable to be disturbed from two sides, in the first case the needs of the persons do not conform to the circumstances, and in the second case when the conditions are not propitious to the fulfilment of the need. Hence, adjustment requires the balance between these two, even if modification and alteration are essential in both.

## METHODS OF ADJUSTMENT

Every individual has certain definite needs and every individual lives in certain specific conditions. It is within these conditions that his needs are fulfilled. When the conditions are favourable no particular difficulty arises in such fulfilment, but for every individual this is not always possible. A condition that is not propitious for the fulfilment of some need is not in the life of every individual, and such circumstances and conditions always prove obstacles in the satisfaction of the need thus creating problems. Difficulties refer to the conditions that prove obstacles to the satisfaction of a person's needs. As it is, one finds great individual differences in the manner of reacting to these difficulties. But even then there are certain modes of reaction that can be seen in every pattern of reaction behaviour. These methods are roughly the following :

**1. Constructive adjustment.** One very general form of reaction to difficulties is the mode of constructive adjustment, and examples of this mode of behaviour are to be seen everywhere in life. Students in educational institutions are constantly faced with situations that become obstacles to the achievements of their educational and vocational objectives, praise and knowledge of self needs that are basic to them. Most students have recourse to constructive adjustments in hours of study or consulting numerous books and teachers in order to overcome their academic obstacles. Similarly, when a trader is faced with some problem of his trade, he resorts to some constructive adjustment to solve that problem. If a person is in financial straits then the simplest constructive adjustment would be for him to exercise economy in his expenditure. In constructive adjustment, the main feature to be marked is that he offers a lot of facing to the situation rather than running away from, and of making efforts that solve the problem instead of merely postponing it.

**2. Substitute adjustment.** All individuals do not have the ready wit and wisdom to achieve constructive adjustment and thus retain their mental balance in the face of difficulties. A very large number of individuals have recourse to substitute adjustments when faced with difficult situations. This also is a common and usual method of reacting to difficulties. For example, in a large number of cases, when students fail to pass at an examination, then, instead of urging them to work harder, they take it upon themselves to blame the teachers in particular and the entire educational system in general, and daydream themselves into success in future. Some students start avoiding school when they fail while other more enterprising though more censured are the ones who leave home. The question that now arises is whether these reactions are adjustive activities in the situation. A closer observation will reveal that even through such reactions, the individual is trying to satisfy needs that other individuals have solved through constructive and positive adjustment activity. A student failing in an examination is usually defamed and this obstructs his social ambitions and motives. Tensions that are created through this obstruction he tries to end by his activity of running away or transferring the blame on the teachers or by daydreaming of success. Thus, for this reason, these reactions to difficulties are called substitute reactions. Even though direct satisfaction is forthcoming from such activity, yet the unsatisfied motive is indirectly and momentarily pacified, and in this manner adjustment is improved through decrease in tension. It must be noticed that adjustment is not a question of successful results, but one of satisfaction of motives, irrespective of the methods that are adopted, be they normal, originating in disease and mental deficiency. It is often remarked that in weak and lean individuals, the motive of self-respect is suppressed, and in order to overcome this repression, instead of resorting to some form of constructive adjustment, they walk with a swagger, thus saving their self-respect from injury and their mental balance from collapse. Here, it must be remarked that this should not be interpreted to mean that the satisfaction afforded to a motive by constructive adjustment is equal to the satisfaction caused by a substitute adjustment. The facts of the matter are other than this. Reactions of substitute adjustment usually win scorn and ridicule for the person practising them, from other members of society, and this life's ignoble strife can save his desire for competition from being frustrated. Hence, it is evident that the substitute adjustment usually results only in more frustration and suppression. On the other hand, these modes of adjustment are also usually harmful for the individuals are seen trying to attract female attention through undesirable activity since they cannot win it in the normal course, and this usually results in great inconvenience to other more reasonable members of society. One characteristic of proper and constructive adjustment is that not only the individual but the entire society benefits from it, besides improving the individual's social relationships.

**3. Mental mechanisms.** Another mode of reacting to difficulties is that of mental mechanisms, main among them being projection, compensation, rationalisation, etc. As a general rule, the consequence of these mechanisms is not good either for the individual or for society. Yet, in some degree or other all or some of those mechanisms are to be found in every individual, hence no individual can be declared abnormal on their account. It is only when one of them develops out of proportion that symptoms of abnormality can be discovered. Normally, a tendency to overlook one's own fault and to blame others for one's failures is only naturally present in man, but if a person is observed doing this all the time and unduly regarding everyone else his enemy, then his conduct will undoubtedly be classed as abnormal. These mechanisms are also called the tolls of adjustment since their objective is the attainment of adjustment through various methods.

## KINDS OF ADJUSTIVE REACTIONS

**1. Adjustive reactions.** Adjustive reactions, as is evident from the name, are those reactions that achieve an adjustment between the individual and his circumstances. In this manner constructive adjustment reactions are included as adjustive reactions. As a general rule the simplest method available to a person to satisfy his motive when conditions exist to frustrate them is to redouble his efforts to achieve his satisfaction and to do so with patience and persistence. When poverty besets the normal individual, he does his best to overcome it by earning wealth, working hard and laboriously, and normally he meets with reasonable success. His economic position improves, and most of his motives arrive at a stage of satisfaction. On the other hand, there are other individuals who avoid a condition of stress and controlling emotions and motives in a manner that leads to reasonable adjustment and compromise with circumstances. Consequently, much of their existence is free from frustration. Hence the class of adjustive reactions includes all actions and behaviour that aim at the control and delimiting of this motive or the adjustment of circumstances so that some equilibrium between motives and the conditions of their satisfaction is attained. One very important feature of adjustive reactions is that it benefits the individual organism as well as the community organisms, or at least is not harmful to such community.

**2. Partially adjustive reactions.** All reactions aimed at facing obstacles so as to satisfy motive are not completely and entirely successful in achieving their objective. Some of them succeed only in attaining a partial adjustment. Simple examples of such partially successful adjustive reactions are daydreaming as well as other forms of escape from troublesome situations. For example, a majority of poor individuals, instead of making constructive efforts to ameliorate their condition, indulge in making castles in the air, with the result that their weakness fails to pinch them as it would otherwise do. People of this kind are of a very optimistic bent of mind, and even though they never try they are never frustrated, constant in the hope that their day will turn, that every dog has his day, that some relative will leave them a legacy or that they will win a pool. Some partial and temporary adjustment of a kind is definitely achieved by this escapist dreaming, but no individual can get complete happiness through this kind of imaginative adjustment. Evidently, reactions of this kind do not achieve any considerable adjustment.

**3. Non-adjustive reactions.** Non-adjustive reactions as a class are activities that do not achieve any adjustment at all between the individual and his conditions. For instance, some people do not attend to some motive even when it is persistently and continually being frustrated, and they continue in activities that do not bring satisfaction for this motive. Consequently, from the standpoint of this particular motive, their activities can only be classed as non-adjustive. Poverty, to take an oft-repeated example, is painful for everyone, but many scholars ignore its demands and pass their days in scholarly and academic pursuits. And, these activities in the pursuit of knowledge and pedantry prove non-adjustive reactions for all those motives that are frustrated because of the individual's financial poverty since he makes no effort to satisfy them. Sex instinct is commonly repressed, and when this happens some people, instead of doing something to satisfy it, only choose to repress it all the more, but the efforts at repression and suppression are only non-adjustive reactions, as they achieve no real adjustment at all.

**4. Maladjustive reactions.** These activities, or reactions, do succeed in achieving some adjustment, but as a type of adjustment that is of a wrong kind; it harms the individual organism as well as the community of organism. This class of reactions includes all kinds of adjustive mechanisms or mental mechanisms. Frustration is to some extent avoided and postponed by the individual when he succeeds in convincing himself that someone else is to blame for his failure, but doing so only endangers his mental relationships, and ultimately he and others come to harm. Besides, the person who finds satisfaction in the achievements of other individuals by identifying himself with them gives some appearance of being adjusted, but he neither himself progresses nor does he afford assistance to others in their progress and development. Individuals who choose to satisfy their desires and overcome their frustrations through daydreaming are not likely to succeed in practical affairs of life, and waste their time to no end. Excessive repression that takes place in individuals who cannot find other means of satisfying their motives and drives usually leads to the development of common errors of daily life, abnormal behaviour and mental illness or even derangement. Consequent upon such a condition is much embarrassment for themselves as well as for others. Society glares at and vociferously criticises people who have recourse to mal-adjustive reactions and ultimately it causes them much pain and discomfort.

From the above description it is fairly evident that maladjustive reactions differ essentially from adjustive and partially adjustive reactions in this that while they do lead to some sort of adjustment, they also jeopardise the person's social relationships. Secondly, reactions of this kind are source of many forms of abnormal behaviour and mental diseases. Consequently, people with such tendencies require expert treatment and advice.

## FRUSTRATION

### What is Frustration?

According to J.C. Coleman, "Frustration is the results of the thwarting of motive either by some obstacle that blocks or impedes progress towards a derived goal, or by the absence of appropriate goal object." Conflict with various factors in the environment in search of satisfaction for his desires is a normal condition of human life. No man in the world can entirely fulfil his desires. Failure in the satisfaction of most of our motives is marred by obstacles and troubles. Naturally, our desire or motive remains unsatisfied on this account. Frustration is the natural consequence of such difficulty. It is a kind of hopelessness and disgust. It destroys the person's enthusiasm, his tension in life is increased, and sometimes he becomes the victim of complete despair. Hence, frustration is a mental condition which is resultant upon our failure to satisfy some motive or the other. Main features of a frustrated state of mind are — extremity of tension, sense of inferiority, lack of peace and various kinds of mental mechanisms.

### Reactions to Frustration

Reactions to frustration also succeed in elucidating its nature. Main forms of reactions to it are the following :

**1. Creation of or increase in emotional tension.** A child is naturally and very strongly motivated and inclined to go out of house and to play with other children of his own age. If he is prevented from doing so he envinces definite signs of labouring under great emotional tension, and this tension remains till the frustrated emotion or motive succeeds in finding some mode of release. And this expression can take the normal form or instead it can be manifested through different kinds of mental mechanisms.

**2. Increase in effort.** A healthy person's reaction to frustration is in the form of increased efforts towards overcoming the obstacle causing the frustration. For example, if a student fails to secure good marks at one of the terminal examination, then, instead of being completely discouraged and deprived of the will to try, he redoubles his effort so that success in future may be made possible, and often this does come to pass. Actually, when frustration falls to a person's lot in life, then, he should think upon the causes of that frustration, since it is not essential that the frustration is inevitably the outcome of a low degree of enterprise in the individual. It is possible that the work he is trying to perform is outside his capability, as not many students succeed in studying a subject that interests them not. But if the failure to attain a goal is the result of our lack of effort or enterprise, then the best one can do is to step up to make effort, in complete disregard of the frustration suffered.

**3. Different approach.** Another cause why frustration holds our footsteps in life is often the choice of wrong method of approach. For example, many of the students are not aware of the method of studying that should be adopted for scoring well in an examination, as a result of which they fail to do it, despite their best, concentrated effort. If frustration is the outcome of such faulty orientation, the success can be had for the asking in the future by changing one's method of approach, and quite a number of people intuitively realize this fact. When a sensible man fails to attain his objective through one approach he immediately tries another, and in this manner sticks to trial and error till he discovers the one correct method of action.

**4. Change of objective.** On the other hand, when some people fail to obtain their object, they avoid frustration in this line by changing their very goal. And the goal can be changed in the following ways : first, by reducing the objective and aiming at lower level, and second by entirely adopting a different goal. For example, every student who chooses to study has not the capacity or ability to stand first in an examination : hence if all of them have this object then frustration is only going to be naturally theirs. When this does happen, some students choose to aim at the second division while certain others aim still lower and choose only to succeed at the examination without talking in terms of merit. Frustration is thereby avoided. Other students may even lose their interest in academic pursuit and turn to trade and commerce, where success may or may not meet them.

**5. Feeling of inferiority.** All the reactions to frustration mentioned so far are simple and straight forward and can be seen in a large majority of individuals but there are certain other reactions that are more indicative of abnormal behaviour.

For example, when frustration meets certain people they do not only refuse to change their method but also their aim, in other words, they do not accommodate themselves and, instead, get into the habit of regarding themselves as very weak and helpless, hapless and unfortunate. A tense mental state of this kind is called the feeling of inferiority. A person full of the inferiority feeling looks to his own shortcomings and is always afraid of inviting criticism from and disregard of others. Mental characteristics such as suspicion, jealousy, criticism of others, anxiety, introvert tendencies fear of competition, high emotional excitability towards criticism, very profound reactions to failure, etc., are to be seen in his life. This sense of inferiority is not caused by actual deficiency of interests and abilities in the individual. It has instead been that many unintelligent students do not allow this sense of inferiority to step near them, and despite repeated failures continue to make gorgeous plans of the future, while on the other hand many very acutely intelligent students develop a sense of inferiority even on the slightest failure. Thus, the sense of inferiority is a concomitant not of capacity but of character. Very highly ambitious people have very many frustrations and thus their sense of inferiority once it is developed is also strong. For example, when a student hopes to get a first division and gets a second instead, he is beset by the feeling of inferiority, whereas other students feel very puffed up merely because they have succeeded in passing the examination.

Congruently, it can be reasoned that in order to avoid the sense of inferiority away from him the individual should first of all try to aim at something that is within his own capabilities to achieve, and secondly he should spare no effort to attain this end. There is a proverb : Know what you can do and do it like a Hercules. Success does not come easily when one does not know what one is capable of or one does not pursue an objective with all the ability at one's disposal, after one has become sure that it is within his capacity. It is this simple formula of success that led some common men to the most coveted and revered positions in the world. Ram Murti, a famous wrestler, was a lean and thin person in his youth, and it was through rigid application and continued effort that he became a great wrestler. Hellen Keller was born blind and deaf but through her indomitable courage and unconquerable will she became a wonderful writer and a fine orator, besides becoming a symbol of these qualities for all the world to look up and to emulate. It is evident from these examples that the sense or feeling of inferiority is not bad in itself since it can conceivably spur the individual to great and immense effort which may bring him great success. But if this healthy reaction towards the inferiority feeling does not take place, then, it develops into a very harmful mental complex as a result of which the individual becomes abnormal and a mentally diseased person.

**6. Aggressive behaviour.** Often, the reaction to frustration takes the form of aggressive behaviour. It is proverbially said that the bad worker blames his tools since he wants to transfer the blame for his failure to the tools. It is observed commonly that when people are scolded in office for their inefficient work, they work off their steam and chagrin by being angry with the children at home. When in an aggressive mood, sparked off by frustration, an individual can, directly or indirectly, launch an attack on others, but in quite a large majority of people this wrath turns in upon themselves rather than on other people or objects. They take to beating their heads with their hands or banging it into the nearest wall, while the more disturbed commit suicide. It is because of this close intimacy between frustration and aggressive behaviour which has been observed that some psychologists have cited frustration as an important cause of war, and they have further suggested that if wars are to be eliminated from human society, then such conditions be created in which frustration of every field of life be at their minimum possible. The most dangerous forms of aggressive behaviour are the consequences of sex frustration. Such a fact is out if we study the life history of notorious master born criminals.

**7. Mental mechanisms.** Sometimes the reaction to frustration is evident in the form of mental mechanism, the ones being fantasy, compensation, identification, projection, sublimation and rationalisation. The following are their examples :

(i) ***Fantasy :*** Any motive of a person that is frustrated in the actual world is satisfied in an imaginary world through the medium of fantasy.

(ii) ***Compensation :*** When people are frustrated in their desires in one direction, they compensate for it by attaining success to pre-eminent degree in other directions. An ugly girl, for example, becomes very learned and scholarly.

(iii) ***Identification :*** Many people who find no successes in their lives at all, find satisfaction and pleasure in identifying themselves with different great people and with their children whose success brings them the sense of having themselves succeeded.

(iv) ***Projection :*** When frustrated, some avoid its consequences by projecting their own shortcomings upon others, and by holding them responsible for their failure. Many students console themselves for failing at examination by blaming their teachers and the educational system in general.

(v) ***Rationalisation :*** Again, the consequences of frustration are bypassed by certain other individuals who, instead of probing the cause of their failure, choose to put forward convincing reasons and arguments for their failure to succeed.

(vi) ***Sublimation :*** When frustration comes to the life of certain other individuals they choose to turn into directions accepted and credited by society, and thus find satisfaction for their motives. For example, the consequences of sexual frustration can be avoided by turning to the study of various fine arts.

### Sources or Causes of Frustration

Having gained a fair working knowledge of the nature and consequences of frustration, it is now possible to pursue analysing its sources. The main causes or sources are the following :

**1. Objective beyond one's power.** As has been pointed out, for achieving success it is essential that the individual's objective should be within his power and capacity. Many people pose before themselves objectives that have no regard of their actual capability and are outside their reach. As a consequence their life becomes a tale of frustration and woe, and they always appear disconsolate, anxious, irritable and disturbed. Here it is necessary to understand that according to psychology every individual cannot be made into anything, Hence, an individual should take care to select an objective and aim that is within his power, and having done so, should exert himself to the very utmost.

**2. Lack of requisite effort.** But when frustration meets some effort of ours it should not be taken for granted that it is outside our power, since the failure may be due to lack of necessary effort, or due to a wrong approach and defective methodology. These difficulties can be overcome with ease.

**3. Competition.** Frustration would have been an unknown phenomenon in human life if every pleasure and all the good things of life had been freely available, as are water and air. But this is not the condition with regard to most physical prerequisites. There are very many things and qualities such as wealth, money, land, property, beauty, attractive personality, great character, fame, etc., in which there is not enough of it to go round, as the saying is. The desire to possess them is present in every individual, and a degree of cut-throat competition exists between all people for them. Frustration and failure come to many in this unequal struggle, and bliss only to a very few.

**4. Social and cultural obstacles.** Another very fundamental cause of frustration consists in the taboos inflicted upon the manifestation of our motives by society and culture. In his book *Civilization and its Discontents,* Freud, the famous psychoanalyst, has shown how man has had to pay the price of civilization in terms of frustration and mental agony. And among the various social and cultural taboos the most effective and the most powerful is the one concerned with sex instinct and its manifestation, and Freud has indulged in a detailed consideration of the mental aberrations and abnormalities resultant upon such restraint. Anthropologists have found that fewer frustrations are to be seen in the population of ancient tribal people in which social and cultural taboos are fewer than in the allegedly more civilized societies.

**5. Physical causes.** Man exists in a physical environment upon the machinations of which he has little control, hence such physical phenomena and events as flood, plague, earthquakes, excessive rain, drought, etc., are some of the sources of frustration in man.

**6. Political causes.** Every human individual is part and parcel of a political organisation, and the manifestation of many of his instincts is controlled and limited by the state. Hence the result for this control is evident in the frustration of numerous motives that would otherwise have been satisfied. Frustrations arising from the above sources can be simple just as much as they can be complex. Simple frustrations are very much a part of every person's life and are often a spur to one's activity since they increase our enthusiasm to achieve some end that is eluding us but the arising of complex frustrations can lead to a person becoming tendencious towards abnormality and mental disease. Such states and calamities can be avoided if we try to keep a sane and healthy outlook in these frustrations. And the first step towards such a healthy and sane outlook is the clear realisation that frustration is a natural and inevitable part of human life. Many thinkers have gone so far as to opine that frustration is essential if success is to be attained and prosperity achieved. Secondly, when a frustration thrusts itself on our mind we should consider it with a cool mind, search for its causes, and make an effort to get rid of them. In this manner we can evade the worst consequences of frustration.

## STRESS

The term stress in medicine and biology today is used in a number of different ways. It may refer to external forces or conditions experienced by the organisms, or to the reaction of the organism to these. When applied to external forces the term stress is similar to its use in physics and applies to an external stimulus or force which is strain-producing, or potentially strain-producing, to the person to whom it is applied. Anything may be considered a stress if it threatens the biological integrity of the organism, whether directly by its physical or chemical properties or indirectly because of its symbolic meaning.

Selye uses the term 'a state of stress' to denote a specific syndrome occurring in the body in response to certain agents to which he refers as 'stresses'.

In medicine and psychiatry, the term stress is usually used to denote various psychosocial situations which can produce disorganisation of behaviour, including physical and mental illnesses.

A convenient definition of stress is any stimulus or change in the external or internal environment which disturbs homeostasis which, under certain conditions, can result in illness. According to Coleman, "Stress, like a motive, may be partly or wholly unconscious, though the presence of uneasiness or anxiety may be the clue that stress is present. Stress is inevitable and sometimes chosen voluntarily : mental health results not from lack of stress but ability to cope with it satisfactorily."

Stress cannot be considered in isolation. We need to know what stimuli or situations are potentially stressful and we need to know the effect produced by such stresses on the organism and, finally, the pathways and mechanisms mediating the organism's response to stresses.

**Stress, Distress and Disease**

According to W.L. Linford Rees, "Stress can be defined as stimulus or change in the external or internal environment of such a degree in terms of strength or intensity or duration as to tax the adaptive capacity of the organism to its limit, and which, in certain circumstances, can lead to a disorganisation of behaviour or a dysfunction which may lead to disease. What may constitute a stress may consist of physical stimuli, infections (bacterial, viral or fungal) or allergic reactions, or may refer to a whole series of stimuli or change in the social or psychological spheres of life".

**Stresses and Coping Mechanisms**

Selye's (1950) definition of a stress is one which evokes the manifestation of a General Adoption Syndrome. Thus this is a physiological response, and the effect of the stress can be measured in terms of action on the hypothalamus, the adrenal cortex, the sympathetic-adreno-medullary system, and the secretion of different hormones. Physiological stresses differ from psychical stresses in that the power or force of the psychosocial stress will be determined not only by its inherent threat but also by the way in which the individual perceives and appraises the significance of the potentially challenging event, and what degree of threat he perceives as appertaining to the stimulus situation. When an event is perceived as being harmful or threatening, a variety of coping mechanisms may be used as a defence. Reality may be discounted by denial, which is a very common mode of dealing with distressing events, including illnesses like cancer, leukaemia and myocardial infection. The degree of subjective distress may be modified by displacement, *e.g.*, anxiety or hostility into smiling or laughter, into sleep, or into eating, drinking or smoking. Other coping mechanisms are rationalisation and self-deception (which are merely manifestations of denial) and withdrawal from the stressful stimulus or situation. These coping mechanisms can ameliorate the experience or distress as well as its bodily concomitants. According to W.L. Linford Rees, "Distress denotes an unpleasant emotional experience which may arise in response to environment influences or to changes in some internal environment, or as a reaction to some disease or disability." To quote W.L. Linlord Rees, again, "Disease is a notoriously difficult term to define, but for pragmatic purposes the term disease is used to denote disability arising from bodily or mental malfunction which imposes difficulties in coping with everyday work and responsibilities, interferes with well-being and produces distress."

The theme is shown in the following figure. We will consider the ways in which stresses produce distress in the individual and in which, in certain circumstances, they may produce disease, which in turn can also cause distress by the threat of the illness itself, or the disability it causes.

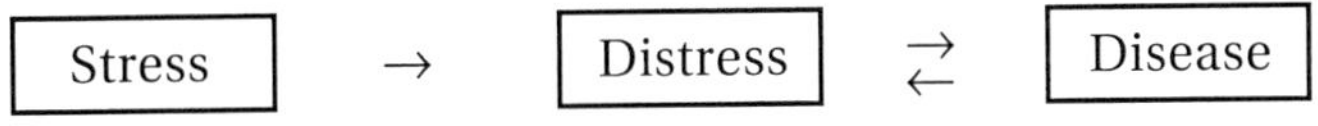


**Sequences of Events**

The sequence of events which occur in the mediation of the effects of stimuli which may be physical or may be psychological stresses on the individual. The individual's response to such stimuli will be influenced by genetic-constitutional factors and by the environmental modification of his genetic make-up.

**Previous Experience**

Previous experiences, particularly in childhood, may also influence the susceptibility to respond to psychosocial stresses. These stimuli, acting on the individual, give rise to bodily changes involving hypothalamic pituitary control of adrenal and other endocrine glands and a variety of biochemical and physiological changes which may constitute the precursors of disease, and these in turn, if they continue, lead to disease. These changes may be modified at all stages.

**Coping Mechanisms**

We have noted the effects of coping mechanisms. It is sometimes possible to modify the response of the individual by changing the internal environment, *e.g.* at the premenstrual phase. It is possible to modify the mechanisms involved in the precursors of disease by psychotropic drugs or psychological means to prevent the changes actually leading to disease.

## STRESS AND LIFE CHANGES

Holmes and Rahe quantified life events giving point value to life changes that require adaptation. They found that there was a critical level at which too many of these events happening during a one-year time span to one person, put that person at great risk of illness. Of those people who accumulated 300 points in one year were 80 per cent at risk of illness in the near future, with 155 to 299 points, 50 per cent became ill in the near future. Of those with fewer than 150 stress points, 30 per cent became ill shortly after the life events.

**Social Readjustment Scale**

| | | |
|---|---|---|
| 1. | Death of spouse | 100 |
| 2. | Divorce | 73 |
| 3. | Marital separation from mate | 65 |
| 4. | Detention in jail or other institution | 63 |
| 5. | Death of close family member | 63 |
| 6. | Major Personal injury or illness | 53 |
| 7. | Marriage | 50 |
| 8. | Being sacked from work | 47 |
| 9. | Requirement from work | 45 |
| 10. | Changing to different type of work | 26 |

It has been found that situations relating to occupation, marriage and parenthood were the most likely to produce anxiety and depression. The life changes affected both sexes but women were more vulnerable, also the poor and disadvantaged groups were more vulnerable. The change created significant strain when it was unexpected and when it not only involved adjustment to a loss, for example a job, but the need to adjust to a new status that involved further hardships and problems.

Loss of work constitutes a stress and may tax the adaptive capacity of the person to the maximum, particularly, if it means marked loss of financial status, marked loss of prestige, or creates additional problems with the family.

### Psychological Phases in the Event of Unemployment

Following the event of unemployment, the individual goes through a series of psychological phases :

**1. Shock and disbelief.** Initial response, as in bereavement, is one of shock and, depending on the circumstance, disbelief. During this phase the worker maintains a certain degree of optimism, regards his loss as only temporary and tends to look at his new situation as if it were a long deserved holiday. He will further stick to this idea if he has received considerable redundancy settlement. This is time when the handyman about the house comes to the fore and completes overdue jobs about the house.

**2. Reality Inescapable.** This is one in which the reality in all its harshness becomes inescapable. The holiday feeling is over, money is getting short and there are no more jobs to do around the house.

The first attempts at job finding having been unsuccessful, the 'unemployed identity' slowly develops. The day is spent in forced and meaningless leisure and there is a feeling of inertia with its debilitating effect on personal self-esteem. The concept of time changes drastically, days will seem to fly past with nothing to distinguish them or to remember them by. They often lose interest in what day of the week it is, they feel exhausted and lacking in energy and most of the day is spent in bed. Tensions develop between members of the family. Petty disagreements are likely to become full blown arguments. An adjustment during this period will depend on whether the ex-worker felt he was sacked unjustly or selectively, or on his ability to accept a low status job if these are the only ones available, and on the extent to which support is provided by the family.

**3. Unemployed state.** The third phase is defined by Fagin as the 'unemployed state'. A new non-occupational identity has now been established with the necessary psychological adjustment. The anxiety and depression characteristics of the earlier phase lift and the family and the individual settle down to the new standards and a different way of life. The job seeking is not done regularly and actively but in a haphazard, casual way, without any real hope of change. Social activities are curtailed, for emotional and financial reasons. At this stage there is a general feeling of inferiority, submissiveness and inability to provide sufficiently for himself or his family. This has been called the broken state.

**4. Influence on personality.** The unemployed state as it continues in time has an indelible effect on the individual personality which will remain unchanged even in future situations of economic prosperity and full employment. There is statistical evidence to indicate that with longer past periods of unemployment, there is an increased chance of losing their jobs through inability or redundancy.

**5. Influence on health.** Kasl and Cobb carried out an interesting prospective longitudinal inquiry on the effect on the health of employees when a firm closed down in Pakistan. Blood pressure recordings taken at monthly intervals revealed that blood pressure rose during the time that closure was anticipated; and continued at this higher level for those remaining unemployed, only returning to normal levels upon, or a few months after, re-employment. The increased blood pressure readings were correlated closely with measures of depression, irritation and loss of self-esteem. Increased serum uric acid levels followed the same pattern as the blood pressure.

**6. Influence on family life.** Entire families are likely to be affected by the consequences of unemployment by the wage-earner. Jahoda studied the effects of unemployment on family life during the great recession years in a village in Austria. Families lost interest in events, and were broken apart owing to forced and unwilling emigration. The women seemed to bear the greatest burden and assumed a central rote in the family. Jones found similar disruption of the family in unemployment areas of the Welsh valleys.

The most vulnerable groups are the extreme age groups, the young and the old workers, the unskilled, the immigrants, the disabled and the executive class. The professional and managerial staff suffer dramatic psychological changes following redundancy as shown by Hardy and Cooper and Tarrant.

**Effect on Morbidity and Mortality**

Harvey Brenner found an increase in deaths due to heart and kidney disease, cirrhosis of the liver, homicides and higher rates of admissions to mental hospitals and prisons among the unemployed. Harvey Brenner, who was a leading research worker in the field, found in a number of studies a relationship between the state of economy and the state of an American subject's physical and mental health. He found that as unemployment increases, so do mental hospital admissions and the suicide rate. He found that it is not people with a previous history of mental disorder and hospitalisation who account for the increase in admissions. Studies in the United Kingdom from 1950-56 also revealed that hospital admissions rise with unemployment. Women show a greater sensitivity to economic change and that the two groups most at risk are women between 20 and 24 and men between 35 and 44. It is reported that the unemployed suffered much higher levels of anxiety, guilt, hostility, self-criticism, personal distress and were comparable to a group of mixed neurotic disorders. George Brown, in his survey of depressed women in South London, found that one of the factors that made them vulnerable to depression after certain life events was lack of employment outside the home.

## QUESTIONS FOR EXERCISE

1. What is adjustment? What is its importance for human life? Explain fully the meaning of adjustment. What are the maladjusted reactions?
2. Critically explain the criteria of personality adjustment. What are the common modes of reaction to difficulties?
3. Distinguish between adjustive, partially adjustive, non-adjustive and maladjustive reactions and point out their distinctions.

4. What is meant by frustration? What are its sources and forms of reactions?
5. Write short note on Stress.
6. Show the relationship of stress and life changes with particular reference to event of unemployment.

# 19

# Psychology of Mental Hygiene and Mental Health

## What is Mental Hygiene?

Mental hygiene is the science that creates a personality in every individual in society that makes for good adjustment with the environment, that attains a proper synthesis between the intellectual, emotional and physical aspects, that is satisfied and optimistic, that experiences a minimum of tension and conflict in its conduct with other individuals in society. The aim of mental hygiene is the evolution and development of a properly adjusted and balanced personality. Briefly, the following can be its objectives :

1. **Treatment and remedying of mental defects.** Defining mental hygiene, Lawrence F. Shaffer has written that mental hygiene or the science of mental health is concerned with the prevention of inadequate adjustment or with those processes or methods which adjust the maladjusted individual. This first function of mental hygiene is the curing of ailments, defects and imbalances.

2. **Preventing of personality complications.** But the curative aspect of hygiene does not exhaust its possibilities. This science prevents all kinds of personality disorders, since all mental diseases originate in them. According to Thomas V. Moore, mental hygiene is that science which studies the human personality, and its deviations, from the curative standpoint. In this manner, another objective of mental hygiene is the curing or removal of abnormalities of the personality, since it is only in the absence of such aberration that the individual can be balanced. Abnormality leads to imbalance, all kinds of mental conflicts and disease. Prevention of such diseases takes

the form both of curing them as well as prevention of further procreation from such parents since diseases are likely to be transmitted through heredity.

**3. Safeguard of mental health.** The most comprehensive function of mental hygiene is the safeguard of mental health. According to D.B. Klein, mental hygiene prevents mental aberrations and advances mental health. Mental hygiene consistently stresses the development or creation of such qualities in the individual as optimism, confidence, cooperation, emotional adjustment and maturity, etc. It points out the means of improving the adaptability and efficiency of individuals.

## ASPECTS OF MENTAL HYGIENE

From the description of its objectives it is apparent that mental hygiene has three prominent aspects — curative, preventive and preservative. In its curative aspect, it indicates ways and means of curing mental deviations, defects and imbalances. Ways and means of preventing them or counteracting them are suggested by it under its preventive function while in its preventive guise it puts forward rules and suggestions by following which any and every individual can ensure his mental health.

## WHAT IS MENTAL HEALTH?

On the basis of the foregoing description of its meaning, its objectives and its various aspects, it is possible to design a makeshift description and definition of mental hygiene. This will further help to clarify its meaning and promote its scientific enquiry the precise definition of the subject matter, even if it be incomplete to some extent. Some of the definitions of mental hygiene have already been given. One or two definitions are more comprehensive, as for example, in the *Encyclopaedia of Modern Education,* the definition of mental hygiene has been given as that approach to human adjustment and achievement which is related to the prevention of emotional maladjustment and preparation of the individual for skilled working. According to the *Dictionary of Education,* mental hygiene is the science which studies the principles and practices of preventing mental disorders and promoting mental health. Both the above definitions, though better than others, are yet incomplete since they do not emphasize all the three aspects of mental hygiene.

Thus, mental hygiene is that science which studies laws and means of curing and preventing mental diseases, personality disorders and complications; it also discovers creative measures for the balancing, adjustment and healthy development of personality.

## SCOPE OF MENTAL HYGIENE

Mental hygiene comprehends the curing of mental defects, diseases, and abnormalities as well as the prevention of such abnormalities, beside the active preservation of mental health, balance, pleasure and adjustment, etc., of the individual. Evidently, then, the scope of mental hygiene is very vast. It comprehends the entire life of the individual. Every individual stands in need of mental health. Young children, men and women experience difficulty in adjusting to new circumstances which lead to mental complications and difficulties, that, in turn, endanger mental health. Hence, it is they who stand in greatest need of mental health and hygiene. In old age, when man is past his prime, his energy is on the decrease. There are very few ways in which he can pass his time, his children are busy in the affairs of their own families, while the young girls in the family have gone to their husbands. When retired from service, even the source of income is blocked. And one foot is already in the grave, as they say. Some or the other minor ailment of the body is always present, hence it is at such times that mental health is challenged the most. If, in such a state, one is to lose one's life partner, it is the last straw for the poor individual. What greater shock can there be for an individual to have his mother die at an early age, and the wife to die in old age? Hence, mental hygiene is needed very greatly by the old and senile people. Besides children and senile folk, some adults in the prime of life also require mental hygiene since their mental balance is disturbed and personality disordered for some or the other reason. Such an individual can be recruited from lists of drunkards, confirmed alcoholics, gamblers, corrupt individuals and people who frequent prostitute homes, etc. They are themselves mentally diseased persons, but they are also potential threats to the mental health of society in general. Their personalities are disorganised and they improve the social disorganisation of society. And the list of sufferers is completed by people who have already lost their mental balance, who are prey to mental defects, diseases and aberrations. They require mental treatment and cure.

## MENTAL HEALTH AND MENTAL HYGIENE

Curative and preventive aspects of mental hygiene have been depicted clearly in the foregoing description, but its preservative aspects remain to be delineated. Hence, even healthy individuals require mental hygiene as they stand to benefit by its preservative function. In other words, people who are healthy from the mental standpoint are also in need of mental hygiene. In practical life, there is no individual who can be declared completely healthy. Secondly, even if he is healthy at one moment there can be no guarantee that he will continue in the same state of health. Man's adjustment to the environment is not a static condition but rather a gradual dynamic process. The question of adjustment is for ever present before the individual since man's condition is for ever changing somewhat. Hence, there is no saying when an individual, who is at present manifesting the most perfect adjustment, may have cause to lose his mental balance. Consequently, he requires mental hygiene to see to it that he is not deprived of his mental bliss and happiness.

From the above description it is evident that the scope of mental hygiene is not contained by any considerations of age since it is required by young, old, adolescent, man, woman, the healthy and the unhealthy alike. Its sphere extends from the home to school, factory, office, shop, market, meetings, society, in fact everywhere. It is needed in all human relationships and activities.

### Value of Mental Hygiene

Description of the meaning and scope of mental hygiene also helps to clarify its value. Its value and efficacy consists not only in the curing and preventing of mental health in the individual fortunately blessed with it. It is of value for young, old, men, women, boy, girl, healthy, insane, in fact for everyone. Even able-bodied beings require physical hygiene for its values and significance. Hence, the requirement of mental hygiene in every sphere of human life — home, school, playground, office, profession, factory, mill, shop — has its value.

Yet, this does not imply that mental hygiene possesses the same value in every sphere. Just as physical hygiene is required most by the diseased individual or one who is potentially diseased, mental hygiene is most needed by an individual whose mind is already disturbed or by one who is likely to be deprived of his reason, one who is under such strain that there is a likelihood of his collapsing under it. Mentally diseased individuals include unbalanced, eccentric and disturbed individuals as well as those who are actually insane. And individuals who can be considered potential patients of mental hygiene are the senile, adolescents and the corrupt persons. Similarly, in the normal course of human life, mental hygiene is required wherever there are human relationships, yet it is most essentially needed in the home and the school since these are the two institutions which are the greatest preservatives of mental health. Hence, a complete comprehension of the value of mental hygiene can come only when one has understood its importance for the school and the home, as well as for mentally diseased persons, adolescents, senile people and corrupt persons.

**Mental hygiene in the family.** Most psychologists are of the opinion that the influences that mould the personality of a child during the first five or six years of his life determine his conduct throughout his future existence. It is in the family that the child learns to express, control and refine or modify his emotions, thoughts, feelings and impressions. It is in the family that he develops the qualities of affection, sympathy, brotherhood, etc. His conduct towards his equals, his juniors and his seniors is moulded and formed in the family. Hence, if some situation or circumstance in the family affects him adversely, his mental health is apt to suffer. Hence, it is evident that if the mental health of the future citizens of nation is to be ensured, it is essential that mental hygiene be introduced into the family. It is not only as a child, but also as husband and father, wife and mother, that one is under family influence. Family, as an institution, is with an individual from the time he steps into the world to the time he steps out of it. Mental disease or ill-health in even one member of the family has its repercussion on the other members. Hence it is as important to safeguard mental health in the family as it is to prevent and cure mental imbalance if it is present there. Without this, the peace and calm of family life becomes an ephemeral existence. Means of curing mental ill-health and its prevention will be described at a later stage.

**Mental hygiene in school.** Following the family, another institution that casts important influence upon the child's development is the school. In school, the personality is influenced by his teachers and colleagues. It is in school that he learns lessons of self-dependence, self-confidence and reliance. Now he cannot seek protection in his mother's lap from the problems that confront him, neither can he look up to his father to save him. Hence he is compelled to conduct himself desirably towards all on his own initiative. And in this effort, it is only natural that he finds frustrations that endanger the balance of his personality with mental difficulties and complexes. Mental hygiene in school is important for preventing such unhealthy development and for preserving mental health.

**Mental hygiene in adolescence.** As it is, mental hygiene is of importance throughout an individual's life, but it assumes greatest importance during adolescence. Adolescence is the most volatile stage in the development of personality. Mental, physical and every other kind of development takes place during this stage. Young boys and girls manifest signs of approaching adulthood. The male member develops his beard, and his voice breaks. In girls, the breasts begin to develop, and various parts of the body begin to round out. This physical development is accompanied by mental development, due to which they do not appreciate being treated as children. They prefer to be counted among the adults and in this fresh eagerness for adulthood, many boys are seen using the blade prematurely in an effort to acquire a beard quickly. Imagination and emotionality are at their highest pitch while the adolescent is passing through this period. Interest in the other sex manifests itself in many peculiar fashions, and curiosity concerning sex increases very much. The adolescent is further anxious about his future and his livelihood, regarding which he develops ambitions and dreams constantly. From this vivid description of the various problems that confront the young folk during this stage of their life, it is evident that it is now that there is greatest need for preventing mental quirks and imbalances and for ensuring mental health.

It has been pointed out earlier that in old age, maintaining a sane outlook on life becomes something of a problem, hence the old men have much to gain from mental hygiene, its ways and means. Another class of men and women who stand to gain much from this science is that of the corrupt and evil-minded — alcoholics, criminals, prostitutes and other antisocial elements. Many of their mental problems can be solved through the ways and means suggested by mental hygiene. In this manner, mental hygiene is an integral part of human welfare and life. It finds application everywhere, although reaping of the greatest possible benefit from it depends upon the skill of the person using it, and the ability with which he can control the circumstances. Mental hygiene is a science. It makes a study of the ways, means and rules that preserve mental health, prevent mental disturbance and cure mental diseases. Hence mental hygiene can benefit every sphere of life such as personal, family, social, national and international relationships, interrelations between various classes, sexes, age levels, colours, communities, races and peoples. This is the value of mental hygiene and it is not influenced by the very little benefit that is derived from it in practice. Being a science it is neutral, and in no position to bestow gifts and benefits upon people of its own accord. It is for man to reap a rich harvest from it. Its value does not deteriorate if man chooses to neglect it, since its value is proved and beyond doubt.

### Importance of Mental Hygiene in India

It would be in keeping with the context to point out the special significance that mental hygiene has for India. In India there are many problems at the national level, the solution of which depends considerably on mental hygiene. One such problem is the presence of communal tensions between Hindus and Muslims, as well as other communities. Yet another problem is the lack of discipline among students of universities and colleges. And another problem that has more recently reared its ugly head on the horizon is that of regionalism, one example of which was the agitation for Khalistan. The riots of Assam are additional proof of its existence. Language is another aspect of life in India, that has led to much tension and conflict. Crime in India, and particularly the example of juvenile delinquency, is primarily a matter of mental disturbance. The greatest obstacles to democracy in the country, corruption and partyism, are the result of mental aberrations. Of course, this harangue is not suggested as the only solution of these problems. What is implied is that in these and other problems involving human relationships there is also a mental aspect into which only mental hygiene has access. Hence, in so far as that particular aspect is concerned, the importance of mental hygiene need not be expressly pointed out. If the situation is looked at from this standpoint, it is quite possible that people who mould the destiny of this nation may find some reasonable solutions for such problems.

## MENTAL HEALTH

### What is Mental Health?

In the book entitled *Mental Hygiene in Public Health,* P.V. Lewkan has written that a mentally healthy individual is one who is himself satisfied, lives peacefully with his neighbours, makes healthy citizens of his children, and even after performing these fundamental duties has enough energy left to do something of benefit to society.[1] Possessing mental health, an individual can adjust properly to his environment, and can make the best effort for his own, his family's and his society's progress and betterment. In *The Human Mind,* K.A. Menninger has written, "Let us define mental health as the adjustment of human beings to the world and to each other with a maximum of effectiveness and happiness. It is the ability to maintain an even temper, an alert intelligence, socially considerate behaviour and a happy disposition." The chief characteristic of mental health, it is evident, is adjustment. The greater the degree of successful adjustment, the greater will be the mental health of the individual. Lesser mental health will lead to lesser adjustment and greater conflict. The healthy individual can interpret any new situation and adapt himself to suit it. He maintains a healthy and benevolent attitude towards life. He is aware that difficulties visit everyone in life, so that running away from them is cowardice. They can be solved only by squarely facing up to them with courage.

---

1. Lewkan, P.V., *Mental Hygiene in Public Health,* McGraw-Hill, 1949, p. 68.

### Mental Health and Mental Hygiene

In this manner, mental hygiene is a way of life in which the individual's adjustment to his environment is maintained intact. N.E. Cutts and N. Moslay have also stressed the element of adjustment in mental hygiene. According to them, we can say that mental health is that ability by means of which we establish our adjustment with the difficult situations of life and mental hygiene is that means or tool which makes this adjustment possible.[2] This definition also helps to reveal the relation between mental health and mental hygiene, as well as the difference between them. Mental hygiene is the means to mental health. In other words, mental hygiene is that science which studies the laws and means of achieving mental health, of maintaining it as well as doing away with mental ill-health. Mental health is the end, and mental hygiene the means.

### Traits of Mental Health

In order to understand the full implications of mental health, it would be advantageous to know the characteristics of a person who enjoys mental health. Actually, mental health, like physical health, is also a condition. And this condition can be recognised by its characteristic features. Roughly speaking, a mentally healthy individual would exhibit the following symptoms :

**1. Self-evaluation.** A mentally healthy individual evaluating himself properly is aware of his limitations. He easily accepts his faults and makes efforts to rid himself of them. He keeps an eye upon himself so that he may be aware of his own tendencies and that he may be in a position to divert them in the desired directions. He introspects so that he may analyse his problems, prejudices, difficulties, etc., and reduce them to a minimum.

**2. Adjustability.** It has been pointed out earlier also that one special characteristic of a mentally healthy individual is that he adjusts to a new situation with the least delay and disturbance. He is never disturbed of what might have been. He does not try to think of old age when he is young and think of his youth when a senile crank. He makes the fullest possible

2. Cutts, N.E. and Moslay, N., *Practical School Discipline and Mental Hygiene*, Houghton Miffline Co., Boston, p. 4.

use of existing opportunities and adjusts to every new situation that presents itself. This does not mean that he is a rolling stone that gathers no moss, but has his own ideas, notions, opinions, is a cool individual who deals coolly and patiently with every novel circumstance, without fear, disturbance, anxiety, complaint or a desire to avoid them. He is aware of the fact that change is the principle of life, he is ever prepared for change and always finds some suitable mode of adjustment. He has every desire to benefit the society, with a show of intrepidity if its benefit lies that way. Usually, he is calm, collected and indomitable even in the face of extreme adversity. Having force of character and will, he often changes circumstances to suit him rather than change himself to suit the situation. Gandhi, Christ, Mohammed, were people of this mould and class. Impatience with circumstances is not to be condemned but what is to be condemned and criticised is the tendency to run away from them and to cry over them. The weak individual becomes satisfied with circumstances and diseases. The great person loses his satisfaction with circumstances and strains every sinew to change them according to his own wishes. In fact, the most important aspect to adjustment is one's own mental condition rather than the external situation. A proper mental attitude gains a kind of immunity from the external situation affecting their peace and calm and balance.

**3. Maturity.** Intellectual and emotional maturity is another peculiar sign of mentally healthy individual. The mature mind is constantly engaged in increasing his fund of knowledge, behaves responsibly, expresses his thoughts and feelings with clarity, and is prepared to sympathise with another's feelings and viewpoints. And in maturity, sexual maturity is very important. The healthy individual behaves like a balanced, cultured and sensible adult in all matters.

**4. Regular life.** Habits are an important element in maintaining mental health. Forming proper habits in matters of food, clothing, the normal routine of daily life leads to their becoming systematic and regulated, which in the long run, economies upon energy and time. Many people are seen worrying over the most trifling thing in their routine. Some women experience such acute difficulty in determining the sari and blouse that they should wear outside the house that it leads to considerable mental pain and complication. Some individuals are always conscious of the fact, erroneously, that their tie is not straight, and they spend much time in knotting it correctly, in spite of which they can be seen fiddling with it all the time. Such nervous behaviour is not a sign of mental health. Healthy persons perform most of the common functions of life with quick assurance and a show of naturalism, without any bother and fuss. Their life is a model of regularity, balance and measured calculation.

**5. Absence of extremism.** Aristotle believed that the ideal man lacks excess in any and every direction, and the principle that excess of anything is bad is a golden rule as far as mental health is concerned. Whatever the instinct, if it is allowed to dominate an individual, it will bring him to harm and endanger his mental health. Some women go through any amount of criticism and degradation besides pain but they cannot forego their habit of quarrel. An unnecessarily courageous individual is often a prey to accident. And for the voluble person there are many occasions or regret and painful recollection of what might have been. Oversexed individuals lose their health reserve very quickly. Excessive ambition is another trait that never lets its possessor rest. Hence, in order to maintain mental health, one's life should be integrated, interests should be wide and the personality balanced. Extremism is no well-wisher of mental health.

**6. Satisfactory social adjustment.** As has been pointed out, from the point of view of mental health, a healthy individual maintains good adjustment with social situations, and is engaged in some or the other project intended to benefit society. And this is because in modern society the proper development of everyone's personality can take place only if there is mutual cooperation. Social relationships are a part of everyone's life. The greater the balance of these social relationships and the greater simplicity, the better will be the individual's mental health. Improper conduct on the part of others can be the cause of both mental problems and diseases. Hence, proper behaviour and proper feelings are essential for everyone.

**7. Satisfaction from chief occupation.** For mental health it is essential that everyone should find satisfaction from his chief occupation, his vocation. The individual who studies only to pass the examination and finds no pleasure in his work is neither a good student nor a healthy individual. A helpful professor teaches without worrying about the financial implications of his profession, an author writes, a businessman trades and a labourer labours but with interest. Money is the result of work but if one works only for it, that much time is obviously a waste. If the work interests an individual, it will yield more money, but at the same time, a proper utilisation of time will bring an increase in his pleasure and happiness. In fact, if one works for interest, one maintains it even in the event of a loss in trade or at least, the pain of loss is considerably lessened.

This description does not exhaust all the elements that a mentally healthy individual manifests, but it is a sufficiently suggestive picture of mental health. It can be imaginatively built upon. In this manner, mental health is that condition in which the individual manifests self-evaluation, adjustment, maturity, regular life, absence of extremism, satisfactory social adjustment and satisfaction from his chief occupation. Complete mental health is an ideal. Any individual who possesses the greatest number of these qualities will be nearest the ideal.

**Preservation of Mental Health**

The question that now arises is : How can mental health be preserved? It mostly happens that many students, particularly children and adolescents, cannot clarify their difficulties and problems so that they require guidance from their parents, teachers and psychologists. It is for the guide to understand the adolescent and to sympathise with him, and to offer him affectionate advice. Scolding or punishing them is not very efficacious. They should be given the opportunity of expressing their desires and mental tendencies.

**Mental Health of Family**

Family has the greatest importance in maintaining a condition of mental health, and within the family the greatest burden of responsibility is on the two parents. What is mostly needed in this connection is the creation of a suitable atmosphere in which the child's personality can adequately develop. A child's delicate and sensitive personality is influenced by the character of parents, their mutual behaviour and relations, their behaviour towards the children, the child's relations with brothers, sisters, and other relatives in the family. Hence, it is essential that these be healthy. There can be no hard and fast rule as to how the parents should behave towards the child under certain conditions; all that can be justifiably said is that they should consciously give the child every chance to develop his personality freely and without restraint. It is for them to prevent the child from treading the wrong path but they should not try to make him follow them in all things. The least they can do is to prevent any situation that causes repression in the child. All other things depend upon the parent's insight into child and adolescent psychology, their patience, their labour and experience.

### Mental Health at School

Following the family, the other institution that has responsibility of promoting mental health in children is the school. It is the school that has the greatest influence, after the home, in forming the child's personality. And even in school, the most important factor is the atmosphere existing there. In a healthy atmosphere the children adopt discipline and other qualities of their own. There is greater fear of some children being spoiled in school. Such children should be specially attended to and given definite and expert guidance. The greatest need is for providing each child with work adequate and proper to the need of his personality. Hence, it is essential that the backward and the brilliant children should be given special treatment. Teachers present an ideal to the children in their charge, hence their character and conduct should be such as can be profitably imitated by the children. Pupil personnel service should be introduced to remove the difficulties with which the children are faced from time to time in school.

Briefly, in school the teacher should keep the following factors vividly in mind if he has to preserve mental health, prevent mental disturbance and promote mental health among his students :

**1. Discipline.** As has been pointed out earlier, discipline in the school has an important influence upon the mental health of students. But this discipline should never be very strict since such conditions will lead to mental ill-health. Thus, discipline should be exercised not through creating fear of punishment but through arousing feelings of responsibility and the desire to be law-abiding among the students. True discipline is self-discipline. And discipline in college should be maintained by selecting its guardians from among the students themselves. It develops feeling of responsibility among the students.

**2. Affectionate behaviour.** It is only too evident that affectionate behaviour towards students on the part of teachers has good effect on the former's mental health. It will inspire him to obey the teacher, respect him, to do nothing that may incur his displeasure. A teacher should maintain the same loving attitude towards all his students. Any discrimination in this treatment injures the feeling of students.

**3. Play and recreation.** Mental disturbance and imbalance are created by the repressed motives surging in a student's brain. They can be given opportunities for healthy expression through games and other forms of recreation. Play and recreation have a cathartic effect.

**4. Sex education.** In adolescence, the morals of young boys and girls show alarming tendencies to proceed to degradation because of the sexual instinct, alternately its repression leads to much mental distress. Teachers should make use of psychological weapons to remove any sexual deviations that may be embedded in the mind of students. And for this, the best way is to provide young boys and girls with the necessary elementary sex education. This will help them, on the one hand, to develop a healthy attitude towards sex and prevent them from forming harmful complexes, as well as assist in their physical, mental and emotional development, on the other; they can then later on become well developed and integrated individuals.

**5. Educational guidance.** In order to maintain a state of mental health, it is essential that they be given subjects that conform to their requirements and abilities, and their educational problems solved. Taking personal advice of a psychologist in this connection is called educational guidance.

**6. Personal guidance.** Many of the problems that arise before the student are such that they cannot be solved by the student himself; hence he needs the personal guidance of the psychologist to solve them.

**7. Vocational guidance.** Every individual is compelled to adopt some one or the other profession once his education is complete, and he begins to worry about it even while he is still engaged in his academic pursuit. The knowledgeable teacher can hclp his students in their choice of a suitable career.

**8. Formation of good habits.** Mental health depends upon good habits. Hence it is desirable for the teacher to help student in the formation of good habits regarding a regular life, balanced diet and exercise, good behaviour and high thinking, etc.

**9. Balanced curriculum.** The curriculum in school should be such as to develop all aspects of the student's personality, to increase his fund of necessary knowledge, and to avoid all unnecessary strain on the mind. The integrated development of the students can be promoted through the organising of various kinds of extracurricular activities in the school and college.

**10. Balanced home assignment.** It is improper to think that if the child is given too much homework to do, he will not have the time to indulge in destructive and naughty pranks as he will be too busy. Loading them with too much homework only leaves them worried and anxious, with the worst influence upon their mind. Hence, the homework required of them should be carefully and sensibly formulated.

Finally, it may be stated that the prevention of mental imbalances is a problem of social and national importance. For this, efforts will have to be made to get rid of circumstances of social disorganisation, exploitation, corruption, various tensions and conflicts, crimes, alcoholic effects, etc. The defects of urban life in the form of excessive crowding, unhealthy small house, promiscuous mixing of the sexes, and noise will have to be eliminated. Suitable and interesting work for all will have to be provided, in addition to opportunities of health and recreation. It is only through efforts at the national level that proper and effective prevention of mental maladies can take place. And for this, cooperative effort on the part of government, teachers, social workers and sensible people in the public, will be necessary.

## QUESTIONS FOR EXERCISE

1. Enumerate and explain the basic principles of Mental Hygiene.
2. Write short note on Mental Hygiene.
3. Write short note on Mental Health.
4. What do you understand by a problem child? How will you reform him?

# 20

# Mental Retardation

### What is Feeble-mindedness?

Feeble-mindedness, as is evident from the term, is a condition in which one is possessed of a brain that is less than normally acute. Following are some definitions :

**1. Woodworth.** "Feeble-minded persons are so deficient in intelligence that they cannot manage their own lives without supervision." Evidently, the feeble-minded individual is a problem for his own family and society at large. In this manner, feeble-mindedness is a kind of mental deficiency.

**2. J.D. Page.** "Mental deficiency is a condition of subnormal mental development, present at birth or early childhood and social inadequacy." It is evident from this definition that the feeble-minded person has less mental capability and capacity than the average individual. In fact, mental deficiency, feeble-mindedness, weak intellect, retardation are words or phrases that mean practically the same thing.

### Problems of Feeble-mindedness

As has been pointed out earlier, the individual with a feeble mind is likely to prove a problem for his family, society and group, particularly in the modern period when life itself is so fast. It is for this reason that in modern civilised societies much attention is being paid to their training and education, so that methods of behaviour can be evolved for them which will enable them to lead harmless, fruitful and valuable lives. In many such nations, legal standing of feeble-minded person has been determined. From this standpoint, every child who is far behind the other children in his class in studies can be considered to be feeble-minded, and there has been much emphasis upon the special training of such children. In the same manner, the feeble-minded adult is one who cannot adequately earn his livelihood, and cannot live well in society. Society accepts the responsibility for the well being, existence and subsistence of such individuals since they can otherwise turn criminal and antisocial. As a general rule it is quite possible to teach the feeble-minded individual to earn his livelihood but so far psychology has not succeeded in evolving any technique whereby their intelligence level can be improved. In fact, it is difficult to do anything for the moronic and feeble-minded because their intelligence has been impaired by heredity while the unintelligent can be trained for some useful minor profession. And for this what is required is to understand their limitations and to create an environment which takes into account such deficiencies.

**Feeble-mindedness and Intelligence-testing**

One chief characteristic of feeble-mindedness is the deficiency in intelligence, and normally a child with an intelligence score of less than 70 can be considered feeble-minded. Hence, intelligence tests can be employed to reveal the presence of feeble-mindedness in children. But with this object in mind, it is best to use the non-verbal individual class of intelligence tests since in such individuals linguistic or verbal ability is also very low, and feeble-mindedness is an individual trait, not a general one. Thus, the teacher can use intelligence tests to discover feeble-minded students in his class, and can then make arrangements for their special education and treatment. It is essential that the difficulties of such children be taken into account and special curriculum and extracurricular programme be created.

**Antisocial Behaviour and Mental Deficiency**

The phrase antisocial behaviour has reference to all activity that contradicts society and undermines the work for its success : all crimes fall in this category. On the other hand, feeble-mindedness concerns the deficiency in an individual in respect of mental ability when compared with a normal individual. Many thinkers believe that there is a relation between mental deficiency and antisocial activity and the view is correct and tenable to the extent that antisocial activity rate is higher among feeble-minded individuals than among the normal population, but no causal or inevitable relationship can thereby be established between antisocial activity and mental deficiency. It is a fact that some feeble-minded individuals do not indulge in any antisocial function. What must be remembered is that the feeble-minded rarely escapes capture even if he indulges in such activity whereas the normally intelligent person escapes retribution much morc easily. Hence, it is evident that among criminals who are apprehended there is a large percentage of feeble-minded people. Secondly, the feeble-minded normally live in a poverty-stricken unedifying environment, as a result of which it is only natural for their social behaviour to take on the appearance of being antisocial. But, on that account, their behaviour should be considered the outcome of a defective and poor environment rather than that of feeble-mindedness. Yet, there can be little doubting the fact that mental deficiency is an important element in antisocial and criminal behaviour because in such individuals there is no full or proper development of normal understanding and the ability to reason, and as a consequence they do not understand the implications of their own behaviour. Much of their behaviour is controlled by the chance impulse, and is right only with reference to that impulse. Law does not hold such individuals responsible for crime since the criminal does not understand his action or its outcome. Finally, it can be said that mental deficiency is an undesirable and indirect cause of antisocial behaviour.

## DEFICIENCY AND DEFECT

Deficiency implies the lack, or absence of something whereas defect is attributed to a condition resulting from injury or deformation. In this manner mental deficiency means the feeble-mindedness or lack of adequate mental ability whereas mental defect implies the mind being impaired, injured or rendered defective. Nevertheless, the relationship between deficiency and defect, in the case of mind, is a near one. Deficiency can also be caused by defect.

### Characteristics of Mental Deficiency

Before coming to the types of feeble-mindedness it would perhaps be better to become acquainted with its chief characteristics. It need hardly be pointed out that on these grounds, the feeble-minded person can be distinguished from the normal individual. Roughly speaking, mental deficiency has the following characteristic conditions :

**1. Limited intelligence.** As has been pointed out at an earlier stage, mental deficiency is the lack of intelligence; in that condition, the person is unintelligent. Intelligence is the ability of man in various fields, such as learning, skills of different kinds, adjusting to novel situations and problems in life, benefiting from previous experience, creative and abstract thinking, making decisions, avoiding errors, overcoming obstacles, and foresight in various subjects, etc. In a condition of mental deficiency all these abilities are found to be less efficient than in the normal individual. In an unintelligent person, intelligent activity is difficult and laborious, his training is slow and even what is assimilated is more by rote learning than by any true understanding. Such a person cannot correct his errors easily, even when he gets to understanding them, and despite much repetition continues to make mistakes. In this class of individuals, the most intelligent can be made to learn a little bit of reading and elementary arithmetic. But even then if there is no constant revival of that learning it is soon forgotten. Yet, from this is cannot be concluded that they are completely lacking in intelligence, since they do have intelligence but it is less than in the normal individual. Even in the most serious case of mental deficiency, the person suffering has some elusive spark of intelligence; consequently it is not possible to make a clear-cut demarcation between the intelligent and the unintelligent, it being more a matter of degree than of quantity. As intelligence increases in people, they can be classified into various classes, such as are shown in the following table :

| *I.Q.* | *Classification* | *Percentage* |
|---|---|---|
| 140 or above | Very superior | 1.5 |
| 120-139 | Superior | 11.0 |
| 110-119 | Bright | 18.0 |
| 90-109 | Average or normal | 48.0 |
| 80-89 | Dull-normal or backward | 14.0 |
| 70-79 | Very dull | 5.0 |
| 00-69 | Feeble-minded | 2.5 |

This table has been extracted from Garret's *Great Experience in Psychology*. Sometimes, to begin with, the mentally deficient individual appears to be normal, but soon his progress shows signs of slackening, and he lags behind the other children or adolescents.

**2. Social inadequacy.** Feeble-mindedness was defined in 1904 by the Great Britain Royal Commission, and American Association for the study of feeble-mindedness, in a way that stressed and brought to the forefront its social and economic aspects. In this manner the person suffering from mental deficiency is inadequate from the social point of view. It is not possible for him to protect himself from the normal hazards of life, and he lacks self control and the means to earn a living. In childhood he is in constant need of assistance from external quarters. And, even till he has grown to a good age, such an individual needs assistance in such simple activities as eating or dressing. His relatives have constantly to protect him from common hazards, and even when he is playing with other children of his own age, it is necessary to keep an eye on him. Being behind children of his own age in everything that he does, the backward child prefers to play with children younger than himself.

Even when he becomes an adult, the backward individual does not become self-sufficient in any important respect. In the report of the British Mental Deficiency Committee published in 1939 it was said that among the mentally deficient people, only 14 per cent were nearly self-sufficient whereas 46 per cent contributed somewhat to the earning of their livelihood, but the rest did nothing. In females who are mentally deficient, this rate of dependence on external assistance is even greater.

Besides being dependent upon others for mental help, these feeble-minded individuals cannot solve their own social and personal problems. If they are not properly looked after and controlled, they are usually caught in undesirable activities such as crime, theft, murder, arson or sexual violation, etc. In the case of such behaviour of feeble-minded person there is no underlying immoral conception or trait, because he is incapable of making a distinction between the good and the bad, and his actions are more instinctive than deliberate. Often he is not even aware of the consequences of his action. When tempted he will steal, when irritated he may strike or kill another person, and under stimulus he may commit some sexual crime, so that his behaviour has to be sympathetically controlled if it is to conform to social norm. In his study, A.H. Wood has studied mental deficiency and defined it as a condition of inadequate mental development in which quantity and quality are lacking to such extent that the individual cannot skilfully and adequately adjust to his social environment. To quote him : "A condition of incomplete development of mind of such a degree of kind as to render the individual incapable of adjusting himself to his social environment in a reasonably efficient and harmonious manner and to necessitate external care, supervision, or control." Apparently, mental deficiency is to be recognised not only on the basis of intellectual incapacity but also by the degree of social inadequacy.

**3. Deficiencies of other mental functions.** Man's mind functions in the form of a whole hence the deficiency of mental power influences all the powers and functions of mind. Feeble-minded individual cannot concentrate on anything for long because his attention wanders very easily. Interests are only too few, and he cannot apply himself to anyone for any length of time or with any real degree of tenacity. His power of comprehension is low and the range of memory rather narrow. He can remember only the simplest of things, besides which proper association between words and pictures is difficult for him. Imagination and the creative impulses are also low if not absent in such individual. Comparatively less feeble individuals are often found daydreaming, but in a more advanced condition the mind is often a blank. Thinking is very difficult for such person.

**4. Defects of drives and emotions.** Lacking mental power, the mentally deficient individual also suffers from defects of drives and emotions that creep in because of the innate deficiency. Very feeble-minded people show even the lack of such a vital drive as that of self-preservation. They are incapable of even showing their own hunger or thirst, it is difficult for them to escape impending danger, their emotional life is sometimes worse than that of animals. But in certain less feeble-minded people, the basic physical drives are often very well developed, although the age of development concerning heterosexual relationships does not seem to exist. Normally, their effective experiences are limited to pain, pleasure, fear, surprise, anger, hatred and other simple emotions. In the comparatively lesser feeble-minded people emotions have a very nearly normal expression but their emotions have the normal person's depth, profundity and sensibility. Complex emotions are almost completely absent and they do not understand respect, duty and morality.

**5. Defects of personality.** In the absence of a required power of mind, the personality does not maintain its organised appearance, so that among the feeble-minded people only very few exhibit a personality that is valuable in respect of dynamism, courage or any other quality. And not merely in respect of the good qualities even in the case of bad qualities they do not show any real strength or driving power. Normally, the feeble-minded individual is possessed of an unattractive, unstable and easily influenced personality. As in normal people, the feeble-minded also shows variations of personality, but comparatively, the variety to be found is nominal.

**6. Organic defects.** In any mentally deficient individual one can observe many physiological and motor defects, because in childhood he takes longer than the ordinary child to learn to talk, move or perform any other activity. Even activities requiring very little skill are not easily acquired. Their speech is often marred by stuttering and their gait by stumbling, their sensory acuity is much less than that of the normal individual. Very feeble-minded individuals are not even capable of distinguishing various kinds of smell and tactual sensations. They also remain far behind the normal individuals in respect of motor mechanical dexterity, many of them being short-stature and sickly. Their physical energy is far less than that of the normal person. They cannot combat disease with the result that death rate among them is higher than in the normal population. As mental deficiency increases, so does physical incapacity.

## Kinds according to Mental Defect

Feeble-minded individuals are divided into the following three classes according to the extent of mental deficiency or damage :

**1. Idiots.** Such people cannot protect themselves against the normal hazards of life; they have the least degree of intelligence. They cannot evade an oncoming vehicle, are fully capable of putting their hand in the fire or of wilfully jumping into deep water. They cannot keep themselves clean, neither can they dress themselves. Idiots of the worst kind cannot even eat their own food or fulfil any other physical requirement. Their linguistic ability is limited to the knowledge of a few common words.

**2. Imbeciles.** They have greater intelligence than the idiots, and they can learn to evade ordinary danger, to speak but not to write. The worst among them cannot learn any work, while the normal imbecile cannot indulge in any productive activity. Some of the more intelligent imbeciles can be taught productive work through much diligent training and control, while the best of them can perform bodily functions, but even they require constant vigil and supervision for any productive effort.

**3. Morons.** Morons form the greatest number of feeble-minded people, and they are the most intelligent among their coterie. They can be trained to work regularly without constant supervision, and to do works of simple skill. Their more intelligent members can be taught such work as looking after animals, baby-sitting, carpenter's work, lathe-work, sewing machines and the like. But if they are to follow such work with a view to earning money, they need the supervision and employment of a sensitive and sympathetic individual who can and is willing to understand their limitation. Without such interest and care, they waste whatever they earn, besides wasting their time to no end. In such cases young moronic girls are often easily led along paths of corruption and prostitution and moronic young men can be led to crime. Generalising upon their condition, it can be said that the morons cannot do any novel or complex thing with success.

### Differences among the Above

Mental and psychological distinctions among the three classes of beings pointed out above lead to certain distinct physical traits in them. The average moron, for example, is better built, taller and more robust than idiots or imbeciles and lives to a longer age. Similarly, the average imbecile as compared with the average idiot, has a better physique, lives longer and has fewer physical shortcomings or defects. Here it should be remembered that one clear-cut distinction between the three classes is possible; the classification being essentially artificial, the classes in fact overlap. Among the feeble-minded people the greater portion is that of imbeciles who number more than idiots, while morons are in greater number than either of these two classes. According to the report prepared by Lewis, out of every 100 feeble-minded individuals. 5 are idiots, 20 imbeciles and 75 morons.

Since imbeciles and idiots stand in greater need of care and supervision, in every institution meant for the care and treatment of the feeble-minded they outnumber the morons very considerably. According to the report concerning patients in mental institutions prepared by the commerce department of the United States of America, situated in Washington, of every 100 patients admitted to such institutions annually, some 15 are idiots, 30 imbeciles and 45 morons while the rest defy classification.

**Inverse Proportion between Mental Deficiency and Cultural Levels**

Family background of the individuals belonging to these three classes also shows certain subtle variations. Morons are to be found at almost every level of society, yet even among them the greatest percentages are drawn from slums and backward areas. Moronic children are to be found in greater number in families in which unskilled labour is a source of earning while children coming from the commercial or skilled labour circle are mentally on a better level. On the other hand, idiots and imbeciles can be seen spread over the entire social stratum without any distinction of class. Lewis made a study of certain representative areas of England and Wales, and demonstrated that 11 per cent morons, 30 per cent of imbeciles and 33 per cent of the idiots came from very good and respectable families while 62 per cent morons, 35 per cent imbeciles and 27 per cent idiots came from poor and very poor families. From the above statistics one can deduce that feeble-minded individuals of a lower class come from respectable and highly cultured families, a fact that is also borne out by a study of their relatives. According to the study conducted by L.S. Penrose, the family relatives of morons showed far greater mental deficiency than the relatives of imbeciles and idiots, while intelligence tests revealed that relatives of morons have a lower I.Q. than relatives of imbeciles and idiots. The question that is now posed is that why is there such an inverse ratio of proportion between mental deficiency and culture levels? One solution has been found by the explanation that majority of idiots and imbeciles suffer from injury during delivery or from the glandular defects. Another explanation has been offered. While the feeble-minded children of a lower class are the outcome of recession of hereditary factors, the morons result from an infection of genetic factors. In other words, heredity works in different ways in feeble-minded children belonging to the higher and lower social orders. Among feeble-minded people belonging to the lower classes, the parents have average or above average intelligence, but to their children they impart such genes as cause mental deficiency.

**Tredgold's Classification**

Among the very many classifications made in connection with mental deficiency, the two most famous are Tredgold's and Lewis's. Both will now be considered in brief.

In his book *Mental Deficiency,* A.F. Tredgold has divided feeble-mindedness in two parts — primary and secondary. They can be described in the following manner :

1. **Primary mental deficiency.** This division includes all those who have independent social adjustment. According to Tredgold, some 80 per cent of mentally defective people fall within this category. And of these 5 per cent are mongols.

2. **Secondary mental deficiency.** This comprehends the functional kind of mental deficiency, in which there is a fundamental or hereditary defect but undesirable external influences have retarded mental progress. Hence, secondary mental deficiency is not innate, but acquired. For example, a child can become feeble-minded through injury to the brain before or after birth, the deficiency depending upon the extent and nature of injury. In injuries inflicted before birth or during infancy the influence towards mental deficiency is much greater than injuries suffered much later.

This particular classification of mental deficiency has been objected at to on the ground that in most cases of mental deficiency it is difficult to ascertain whether the condition is the outcome of heredity or later accident. As Tredgold himself accepts, certain mental deficiencies caused by defective environment are present even in the cases of primary deficiency.

E.O. Lewis divides mental deficiency into the following two classes :

1. **Subcultural.** Majority of the mental patients fall within this category. They differ from the normal individual only in respect of quantity. They represent the lowest level of intelligence in the general population. In appearance they resemble the normal individual; they are more intelligent than the normal kind of feeble-minded people. Much of their mental deficiency is the outcome of heredity, and they are to be found in slum areas.

2. **Pathological.** Mentally deficient individuals belonging to this class differ from the normal individual in the same way in which a pigmy differs from the average person. Their physiological condition differs from the normal and is quite defective. At the root of their defects is some organic defect or abnormality. Every strata of society has its pathological defectives.

This classification of Lewis is similar to Tredgold's in many essential respects although in his second class he has comprehended many people whom Tredgold would place in the first category.

## CLINICAL TYPES

But among the classification of mental defectives, the most famous is that of clinical types, in which there are simple, mongols, microcephalic, hydrocephalic, cretins, idiot savants. These various classes will now be considered briefly :

1. **Simple.** This class includes those mental deficients who most nearly resemble normal people and between 60 and 70 per cent of mental deficients are found in this class. Compared to the normal individual, the chief difference that they exhibit is that they are not attractive, while their minds do not show any peculiar difference. They tend towards short stature and some physiological defects. But about two-thirds of them are

morons and the rest imbeciles. Mental deficiency is normally believed to be hereditary, although environment and education have their requisite effect. Majority of the feeble-minded children are the offspring of feeble-minded parents or unskilled labourers. And the I.Qs. of the brothers and sisters of feeble-minded children vary between 80 and 95. But a small percentage of feeble-minded children are also found in the best of families, their brothers and sisters being conspicuously intelligent.

**2. Mongols.** Mental defectives of this class have been given this particular name because roughly speaking, they resemble the mongols who inhabit Asia. Mongolian deficiency is to be found in the white as well as black races, in the East as well as West. Further, it is found in all kinds of economic circumstances, affluence and poverty 50 per cent of feeble-minded children are of the Mongolian type in their first year, but later on their proposition in the group of mental deficients is reduced to 6 per cent. This occurs because a majority of the mongols die as infants.

Mongol children are ostensibly alert and very active but intelligence tests reveal that almost two-thirds of them are idiots and imbeciles. Linguistic ability is ahead for them to matter, so much so that some of them do not even learn to speak at all. As a general rule their personality is affectionate, cooperative and gentle. Physical characteristics of the mongols are not evident equally in all Mongoloids, and in some they are altogether absent. Even then there is so much similarity between them that observers mistake them for brothers and sisters. Chief physical characteristics of the mongols are small and round head, flat front and back portions, high cheek-bones, sunken eyes that are bent downwards, thick rough and corrugate tongue, defective lines of mouth and nose, small stature and less than average weight, thumb and small fingers disproportionately small, much space between thumb and finger of the foot, very big size of ears, late teething and badly arranged teeth, very thick and twisted lips, joints very loose and flexible, etc.

There are many different opinions concerning the main causes of Mongoloid kind. According to scientists, the main causes of this are syphilis, alcoholism in the parents, influence of defective percentage, lack of vitamins, imbalance of glands, excessive or defective methods of birth control, excessive weakness of the mother, injury to the embryo while growing, incomplete development in the embryonic stage and defective heredity. Studies have revealed that two factors contribute mainly to the birth of mongol type — heredity and environment during pregnancy. Studies conducted by Bleyer and Penrose have indicated that the mothers of mongol children are older than the mothers of normal children and often such a child is the offspring of that family. His father, too, is quite as old. From this it appears that the main cause of mongol characteristics is a compact of defective or embryonic state, lack of nutrition and lack of glandular secretions of a kind, a state which is characteristic of women who have grown old. Contrary to such an opinion, some scientists have suggested that mongol children can be born of any woman of any age belonging to any particular condition of society, and that such women also give birth to normal children. This criticism does not invalidate the previous theory because it is possible that the defects of pregnancy that make one child a mongol may not be present in the next or previous pregnancy. Cases of twins have also been adduced to forestall the above theories concerning the birth of mongol children because in many children it was seen that while one child was mongol, the other was quite normal. Now, if the condition of the mother was such as to give rise to mongol children, it should have affected both the twins. This deduction from the example of twin children is upheld by the heredity theory. It has been observed that in the case of twins where both were mongols they were of the same type, but where the sex was different only one was mongol. All such experiments and observations have served to emphasize the importance of heredity in the mongol type of mental deficient. From the observations of Penrose, it appears that in the general population, one out of every thousand children is a mongol but within a family in which there is a mongol, one child out of every 50 will be a mongol. This, too, has only stressed the importance of heredity for mongol deficients.

**3. Microcephalic.** These people are called pinheads because their heads are extremely small, and the number of such mental deficients among feeble-minded people in general is about 1 per cent. The circumference of their heads is 17 inches, and the weight of their brain approximately one-fifth of the normal person's brain. In their head the forehead is sunken, the rear part of the head is flat and their hair rough and stringy. Their brain is undeveloped. Emotionally, such people are affectionate, obstinate and excitable. They give expression to their emotions. The spinal cord in such cases is thinner than normal, and they have a short span of life. Normally, they cannot do any valuable work, but those among them who are hardworking can do something towards earning their livelihood. As often as not, their mental condition is likened to that of the idiot. Actual causes of their mental defects have not been discovered. According to some scientists, the women who are given pelvic X-rays give birth to microcephalic children. Murphy examined some 53 such women and found that 26 per cent of their children were microcephalic feeble-minded.

**4. Hydrocephalic.** In the mental deficiency of this kind, as is evident from the name, some liquid collects to excess within the brain and spinal cord so that the size of the head increases its circumference which varies from 27 to 30 inches. When this aggravation is in the brain it is called inner hydrocephalus but if the liquid collects between the brain and skull it is called external hydrocephalus. This second kind of defect does not cause any mental deficiency or feeble-mindedness, while the first one invariably does. In individuals belonging to this class, the head is round and disproportionately big in comparison to their faces, the skin is very thin and the veins swollen. This condition can occur before birth as well as after it. When it occurs during pregnancy such infants do not live, but if it develops after birth such children never grow to be healthy; they are afflicted with different diseases. Imbeciles, morons and idiots can all be seen-in this class; by nature they are jovial, happy and affectionate, always prepared to cooperate. They form 1 per cent of the total feeble-minded population.

**5. Cretins.** In this class of feeble-mindedness, there are 1 per cent individuals; their physical development is very redoubtable. In stature they are very far short of the average, so much so that in complete adulthood they are no taller than three feet. They also do not develop any other signs of adulthood. From six months to two years, the cretin child begins to show signs of physical development in which the hands and feet are very small, the skin rough and hanging, big tongue, a swollen face, thick lips, unattractive head, short and thick neck. Such a child teethes rather late, and learns to speak even later; his movement and other motor activities are unattractive. From the emotional standpoint such children are indifferent and slow, although by nature they are peaceable, affectionate and soft-spoken. Thyroxin, the glandular excretion of the thyroid gland, is the main cause of cretinism since its deficiency brings about this condition. If the thyroid gland is operated upon, some favourable changes can be caused.

**6. Idiot savants.** Among the people suffering from feeble mindedness there are some people in whom certain specific abilities are developed far above the normal level. Abilities of this kind are the sensations of sight and touch, ability to paint, musical taste, memory, mathematical ability. Individuals of this kind even though they are feeble-minded, perform remarkable feats like telling the day which will be on a particular date in some future year. A person of this kind told Page of one such day in the future within three seconds. But in intelligence tests their I.Q. varies between 45 and 68, while their mathematical ability is equivalent to that of a student in fourth class. Although it is remarkable that one should be able to tell instantly the day and date of some future year yet for this reason alone they cannot be classed among the savants, because they themselves cannot explain the process by which they arrive at their answer.

## CAUSES OF MENTAL DEFICIENCY

Causes of mental deficiency or mental defects are the following :

**1. Heredity.** One major, and probably the most important, cause of mental deficiency is heredity, a view that is borne out by the study of twins and their family. Between 50 and 75 per cent of mental defectives come from families in which intellectual weakness or less than average intelligence is the rule rather than the exception. Studies conducted by Hopwood, Kriks, Keiser and Pehrose have indicated that one major cause of mental defects is the feeble-mindedness of parents. In twins it is very rare that one child be normally intelligent and the other feeble-minded. Studies that Rosanoff and his associates conducted have indicated that 91 per cent of identical twins and 53 per cent of the fraternal twins show mental defectiveness, as a general rule. Other psychologists have advanced statistics that confirm such a view.

**2. Abnormalities of brain.** In 25 per cent of the class of mental deficiency, the root cause is some abnormality of the brain which can be caused by any injury during birth, any infectious or contagious disease, imbalance of glands, psychophysical conditions, etc.

**3. Alcoholic parents.** It is the view of certain people that excessive drinking or alcoholism in the parents can lead to mentally deficient children being born to them. But this view has no scientific basis or support. In fact, the intelligence of the children of alcoholics is determined not by the extent of their parent's alcoholism but by the latter's intelligence. If they are themselves unintelligent, their children will, in all likelihood, be unintelligent, but if they are intelligent their children might also prove to be intelligent.

**4. Consanguinity.** It is a widespread belief, almost universally held, that sexual relationships with blood relatives lead to defective children being born. Such a view has been put forth even in the Gita. What is almost certainly true in such an opinion is that the case of sexual intercourse with blood relatives can advance the danger of defective genes becoming concentrated and manifesting themselves in the defects in any child that is born. But if there is no defect in either of the two parents, then defective children, caused by the mere fact of sexual intercourse with blood relatives, will not be necessarily born.

From the above explanation it is apparent that the most important cause of mental deficiency is heredity, but the factor within heredity that results in mental deficiency has not been determined. And, in fact, in order to reach any definite opinion on the subject of mental deficiency and its causes, it is essential to have much more research and experimentation. Often, more than one causes cooperate to bring about mental deficiency, and it is difficult to trace all such causes.

## CURE AND PREVENTION OF MENTAL DEFICIENCY

From the point of view of cure, mental deficiency is not a disease that can be cured by any drug or training, yet even then it is necessary to take steps towards the prevention and treatment of mental deficiency because such measures have some beneficial influence, however little. It has generally been experienced that through adequate training and guidance even morons can be helped towards making their lives profitable and useful in some degree. Self-dependence, of a kind, can be bestowed upon these otherwise deficient creatures. And, almost all feeble-minded individuals, within certain limits, can be trained to keep clean, look after themselves and value certain social qualities which make them more acceptable. But the precondition of any success in this direction is that the training should begin in infancy. It is only natural for progress to be very slow in a venture of this nature, but the attempt will be commendable from every standpoint — the child's, society's, as well as the parents'. Organised training and effective guidance can help many helpless, pained and otherwise useless people to become less of a burden to society and lead more rich and constructive lives. They can be made useful members of society. Hence, psychologists have put forward certain suggestions for the training of mental deficients, the cure and prevention of mental deficiency.

**1. Education of parents.** Parents of children who are mentally deficient need to be more sympathetic and understanding than the normal child's parents. They must realise the fact that their child is suffering from a permanent mental defect. Many parents do not accept this fact even when it has been clearly pointed out to them, so that instead of discovering the shortcomings of the child they continue to blame the teacher for the child's failures. On the other hand, even when they do accept this inevitable fact, they develop a fixation in their mind that the child can be made completely normal through the use of drugs or by some kind of special training. And because of this blind faith they waste much valuable time and resources in the futile efforts to render their child normal. In any such condition it would perhaps be best if the parents recognised immediately that if the child's future is to be improved it is essential to create favourable conditions within the house rather than searching for some magical cure. If the child's personality is trained, benefit can be achieved. Thus, the first step towards the child's improvement is the parent's adoption of a realistic and correct attitude.

**2. Home training.** As has been pointed out earlier, the most natural and the best place for the training of mentally deficient children is their home. Every child stays at home in his infancy and may continue to live at home even after they have grown beyond childhood. What essentially separates them from the mentally deficient children is that the latter only require greater training or greater patience in the trainer. Sometimes mothers disregard their defective children but this has an adverse effect upon their emotional development. On the other hand, other mothers pamper them with so much care and protection that they can never become fully independent. It is essential for the mother to have a healthy attitude towards her children, whether normal or abnormal, but all the more so towards the defective child. In particular there should be no difference in her attitude towards the normal children and abnormal child. Being aware of the mental shortcoming of the child, the mother should do her very best to train the child in keeping clean, eating his food, gearing his clothes and being able to put them on, walking, talking, etc. As the child grows up, he should be given his normal responsibilities and duties without hesitation so that he can become self-dependent, Particular attention should be paid towards moral conduct and training of the personality. Every effort should be done to prevent them from all improper actions. If there are some normal children in the family, they should be taught to look upon the mentally defective child as a responsible member of the family, but tempered with sympathy. The defective child should not be prevented from playing with other children in the neighbourhood but it should be observed if other children take advantage of his shortcoming or if they tease or irritate him on that account. In this manner, the most important element in domestic training is that the parents should train the child with patience and persistence in order to make himself dependent, and also that they should create such an atmosphere within the home that the child may not develop any inferiority complex.

**3. School training.** After his life within the family, the child steps into a larger world of the school. From the educational standpoint, idiots and imbeciles are considered a waste of time; therefore, only morons are sent to schools. Even they cannot keep up with the normal children in school and are quite backward. Backward children have their own individual problems, and since they have very low intelligence quotient they need to be taught many things by others. A backward child shows no inclination towards leadership; instead he needs the affection, understanding and sympathy of his luckier mates. If the child is very backward, with an I.Q. of less than 70 then he cannot be educated or trained in the normal kind of school. He should be sent to specialised schools. If a child continues to fail in the same grade year after year, his mental and emotional adjustment is further endangered and because education in the classroom is meant for the average child it is only natural for the backward child to meet with failure. But failures in school tend to develop and fix in his mind the notion that he will also be failure in life. Much of his ambition, the motivation for effort, is destroyed and he becomes frustrated and disappointed. Social adjustments also present numerous problems to the backward child. In a group he fails to grasp easily even the smallest fact that is placed before him, and understand them. Hence, other children tend to avoid him or ridicule him. Leadership can be engendered in him only if he keeps company with children much younger in age but his equals in mental level. But then, such children keep away from the backward child because physically he is more developed than any of them. Grown-up adults only scold him from time to time instead of paying any attention to him. His condition does not improve either in adolescence or adulthood, and he is often the butt of everybody's jokes. And group activities are often beyond him because they are on a level which is too high for him to attain.

Many of the feeble-minded children can be improved. But children who have intelligent quotients of 70 or less cannot be educated in the ordinary school; instead they have to be referred to specially equipped schools. Children with intelligence quotients between 70 and 85 can be educated and improved in ordinary schools despite their handicap. Many such children can even be rendered almost completely normal, and they can attain normal success in school as well as in later life. If they are slightly encouraged and praised in their success, they can be induced to learn the simpler process. But for this the teacher will have to make the appropriate change in curriculum, method of teaching, his behaviour towards the children, etc. For children with I.Qs. between 70 and 85, there is no need to treat them separately from average children; they only require special attention and some additional care. But in the case of children with I.Qs. below 70, a separate and especially prepared curriculum is required. The following adjustments must be made :

(a) ***Curriculum :*** Often the main reason why children repeatedly fail in some class is that the curriculum is not appropriate for them; hence the teacher must make an effort to adjust the curriculum to fulfil the needs of the backward children. Only such subject should be taught that can benefit the feeble-minded; all the complex and subtle subjects should be avoided. Besides, the entire course should be oriented in such a manner that it may help the backward child in adopting some useful profession in the future after he has completed this fundamental course. Basic education in particular, should be emphasised in any such curriculum, besides which the children can also be profitably taught some profession.

(b) ***Method of teaching :*** The chief quality of any method of education is that whatever it imparts to the students should be grasped and acquired by them. Hence, for different levels of students, the methods of education should be suitably varied. Evidently, any method found suitable for the average child cannot prove efficacious for the feeble-minded moron, and therefore any method of education applying to him should be varied. It must possess the following characteristics :

(i) Speed of teaching should be low;

(ii) Every lesson should be repeated many times;

(iii) The programme for teaching should not continue for long stretches;

(iv) Concrete objects should be employed;

(v) The project method should be used;

(vi) Physical or motor activity should be stressed;

(vii) Should be varied with occasional tours and picnics;
(viii) Moral education in particular should be emphasised;
(ix) Boys and girls should be educated separately.

(c) ***Ability and behaviour of teacher :*** An able teacher provides an atmosphere for the feeble-minded children in which they can find success. This helps to stimulate their pride and self-confidence, with the result that they tackle circumstances that are much more complex. Hence the ability and behaviour of the teacher count for much where treatment of backward and feeble-minded children is concerned. In this respect the following things are important :

(i) The teacher should be trained;
(ii) He should have knowledge of various examinations;
(iii) He should establish close and intimate contacts with the students;
(iv) His behaviour should be affectionate and sympathetic.

If any real improvement in the feeble-minded child is to be affected out, for the improvement of such a child; much importance attaches to the attitudes of parents and the kind of atmosphere and environment in which the child is required to live. Many parents do not take particular notice of the child's feeble-mindedness because they believe that gradually the child's mind will take care of it self. But when nothing of the sort happens even when the child arrives at the age of ten, they become disappointed and apathetic to such an extent that they do nothing about it. But with effort, persistence and sympathy, the feeble-minded child can be trained to adopt some simple profession or vocation, and success of a sort can be brought within his reach. But for this the teacher and parents, must cooperate, and use psychological techniques that are appropriate guidance in the choice of school subjects or of a profession later on, and his development must be considered at length in school no less than at home. And for the care and treatment as well as education of very feeble-minded children, the state should provide institutions with the necessary funds. Only on this scale can the problem of feeble-minded children be solved within the limit of possibility.

**4. Institutionalisation.** One way of curing mental deficiency is to place such individuals in institutions where they can be treated. According to Page, a psychologist, some one lakh feeble-minded people live in such institutions in the U.S.A., about ten thousand new inmates being added each year. In all such institutions there is a constant flood of applications, and if feeble-minded people could avail of them. In India, on the contrary, such institutional facilities are almost not available though in such a big country there is far greater need for such services. Mental patients who are admitted to such institutions are of two kinds, the first are idiots and the very feeble-minded, or even handicapped children whose parents are unable to look after them, and the second kind are morons who are slightly better and who need to be kept in such institutions on account of some or the other criminal tendency that they manifest. Persons belonging to the second group do improve, and after a short period of training in social adjustment they are released.

**5. Care by other families.** Another method of caring or treating feeble-minded defectives is to leave them in villages in the care of some particular family. In Belgium and in certain other nations, this system is catching one.

**6. Occupational training.** As is evident from the term, and has already been indicated, there are many persons among the mentally defectives, who can be trained to take part in certain professional activities so that their lives become at least partially useful. They can be made self dependent to some extent. Adult feeble-minded persons, after adequate training and guidance, can take up such jobs as agriculture, washing, animal husbandry, poultry farming, etc. The moronic among them can turn to such work as that of the carpenter, tailor, skinner, but normally only in cooperation with other persons, and besides it they can also look after farms, poultry farming units, animal husbandry units and various kinds of elementary engineering units, etc. Grown-up feeble-minded women can also indulge in certain domestic activities of a more or less elementary nature. But grown-up moronic women can turn to all kinds of domestic work as well as the work of labourers in factories. It is only natural that such persons would not be skilled in their works. Hence, many employers would not hesitate to employ them so that they can also thereby become independent.

**7. Sterilisation.** Many scientists hold the belief that feeble-minded individuals give birth to defective offspring; hence in order to limit the number of feeble-minded people being born into society it is essential that the feeble-minded people be sterilised, thereby the possibility of their begetting even worse children is obviated. Even then many kinds of mentally defectives would escape such measures, so that it is practically impossible to completely put an end to feeble-mindedness in the country. Besides, it has already been pointed out that many normal parents give birth to abnormal children. According to Blacker and Myerson, only 15 per cent of all mentally defective individuals are the offspring of parents who are themselves suffering from mental deficiency. Of the rest, almost all are begotten by normal parents who have certain defective genes due to which some of their children turn out to be defective. From this it appears that even by sterilisation no more than 15 per cent of the mentally defective people can be prevented from being born. This suggestion for the sterilisation of the feeble-minded is based on another false notion that such people give birth to more offspring than the normal couple. According to the report of the Departmental Committee on Sterilisation, published in 1934 in London, such a view is not based on facts because idiots and imbeciles give birth to very few children. Some morons have large families, but even among them the majority have either few children or none at all.

But some other people have also advanced the need for sterilisation, though on social grounds. This suggestion has been advanced particularly with a view to benefiting feeble-minded and mentally defective women because while such men are almost never married, the women do get married; and some of them give birth to children even without getting married. Hence, if they are sterilised their lives can become easier and more pleasant and they will also avoid giving birth to legitimate or illegitimate children who will be a burden to society. If they are not sterilised then such women will have to be kept in institutions that will naturally prove rather expensive. For these reasons, this suggestion has been adopted in many countries. In California, U.S.A., there has been conspicuous success in reducing the percentage of feeble-minded and mentally defective people in the population, through sterilisation.

Certain other methods have also been employed in the cure, prevention and treatment of mental deficiency, in addition to the ones mentioned above. Medicines, particularly for mental deficiency arising out of birth, injury, glandular complication, or contagious diseases, have been discovered. Guidance through lectures is another method. There can be no doubting the fact that if the feeble-minded individuals are given adequate social and professional training, and if their domestic environment is improved to conform to their needs then the majority of them can be made independent. And in this way, a complex social problem can be solved to great extent.

## QUESTIONS FOR EXERCISE

1. Define feeble-mindedness. Describe the major problems of feeble-mindedness with suitable illustration.
2. Distinguish between deficiency and defect. Bring out the mental traits of various types of mental deficiency.
3. Discuss the characteristics and causes of the clinical types of mental retardation.
4. What are the causes of mental deficiency? Suggest cures.

# 21

# Mental Illness : Psychoneurosis and Psychosis

## Historical Background

The history of mental diseases is quite as old and distinguished as human life itself but the analysis and cure of mental disorders on a scientific basis is a much recent innovation. Fourteenth century saw the establishment of a mental hospital in London, and the establishment of such an institution indicated that people were beginning to understand that the mental diseases were not the outcome of ghostly visitation or spirit's experience. It was also realised that the mental patient needs help and treatment, not deserves punishment. Ever since then, the cure and treatment of mental diseases have seen increasing research and study, and the most important contribution to this field was made by U.S.A. after its Independence.

## Discoveries concerning Psychoneurosis

As is evident from the nomenclature, psychoneurosis implies disorders of mind and nervous system. The first to make a detailed and systematic study of them was Charcot of Paris. Janet's book *The Major Symptoms of Hysteria* contains his study of hysteria and the conclusion at which he arrived thereby. But the study conducted by both Janet and Charcot lacked the necessary profundity. Dr. Sigmund Freud of Vienna made studies of subjects concerned with mental disease that have never been rivalled or even paralleled before or since. Freud not only put forward his own point of view, he even encouraged research in many different fields, and many of his followers, the modern Freudians in particular, have made valuable contributions to information in the field. Among them, the name of Karen Horney deserves special mention.

## NATURE OF PSYCHONEUROSIS

Many different researches have indicated that different bodily disorders in man also result in some mental distortion, and similarly mental complexes succeed in causing physiological disturbances. In fact, in modern world, the concept of duality of mind and body has been absolute since everyone agrees that mind and body influence each other. Hence the phrase mental disease should not delude one into thinking that they are primarily diseases of the mind and that they have no influence upon the body. The truth of the matter is that most diseases are psychosomatic in nature. In distinguishing them from physiological disorders, all that is implied is that mental diseases are mainly in respect of origin and characteristics, and that their initial cure should also be psychological.

## KINDS OF PSYCHONEUROSIS

Of course, there are many kinds of mental diseases that have come to light in recent years, but generally speaking, mental diseases allow of a division into two main classes — psychosis and psychoneurosis. In order to evaluate the differences between them, it is essential to study them individually, as it is also the logical way of examining their respective natures.

## CHARACTERISTICS OF PSYCHONEUROSIS

In order to know what a psychoneurosis is, it is essential to know its characteristics or symptoms, the main ones used being the following :

1. Psychoneurosis is the term used to denote mental disease of an ordinary kind, since in it fatality does not result from the disorder.
2. It also does not cause much physical pain and discomfort.
3. In such patients, the powers of speech and thought also remain intact and in order.
4. Patients also do not suffer from delusion and hallucination.

5. In them, the patient behaves in a normal manner; he does not revolt against social customs but understands reality.
6. In them, the patient also does not evince any absence of self-control and self-dependence.
7. They are mostly caused by frustrations, conflicts and mental tensions.
8. As they have their origin in psychological causes, they are also to be treated according to psychological methodology.
9. In them, mental and hereditary elements or factors play an important part, and chemical or psychosomatic causes very little.
10. As the patient maintains the normality of his personality, he understands his difficulties and can help the psychologist in curing them.
11. These diseases can be cured by suggestion, hypnosis, psychoanalysis and re-education.

## PSYCHONEUROSIS AND PSYCHOSIS

Before going on to a detailed account of the psychoneurotic diseases, it would perhaps be best to distinguish them from the psychotic disturbances. According to Dorcus and Shaffer, "The outstanding distinction between the psychoneurosis and the psychosis is that in the former only a part of the personality is affected, while in the latter the change involves the whole personality." Meyer describes it by saying that the psychoneurosis is a part reaction, while the psychosis is a whole one. In this respect, the following points are to be noted :

1. Compared to psychoneurosis, psychosis is more complex and profound.
2. Hence, due to psychosis, the individual loses his self-control and social balance whereas this does no occur during a psychoneurosis.
3. In this manner, while the behaviour of the psychoneurotic is normal, that of the psychotic shows signs of abnormality, lack of meaning, inexplicability and antisocial tendency.

4. Contrary to psychoneurosis, psychosis creates tendencies towards hallucination and delusion in the patient.
5. Contrary to psychoneurosis in psychosis, the powers of speech and thought are unrelated, meaningless, illogical and abnormal.
6. As the patient suffering from psychosis loses his self-control, he often exhibits a tendency towards suicide, and for this reason he has to be carefully looked after. In the case of psychoneurotic individuals care of this kind is not essential.
7. In contrast to psychoneurotic patients, the psychotic patients suffer a very great and significant change in personality, and to such an extent that they do not realise their faults with the result that they do not cooperate with the psychologist who is treating them.
8. While psychoneurotic disorders can be cured and removed through psychological techniques, not much benefit accrues in the case of psychosis, but some good can be done by chemical and physical treatment.

From the above-mentioned distinctions of psychoneurosis and psychosis, it is apparent that the first division includes normal mental diseases while the latter contains more complex disorders of the mind. But the main diseases of both classes are primarily related to the mind and both make social adjustment of the individual difficult. In both cases, people connected with the patients undergo certain usual stresses and strains, and the truth of the matter is that the difference between the two is more of quantity than of quality. One is more intense than the other. When a psychoneurotic disorder gains in complexity and becomes difficult to treat, it turns into a psychotic defect. So long as the patient continues to help in his treatment, and maintains his balance of life, he will be considered a psychotic. When this stage of the disease is reached it becomes impossible to cure the patient through psychological techniques, and the cure itself is not easy any longer. He needs special treatment and cure, spread over a very long period of time with the result that it is convenient to place him in some mental institution. So far he had been only a source of infinite nuisance and bother, but now he can also be dangerous since his personality changes completely and he does not recognise any person. In legal terminology, such people are considered insane, and they cannot be held responsible for any of their actions.

## KINDS OF PSYCHONEUROSIS

Neurotic disorders are ordinarily considered to be of five kinds :

1. Neurasthenia
2. Anxiety Neurosis
3. Anxiety Hysteria
4. Obsessive-Compulsive Neurosis
5. Hysteria

Here the first kind of neurosis, neurasthenia, will be considered at some length, the others being treated of in the following answers to related questions.

### Nature of Neurasthenia

Coleman has written, "Neurasthenia; older term of aesthetic reaction characterised by chronic mental and physical fatigue and illnesses." This term neurasthenia was first used by the American scientist Beard in 1880 in the sense of nervous exhaustion. But after him, the term lost this connotation and was used in a different sense by the following scientists. Nowadays it is employed to denote the mental disease in which the patient constantly complains of physical and mental exhaustion, and some people do not even recognise in it a distinct mental and physical exhaustion which are also evident in other diseases if that disease is not granted a distinct status. Yet this particular view has not won many followers to its ranks among scientists because the majority of those who know best in such matters incline to the view that it in itself constitutes a mental disorder.

### Symptoms of Neurasthenia

Fatigue is a factor that every individual experiences at some time or another, hence in order to comprehend the true nature of neurasthenia it is essential to understand the kind of a fatigue it involves, that also causes it to be regarded a mental disease.

The following differences between normal fatigue and neurasthenic fatigue are apparent, and should be noticed :

1. Normal fatigue and exhaustion are easily got rid of by rest, but the fatigue of this disease does not leave the patient who always feels exhausted.
2. Common fatigue is a temporary state of the body but this disease is more permanent.
3. Normal exhaustion is normally the outcome of mental or physical effort but in this disease fatigue remains even when no exertion has been done.
4. Normal fatigue is concerned with muscles, but in this disease no connection between fatigue and muscular exertion is noticeable. In this connection, the research of Hartenbeg deserves mention.

### Kinds of Neurasthenia

Psychiatrists and psychoanalysts treating neurasthenia divide it into two classes — acute or secondary neurasthenia, and chronic or primary neurasthenia. It is essential to understand the difference between the two here :

**1. Acute or secondary neurasthenia.** This can be caused by any disease of the body that undermines the constitution or otherwise leaves some kind of poison or toxin in the body. It is also caused in nurses and other people similarly employed if they work for long periods without adequate rest and relaxation. This is also true of other occupations in which work is done over long periods continuously, without intermittent rest. This disease is sometimes also observed in the case of soldiers. In this disease, the only symptom that is observed is that of fatigue, no other mental disorder to be observed, but the patient constantly complains of insomnia and lack of appetite. He tends to irritability and finds it difficult to concentrate on any work. Even the slightest effort leaves him tired and exhausted, debilitated and run down. Emotional control is often lost with the result that he tends to be censorious. His head tends to heaviness, his memory becomes weak and he does not enjoy doing anything. Besides these psychological symptoms, the patient also exhibits certain physical signs of the disease. Fatigue is a normal condition but it is often accompanied by a wide fluctuation in the rate of pulse, it changes from very high to very low. He tends to perspire much and his heart beats at a rapid rate. In sexual intercourse he does not have any success because before complete erection, the seminal fluid is ejected. As it is, his sexual drive or vitality is low, but even then ejection takes place without full excitation.

**2. Chronic or primary neurasthenia.** In this the patient often appears disgruntled and discouraged, depressed and fatigued. This fatigue is not got rid of even by prolonged rest, and besides fatigue some or the other part of the body constantly gives signs of pain such as head, back, leg, etc. Irritability, anxiety and a tendency to being completely self-centred are apparent. Being normally unable to achieve satisfaction in sexual intercourse, he is sometime seen having recourse to masturbation. Often he becomes considerably anxious about the state of his health. He shows signs of indigestion and easily becomes excited over the smallest incident.

**Causes of Neurasthenia**

The following causes of neurasthenia are recounted by different psychiatrists :

**1. Weakness of central nervous system.** This cause of the disease has been mentioned by Janet, and according to him, the weakness of the central nervous system is the cause of fatigue, weakness, dissatisfaction and mental disorganisation. But Janet's views have not been supported by experiments and studies.

**2. Laziness and inactivity.** According to White, the cause of this disease is underwork, and due to laziness or inactivity the patient considers himself exhausted even after doing very little work. This leads to physical symptoms of bodily exhaustion. White's views do not have any particular value.

**3. Auto-intoxication.** Some psychologists believe that the main cause of this disease is auto-intoxication, but this view, too, has not been proved.

**4. Heredity.** In the opinion of some psychologists, heredity is the cause of this disease, but the study of patients does not bear out this view.

**5. Over work and anxiety.** Some people attribute neurasthenia to overwork and anxiety, but the opinion has no factual basis.

**6. Mental disintegration.** According to Coriat, the cause of this disease lies in mental disintegration which in turn is caused by abnormal fatigue and emotional experience. There can be no doubt that mental disintegration is an important cause of neurasthenia but other causes are also important.

**7. Lack of excitement and frequency of discharge.** Freud and his followers trace this disease to lack of excitation and frequent discharge of seminal fluid or semen. It should be held clearly in mind that according to Freud, the actual cause is not physical but conflict that goes on within that patient's mind behind this. And conflict is caused by the habit or desire to masturbate on the one hand, and the idea that it is bad, on the other. There cannot be much doubt that mental conflict is the cause of this disease, but this mental conflict cannot be traced only to sexual causes. According to some psychologists, it can be caused also by a sense of inferiority and self-projection. Whatever may be the fact it can be stated that mental conflict is the cause of neurasthenia.

**8. Desire to escape disturbing situation.** According to Wolf, a famous psychologist, the main cause of neurasthenia is the desire to evade a disturbing and painful situation, and the escape is achieved when this disease develops in the individual. But psychological analysis and researches have established that almost every mental disease is a mechanism designed to evade difficulties of adjustment to circumstances.

**9. Emotional tension and conflict.** According to certain other thinkers, the disease is caused by emotional tension and conflict.

**10. Introverted personality.** Some people believe an introverted personality to be the cause of neurasthenia.

In fact, the various causes of neurasthenia that have been mentioned above are important in different circumstances, and the root of the matter is difficulty of adjustment, whether social, sexual or of any kind.

**Cures of Neurasthenia**

The following conditions are essential for a cure of neurasthenia :

**1. Rest.** The patient should be allowed as much rest and

comfort as he can take and excitement should be denied to him.

**2. Nutritive food.** The patient should be fed with nourishing food but no alcoholic or other stimulant should be administered to him.

**3. Psychological method.** In this disease, no medicine has any benefit for the patient, hence psychological methods such as hypnosis, re-education, psychoanalysis, etc. are employed, and they do benefit the patient.

## ANXIETY NEUROSIS

### Definitions

**1. Fisher.** "Neurotic anxiety is a reaction to unapproachable inner or subjective difficulties of which the individual has no idea."

**2. W.L. Linford Rees.** "The term anxiety state refers to a disorder in which anxiety is the primary and dominant part of the clinical picture, with the mood change being relatively fixed and persistent and of such a degree as to affect well-being, efficiency and normal adjustment."

**3. J.C. Coleman.** "It is characterised primarily by diffused free floating anxiety which does not seem to stem from or be directed toward any particular situation or object."

Anxiety is a normal emotion which in moderate degree can be a helpful force by increasing effort and alertness. In excess anxiety imparts effectiveness and is a handicap.

Anxiety states vary in severity and duration. Thus they may be acute and mild or chronic mild or severe. The prevalence of anxiety states in the United Kingdom has been variously given as 2-5 per cent of the total population and 7-16 per cent of psychiatric patients.

Anxiety is a common feature of many clinical states and may be found in any medical and surgical condition. It may form a prominent feature of many psychiatric illnesses. It is frequently found in depressive illnesses and in its most severe form in agitated depressive states. It is also found in obsessional states and is an essential feature of phobic conditions. Anxiety also occurs in acute toxic confessional states and may occur in any form of dementia particularly when the sufferer has to attempt tasks which are at or beyond the limits of his capacity. It is not infrequent in mentally handicapped patients when they try to undertake tasks difficult for them. It may occur in any form of schizophrenia and is very marked in the form known as pseudo-neurotic schizophrenia, and contrary to popular belief anxiety may be present in conversion hysteria. Anxiety may be an integral part of epileptic phenomena particularly of the temporal lobe variety.

**The Biological Significance of Anxiety**

Throughout the animal kingdom, an animal in danger shows all the bodily and behavioural manifestations of anxiety.

Cannon has shown that, during such situations, the body becomes mobilised for action either for fight or flight and that the mechanisms involved include the autonomic nervous system, the locomotor system and other changes throughout the body which serve to increase the organism's ability to deal with the threat by action. The sympathetic part of the nervous system is predominantly involved but certain aspects of parasympathetic activity come into action, *viz.*, those subserving the need for total mobilisation for activity, *e.g.*, the sacral parasympathetic causing evacuation of the bladder and bowel.

Various changes which occur alert the animal, increase awareness and responsivity to various stimuli and serve to bring about more effective blood supply to the muscles of locomotion, where it is most urgently needed during an emergency, the rate of respiration is increased to cope with the increased demands of oxygen by the muscles, heart rate is increased to pump the blood round to the muscles where it is needed. The blood vessels to muscles and heart tend to be dilated whereas the arterial to the skin and digestive tract, where food and oxygen are not urgently needed, are diminished, so that there is redistribution of blood supply to the vital organs of circulation and locomotion. Muscular tone is increased so that the animal can go into action without delay. Dilation of the pupils and increased alertness in response to stimuli also help the organism in being effectively aware of the environment.

In some animals, pilo-erection makes the animal look more fierce. In man, anxiety just inconveniently produces goose pimple without serving any obvious beneficial effect, biologically or otherwise.

### Anxiety Neurosis and Anxiety Hysteria

The anxiety of an anxiety neurosis differs from normal anxiety on the one hand and from a hysteric anxiety on the other. Anxiety hysteria will be considered in detail later on, but here it is essential to point out that in it the patient's cause of anxiety is abnormal, and he projects his own difficulties on the conditions outside himself. But in anxiety neurosis either of these two conditions are not in evidence. Here it should be noted that although the patient is not aware of his causes for anxiety, yet he imagines one in order to lead an air of rationality to his worry.

### Kinds of Anxiety Neurosis

The following are the two classes into which anxiety neurosis is divided :

**1. Acute anxiety.** In this all the above symptoms appear in their most intense form and condition.

**2. Chronic anxiety.** In this the symptoms natural to the condition are neither momentary nor intense but more permanent and continuing. It takes the following two forms :

(a) ***Free floating anxiety :*** In this the patient is completely unaware of the causes of anxiety, but he continues to be worried and restless.

(b) ***Channelled or bound anxiety :*** In this the patient attaches his anxiety to some specific condition or circumstance, but bound anxiety only succeeds the stage of free floating anxiety.

## ANXIETY HYSTERIA

### Clinical Features of Anxiety States

**1. General appearance and behaviour.** A person with an anxiety state has a tense, anxious, apprehensive attitude and demeanour. Increased muscular tension is shown in his facial expression, posture and his difficulty in relaxing. Characteristically he sits on the edge of the chair during an interview and jumps at any sudden noise.

When muscular tension is marked, tremors of the hands, knees and sometimes other parts of the body are noticeable.

Palpebral fissures tend to be wide and pupils dilated; the mouth tends to be dry so that the patient can be observed licking his lips and moistening his tongue.

**2. Mood.** The patient is in constant state of worry and usually looks apprehensively ahead, anticipating problems and crossing his ridges before reaching them fearing that dangers and catastrophes lie awaiting him around the corner. He is apprehensive about his health, family, finances, about his abilities and other aspects of his life. He seeks constant reassurance. His thoughts are concerned with worries for the present and the future. Speech is often rapid and may exhibit stammering or hesitancy.

**Bodily Concomitants of Anxiety**

These are to be seen as changes in locomotor system, sudomotor system and the autonomic nervous system control of functions of various organs and systems. An understanding of the physiological basis of these will enable one to understand the patient's symptoms and to be in a better position to explain and reassure him effectively.

**1. Muscular system.** Increased tension of the voluntary musculature is characteristic of anxiety states and has been referred to already. Symptoms directly referable to increased muscular tension include tremors, aches and pains in various muscles of the body, for example, pain on the back, limbs, neck and side of the head. One type of headache is due to increased tension of the scalp muscles.

A useful diagnostic test is that the pains arising from increased muscular tension disappear with a small quantity of intravenous 10 per cent sodium amytal, *viz.*, one or two injected intravenously slowly. The pain will go long before there is any interference with the patient's consciousness and when the patient develops feeling of relaxation. Sodium amytal in this dosage has no analgesic effect and produces this by producing relief of anxiety, tension and, concomitantly, reduction of muscular tension.

**2. Cardiovascular system.** Tachycardia and the subjective experience of increased rapidity and forcefulness of heartbeat, palpitations, are common effects of anxiety. The patient often becomes worried about this and develops fears of heart disease which further increases his anxiety thus creating a vicious circle. Precordial pain is frequent which, again, the patient tends to assume is evidence of heart disease, but precordial pain in young people is invariably due to psychogenic factors. It has its origin in the intercostal and pectoral muscles and, if it were necessary for this to be proved, an injection of local anaesthetic into these muscles would immediately abolish the pain.

Blood pressure is often increased, systolic pressure being mainly affected, and it usually soon returns to normal. During physical examination, initial readings tend to be much higher than subsequent readings, which provides evidence of the effect of anxiety and apprehension on level of blood pressure.

Pallor and cold, blue extremities are evidence of vaso-constriction in the arteries supplying the skin.

**3. Respiratory system.** Anxious patients tend to have rapid, shallow breathing, sometimes frequent sighing and, in general, to show much poorer effort tolerance than is characteristic of their normal states.

**4. Gastro-intestinal system.** Decrease of salivary secretion gives rise to characteristic dryness of the mouth. Epigastric tremulousness, nausea, dyspepsia, bowel urgency, frequency of diarrhoea are common.

In some patients, anxiety and tension produce spasm of the large bowel, giving rise to constipation.

It should be noted that, in some people, anxiety makes them eat more because eating gives them relief of tension and may serve as a substitute for love and affection. As a rule, appetite is diminished in anxiety states.

**5. Sudomotor system.** Increased sweating in anxiety states is typically emotional in distribution, *i.e.*, from the palms, the axillae and forehead. The cold, moist palm is typical of a person suffering from an anxiety state, in contrast to the warm, moist palm of a patient suffering from thyrotoxicosis.

### Aetiology

The principle of multiple aetiological factors can be clearly seen in the genesis of anxiety states. Aetiological factors may be conveniently considered as (a) extrinsic or environmental and (b) intrinsic or constitutional, or they may be classified into (1) predisposing factors and (2) precipitating factors.

**1. Genetic and constitutional predisposing factors.** It was demonstrated in World War II that a person's constitution determines the degree of environmental stress that he could cope with before developing a psychiatric illness, such as an anxiety state. The constitutional predisposition included genetic factors, probably a number of genes of small effect.

Genetic factors may be manifested in a number of ways :

1. By determining the predisposition to breakdown;

2. Determining, in part, personality type and stability;

3. Determining physiological features such as autonomic imbalance and, possibly, certain neuro-endocrine mechanisms which may be important.

Genetic factors cannot be considered in isolation because parents and siblings with anxiety states or other psychiatric disorders may also exert a direct influence on the person and influence his personality disposition and may cause him to develop certain traits of personality which are conducive to the development of anxiety and distress, the tendency to be very sensitive, the tendency to be timid, apprehensive and unassertive and the tendency to emotional instability over minor frustrations. It has been suggested that people of introverted personality tend to develop conditioned responses more readily and tend to learn anxiety reactions more rapidly than extraverted persons.

**2. Physical factors.** These include fatigue, exhaustion and infections, particularly virus infections which may leave depression and anxiety persisting for many weeks after the physical aspects of the infection have passed off.

**3. Endocrine factors.** In hyperthyroidism, anxiety is a common feature. Similarly, changes in the hormonal balance of the body which occur at puberty, following childbirth and at the menopause may be associated with emotional liability and increased tendency to anxiety.

In some women, the various psychophysical changes comprising the premenstrual tension syndrome are particularly associated with development of anxiety and tension.

It should be remembered, too, that certain addicts develop very marked anxiety as a part of the withdrawal effects of the drugs. Originally, people may take barbiturates for the relief of anxiety but, if they take a sufficiently high dose over a long period of time, they become physically dependent and when the drug level of the barbiturate decreases, they develop marked anxiety which leads to the taking of further barbiturates, thus creating a marked vicious circle and increasing the problems of addiction.

Similarly, increased anxiety can follow the intake of alcohol and, again, one can get alcoholism developing as a part of this mechanism.

**4. Psychological factors.** Psychosocial stresses may be acute and severe or may be prolonged. Every person has his breaking point. Some people are more vulnerable to certain stresses, for example, financial or marital whereas others are mainly affected by threats to their status and prestige. Severe stresses include accidents, frightening experiences, bereavement, prolonged stresses relating to interpersonal problems, to marital, financial and occupational worries and conflicts.

(i) ***Stresses :*** Stresses tend to have a cumulative effect and sometimes the experience of a series of stresses or prolonged stress combined, perhaps, with infections or fatigue, may be the culminating point which leads to the development of an anxiety state.

(ii) ***Conflicts :*** Conflicts relating to any sphere of a person's life may be associated with anxiety. Desires related to instinctive drives and the conflicts imposed by the person's standards or the requirements of society or, indeed, conflicts about any wish can lead to the development of anxiety.

(iii) ***Tension :*** Anxiety and tension may become part of the life pattern of successful businessmen. They live in a constant state of tension and over-activity and are unable to relax and some remain well for years without much rest or recreation. Others become increasingly fatigued and depressed and ultimately break down with a psychiatric or psychosomatic disorder.

(iv) ***Pressure of work:*** In some persons, the relief of pressure of work, such as holidays or weekends, leads to increased anxiety unless they are able to channel their energies into substitutive activities.

**The Occurrence of Anxiety in other Disorders**

Anxiety may occur in practically all psychiatric disorders but here it is a part and not the predominant and primary component of the clinical picture for example :

**1. Schizophrenia.** Anxiety may be prominent in many forms of schizophrenia; the diagnoses will rest on the discovery of features which are indicative of schizophrenia.

One type of schizophrenia, referred to as pseudo-neurotic schizophrenia, may cause difficulties in diagnosis. Here the anxiety is overwhelming. It is a state of pan-anxiety but careful observation will illustrate deterioration of personality, emotional incongruity and other features which indicate the true nature of the disorder.

**2. Depressive states.** Anxiety is a frequent component in depressive illnesses. In those illnesses which are a reaction to environmental difficulty, anxiety is particularly prominent but it may also occur in endogenous depressions and is particularly intense in agitated depressions.

In patients developing anxiety for the first time after the age of 40, in the absence of any organic disease, one should bear in mind the possibility that this may, in fact, be a depressive state in which the main manifestation to the observer is anxiety.

Anxiety occurs in acute organic states such as the delirium; also in cases of organic dementia, and is related to the emotional liability of those patients and also to the difficulties of adjustment which the dementia imposes on them.

**3. Post-concessional syndromes.** These are often associated with anxiety and irritability.

**4. Anxiety symptoms.** These are common in all psychosomatic disorders and in almost all physical disorders, depending on a variety of factors including the patient's reaction to the illness and the threat which it presents to him.

**Prognosis**

This will depend on the strength of the predisposing factors and the personality of the patient, his habitual modes of reaction, the role played by organic and endocrine factors in predisposition and the extent to which these can be modified.

Factors of good prognosis are an acute onset, short duration of symptoms, stable personality, good work record and good general previous adjustment. Factors of poor prognosis are family history of neurosis, neurotic traits in childhood, poor work record and other evidence of difficulties of adjustment, unstable personality and the extent to which various circles have developed in the perpetuation of symptoms, such as worry about somatic effects of anxiety and, in the case of phobias, avoiding situations which were previously associated with phobias.

**Treatment**

The steps in treatment include :

1. First of all, taking a full history;
2. Thorough physical examination;
3. Discussion, explanation and positive reassurance;
4. General support and management, giving further explanation, encouragement and guidance in coping with their problems;
5. Social measures dealing with problems of work and home, as far as they can be modified;
6. Symptomatic treatment and the use of anti-anxiety drugs to relieve symptoms and to encourage resumption of normal activities;
7. Psychotherapy if indicated and according to the needs of the case, *e.g.*,
   (a) Shorter supportive;
   (b) Prolonged and intensive psychotherapy;
   (c) Group therapy.

**General Strategy of Treatment**

In the treatment and management of anxiety states, investigation is an integral part of treatment. The first step in treatment is the taking of the history in which the patient is allowed to talk about his past and present problems and life situations freely with minimal interruption from the doctor. The interview enables both the physician and the patient to see what factors in the environment, in interpersonal relationships or in the patient's own conflicts, may have contributed towards the development of his anxiety state. In also enables the physician to develop rapport with the patient and can be the beginning and the foundation of a good doctor-patient relationship.

Physical examination can also be an important part of treatment. If there is no evidence of physical disease, the nature of the patient's symptoms must be explained to him in terms suitable to his intelligence, education and personality and it must always be remembered that a negative reassurance is not enough. It does not usually satisfy the patient to be told that there is no physical basis for his symptoms. This must be accompanied by a positive explanation of the nature and basis of his symptoms in terms which he can understand. The physician can also help him to understand the relationship between life events and stresses in the development of his illness, and can help him either to cope with or to modify circumstances if this is feasible.

If anxiety is mild and causing minimal incapacity or suffering, there may be no need for pharmacotherapy. If the anxiety state is sufficiently severe to interfere with well-being and adjustment and cause considerable incapacity, pharmacotherapy will need to be considered along with other methods of treatment. But anxiety hysteria is not merely phobia, because there is more of anxiety in it. Besides, the anxiety is also permanent in nature, so much so that the personality is transformed. In anxiety hysteria, the sufferer is afraid of circumstances which do not frighten the normal person, such as dark places, heights, etc. For example, a young woman always asked her mother and father to accompany her wherever she went because she was frightened to going alone.

## OBSESSIVE — COMPULSIVE NEUROSIS

In a general sort of way, compulsion is to be found in some degree in every sphere of life, such as the inability to believe without re-checking that the door is closed, even though it has only just been closed by one and the same individual. Hence, he is more or less compelled to go and took at the door to confirm it in its closed condition. This form of compulsion common to life is of a different order from the obsessive — compulsive neurosis because by repeating an action the normal individual is thereby rid of that compulsion, but for the mental patient there is no end to it. In the example quoted above, the individual finds his peace after he has run to the door once or twice, and he is free to concentrate upon any other activity. A mental patient, on the other hand, may go to the door many times but his compulsion and sense of uncertainly will not be removed. But the difference between ordinary compulsion and neurotic compulsion is not merely one of degree but also of kind, since there are certain kinds of compulsion that cannot be considered normal. If a person finds himself compelled to commit arson, murder or theft, then it can only be called a neurotic compulsion.

**Obsessions**

Obsessions can occur as symptoms in many psychiatric disorders or they may constitute the entire illnesses which are then referred to as Obsessional States.

1. **W.L. Linford Rees.** "An obsession is a content of consciousness, that is, an idea, an impulse to action or an emotional state which, when it appears, is accompanied by a subjective feeling of compulsion which the patient tries to resist but cannot get rid of."

2. **Fisher.** "An obsession is a mental or implicit activity of a fairly specific nature which the individual recognises to be irrational but over which he has little or no control."

3. **J.D. Page.** "An obsession is a spontaneously recurring thought or impulse that persistently intrudes itself into the patient's mind even against his wishes."

The most important diagnostic features are the feeling of compulsion accompanied by a tendency to resist the latter being the most important criterion of all. Obsessional symptoms may or may not appear to be nonsensical to the patient. They are characteristically alien to the patient, but in spite of this he always recognises that they arise from him. The realisation that the obsessional idea, feeling or impulse to action is irrational is less important as a diagnostic criterion. The tendency to resist the obsession is the most important and characteristic feature. Obsessional thoughts tend to be recurrent and often associated with a great deal of anxiety and distress. In some patients the obsessional symptoms and the associated distress can occupy most of their daily lives. In others, the obsessional symptoms come on intermittently with intervals of comparative freedom.

**Compulsions**

**1. W.L. Linford Rees.** "The term compulsion is applied to an obsessional impulse to carry out certain acts, such as having to do things in a certain way, or to repeat them a certain number of times, to touch various objects, to carry out cleaning operations by repeated washing, and so on."

**2. Fisher.** "A compulsion is an overt activity of persistent and fairly specific character which the individual recognises to be irrational and incongruous with the situation in which it occurs but over which he has little or no control."

**Traits of Obsessional Personality**

It is important to differentiate obsessional traits of personality from obsessional symptoms. The obsessional personality is characterised by over-conscientiousness, meticulousness, tidiness, reliability; by being parsimonious and persevering, and by a tendency to pay a great deal of attention to detail. The obsessional person often tends to he rigid, to dislike changes in his plans or daily routines and to be generally cautious and timid in his outlook. These are common traits of personality, many of which are socially desirable insofar as they are conducive to reliable work and socially acceptable behaviour. If they become very marked and develop the features of compulsion and resistance, they then become obsessional symptoms. It should be noted that the obsessional personality is very common in the normal population and is found in association with anxiety states, depressive illnesses and variety of psychosomatic disorders, and although it is correlated to some degree with obsessional illness, it is by no means always present in those who develop obsessional illnesses. Various surveys have shown that about one-third of obsessional states are free from previous obsessional traits of personality.

According to W.L. Linford Rees, "The anankastic personality is a term which denotes certain personality characteristics which include obsessional traits. The anankastic personality is characterised by a strong sense of personal insecurity, associated with excessive caution and conscientiousness. The essential traits are timidity, rigidity often with the extreme self-control and excessive tendency to doubt."

### Differential Diagnosis

Obsessional symptoms must not be confused with the following.

**1. Habit patterns.** These are learned reactions of behaviour which we carry out easily and automatically. There is noted feeling of compulsion or a tendency to resist.

**2. Habit spasms or tics.** These are involuntary movements which are not necessarily accompanied by feelings of compulsion or tendencies to resist.

**3. Rituals.** These are certain acts based on superstitious beliefs which are carried out to ward off dangers or misfortune. They are carried out deliberately and, although there may be varying degrees of compulsion to carry out such acts, there is no tendency to resist. Certain types of behaviour of children, such as avoiding walking on the lines of the pavement, are usually carried out deliberately without exhibiting any tendency to resist them.

### Obsessional Symptoms

**1. Obsessional thoughts.** Obsessional thoughts, ideas, words or mental images appear in consciousness against the person's will and despite resistance. John Bunyan suffered very greatly from obsessional thoughts relating to religion. The obsessional thoughts are distressing and repetitive and mental images may take the form of distressing or horrible scenes, sexual images which the patient tries to resist but cannot get rid of and all are associated with emotional distress.

**2. Obsessional ruminations.** Here the patient is compelled to ruminate over questions which have no ready answer, such as 'Who created the God?', 'What is the purpose of life?', etc. These recurring thoughts distress the patient. John Bunyan, for example, suffered from luminations about God.

**3. Obsessional doubts.** These often relate to whether certain actions have been carried out, such as putting a letter in a pillar-box, turning off the electric light switch, turning off gas taps and water taps.

**4. Obsessional vacillations.** These may occur when there is a choice of two alternatives, even when it is unimportant as to which one is chosen, such as deciding which of two turnings to take at a turn in the road.

**5. Obsessional phobias.** It should be remembered that the majority of phobias are not obsessional. They are learned phenomena whereby a fear becomes attached to some object or situation. A phobia is an irrational fear of such things, some phobias may be obsessional and in this instance they have the characteristics of obsessional symptoms hi that they are accompanied by repetitive feelings of compulsion associated with resistance and emotional distress.

**6. Compulsive actions.** Motor activities of an obsessional kind are referred to as compulsions. Compulsions are an irrational impulse to perform some form of action. Examples of obsessional compulsions are tendencies to carry out acts a certain number of times, such as switching off electric lights, undressing and dressing, the tendency to count things and do things by numbers, the tendency to carry out certain activities like washing and cleaning repetitively.

A soldier patient during the war had a compulsion to part his hair exactly in the middle. In the morning he spent half an hour in an attempt to get it right, first parting it to the left of the middle line and then to the right of the middle line until eventually it was more or less correct but never completely to his satisfaction. He had a compulsion to do things four times; on going to bed he had a compulsion to touch things four times. All this made his life very complicated and difficult; he was able to save himself a little time by touching things with his four fingers. He also always had to start doing things on the right, the right hand or the right foot, but customary procedure in the Army is by the quick march and this used to put him off for the rest of the day.

Patients with obsessional states have varying degrees of anxiety, tension and distress and may have secondary depression.

It has been found that about one-fifth of obsessive-compulsive states have depressive symptoms and one-eighth symptoms of anxiety.

**Obsessions in Other Illnesses**

Obsessional symptoms may occur in the following psychiatric illnesses :

1. **Schizophrenia.** It is probable that the occurrence of obsessional illness in schizophrenia represents the occurrence of two disorders rather than a single illness. There is some evidence that persistent obsessional symptoms may inhibit the development of schizophrenia. Ominous signs are the development of a loss of anxiety and concern about the illness and a decrease in tendency to resist.

2. **Depressive states.** It has been estimated that some 20 per cent of patients with depressive illness have obsessive — compulsive symptoms, and a third have obsessive — compulsive traits of personality. These figures are even higher in patients suffering from depression during the involutional period. It is also noteworthy that patients with an obsessive — compulsive illness may develop a typical depression as a secondary reaction. Another association is the tendency for obsessional symptoms to appear only during attacks of depressive illness, and in this situation the obsessional symptoms usually resolve with recovery from the attack of depression, whether this occurs spontaneously or as a result of treatment by drugs or other means.

3. **Organic brain diseases.** The occurrence of obsessional symptoms in organic brain disorders has aroused a great deal of interest and speculation in encephalities lethargic, sometimes patients develop obsessional symptoms having previously been free from the disorder.

Sometimes obsessional symptoms occur only when the patient develops oculogyric crises. It is interesting that some metallic positions, particularly those which produce extra-pyramidal symptoms, may also produce obsessional symptoms as for instance, manganese poisoning.

**Prognosis**

The illness may come on in attacks and episodes with intervening periods of freedom, or they may last for longer periods with exacerbation, and during the intervening periods the symptoms may be less distressing to the patient, although they are still present. Environmental stress may act as precipitant in some patients. The illness may show spontaneous recovery and when this takes place it is more likely in the early years of the illness. In those patients in whom the obsessional illness has gone on for many years, five years or longer, the probability of spontaneous recovery or complete recovery in response to treatment decreases.

About one-half of the patients develop their main illness before the age of 20, and only 4 per cent start after the age of 35 years.

Studies of the outcome of obsessional states give different figures for the degree of recovery, ranging from 25 per cent to 50 per cent over a follow-up period of five to ten years. The prognosis is, on the whole, favourable for obsessional states which develop as part of a depressive illness as they disappear with recovery from depression. A reflexively early age of onset tends to carry a poor prognosis. A marked obsessional permorbid personality and severity of clinical picture on first admission are also regarded as unfavourable prognostic factors.

**Social aspects.** Most authorities find that the families of obsessional patients have significantly higher incidence of obsessional disorders than the corresponding control groups, whilst there is evidence that genetic factors predispose to the illness. There is also evidence that a strict tyrannical upbringing with insistence on rectitude, obedience and cleanliness may also be contributory. It has been found that patients are often ill for many years before being referred for outpatient or inpatient treatment. They form a small proportion of patients admitted to hospital, between 2 per cent and 3 per cent.

**Obsessional Personality**

The obsessional personality is described as being meticulous, conscientious, orderly and punctilious. These are clean, punctual people paying a great deal of attention to detail and being trustworthy, reliable and tending to take their work home in their minds at night.

They are precise, careful, cautious, pedantic and conservative. They dislike change and get very disturbed if their plans have to be altered. They become creatures of habit, rigid, unadaptable people. As employees they are appreciated, the salt of the earth, dependable and will work at their best without supervision. They set themselves very high standards and tend to be anxious.

Obsessional personalities are common in the community and are not necessarily related to obsessional illness. Some of them can develop obsessional states but there are many patients with obsessional states who do not have this type of personality before the illness.

Obsessional personalities are of importance in predisposition to the development of anxiety states and various psychosomatic disorders.

**Psychopathology**

According to psychoanalytic theory obsessive — compulsive illnesses are associated with conflicts and regression at the anal-sadistic phase of psychosexual development. In favour of this is the frequency with which patients are preoccupied with aggression or dirt, either in their personality or in their symptoms. The mental mechanism, underlying an obsession involves a conflict between drives which seek expression such as sex drives, self-assertion, aggressive drives, on one hand and the controlling forces on the other. This conflict is dealt with by displacement and substitution into an obsessional symptom, and sometimes the obsessional symptom may symbolise the nature of the conflict, for example the hand washing compulsion may symbolise the getting rid of dirt, that is resolving guilt feelings about sexual problems.

Proponents of the learning theory suggest that certain phobias and obsessional symptoms may involve learning mechanisms, particularly as the obsession is associated with anxiety. As a compulsive act relieves the anxiety this will produce a reinforcement which will be conducive to its perpetuation and eventually, because of its capacity for reducing anxiety it becomes fixed by learning as a pattern of behaviour.

**General Management**

Associated anxiety and tension can be relieved by appropriate tranquilly sedative drugs. These will help to make the patient's life more bearable and will make it easier for him to learn to adjust himself to his illness. Many patients will recover on a simple regime of this kind.

If the obsessional symptoms are part of a depressive illness, the treatment is that of the depression, either by antidepressant drugs or, if severe, by electro-convulsive therapy. Psychotherapy is of more value in explaining the psychopathology and genesis of symptoms than psychotherapeutic approaches because of the strength of the patient's defences and the rigidity of his personality. Hallucinogenic drugs, such as lysergic acid and phencyclidine have been used to make the patient more accessible to psychotherapy.

**Treatment of Phobias and Obsessional States**

The treatment of obsessional symptoms has been revolutionised by the introduction of new techniques of behaviour therapy. In addition behaviour therapy may be combined with pharmacological methods of treatment. Specific phobias, including morbid fears of animals, such as dogs or spiders, or defined events, such as heights or thunderstorms, can be treated with systematic desensitisation which involves a gradual exposure in increasing intensity to the phobic situation, usually with a state of relaxation induced to prevent the evocation of anxiety. Flooding, which involves a more rapid, intense exposure to the phobic stimulus, is useful in the treatment of general phobias including agoraphobia.

The common feature of systematic desensitisation and flooding is that there is either a gradual or a sudden exposure to the stimulus which enables the patient to adapt to it. Compulsions are often related to cleaning activities, avoidance, repetition or checking, usually resulting in a reduction of anxiety and subjectively they are considered to avoid disasters or ill-fortune. For example, hand-washing can be treated by behaviour therapy involving contact with the feared contaminant and prevention of washing. This has been termed apostrophic therapy because apostrophic means turning away or dissuading. Flooding associated with modelling, in which the therapist carries out the contact with the phobic stimulus or object, can also be carried out with response prevention. Other workers have shown that deliberate contamination and allowing washing to take place is also quite as effective as that achieved by response prevention. Obsessional slowness has been treated by behavioural techniques including prompting and pacing by the therapist, and also shaping, which is achieved by graduating the tasks and giving reward in the form of praise or approval when they are achieved. Obsessional ruminations are not helped by systematic desensitisation; they are more effectively treated by thought stopping. The thought stopping technique requires the patient to think his obsessive thoughts deliberately, the therapist then makes a sudden loud (aversive) noise and shouts 'Stop'. This appears to interrupt the induced rumination and the patient is then taught to shout 'Stop' each time he deliberately produces his distressing thoughts. After some practice he whispers 'Stop' and eventually uses a sub-vocal command. The technique of paradoxical intention is in some ways similar. Six sessions of instructions in deliberately magnifying and exaggerating obsessional ideas have been found to produce a marked decrease in the occurrence of obtrusive unwanted thoughts.

## HYSTERIA

Hysteria is one of the more commonly seen mental diseases, and some people are of the opinion that it happens to women only, but in fact it is a question merely of women being inflicted with it more commonly than the other sex.

### Definition

In the words of W.L. Linford Rees, "Hysteria is defined as a disorder in which the patient develops symptoms and signs of illness (mental, physical or both) for some real or imagined gain without being fully aware of the underlying motive."

Frequently the term hysteria is misapplied to histrionic or uncontrolled behaviour, whereas it should be reserved for psychogenic illnesses having a motive of gain.

Hysteria is protean in manifestation and may simulate any disease.

The mental mechanism underlying the formation of hysterical symptoms is a process of dissociation whereby certain dynamically important experiences (usually psychic traumata) become separated from the mainstream of consciousness in predisposed individuals under conditions of stress. The development of the hysterical symptom usually enables the patient to escape from a difficult situation. It is on account of the gain resulting from the illness that hysteria has been confused with malingering.

A malingerer is a person who claims he has symptoms when he knows he has none, whereas the hysteric has genuine symptoms.

### Forms of Hysterical Reaction

The varied manifestations of hysteria can conveniently be classified into three groups.

**1. Dysmnesic.** These exhibit the following symptoms :

(i) Amnesia

(ii) Fugues

(iii) Somnambulism

(iv) Twilight states

**2. Conversion hysteria.** These exhibit the following symptoms :

(i) ***Motor :*** Paralysis, paresis, tremors, rigidity, abnormal gait, ataxia, fits.

(ii) ***Sensory general :*** Anesthesia, paraesthesia, hyperalgesia and pains.

(iii) ***Sensory special :*** Visual difficulties, blindness, deafness, loss of taste, loss of smell.

(iv) ***Visceral :*** Vomiting, retention of urine, constipation.

**3. Quasi-psychotic state.** This is also known as Ganser syndrome.

**4. Hysterical superadditions to physical diseases.** This includes hysterical prolongation of illness and certain latrogenic disorders.

It should be noted that all hysterical manifestations involve functions which are under the control or the influence of volition. This applies to the voluntary muscles concerned with vomiting, retention of urine and dyschezia. A great deal of confusion occurs because some authorities describe as hysteria manifestations symptoms which are the bodily manifestations of emotional tension mediated by the autonomic nervous system.

**1. Dysmnesic.** These forms of hysteria include amnesia, fugues, somnambulism, hysterical fits, multiple personality.

(i) ***Hysterical amnesia*** **:** These may cover a short period of a person's life or may cover a large part of it or even the whole of it. Amnesia may or may not be associated with loss of personal identity. Amnesia usually occurs to escape from intolerable anxiety and distress about some problem or difficulty or situation in which the patient finds himself.

Amnesia is sometimes claimed as a defence when the patient has committed a criminal offence, but hysterical amnesia is not accepted in law as mental illness and therefore the patient is held to be responsible quite irrespective of the presence of amnesia.

As a deterrent during World War II and to avoid epidemics of amnesia, notices were sometimes put up that any soldier losing his memory would be dealt with disciplinarily in the same way as he would if he lost any other part of his equipment.

(ii) ***Fugues :*** Fugue is a state of wandering, with amnesia for the period during which the wandering occurred. Again, the fugue is usually determined by a need to get away from some intolerable situation.

It should be noted that fugues may be of three kinds :

(a) Hysterical, (b) as a manifestation of a depressive illness in which the patient is extremely distressed, wanders around, sometimes contemplating suicide and, because he does not register clearly what is happening to him, he is unable to remember the events which occurred during the period of wandering and (c) manifestations of organic mental states, for example post-epileptic phenomenon, or wandering in a state of confusion.

(iii) ***Hysterical fits :*** Hysterical fits may sometimes create confusion in diagnosis because of superficial similarities to grand mal-epilepsy, but the following features will serve to distinguish between them.

Epileptic fits, on the other hand, can occur during sleep and on out of the blue without being necessarily related to what has happened immediately before in the patient's experience; they may occur in dangerous situations such as working at heights or whilst swimming in the sea. All these situations are dangerous with epileptic fits.

There is no real loss of consciousness as in epilepsy, no sequence of tonic and clinic phases, no tongue-biting and no incontinence. Hysterical fits consist of purposive movements of both the limbs including struggling, fighting, scratching, clawing.

Thus, if during a fit, the patient gives evidence of any purposeful movements, such as fighting or resisting or talking spontaneously, answering questions or deliberately attacking or biting, this indicates that the patient is not unconscious, that the cerebral cortex is acting and therefore it is not epileptic. Hysterical fits can go on for much longer than a single major epileptic fit.

**2. Conversion symptoms.** These include the following :

(i) ***Hysterical motor conversion symptoms :*** These may consist of paresis or paralysis of limbs or other parts of the body. They never involve single muscles but symptoms.

Hysterical gaits tend to be bizarre and are not similar to any organic neurological gait; similarly, hysterical weakness is when the patient is asked to contract the muscles of the limb, contraction of both against and antagonist will occur.

(ii) ***Sensory conversion symptoms :*** Special senses *e.g.*, hysterical blindness, hysterical deafness, hysterical anaemia, hysterical loss of taste will occur for some special reason which determines the selection of the particular sense modality to be affected. Sometimes it may be the patient's weak point, for example myopia may be the determinant of the development of hysteric blindness in certain traumatic situations when the stress is sufficiently severe, or may be determined by the occupation of the person, for example a telephonist, or it may be determined by a desire not to hear.

(iii) ***General sensation :*** The most common hysterical symptom affecting general sensation is anaesthesia of the skin; this corresponds to the patient's idea of anaesthesia and is usually of a glove and stocking distribution and stops at one of the joints, wrist joint, elbow joint or shoulder joint and is quite different from the distribution or loss of sensation due to any affection of the sensory nerves.

**3. Quasi-psychotic state.** This usually takes the form of hysterical pseudo-dementia or Ganser syndrome, which is characterised by tendency to give approximate answers. The answers are incorrect, but near enough to show that the patient has the mental capacity to work out the correct answer, and behaviour again corresponds to the patient's concept of what mental illness is. This condition most commonly occurs in penal institutions.

**4. Hysterical superadditions.** Hysterical Superadditions can occur in any physical disease for motives of gain, such as gaining attention and sympathy. Any illness may similarly be prolonged by hysterical mechanism. Some inorganic illnesses are hysterical and brought about by suggestion.

### Aetiology

At one time it was believed that genetic factors played an important role in the predisposition to hysteria, but twin studies have thrown considerable doubt on this and hysteria is nowadays regarded as a reaction to environmental problems in which the patient's personality plays an important part in determining the mode of reaction. Environmental circumstances determine the time of development of hysterical symptoms. A specific type of hysterical personality has been described which is characterised by the need to exaggerate, the need to be in the centre of attention and to give an impression to the outside world of being better than one is, of tending to manipulate people and situations for some personal need, to have shallow emotional reactions but which are often demonstrative and dramatic and histrionic, a tendency to be untruthful and to exaggerate statements and claims. Many patients feel they have been deprived of affection and approval which it is very difficult to satisfy. When they do get the attention and approval which they need, they test the person who gives it to such an extent that very often this produces a withdrawal of affection. Hysteria may be regarded as a protective mechanism to safeguard the person from stresses and strains of life and anxiety which are difficult to tolerate.

**Causes of Hysteria**

In earlier times of gullibility hysteria was believed to be the consequence of a visitation from the otherworld, but now many of its causes have been unearthed due to a minute and detailed analysis of its psychological roots. But only the main causes will be mentioned here :

**1. Emotional tension.** Very severe or intense emotional tension can result in an individual due to the various problems of life, extreme frustrations and disappointments, failures and particularly sexual dissatisfactions, and this element plays an important role in causing hysteria.

**2. Age.** Hysteria is a disease peculiar to adolescence and early youth because this is the age in which one is especially susceptible to various problems. Mental tension at this stage is very strong.

**3. Defective discipline.** One cause of hysteria among children and adolescents is the defective nature of discipline among them. Whenever discipline is more extreme or less effective than it can ideally be, there is the improper and unbalanced development of self-control in the individual. Synthesis is thereby denied to his personality and he is hysterically bent.

**4. Hereditary defect.** It is the opinion of some scholars that the tendency to hysteria is a hereditary defect, but the extent to which hereditary defects contribute towards a hysterical condition has not been ascertained as yet.

**5. Low intelligence level.** Upon examining hysteric patients among soldiers Hollingworth found that they have a low level of intelligence and as a general rule, lack of intelligence may be interpreted as one of its causes.

**6. Maladjustment.** One definitely important cause of hysteria is the patient's maladjustment with his own conditions which results in his acquiring feelings of inferiority and insecurity. People of this kind evince sexual deviations, mental conflicts and the feeling of guilt.

**7. Suggestion.** Babinski believes that one cause of hysteria in man is the extreme degree in which man, or woman, is susceptible to suggestion. But the view has not gained much in currency.

**8. Absence of synthesis.** According to Janet, the major cause of hysteria is the absence of synthesis in the patient's personality, but he failed to explain why different patients exhibited different symptoms of hysteria if synthesis and the lack of it were the only cause.

**9. Sexual dissatisfaction.** Freud defined and explained hysteria on the basis of the sexual drive. During youth an individual passes through the phallic stage, and if his sexual desire is suppressed by his super-ego then it leads to mental conflict, and when this conflict takes the form of psychological expression then it is termed hysteria. It is often remarked that the sexual life of patients of hysteria is not normal, and the fact of this disease being predominantly concerned with sex is further borne out by the fact that it is found more in women than in men. This is due to the fact that man's bodily structure permits him easier satisfaction of the sexual impulse than in the case of women. Secondly, whenever sexual life within wedlock is abnormal it is the female partner who is more profoundly influenced, and hence it is apparent that sexual maladjustment is one important cause of hysteria.

In a consideration of the various causes of hysteria, it is sensible to keep in mind all the above causes since in some form or the other each one of them is important. Besides these causes, certain psychiatrists have tried to attribute hysteria to sexual, racial and psychological differences, but it has been established that hysteria is unconcerned with such differences.

**Cures of Hysteria**

Following are the methods that are normally employed in the treatment and cure of hysteria :

**1. Psychoanalytic method.** Through this method it has been possible to cure numerous patients of this disease.

**2. Suggestion.** Suggestion can help to permanently eliminate certain symptoms of hysteria though the disease itself cannot be permanently cured by this method.

**3. Re-learning.** Hysteria can also be cured through re-learning.

**4. Hypnotism.** The hypnotic method has proved of greater importance than suggestion but of less than psychoanalytic method.

It should be borne in mind that hysteric are suggestible and respond readily to harmful as well as beneficial suggestions. They usually crave attention but the more attention paid to their symptoms the more implicit will be the suggestion that these are serious and the longer will they tend to persist.

The hysterical symptom should as far as possible be ignored and no notice taken of any worsening of the symptom, but the slightest improvement should be encouraged. The patient must be persuaded by those with whom he is in contact to carry on living as normally as possible. Keeping a patient with hysterical symptoms in bed or helping a patient to walk with a hysterical gait only serves to impress the patient know that he is ill and needs support. Every effort must be made to make the patient assume responsibility for his functional revelry, and the more active part he can be made to play in treatment the better. The general rule in management is firmness and, what is even more important, it must be consistent firmness.

Sometimes symptoms will disappear if they are completely ignored, but it is sometimes necessary to tackle the symptom actively in order to prevent habituation and capacity due to the symptom, and early removal makes it possible to bring the patient to face his problems and be guided to a more salutary solution.

The best method undoubtedly is to produce full function recovery in one session. It is, therefore, important for the patient to allow himself ample time for the therapeutic session and to be prepared to carry on with his treatment until full functional recovery is achieved.

The following procedures are useful tactical aids in some patients :

(1) hypnosis and (2) intravenous barbiturate narcosis.

Both of these will help to elicit further information about the psychopathology of the disorder, as well as increasing the patient's suggestibility to beneficial persuasion.

When the patient has recovered from his symptom, he will often become more anxious because now he has to face his problems more directly. It is now necessary to discuss with the patient his reactions to life's difficulties. The hysteric tends to give in readily and retreat into illness in the face of difficulties, and the patient must be guided in dealing with the problems which precipitated his illness in a more satisfactory manner.

Hysterics tend to attempt things beyond their capabilities in order to impress people. They must be encouraged to accept their limitations and work within the limits of their abilities, and at the same time, to learn to gain satisfaction from whatever assets they possess.

## CONVERSION HYSTERIA

### Definitions

**1. J.C. Colemen.** "Conversion reaction is a neurotic defence in which symptoms of some organic disease appear without any underlying organic pathology."

**2. N. Cameron.** "A conversion reaction is a process whereby an unconscious conflict is transformed (converted) into a bodily symptom which reduces tension and anxiety by expressing conflict symbolically."

### Symptomatology

**1. Sensory symptoms.** These include anaesthesia, hyposensitivity of different sense organs.

**2. Motor symptoms.** These include paralysis, trembling, tics, stereotypes, blinking, unconsciousness, etc.

### Aetiology

Following are the general causes of convention hysteria :

1. Sense of insecurity due to sexual reactions.
2. Urge to avoid unpleasant situation.
3. Escaping dangerous situations.
4. Sense of guilt and self punishment.
5. Suppression of dangerous emotions.
6. Revenge against strict and cruel behaviour.
7. Escaping future difficulties.

### Treatment

Treatment of conversion hysteria requires prolonged psychotherapy so that the patient may be able to face reality.

## FUGUE STATES

According to Fisher, "Fugue is a hysterical attack (accident) in which the individual forgets his personal identity and leaves his physical surrounding." The term 'fugue' is of Latin origin and implies running away or escaping. In psychopathology one form of hysteria is known as hysteric fugue in which the individual is compelled by a concealed impulse to run away from home and wander about for many days. When he recovers his normal state, he returns home but forgets all that occurred during his fugue condition.

As in the case of other mental diseases, fugue also has its root in excessive repression. It is a fact of normal psychology that the desires that one represses find their satisfaction through some other medium. Now, if this person suffers from some serious psychological or emotional shock then his repressed desires find expression in the form of fugue, and he escapes from his domestic environment. This desire to escape is not of momentary or instantaneous origin since it also contains another desire to stay at home in order to spare other members of the pain, but gradually the desire to escape overcomes the tendency towards filial responsibility, and the individual does escape.

A stage of fugue may last for any time period from a few hours to a few years and as has been remarked, during it the individual has no recollection of his past life. Although he retains consciousness enough to make a pretence of running away as well as of looking after himself, yet during the fugue state he is unconscious. When the fugue attack is over, the person does not recollect anything that may have occurred during the period of attack, although the period preceding the fugue is again recollected. Janet has described a case of fugue in approximately this manner :

Rue was a poor boy who lived in a town with his mother and was employed in a grocer's shop. After working some years at this job, he fell into the habit of going to the bar where he used to keep company with sailors and would listen to their tales of sea life with much interest. He also used to dream of visiting the places that they mentioned. But as the habit of drinking grew on him, his personality gradually proceeded towards disorganisation, and he would even forget to return home after drinking but would instead roam in the streets of Paris. His mind was constantly echoing the desires that he should somehow reach the countries of which the sailors had told him. In order to give substance to this dream he once ran away from home, and after facing numerous difficulties succeeded in securing a job on board a ship. Many months after he had run away from home he was given alcohol to drink on the occasion of some festivity. When he heard the date, he suddenly shouted, 'It is my mother's birthday.' Immediately he recollected his home, and simultaneously forgot all that had happened to him after he had run away from home. From this it is evident that a shock can end a condition of fugue.

## SOMNAMBULISM

Somnambulism also is a Latin term meaning walking in one's sleep. It is often found in a hysteric person, and the symptom of the hysteric person is called hysteric somnambulism. Besides the hysteric person, somnambulism is a condition that can be seen in the individuals who are otherwise normal. In this condition the individual comes under the influence of some feelings, memories or concepts and acts upon them while actually asleep in the manner of puppets. As to the causes that lie at the root of such activity, even the patient himself is not aware of them. In this manner it is a condition of mental disorganisation, a condition in which the individual's complexes or sentiments are not organised and synthesised, and do not find expression in normal life. Hence, they are expressed through abnormal behaviour. In this abnormal condition, the distorted thoughts gain control over the individual's normal personality and guide him into mechanical behaviour. In this manner, in such a condition the person's normal life does remain undisturbed, and the primary mental organisation becomes subordinated to the somnambulistic secondary mental organisation. When the strike of sleep-walking is over, the individual returns to normalcy and forgets all that is conjoined to the condition.

In order to understand the above law of somnambulism, it is essential to examine a case mentioned by Janet.

A twenty-year old girl named Irene had become ill following the prolonged and painful death of her old mother; the conditions accompanying the death were very painful and dramatic. Her mother was affected by tuberculosis, and the disease had reached its highest point. Irene and her mother had lived in a simple lodging. Just before her death the mother had felt severe constriction in the throat and vomited blood as well as death coming as a relief following many days of suffering. And Irene had tried to achieve the impossible by looking after her with courage and devotion, fighting with all her might. She used to knit and stitch in order to earn a living, and would spend the nights by the mother's bedside, and when the mother died she even tried to cremate her body. She stood the corpse on its feet but it fell down, and she had much difficulty in carrying it to the bed. After the burial of her mother, Irene's behaviour started exhibiting signs of abnormality, the main symptom taking the form of somnambulism. She would remain in the somnambulistic state for hours together and would re-enact the entire scene of her mother's death with the skill of an experienced actress. In this enacting she would sometimes describe the entire scene in terms of questions and wait for the answers, but at other times would ask questions and not wait for the answers. Again, she would sometimes appear to be taken by fright in visualising or perceiving the painful scenes again. At yet other times, she would have delusions of words and actions in order to take part in the acting. In her dramatics, following the death of the mother, the daughter would be inspired by the thought of death and would prepare to commit suicide, and this fact she would express as if she were asking her mother for advice. Under the influence of experience in her own life, she would imagine committing suicide by being overrun by a locomotive, imagining that she was lying on the railway track she would prostrate herself on her room floor and await death with anxiety and fear, and at such time she perfectly acted the role of being cut to death under the locomotive wheels. She would gaze continuously at the imagined train, and sometime later would fall back with a shrill scream as if she had been cut to death. But then she should immediately get up and start enacting another scene, and soon after she returned to her normal state.

It is evident from the above example of somnambulism that in it there can be repeated remembrance of actions in an indefinite manner, and in every remembrance the association between motion, spirit and words is mentioned. Once the fit of somnambulism is over suddenly or gradually he returns to his daily activities as if nothing had happened. This occurs because the patient has no recollection of his environment and actions during the fit.

## PHOBIAS

### Definitions

1. **W.L. Linford Rees.** "A phobia may be defined as an irrational or morbid fear in relation to a thing, situation or stimulus which normally would not evoke such fear."

2. **Coleman.** "A phobic reaction is a persistent fear of some object or situation which presents no actual danger to the patient or in which the danger is magnified out of all proportions to its actual seriousness."

3. **N. Cameron.** "A phobic reaction is an attempt to reduce internally generated tension and anxiety by a process of displacement, projection and avoidance."

A phobic reaction is a form of fear which is out of proportion to the danger of the situation, cannot be explained, is beyond voluntary control and tends to lead to avoidance of the feared situation or stimulus. Certain fears, however, cannot be avoided by escape from the stimulus, *e.g.*, fears of disease, death or one's own harmful impulses. The patient experiencing a phobic reaction can experience all the distressing mental and bodily concomitants of anxiety. Many patients become preoccupied with the possibility of encountering the phobic object or situation and suffer greatly as a result of such anxious apprehension. They may also become afraid of the experience of anxiety, *i.e.*, they become phobic, a mechanism which intensifies the distress and disability associated with phobias.

Characteristically, because of the unpleasantness of the emotion of anxiety, the patient will tend to arrange his life to avoid the phobic stimulus, thereby greatly restricting his daily activities.

Phobia denotes an abnormal or irrational fear. Normally fear is a reaction to dangerous conditions or objects and is appropriate, but a person having a phobia has no proper cause of his fear. Thus, phobia is fear without any basis. People afflicted with disease are afraid of enclosed spaces, height or even crowds. The patient is also aware of their arbitrary and idiotic nature but he has no way of getting rid of it or of understanding and analysing the reasons why he contracted it in the first place.

**Kinds of Phobia**

Main among the many fears concerning the environment are the following :

1. Agora-claustrophobia
2. Social phobias
3. Animal phobias
4. Other specific phobias
5. Illness phobias
6. Obsessional phobias.

**1. Agoraphobia.** This is one of the commonest phobic disorders seen in clinical practice. About 75 per cent of patients are women and the onset usually is between 15 years and 35 years. They tend to show generalised anxiety as well as phobic fear reactions. They may also be depressed and have obsessional symptoms or depersonalisation. They have fears of going out alone, of going into crowded or enclosed place. They do not show any increased tendency to condition easily and do not respond well to desensitisation therapy.

**2. Social phobias.** These again are most common in women and have their onset between 15 years and 30 years. They have fears of social situations and activities, *e.g.*, eating, drinking, writing or reading in company.

**3. Animal phobias.** These are less common and differ from the above in having their origin in childhood and usually being monosymptomatic fear of a single animal species. There is usually no general anxiety. The large majority of sufferers are women. On psychological testing, they condition rapidly and extinguish slowly. They respond well to systematic desensitisation.

**4. Other specific phobias.** These include phobias for thunderstorms, heights, winds, darkness, etc., are usually monosymptomatic phobias with no generalised anxiety or associated symptoms such as depression or depersonalisation. They respond well to systematic desensitisation.

**5. Illness phobias.** These patients are preoccupied with fears of disease like cancer, heart disease, venereal disease, death, etc. The symptoms superficially resemble obsessional symptoms but do not include the tendency to resist the preoccupation,

**6. Obsessional fears.** These fulfil the criteria for obsessional symptoms in that they are associated with a subjective feeling of compulsion which patients try to resist but cannot get rid of although they may realise that they are irrational. Examples are fears of harming people, fears of contamination leading to compulsive hand-washing.

### Phobia and Normal Fear

Fears of the kind mentioned above do not have rational and specific causes like ordinary fear. Normal fear has causes that can be comprehended, for it would be natural for a person saved from drowning to be afraid of water. But, on the other hand, phobias are abnormal and neurotic fears, of the causes of which the patient is not aware but as reaction to which he appears violent. Such fears lead to much inconvenience for the patient, but if their causes are known then their influence is reduced and sometimes entirely eliminated. Bagby and Shaffer have mentioned the normal characteristics or symptoms of phobias as follows :

1. Phobia dates back from some singular traumatic condition which is occurred probably in infancy when the child has been severely frightened.

2. At the root of phobia is some painful and disgusting experience which is conjoined to some tabooed or shameful activity, as a result of which the patient does not like to think of it and neither can he discuss it with others. Hence this experience passes out of the mind through protective forgetting or repression.

3. Phobia is a permanent fear since the guilt consciousness attached to the basic conditions or situations of fear prevents

it even from being brought into conscious memory. Besides, excessive fear of the object prevents all favourable associations that can put an end to the basic experience of fear. Phobias that are the consequence of repression can be eliminated by achieving satisfactory relations with one's parents or one's guide.

4. Although phobia arises out of fear caused by a specific condition yet it can spread to a large class of objects.

5. When the repressed, traumatic experience at the root of phobia is brought on to the plane of consciousness through free association, the analysis of dreams and other psychological techniques, then its intensity is considerably reduced because the patient understands it. Bagby has related a very interesting case of ochlophobia.

A young lady came to a psychiatrist to rid herself of the fear of crowds. Whenever she became surrounded by a number of people, she became obsessed by the fear of being crushed or suffocated to death. She was aware of the basically irrational nature of this fear but nevertheless spent the life of a prisoner within the precincts of her own house. When ill she could not bring herself to travel by crowded buses or trains, or to purchase things from large and crowded shops. This fear had been with her since childhood, but of its cause she knew nothing. With the help of free association she revived the memory of a very dangerous experience that she had long forgotten. When she had been an infant her parents gave her permission to witness a passing crowd of circus procession but with the injunction that she were not to follow it into town. But the excitement and attraction of the circus was such that she finally reached the centre of the town where she suddenly found herself surrounded by tall and grown-up adults. She tried to force her way but did not succeed, and started crying. Seeing her cry a gentle-hearted person presumed that she could not see and helped her to the front row, near the centre of activity. After sometime her fear ended and she stopped crying, soon after which she returned home. But under the circumstances she could not relate the incident to her parents, and the entire experience was forgotten. It was made to revive through free association, and thus when she came to know the cause of fear she gradually managed to control it.

**Psychogenic Kinds of Phobia**

Phobia has been classified into three classes from the psychogenic standpoint :

**1. Ordinary concrete phobia.** In this, as is evident from the term, the individual is afraid of some concrete stimulus, and as time passes this original stimulus is forgotten, although fear of a similar stimulus is always retained. If now the person is reminded of the original stimulus, his fear can be removed. In the generation of a phobia, besides the condition of fear, another factor that plays an important role is the individual's immediate objective. One example of a concrete phobia can be examined.

A twenty-year old lady of culture was very much afraid of running water. As a result of this fear she would lock up all windows and doors while travelling so that she may not observe running water in brooks and rivers. Detailed investigation revealed that at the root of this phobia was an incident that had occurred some thirteen years earlier. In her seventh year she had gone out with her mother and aunty, but the mother had left her with aunty and returned. While with her she started running around in the hilly terrain although admonished by the aunt not to do so. Later on her aunty found her; the girl was stuck between two rocks with a stream of water flowing continuously over her head. The young girl was very frightened, and she requested the aunty to keep the incident a secret, which she had done. But immediately after her aunty left, the girl developed an abnormal fear of running water, twenty-three years later the aunty was told of the girl's condition while revisiting the family. She then disclosed the original experience after knowing which the girl lost her abnormal fear.

**2. Symbolic concrete phobia.** In this the individual is afraid of certain concrete objects but he considers them in symbolic form rather than their own. Fisher has described a case of this kind.

A young girl was constantly beset with the idea that her mother would stab her with a particular knife lying in the kitchen. This fear was so strong in her mind that she could sleep only after her mother had gone to sleep. She was aware that her fear had no rational basis but she was nevertheless frightened of touching that knife, and on the other hand she was also attracted to the knife and did not consider destroying it. She was a well, educated and sensible young woman. She had two elder brothers, she loved her father very much although he had been dead for quite some time and continued to see him in her dreams. Towards her mother her feelings were those of fear, jealousy and sympathy.

On analysing the case it was discovered that when young, the girl used to sleep with her parents, and to play with her father in the morning. She was very much attached to her father. Further analysis revealed that when she was ten years old, one of her brother used to come to her in the night, thus causing her much mental anguish, but she concealed this fact from everyone else. Contact with the brother made her conscious of many facts concerning sex, and she had also inferred the relations between her parents. In view of this knowledge her attraction for the father had grown up while she felt the need to control such impulse. Due to this injury to her moral concepts, she tended to keep quiet and somewhat lost. The experience with her brother caused her physical and mental pain, but also at the same time the knife, in her mind, became the symbol of sex. Due to this emotional attachment with sex she could not bring herself to destroy the knife and all dreams concerning her father that she saw were of a pre-eminently sexual nature. Consequently, she had formed criminal feelings concerning her mother, and it was due to this that she feared being stabbed by her mother. In this way, this abnormal fear was a self-defence mechanism on the part of the girl to protect herself from her sexual urge towards her father.

**3. Symbolic abstract phobia.** While in the case of symbolic concrete phobia, a person fears a particular object or person but in symbolic form, in the case of symbolic abstract phobia he fears the symbolic form of some abstract thought or motive. In this the stimulus is within the individual, not outside him. As a consequence of painful experience during childhood, the individual finds himself incapable of applying all his energy towards extrovert behaviour in his personal and social life. Due to this, his mental power became self-centered. As a result he began to exhibit signs of phobia.

## TICS

A tic is an involuntary, irregular and sudden movement of some part of the body, such as eye, mouth, fingers, etc. Chorea is the name given to the active irregularity caused by tic. Psychologists have effected a distinction between hysteria and psychasthenic tic. In this first kind the individual is not aware of a tic, and the moment he becomes aware of it the tic stops. In the other case the person is aware of the tic while it occurs. The first kind of tic is the outcome of personality disorganisation or disintegration while the other is caused by repression. One example of tic is the case of a soldier who felt a tic in the muscles of his jaw and throat while eating, and as a result his face would assume a look of anger and ferocity. He had no idea how the tic had started. When he was hypnotised during his treatment he remembered a scene that he had completely forgotten, in which he was concealing himself in enemy territory. During this time he saw the enemy ill-treating a colleague of his, and this filled him with extreme anger, but he was immediate hit by a bullet and he lost consciousness. In this conscious state when the soldier remembered the incident, the tic stopped.

From the above example it is apparent that a tic stops when it becomes conscious, and hence it cannot be attributed to habit. Its intensity and frequency both depend upon the mental condition of the subject. In a calm moment, the tic is almost absent but when excited it is both intense as well as very frequent. Normally all kinds of tic can be cured.

It has been mentioned that a psychasthenic tic cannot be stopped even when the individual is conscious of it. One example of such a tic is the following case :

A young lad got a tic in his left cheek in the presence of any girl; this condition had worried him for the last three years. Analysis revealed an incident that had occurred earlier and formed the background of this tic. When he was 15 years of age, while talking to a girl of his acquaintance, the girl removed a fountain pen from his pocket in order to tease him. When he tried to forcefully take it away from her, she dropped the pen in her blouse. This excited the boy but also perplexed him, and there he had first experience of his embarrassing tic. This young lad had spent his infancy and childhood in an atmosphere of oppression in which his mother and sister had bossed him, with the result that he had a tendency to recede into the background when females were around. When he grew up he determined not to be thus coerced by the weaker sex. When the girl silently challenged him to remove the pen from her blouse, his determination to assert himself came to the fore, but as yet his tendency to be oppressed by women had not been destroyed. Hence he experienced the tic and his attention was withdrawn from this difficult situation.

## WAR NEUROSIS

Neurosis to be found in soldiers during a war period are called war neurosis. They are to be seen mostly during days of actual combat.

### What is War Neurosis?

During the First World war psychologists succeeded in discovering the concept of shell shock while during the Second World War they found the notion of combat fatigue. It was erroneously believed that in both these concepts implicitly the idea was that mental symptoms were caused by actual shell burst or combat fatigue whereas in truth what actually occurred was that these physical occurrences gave rise to psychological tension which resulted in certain mental characteristics. Consequently, psychologists invented the term 'war neurosis' to suit all neurosis that had their origin in the condition of war. In the days of the Second World War psychologists observed that individuals suffering from war neurosis could conveniently be divided into two classes. The first class included individuals who had a properly healthy personality and who had led satisfying lives of a civilian or soldier before the outbreak of war. When such fundamentally healthy individuals became involved in incidents that gave them very bitter experiences, then they exhibited certain mental symptoms, symptoms which were also seen in conditions of inadequate training, physical fatigue and low morale. Among these mental symptoms the most frequent were remembering of very dangerous and fatal incidents, insomnia, mental or spiritual unrest, being startled, staring with unseeing eyes, expressionless face, physical fatigue, irritability, depression or tendency to avoid all group activity. In the case of normal individuals it is better to term such conditions as combat stress reactions rather than war neurosis. The other class of sufferers from war neurosis includes individuals whose history, symptoms, etc., compared with those of peace-time sick people. In most of them tendencies towards neurosis were present to begin with. They were shy, easily led and self-conscious individuals, who showed an almost complete lack of pugnacity and courage. A majority of them also showed emotional instability and maladjustment even in civilian life. Hence, it can be easily concluded that had they never been a prey to war conditions, there was no less possibility of their becoming neurotic in normal life. It was only natural that when such individuals were forced to face such strenuous conditions as that of war they should develop symptoms of neurosis. They exhibited mostly such signs as hysteria, neurotic weakness, anxiety and compulsive neurosis. Like normal patients they required a long treatment, and when ultimately discharged from the hospital they were considered unfit for further military service.

**Frequency of War Neurosis**

From the statistics made available after the war it appears that the majority of soldiers do not find much difficulty in adjusting to conditions of modern warfare. In certain specific cases many soldiers showed temporary signs of being depressed, but evidence of neurosis was very small. From the report published by J.B. Dynes, N.N. Springer and S. Peal it appeared that only 2 per cent of soldiers showed an intensity of neurosis that necessitated hospitalisation. On any day during the period of war only 1 per cent of all soldiers in hospitals were there due to neurosis. The major cause behind this was that the soldiers who represented the possibility of developing abnormal symptoms had been weeded out during training itself. In the Second World War some 5 per cent of all the soldiers registered were turned out during training for possessing neurotic tendency and susceptibility. Studies made by R.D. Gillespie, G.N. Raines, and N.C. Kolb revealed that war neurosis is to be found only in the case of new soldiers who have not been properly trained, in inactive, defeated, cowardly soldiers suffering from very low morale, or in individuals who have been through such situations as heavy firing, attack, etc., while they themselves were without means of defence.

**Symptoms of War Neurosis**

Many are the symptoms of war neurosis, the following having been observed by R.D. Gillespie during the Second World War in his examination of neurotic soldiers :

**1. Fear reaction.** This includes the normal reactions signifying fear, such as violent beating of the heart, shivering, looking with an unwavering glance, inactivity of the limbs, etc. In state of extreme excitation, extreme intensity of fear is an evidence which sometimes results in mental disturbance and sometimes not. Some patients exhibit such signs of fear as immobility to speak etc.

**2. Psychosomatic symptoms.** War neurosis gives rise to many physical symptoms which have no real psychological basis, and are in fact caused by emotional factors, the main being headaches, ulcers in intestines, disturbed beating of the heart, disturbed breathing, spinning sensation in the head, difficulty in focusing eyes, severe pain in various parts of the body, pain in muscles, stopping of motor and nervous activity, etc.

**3. Conditioned reactions.** Conditioned reactions are those which were present when the traumatic condition that is the cause of the neurosis occurred, and which are also essential for the reviving of psychological and emotional symptoms of that experience. For example, if a soldier has been injured in the arm through bomb blast, he manifests obstacles in the activity of the arm. One soldier had been trapped in a burning tank, and later on, when he had become a patient, tended to be nervous and anxiously excited whenever enclosed in a small space such as elevator. The manifestation of the traumatic condition and its conditioned reactions have been observed to occur at intervals of hours and even days.

**4. Amnesia.** Many of the patients of war neurosis exhibit amnesia concerning the conditions of accident or the traumatic condition which brought about the neurosis in the first place. This occurs in order to shield the individual the pain of that experience. Amnesia of this kind has been observed to occur in relation to experiences that comprehend feelings of crime and self-degradation, in particular. Amnesia also exhibits such conditions as anxiety of an emotional kind, mental disturbance, etc.

**5. Fatigue syndromes.** When soldiers are forced to fight for long periods of time without relaxation, they fight under great stress of tension with the result that they manifest signs of physical exhaustion even when their bodies are not actually exhausted. Such signs include yawning, lack of zest, tendency to hate others, irritability, an extremely critical tendency, anxiety, lack of self confidence, sleeplessness, etc. In its emotional forms, such signs are accompanied by indifference. Such evidences of fatigue are to be seen more particularly in the case of fliers.

**6. Exhaustion syndrome.** Such exhaustion syndromes are to be seen in soldiers who have experienced great personal danger, extreme physical endurance, lack of sleep and adequate food, etc. It manifests itself in such physical symptoms as the drying up and yellowing of the countenance, reduced weight, sleeplessness and motor nervous disturbances. Mental symptoms of this condition are extreme worry, amnesia, indifference and imbecility, but normally individuals suffering from exhaustion syndrome are easily and expeditiously cured.

### Aetiology

War is an undesirable and dangerous activity, and as long as the soldier is engaged in it, he is constantly aware of the possibility of being killed or very seriously disabled. Due, to military laws and the sense of duty he cannot run away to protect himself from such danger, while on the other hand his instinct for self-preservation is equally strong. Hence, it is only natural that the instinct for self-preservation should come into conflict with military law and sense of duty. As a result the patient finds a very feasible solution in the form of neurosis in which he not only evades danger and ensures safety, but also manages to preserve his dignity and self-respect. Once the signs of neurosis become apparent, the soldier is removed from the field of active fighting, permanently or temporarily, whether or not he desires to be so removed. The elucidation of the fact of war neurosis is further borne out by the fact that so long as a soldier is not healed of his wounds he exhibits no signs of internal disturbance but as soon as he is cured and is fit for active service he manifests signs of neurosis. Symptoms of war neurosis are never seen in prisoners of war, and this only further elucidates also that has been said before, because the prisoner is not faced with the possibility of being sent back to fight the war. Yet this explanation does not serve to explain all kinds of war neurosis, since it is quite possible that abnormal behaviour may be the outcome of causes more complex than the ordinary struggle and conflict between self-respect and safety. For example, one may develop a guilt sense by not being able to help a wounded friend and this way also create some mental symptoms as a kind of self-punishment. Similarly, the desire to revolt against strict military discipline may also find expression in some distorted and abnormal reaction. Nevertheless fear is always a part of such reactions, and it can be said that the purpose of neurosis consists in the temporary or permanent withdrawal of the individual from the battlefield while leaving his self-respect intact in this manner consciously. The truth of the matter is that they fight against any such symptoms, and in spite of their presence they want to go on fighting the war. These symptoms and the disturbances have their origin in unconscious forces of the mind, and the soldiers are incapable of controlling them.

**Treatment of War Neurosis**

In both the preceding world wars it was observed that if the patients of neurosis receive prompt attention and treatment they are cured as greater benefit is apparent if the patient is hospitalised as soon as the symptoms appear. Methods of curing these soldiers do not differ from the ones utilised in the case of civilian individual, but some particular methods have proved more efficacious in the cure of war neurosis. The first steps in the cure of war neurosis consists of giving the patient regular and measured rest, comfort, proper food and favourable environment. Some patients also exhibit signs of mental conflict as well as complain of a loss of memory. If it is found necessary to reduce the patient to unconsciousness then this is done with the help of hypnotism, the object of which is to bring the resisting patient to a condition of hypnotism. It is found that in the hypnotic state verbal suggestions have particular strength, but intravenous injections of sodium amytal and pendothal are also administered wherever found necessary. Once the cooperation and approval of the patient are received then it becomes easier to induce him to recollect traumatic experience of war, and thus he can find expression for his repressed emotions. Information gained through hypnotism is discussed with the patient is his conscious state. Psychotherapy has been able to assist in this form of communication with the patient and has also succeeded in curing very dangerous symptoms. The main purpose is helping the patient to a right understanding of necessary adjustment between his duty to return to the field of war and his fear of it. Any benefit that accrues of psychotherapy depends upon the normal personality and tendency of the patient. A majority of the patients decide to return to war field after they have been given some treatment and adequate rest, but such a result of treatment does not appear in the case of soldiers who have a defective personality or contrary tendencies. If they are forced into any action, then even when they have been cured, their original symptoms reappear. Reports on the World War I prepared by R.R. Grinker, J.P. Spiegel, A. Torric, M. Wellman and J.F. Simpson show that some 80 to 90 per cent of patients affected with war neurosis return to a limited or full engagement with armed forces. It appears from this that these soldiers did not suffer from actual neurosis but some abnormal reactions to the experiences of war. Soldiers who are declared unfit for active service show quite satisfactory adjustment in their civilian capacities, yet there are some patients who never recover fully, one cause of which is the pension scheme in America that offers a stipend as long as these symptoms are mentioned. James D. Page, a psychologist has suggested that if the pension system is replaced by a scheme for gratuitous payment of a sum to sufferers then the profit from maintaining these symptoms would come to an end.

## QUESTIONS FOR EXERCISE

1. Explain the nature, kinds and characteristics of psychoneurosis and distinguish it from psychosis.
2. What are the various types of neurotic disorders? Discuss the nature and symptoms of neurasthenia.
3. Write short note on Anxiety Neurosis.
4. Write short note on Anxiety Hysteria.

5. Explain the nature of Obsessive-Compulsive neurosis.
6. What is hysteria? Explain the origin and symptoms of this disorder.
7. Write short note on Conversion Hysteria.
8. Write short note on Fugue states.
9. Write short note on Somnambulism.
10. What is phobia? Illustrate some of its varieties and discuss its etiology.
11. Write short note on Tics.
12. Write short note on War neurosis.

# 22

# PSYCHOTHERAPY

## WHAT IS PSYCHOTHERAPY?

**1. G.W. Kisker.** "Psychotherapy is the treatment of emotional and behaviour disturbances by psychological methods. These methods are of a great many different kinds, with some directed toward individuals and other towards groups."

**2. W.L. Linford Rees.** "Psychotherapy may be defined as treatment involving communication between the patient and the therapist, with the aim of modifying and alleviating illness."

**3. Fisher.** "Psychotherapy is a planned and systematic application of psychological facts and theories to the alleviation of large variety of human ailments and disturbances, particularly those of psychogenic origin."

**4. J.D. Page.** "Psychotherapy means treatment of mental disorders, especially psychoneurosis by psychological techniques."

**5. Landis and Bolles.** "Psychotherapy means acting on the human mind by mental means with the intention of effecting a cure or alleviation of illness."

Psychotherapy consists in the cure of personality-states by the use of the psychological methods and techniques. Such methods of mental cure are not new for they have been known from the earliest times, when hypnotism, suggestion, advice, faith, etc. were used in efforts at curing mental disorders. But these old methods did not ensure success because the root cause of any mental disease was not apprehended and removed. Secondly, in these ancient techniques the patient was reduced to helplessness and complete misery, in the face of such disease. In modern psychotherapy, on the other hand, the patient himself takes active part in the analysis and cure of his disease, and in many cases the doctor remains almost passive. A patient is given the time to think and give expression of his own feelings on the subject, a process in which the doctor interferes almost not at all. At the root of this method of treatment is the knowledge that mental diseases are the outcome of many psychological conflicts and if these conflicting elements are given a chance to find expression, the conflict can be resolved. In these techniques of psychotherapy, a considerable sum of money and period of time are required. Consequently not everyone can benefit from it.

**Process of Psychotherapy**

The chief objective of psychotherapy is to rid the patient of symptoms which make his life a burden to him, and it is the duty of the psychiatrist to help the patient regain his self-confidence and to strengthen his personality so that he can solve his own problems and adjust with his environment. Apparently, it may become necessary to effect the widest possible changes in the patient's personality. The patient may have to reject his affective tendencies, remove all the undesirable characteristics within him, and even change his original outlook on life. In this process the patient himself shoulders a large part of the responsibility because if he does not so desire it, no psychiatrist can make any significant changes in his personality traits. But normally the patient does cooperate for he has come to the doctor for help, and there should be no question regarding his cooperation. What the psychiatrist does is to help the patient cure and improve himself. And for this the first essential is that the patient and psychologist should establish a rapport between themselves. Once that has been achieved the patient learns to have faith in the doctor, and then can have no objection to revealing even the inmost secrets of his heart. Curing of mental disease is almost impossible without this rapport. But while on the one hand this rapport depends upon the patient's own efforts, it depends, on the other, no less upon the personality of the psychiatrist. If the doctor shows the keenest interest in the patient and tries to understand his problems with complete sympathy, he will win the confidence of the patient. To begin with, he may even be ill-treated by the patient who will not show any confidence and faith in him and will not be prepared to open out his heart to the doctor, but an intelligent doctor can dispel all such doubts and attitudes. Rapport having been established, the precondition of treatment is complete. This initial difficulty having been overcome, the doctor may find it difficult to damp the patient's enthusiasm for praising him to all and sundry. Anyway, with his rapport created, half the difficulty facing the doctor is removed, half the battle is won. Now, different psychological techniques are employed to cure the patient.

## SUGGESTION

Suggestion is probably the oldest form of psychotherapy and one used in everyday life. Whenever one person tries to influence another, suggestion usually plays a part. It is extensively employed in advertising, propaganda, religious and political activities. It plays a part in every psychotherapeutic relationship and indeed plays a prominent part in any successful doctor-patient relationship. The best manner of the successful physician is compounded of a large variety of different features — his general appearance, speech, the interest he shows in the patient, his general behaviour, demeanour, his impressiveness and, in general, his 'presence'. Any treatment, whether it is in the form of a tablet, a bottle of medicine or the form of therapeutic procedure, always has an element of suggestion. The colour and taste of a medicinal mixture sometimes have more potent effects by suggestion than the active pharmacological ingredients.

Suggestion is defined as a process of communication resulting in the acceptance with conviction of the communicated proposition in the absence of logically adequate grounds for its acceptance. It therefore involves the active influence of one mind upon another without any necessary logical basis. Treatment by suggestion can be traced as far back as the methods of healing used by the ancient Greeks. The therapeutic methods used in those days involved the invocation of miracles, of which there were two kinds, religious and magical. Interesting examples of religious miracles took place at the Temple of Aesculapius at Epidaurus. Patients came long distances and laid valuable gifts so as to influence the gods favourably. They spent some nights in public prayers and exhortation. Then, in front of the statue of a god, they were given advice in the form of oracles and prophetic dreams.

During the Middle Ages, churches and saints were invoked to cure particular diseases, *e.g.* St. Clare for eye disease, St. Ralph for plague, St. Fiarce for haemorrhoids. By the simple authority of the name and the mere influence of the words, pious personages would sometimes produce remarkable cures, which were regarded as the outcome of divine intervention. Kings used to cure scrofula. Magical remedies in which were all kinds of curious concoctions were used for treating diseases throughout the Middle Ages. Red coral, viper broth, crab's eye and powdered stag's horn were favourite medieval remedies.

Unobtrusive suggestion, of course, takes place in all successful methods of treatment, not only in psychiatry but in medicine and surgery. The benevolent attitude of the long-experienced general practitioner, the smile of the pleasant nurse, the clean smell of antiseptics in hospital, the colour and taste of the medicine can all play an important part by suggestion in promoting the patient's recovery. Suggestion is superficial, symptomatic treatment alone is not enough. It should be combined with a further attempt to deal with the causative factors and the patient should be given some insight into his condition.

Treatment such as massage, radiant heat, sunray treatment, mud bath and colonic larvae owe a large part of their success to suggestion. Some physicians obtain excellent results merely by their personalities and by the suggestions they unconsciously or otherwise give. Suggestion, therefore, probably has the widest use of all methods of psychiatry. It is not only used deliberately by psychiatrists but unconsciously by good nurses, physicians and surgeons all the time. It plays a great part in our ordinary lives in many processes which we tend to think are due to the activity of the intellect but which, on closer examination, are found to operate by the subtle means of suggestion, disguised as intellectual explanation. The hoardings in the street, the reiterated policies of our newspapers, the doctrines promulgated from the pulpit are all suffused with suggestion, although disguised under the category of economical, ethical and political values. Propaganda, in all its forms, relies mainly on the power of suggestion.

The history of the treatment of many disorders shows that any spontaneous improvement occurring during the administration of treatment was put down and attributed to the treatment. Another common factor in all the treatments is that they all had an influence by suggestion. Recent work on the effect of placebo tablets, to which patients developed marked reactions, indicates that inert preparations may exert marked therapeutic effects by suggestion and may also produce marked autonomic and other bodily changes by psychogenic influence.

## REASSURANCE

Reassurance is involved in many forms of treatment and in doctor-patient relationships generally. Patients, whatever they are suffering from, often have anxieties regarding the possibility of more serious diseases or regarding their mental stability. Many patients with mild neurotic symptoms have a severe dread of becoming insane. Patients with various bodily manifestations of emotional tension often harbour fears of cancer or other serious diseases.

All too frequently, patients with psychiatric symptoms are told by their physicians that there is nothing wrong with them. This very often only tends to make the patient more frightened because they know that there is something wrong and they are suffering symptoms and varying degrees of unhappiness and disability. They feel bewildered and more anxious because there feel that their condition has not been properly diagnosed and that there is still something wrong which has not been found. It is important to realise that the negative reassurances of this type are not by any means as effective as positive reassurances.

In patients suffering from psychiatric disorders, the physician should make the patient understand that he realise that there is something wrong but that the trouble is not due to physical diseases and that his symptoms are manifestations of an emotional illness. A description of the nature and the origin of the symptoms should always be given in terms suitable to his intelligence and personality. Such positive reassurance with explanation is much more effective than a mere negative reassurance.

Although many general physicians and general practitioners think that psychotherapy begins and ends with reassurance, this is by no means so and very rarely does it prove to be adequate treatment in itself.

The relationship with the therapist gives the patient a feeling of acceptance and security, even though such feelings may not be expressed verbally. Reassurance is mainly effective for recent or superficial disturbances and is usually ineffective in deep-seated problems and personality difficulties.

Supportive therapy is the most commonly used method of dealing with problems of an emotional nature. The object is to bring the patient to an improved state as rapidly as possible with symptomatic improvement or recovery, so that he is able to resume normal life and activities. Supportive therapy includes guidance in such matters as education, employment, health and social relationships, always letting the patient make the final decision himself.

Environment manipulation attempts to remove or modify disorganising elements in his environment. Social work is the best example of trained, skilful, environmental manipulation.

Persuasion is a therapeutic method based on the belief that the patient has the ability to modify his abnormal emotional processes by will power or by application of common sense. Appeals are made to the patient's reason and intelligence, in order to help him to abandon neurotic aims and symptoms and to regain self-respect. Persuasion, in order to be effective, must be based on a good doctor-patient relationship. The patient must feel that the doctor is intensely interested in him and wants to help him. Persuasion involves explanation of the origin of the symptoms and encouragement to adopt more salutary reactions to his problems. It is probably fallacious to assume that the effectiveness of persuasion therapy depends on the operation of the intellect and it is probable that suggestion also plays an important role. Persuasion as a variety of psychotherapy can be helpful if it is effective in helping the patient's understanding of himself, helping him to relinquish neurotic reactions, tendencies and aims and if it achieves a better genre readjustment. This will minimise the tendency for the patient to develop neurotic reactions or emotional tensions which, in turn, can precipitate attacks of psychosomatic disorders.

Supportive therapy is indicated for individuals with a reasonably stable personality who, up to the present illness, have made satisfactory adjustment but who have broken down under the impact of severe stress in the environment. Supportive therapy can also be helpful for less stable or more neurotic individuals.

## GROUP PSYCHOTHERAPY

The treatment of patients by psychotherapy in groups was first introduced as a time-saving measure but subsequent experience demonstrated that the method had special therapeutic possibilities, which did not occur in individual psychotherapy.

The number of patients is usually six to eight. Some patients do poorly with group therapy; these include psychopathic personalities, patients with low intelligence. The length of the group therapy session is customarily 1-1½ hours and usually held once or twice weekly. Patients are seated around in a circle. In the first session the participants are introduced by their Christian names and the purpose of group discussions is explained.

Group therapy may be conducted :

1. For purposes of re-education with a view to alteration of attitudes and behaviour patterns;
2. For purpose of psychoanalytic therapy.

The possible therapeutic aims and goals of group therapy are :

1. Guidance and practical advice;
2. Education or orientation;
3. Spiritual strength and fellowship;
4. Socialisation;
5. Aberration;
6. Facilitation of associations and the production of deeper material for analysis;
7. Symptomatic relief;
8. Improved adjustment and adaptation to reality;
9. Increased understanding and insight into emotional problem and conflicts;
10. Modification of personality and character.

**Group Analytic Psychotherapy**

This method has been well developed by Foulkes who states that its most significant features are :

1. Seven or eight members meet for 1½ hours, sitting in a circle together with the analyst.
2. No programme or directions are given, so that all contributions arise spontaneously from the patients.
3. All communications are treated as the equivalent on the part of the group of the free association of the individual under psychoanalytic conditions. There is also a corresponding relaxation of censorship.
4. The therapist retains an attitude corresponding to that of the psycho-analyst during individual treatment.
5. All communications and relationships are seen as a part of the total field of interaction, namely the group matrix.
6. All group members take an active part in the total therapeutic process.

The natural history of the therapeutic group is as follows. In its early stages, there may be much anxiety and guilt in individual members. Conflicts are invariably present; these are related to conflicts of a conformity, authority, dependency and change. It is the primary conflict of man as a group animal. The first conflict, therefore, is one of conformity to the group. The second is conflict to authority and authority figures. The third conflict evolves around the problem of dependency. The fourth is conflict of a change.

The natural history of the group usually goes through an initial phase which is termed the 'therapeutic honeymoon', in which great hopes are placed on the therapist; the patient has to orientate himself away from the doctor-patient axis towards the patient-to-patient axis of the group. Patients then usually get down to discussing individual symptoms. The intermediate phase is when the group truly becomes a group. The centre of reference is no longer the therapist alone. They address each other and respond directly to each other with general support and then analyse and interpret their own interactions and feelings. The terminal phase should always be gradual to allow the patient an opportunity to work through the many entities and depressions that in therapy, as in life, associate themselves with endings.

### Group Psychotherapy for Children

This is classified according to the ages namely, nursery, early childhood, late childhood, adolescence; also early adolescence and late adolescence.

The nursery group is about 4-5 children in a small room, with a flat tray divided into two compartments containing sand and water and some toy materials. In the early stages, areas are respected and each child cultivates his own plot. Later, they become interested in other people's work and begin working and playing with each other.

Early childhood ranges from 5 to 9 years age. Groups are formed here, according to Foulkers and Anthony, in conjunction with a sedentary occupation such as drawing, painting or modelling. The period is usually divided into a discussion phase followed by an activity phase. At the end of the discussion period, the groups choose their activity for the day.

Adolescent groups are usually kept to one sex, optimal number about sex.

## HYPNOSIS

Hypnosis is a state of artificially induced increased suggestibility.

The technique of hypnosis usually aims at narrowing the patient's attention and awareness to the hypnotist alone and, although the condition may have the appearance of sleep, it is physiologically quite different from sleep. Electro encephalographic recordings, for example, are similar to those of the waking state.

A part of the patient's mind is 'en rapport' with the hypnotist and hypnosis is regarded by some authorities to be a state of induced dissociation.

There are different levels of hypnosis, ranging from a light hypnotic state to a deep trance.

### Deep Hypnosis

Deep hypnosis, or a deep trance, is qualitatively different from the lighter stages of hypnosis. The patient is extremely relaxed, breathing becomes slower, post-hypnotic suggestions will be executed with amnesia. Suggestions are extremely effective; it is possible to make the subject hallucinate, *e.g.* to visualize scenes or to experience smells.

In a deep hypnotic trance, the patient can open his eyes and remain in a trance; it was for this reason that the terms deep trance and somnambulism were applied to this state.

About 5 per cent of the population can be hypnotised into a deep trance without difficulty; some others can be trained to develop a deep trance with intensive efforts over a period of time.

There are, however, many people who are not suitable subjects for hypnosis and can never be deeply hypnotised.

**Hypnotic Techniques**

A variety of techniques are available for inducing hypnosis :

It is necessary to prepare the patient and to explain what hypnosis means. It is important to explain that it is not state of sleep and, secondly, that it is not essential for amnesia to occur to obtain beneficial therapeutic results.

It can be explained to the patient as a state of relaxation in which his field of awareness becomes narrowed and that in this state, suggestions will be much more effective.

The hypnotist's rate of inducing hypnosis must be governed by the speed with which a patient responds to hypnotic suggestions.

The following are some examples of techniques used :

First of all the patient should be seated comfortably in a chair or lying down on a couch and should be encouraged to let all muscles go loose and relax; to let the body sink down in the couch; to let all the muscles be as loose and relaxed as possible. They are then asked to pay attention to the right hand or the left hand; they are asked that, as soon as they feel any movement in the thumb or fingers, to lift it up to indicate which one it is. Slight movements invariably take place and the patients lift up the appropriate finger. This is then followed by suggestion that the hand and the arm are getting lighter and will rise upwards steadily to touch the forehead and, as they rise, the patients get sleepier. When the hand touches the forehead they go off into a deep sleep. The depth of hypnosis can then be increased by further suggestions, by counting ten and, by the time one has finished counting ten, they will be in a deep state of hypnosis. The advantage of this technique is that one is unlikely to make mistakes and the rate of hypnotic suggestions for induction are governed by the response of the patient.

Other techniques are to get the patient to fixate his vision on a key or a finger or a light and to give suggestions that the eyelids are getting more and more tired and will close, and that the tiredness is passing over the head and down various parts of the body.

Sometimes one can induce a hypnotic state rapidly by getting the patients to hyperventilate and, in some patients, this with suitable suggestions puts them into a deep hypnotic state. If the patient is a suitable subject, hypnosis can be one of the quickest ways of carrying out psychotherapy :

1. For psychological investigation, *i.e.* to elicit the nature of underlying conflicts and problems and to facilitate the recall of forgotten experiences which may be emotionally important.

2. To abstract past experiences.

3. To modify symptoms and attitudes.

4. In the treatment of psychosomatic manifestations such as asthma.

A word of warning here, it is unwise to use hypnosis in a patient suffering from status asthmatics, particularly if they are suffering from the effects of anoxia, endanger the patient. However, in other forms of asthmatic attacks where anoxia has not become a problem, hypnosis in certain subjects can produce dramatic results.

In the treatment of psychosomatic disorders, it is usually necessary to induce deep hypnosis to achieve the best results.

**Signs of Hypnotic Trance**

In order to ascertain that the patient is sleeping under the influence of hypnotism, a certain mechanism is employed. The doctor suggests to the subject that he is in a deep sleep or coma and cannot open his eyes. He follows up with the contradictory suggestion that the subject should open his eyes, but supplements it with the suggestion that he is not capable of opening his eyes. If the subject finds it impossible to follow these suggestions, the hypnotiser can proceed further. Now the hypnotiser tells the patient or subject that his left arm is completely senseless and cannot feel any sensation of pain. If the arm is now injured with any sharp instrument, the patient, even though being injured, shows no signs of having experienced pain. It must be remembered that by the use of an electrical apparatus it is possible to ascertain that the subject's body has reacted to the sensation of pain. The subject is then told that his arms are very hard and heavy, and that he cannot lift them. He is further asked to lift them, but despite his effort he cannot do so. It should be remembered that this partial and temporary paralysis is the outcome of suggestion because as soon as the hypnotiser tells the subject that he can raise his arm he does so facilely. Sometimes the hypnotiser gives certain wrong suggestions to the subject, for example, the subject is told to repeat the song that was being sung, even though in actual fact there is no music in the air.

**Ending Hypnotic Trance**

In this manner after a variety of tests it can be ascertained that the patient is in a hypnotic trance. This trance can be ended quite simply. The hypnotiser tells the patient that on a certain signal he will get up from sleep. One such signal or suggestion can be counting up to the figure of five, and by the time five is reached the patient should be awake. When the hypnotiser has succeeded in hypnotising the subject successfully many times, he can repeat it very easily and in a very short time again.

**Post-Hypnotic Suggestions**

Sometimes the hypnotiser suggests to the subject that after arising from the trance he will perform a certain action. When he has been directed to do some such thing, even in complete ignorance he feels himself compelled to do that action in a semiconscious state. If, for example, he has been asked to call up a certain friend on the telephone the next day at eight, he will do so but if he is asked to explain why has he called his friend, he may possibly have no answer. This influence of suggestion after the hypnotic condition has come to end is called post-hypnotic suggestion, and through this post-hypnotic suggestion many kinds of symptoms of mental disease can be eliminated.

Many are the experiments that have been conducted to discover the condition of a subject in a hypnotic trance. These experiments seem to indicate that, compared with the state of sleep-hypnotic trance approximates to the condition of waking. Many hypnotised individuals keep their eyes open even in the trance and they behave as in their ordinary waking hours, the only difference being that no action of their's is controlled by their own violation, whatever they do is ordered by the person hypnotising them. Hence, as W.R. Wells has illustrated by his experiments, the symptoms of hypnosis can be created even without first achieving the condition of sleep.

**Hypnotism as a Curative Method**

Hypnotism is used to cure patients suffering from a loss of memory as well as patients of hysteria. In the hypnotised state these patients easily recall the forgotten or repressed memory, and through post-hypnotic suggestions these memories are brought to the level of normal consciousness. Direct suggestion and post-hypnotic suggestion have also proved to be useful in the case of other symptoms of hysteria such as muteness, deafness or injury, etc. Besides this, hypnosis can also be used to remove such diseases as insomnia, tension, neurotic habits, abnormal fears, etc. In this manner it is obvious that through hypnosis many of the symptoms of various less complex mental diseases can be done away with without much difficulty.

**Objections to Hypnosis**

In spite of the above uses to which hypnosis can be put, it is subjected to various objections, the chief ones being the following :

1. According to one view, the cure effected by hypnosis remains on the external level and it does not penetrate deep enough to remove inner tension. Hence the cure is purely temporary.

2. According to certain other thinkers, this technique is limited only to such patients who do not object to being hypnotised and can easily be reduced to that state. On the

other hand there are certain other mentally ill people who neither want to be nor can easily be hypnotised, and therefore, this method cannot be used to cure diseases in the latter class of patients.

3. Another objection to the technique of hypnosis is that some doctors cure the persons by hypnotising them on the ground that while they were in a trance state, certain undesirable influences were brought to bear upon their minds or that indecent behaviour has been directed at them. Even though many of these cases are based on nothing more than malicious and imagined objections and sufferings, the doctor certainly loses his reputation.

**Present Standing of Hypnotic Method**

Due to the above-mentioned objections and implied difficulties, the use of the hypnotic method continually declined, and in the present day it has been made use of as a part of psychoanalysis in the form of hypnoanalysis. Yet, there is not much justification in the objections adduced against hypnosis. And yet it is equally true that an unscrupulous individual can certainly misuse the power of hypnosis. In itself hypnosis is a neutral power which can be used for good or bad; what is essential is that it should be put to proper use. And in fact, even when the patient is hypnotised the doctor cannot induce him to do whatever he wishes. Very often if he is asked to do an improper, harmful or dangerous act, he does not accept the suggestion, and instead wakes up from the trance. It is another thing that he may do something wrong while under some kind of illusion wilfully forced upon his mind. For example, if he is told that the revolver he is holding contains no cartridge and then he is asked to take aim and fire he may do so. But examples of accidents occurring under similar circumstances are known even in the waking state. It cannot be denied that in the state of artificial trance, the patient or subject is confident that no such thing is really happening. Besides, the experiments of Erickson have more or less proved that hypnotism cannot be made use of for antisocial activity. In an experiment a hypnotist student was told by suggestion to read the letters of one of his friends. To begin with, the psychologist did not succeed even making repeated suggestions, and even when he did succeed in conveying his meaning to the student, the latter only looked at the empty sections of the letter. When the psychologist ordered him to turn the letter over he did so in such a way that the letter was held upside down in his hand. He was again told to hold it correctly; he then objected that he did not have his spectacles on him. When he was provided with his spectacles he objected that the writing was practically illegible to him, but when the psychologist tried to help him read the letter the student remarked that he could not see anything. From this experiment of Erickson's it appears quite definitely that the hypnotized individual cannot be guided against his inner conscience to any immoral or antisocial activity. If, on the other hand, the patient himself has no objection to some immoral activity, then he may accept the suggestions for such act with alacrity.

Putting it briefly, it is apparent from the above consideration that hypnosis is definitely a useful and adequate method of removing the symptoms of hysteria and other mental diseases. Its peculiar advantage lies in the fact that the hypnotist subject accepts the suggestions of the psychologist not as external commands but as dictates of his own volition. In the case of post-hypnotic suggestion, this is particularly true. Nevertheless, as is apparent from the previous considerations, the uses and misuses of this method of psychotherapy create their own limitations.

## PSYCHOANALYTIC TECHNIQUE

### Object of Psychoanalytic Technique

Sigmund Freud, the originator of the technique of psychoanalysis, was himself a very successful doctor. According to him, the human personality has three elements, the id, the ego and the super-ego. These three elements and the external environment of man are constantly acting, and reacting, and it is quite possible for these elements to come into mutual conflict over something. The conflict results in the gradual manifestation of various characteristics, and they are the cause of all mental diseases. The object of Freud's psychoanalytic technique was to strengthen the ego, knowledge or consciousness of self in man and this can be achieved by resolving it from the grip of super-ego and making it incumbent upon the id. In the words of Allport, "If psychoanalysis can widen the ego's field of vision so that it is able to take over into the unfilled region of consciousness many hitherto hidden portions of the id, reconciling them in them in the process with the demands of the super-ego and the outer world, the patient will then face life more serenely, and his neurotic difficulties will presumably vanish." In order to achieve this objective, the doctor has to bring to the conscious level all motives and desires repressed in the unconscious of a patient. Evidently, this is not simple task because the unconscious mind creates obstacles in the path of direct recognition. It is the task of the doctor to overcome such obstacles and bring to conscious recognition all elements residing in the dark unconscious. Psychoanalysis has this for its aim.

**Process of Psychoanalysis**

In the psychoanalytic technique, the first step for the doctor is to gather sufficient information concerning the patient's symptoms. He now tells the patient to meet him for one hour daily for five days out of the week for a period of one to three years, the actual time of treatment normally occupying a year and a half. Now, if the patient is willing to abide by these terms, the fee is also determined; it varies between five and ten dollars by the hour which the patient has to pay even if he fails to keep appointments. Many psychoanalysts hold the view that if the patient is not charged exorbitant fee the cure is not effective because as long as the patient is not under stress he does not assume the necessary gravity or seriousness needed for this task. If now the patient agrees to the fee, he is requested not to reveal his condition to any other persons besides which the patient is required not to read any books on psychoanalysis or to indulge in sexual intercourse. In the traditional method of psychoanalysis, the patient is asked to lie behind the couch in such a way that the patient cannot see him while he can observe the patient. In such an arrangement, he can observe and note the emotional reactions of the patient while the patient cannot observe him doing so.

**Free Association**

The patient is now allowed to tell his story, his view of life, without any obstacles being put in his way. Often the patient begins his account with description of his experiences of life, particularly sexual experiences, ambitions, difficulties, hopes, fears, etc. He is encouraged to reveal his mind further, and is told that he can talk on any topic that he likes, be it moral, immoral, personal, social, in fact whatever comes into his mind. This method of recounting thoughts that come into the mind of their own accord without any external prompting is called the method of free expression. And in this method the patient manages to reveal many memories, emotions and imaginings that normally do not come to the conscious level of his mind.

**Dream Analysis**

Another technique peculiar to psychoanalysis is dream analysis. Explanation of dreams can help to express many desires, conflicts and thoughts repressed in the unconscious, thoughts and desires that normally do not come to the normal conscious level of life. While dreaming the individual's unconscious mind is functioning, and during this process there is greater independence and freedom. But from this it cannot be deduced that in dreaming there is no censorship. In fact, Freud has indicated precisely the opposite in his dream analysis. This censorship permits only a specified kind of manifestation pressing itself to the conscious mind. And in order to conform to such needs, the unconscious drives and motives adopt various acceptable forms in order to find satisfaction. It is for this reason that the latent content and manifest content in dreams differ considerably. Dream analysis consists in the understanding, comprehension and analysis of the manifest content in a dream in order to unravel its latent content. In this process, the patient is required to relate his dream, and then he is required to reveal himself uninhibited in order to associate the various persons, objects, incidents, etc., of the dream, relevant individuals, objects and incidents of conscious life. Avoiding inhibition implies the complete acceptance of any associated thought, without any logical or thoughtful intervention, that may occur after the dream sequence. Often, irrespective of however much the patient may desire it, the resistance of censorship in the unconscious cannot be eliminated. Thus the analysis of a dream may take long time. There can be numerous forms of this obstacle to dream analysis. Sometimes the patient stops dreaming, and sometimes he cannot make any associations. At other times he talks in an incoherent manner or instead becomes bored with this process and loses his temper with the doctor. He may even fail to arrive at the right time appointed for such analysis or he may announce that he is now fully cured. This resistance to the analysis of dream indicated a very vivid consciousness or awareness of his unconscious and unresolved conflicts and instead of facing them he concocts various excuses in order to avoid such a showdown. In such occasions it is best for the doctor to clarify the patient the reasons for his reluctance so that his cooperation may be obtained.

Analysis of dream can lead to the creation of emotional or affective relations between doctor and patient, but the relationship is one of father and son. When this happens the patient easily recognises his own resistances and can then have little difficulty in relating his fatuously repressed sexual feelings. In the opinion of Freud repressed drives of infancy have an important part to play in mental disease, but by making such repressions conscious the disease can be cured to a large extent. And because emotional relationships are established during the treatment, the patient comes to regard the doctor as the most intimate, important and powerfully attractive individual in the world because the doctor replaces the object of the patient's love. If the patient is a woman she will probably place the doctor on a par with her husband or lover. This transference of affection or emotional attachment during the period of treatment is essential and after the treatment is complete, when no such transference is required, the doctor can again turn such an emotional attachment to its original goal. This process is called counter-transference. In such a condition of emotional attachment the doctor must be very careful how he proceeds because if he becomes attached to the patient in any way, the latter cannot be cured.

It has already been indicated that in psychoanalysis the doctor plays a passive role, confined to a patient and sympathetic hearing of the patient's woes related by himself. During the period of treatment, the patient talks for nearly 95 per cent of the time, which is enough for him to tell the doctor his fears, sins, shameful actions, hopes and conflicts. In this process it is for the doctor to help the patient understand the conflicts that take place between his id, ego and super-ego. In doing this the doctor has to analyse many of the incidents and occurrences mentioned to him by his patient. Obviously, success in such analysis depends very much upon the mutual cooperation and understanding that exist between doctor and patient. The truth of the matter is that in this process the doctor becomes a medium for cleansing the patient's unconscious mind of its love, hate and fears, engendered within it. What the patient does is to replace the original object of these tendencies by the doctor, and when through such transference his repressed emotions find expression it is only natural that the troublesome symptoms come to an end. Cure can now be stopped. Sometimes when the patient offers so much resistance that no transference of emotional attachment is possible, the doctor has to call off the cure without completing it.

**Hypnotic analysis.** In hypnotic analysis, for the first fifteen minutes the patient is allowed free association, but this free association takes place in the state of hypnotic trance. By means of various suggestions the patient is encouraged to recognise and remember his repressed experiences. In this manner the person hypnotising the patient acts as a guide to the latter, helping him to make free association, repeat various kinds of emotional experiences, describe dreams, etc. Sometimes a crystal ball is placed before the patient and he is asked to describe what he sees in it. What the patient does see in the crystal ball are drives and tendencies, in the form of incidents, that lie repressed in his unconscious mind, and this happens because he is hypnotised. But the hypnotic trance is sometimes broken, and a normal analytical technique applied. Nothing final or definite can be said regarding the efficacy of hypnotic analysis in the treatment of mentally diseased persons.

### Defects of Psychoanalytic Technique

Psychoanalysis as a technique of mental treatment has been employed in the cure of various mental diseases, but the method requires a considerable period of time, besides which it also requires the services of a very efficient doctor. Hence, it proves a very expensive cure; consequently very few patients can benefit by it. For example, the complete curing of a patient suffering from psychoneurosis requires the expenditure of some two thousand dollars or equivalent amount in rupees. Because it is so expensive and extended over such a long period of time, efforts have been made to derive its advantages from a more conscious and less expensive method of treatment, and to this end hypnotic analysis is being devised. People who favour this method believe that because of hypnosis, transference is achieved in a much shorter time, and the patient puts up far less resistance. And in this method, the patient can meet the doctor five to six times a week for a period of few months and be completely cured at the end of that time. Briefly, the following are the shortcomings of psychoanalysis :

**1. Expensive method.** As has been pointed out at an earlier stage, this method involves considerable expenditure of time and money.

**2. Useless for some diseases.** It has been further indicated that this technique cannot cure diseases in which the patient and doctor fail to achieve any emotional attachment.

**3. Can succeed only with a particular kind of patient.** For successful treatment by this method, the patient should be between 20 and 40 years of age, and intelligent.

**4. Not more effective than some simpler methods.** Psychoanalysts have contended that their method of treatment is more efficacious than simpler methods but in fact this contention has not been proved correct. Many psychoanalysts have not even deemed it fit to publish the results of their treatments, and from reports that have been published it appears that two-thirds of visiting patients could be cured, and even among them only those who stuck faithfully to the doctor could be declared completely cured. These formed 80 per cent of the latter figure. Yet, impartially considered, it cannot be remarked with justice that the psychoanalytic method is not more effective and efficacious than other simpler techniques, because before any such statement can justifiably be made it is essential to make a proper comparison. And this, so far, has not been done. Freud himself did not treat many elements of the psychoanalytic method as facts, but chose to consider them as economic principles. In his book *Autobiography* summing up the work of his life he could say that he has originated many things, and found many suggestions useless; he has thrown them away. Certainly in the future much will be made of them, but he himself could not say whether this would be much or little. In another context, in another book Freud wrote that if he were asked whether he was in agreement with the ideas put forward there, and if he was, to what extent, he would say that he was not in full agreement with them and that he had no wish to win the approval of others. It is a greater truth, says Freud, that he does not know to what extent he believes in them. One would be hard put to it to discover a more appropriate and adequate criticism of the psychoanalytic technique than Freud's own words.

## SHOCK THERAPY

### Insulin Shock Therapy

Various kinds of shock therapy are now much in use in the cure of structural or motor deformations. Insulin shock therapy was first used to this end by Sakel, a Viennese doctor. In insulin shock therapy the patient is administered an injection of insulin due to which the patient remains unconscious for hours, for the sugar content of the blood is considerably reduced. Rendered unconscious by the induction of insulin, the patient suffers a shock which is manifest in the different deformations of muscles, facial expressions and different nervous changes. Sometimes the patient perspires much, or he may even pass through some fit. Consciousness is induced in the patient again through doses of glucose, injected or administered orally. This method of cure is spread over a period of ten weeks, and is repeated three to five times a week. Insulin shock therapy was first used for the treatment of schizophrenia, but later it came to be used also for affective psychoses. This method does not succeed to the extent to which its success has been almost negligible. While the patients suffering from schizophrenia have certainly benefited from insulin shock therapy, obviously it cannot be used for every disease.

### Metrazol Shock Therapy

Meduna was responsible for evolving another simple method of shock therapy after the insulin method had been used. He caused changes in patients through injecting metrazol into the system. In this technique, the patient is made to lie down, following which the doctor injects metrazol into the patient's arm; the patient becomes unconscious very shortly after the injection. Immediately after this, the patient has a kind of epileptic fit. This process is repeated daily for few weeks. This cure, too, was used originally for curing schizophrenia, but instead, it proved more successful in cases of depressive psychosis. But because of the following shortcoming this method failed to achieve much success :

1. In this method, the period between actual injection and before unconsciousness sets in is a time of acute fear. Hence, many patients do not want to make use of this method.

2. And unless proper arrangements are made, it is possible for the patient to suffer minor injuries in the arms, jaw and spinal cord.

**Electroshock Therapy**

Experiments conducted by two Italian doctors, Cerletti and Bini, led to the development and use of electroshock therapy. In this method, an electrode is placed on the patient's head and a stream of current is passed through the brain, the patient becoming unconscious almost immediately, and then suffering an epileptic fit. When the patient regains consciousness he remembers nothing concerning the treatment. In this technique, the fit induced is less severe than when metrazol is used, and hence it can be conveniently controlled. Secondly, it induces no feeling of fear, and neither is there any possibility of physical injury. Hence this method has proved to be more popular than the metrazol shock therapy method.

**Explanation of Shock Therapy**

Shock therapy has been explained on two grounds, physiological and psychological and hence two kinds of theories have been propounded concerning it. But both kinds of theories are based primarily on conjecture. According to the psychological contention, through such treatment the patient returns to the world of reality, and by passing very acute sensations his consciousness attains a definite reorganisation. According to the physiological contention, by this method the abnormal neurotic conjunctions are broken, the influence is destroyed and the stupor ended.

In actual fact, shock therapy is a practical cure, and it results in physiological as well as psychological change and transformations. It is very true that because of it many cells of the brain are destroyed, and memory is also injured. But in shock therapy the mortality or fatality rate is low. Comparative studies indicate that the smallest number of deaths are caused by electroshock therapy and the maximum by insulin shock therapy.

## PSYCHO SURGERY

Psychosurgery has been considered at length by Freeman and Watts in their book *Psychosurgery*. This technique was first employed by Dr. Moniz of Lisbon in 1935. Through psychosurgery of the brain, Moniz sought to and succeeded in the cure of functional psychoses and psychoneuroses. In this method, a small hole is bored in the patient's head on either side, just under the nerves by which the connection between prefrontal lobes and thalamus are severed.

Psychosurgery is resorted to only when all other means of removing the mental disease have been tried and have failed. Psychosurgery has proved to be very successful in the treatment of involution melancholia and certain psychoneurosis of depression since it can eliminate the feeling of anxiety and depression with the result that the patient who previously appeared depressed, excited or self-conscious now appears happy, light-hearted, gay and free from all worry. Some patients become slow and dull-witted following such an operation, but the majority of patients succeed in achieving a condition similar to the one before the disease overtook them. In the case of such patients, this method has proved to be eminently successful.

## MUSCULAR RELAXATION

Increased muscle tension is a common manifestation of all forms of emotional tension and is responsible for a number of the patient's symptoms, *e.g.*, certain type of headaches are due to increased muscular tension of the skull muscles; pains in the back of the neck, the back and the limbs may be due to increased muscular tension. Tremors are also manifestations of increased muscular tension.

The symptoms arising from increased muscular tension often give rise to additional anxiety, because the patient may believe that they indicate some serious disease and thereby tend to set up a vicious circle. Treatment consisting of training the patient in muscular relaxation is a valuable therapeutic adjunct. It not only can provide symptomatic relief but, in so far as states of anxiety and tension have both emotional and somatic aspects, relief of muscular tension often provides a general alleviation of the degree of anxiety felt.

Muscular relaxation may be helpful in asthmatic subjects suffering from anxiety tension symptoms, particularly when they have neuromuscular symptoms. Also, relaxation may be helpful when combined with breathing exercises, as the latter can be more effectively introduced when combined with training in muscular relaxation.

### Autogenic Training

This method was developed by Schultz for treating patients with anxiety and increased muscular tension by means of muscular relaxation and exercises. The patient learns to relax each muscle group, eventually achieving complete muscular relaxation throughout the body.

Autogenic training has the advantage of being simple and effective, and can be used for groups as well as individually.

Biofeedback and behaviour therapy are two forms of treatment aimed at modifying symptoms or behaviour by methods based on learning theory.

## BIOFEEDBACK

Biofeedback involves the use of technology to provide the patient with information of the current state of the physiological system that need to be controlled to alleviate symptoms. It is used for those symptoms or behaviour abnormalities which are normally outside voluntary control because of poor sensory information from the systems involved. Biofeedback provides information of the physiological state, usually by electronic methods which can be used in order to learn control of the relevant organ or system. Biofeedback has been used successfully in the treatment of tension headaches, also in neuro-muscular rehabilitation, including muscular specified or defective muscular control after cerebro-vascular accidents, in varieties of cerebral palsy, and torticollis. It has also been used successfully in the treatment of severe focal incontinence.

It has been shown that if patients are given feedback regarding the size and frequency of alpha waves in their EEGs, they can learn to control the amount of alpha recorded. Enhancement of alpha activity is usually associated with a relaxed and pleasant feeling. Another frequency from the sensory motor cortex has been used to success in the treatment of some forms of ellipse.

Migraine has been successfully treated by providing feedback on blood flow to the temporal artery. Only limited benefits have been achieved in the control of arterial hypertension. It is possible to achieve reduction in systolic pressure of approximately 10 per cent but this is not sufficient to be of clinical importance in practice.

Promising results have been achieved in the control of cardiac arhythmias. Feedback from cardiac activity is given by three lights, a green one is a signal for him to try to speed his heart, red light to slow the heart and a yellow one to inform him that he is performing correctly. Patients are taught to speed the hearts and to slow the heart rates within a narrow range. Patients are able to learn to identify premature ventricular contractions. A premature beat causes a red light to flash because it comes too fast, followed by a flash of a green light which is triggered by the ensuing compensatory pause. Patients learn to identify this sequence as a premature ventricular contraction and to prevent it.

## BEHAVIOUR THERAPY

Behaviour therapy is the systematic application of principles of learning to the analysis and treatment of disorders of behaviour. The rationale adopted by practitioners of behaviour therapy is that neurotic behaviour and other types of disorder are predominantly acquired and therefore should be subject to established laws of learning. Knowledge regarding the learning process concerns not only the acquisition of new behaviour patterns but the reduction or elimination of existing behaviour patterns.

Behaviour therapy has made tremendous advances in the last two decades and has made impact on the treatment of a variety of symptoms and behaviour disorders which previously had been resistant to treatment. A large variety of new techniques are available including :

**1. Reciprocal inhibition.** Many forms of neurotic behaviour are acquired in an anxiety-generating situation.

Treatment can be used in the suppression of anxiety responses by responses which are physiologically antagonistic to anxiety.

The techniques of systematic desensitisation consist of enquiring first of all into the stimulus situations, which provoke anxiety in the patient, and to rank these stimuli in order from the most to the least disturbing, *i.e.* a hierarchy of stimulus situations.

Then the patient is asked to visualise the least disturbing stimulus when he is in a state of relaxation produced by hypnosis or intravenous anaesthetic such as methohexitone (Brietal).

Whenever marked disturbance occurs the therapist withdraws the stimulus and calms the patient.

Each stimulus is visualised for 5-10 seconds and 2-4 items are presented in each session, each item usually being presented twice.

As soon as the patient is able to visualise the items without disturbance, the therapist moves on the next item in the next session.

Eventually the patient is able to visualise all the former noxious stimuli without anxiety and this ability to imagine the noxious stimuli with tranquillity is transferred to the real life situation.

**2. Implosion therapy, or flooding.** In this method, in contrast to systematic desensitisation, the patient is confronted in imagination or reality with his most feared situation or stimulus at once, and encouraged to remain in contact with that situation until the avoidance response is extinguished.

It is a mistake to regard systematic desensitisation as applicable to classical phobias only. It is in fact useful in the treatment of a wide range of behavioural disorders when one is able to identity the stimuli which elicit anxiety and which result in maladaptive or disruptive behaviour. Sometimes obsessive-compulsive behaviour is stimulated by the anxiety produced by specific objects or situations and can be helped by systematic desensitisation using a hierarchy of relevant stimuli. In stammering it can be used to condition the anxiety associated with a range of speaking situations. Similarly, certain sexual problems such as impotence or even certain type of homosexuality may be amenable to desensitisation therapy. Asthma and dysmenorrhoea have been treated by systematic desensitisation.

**3. Modelling.** This is a technique used with flooding or desensitisation in which the patient sees the therapist enter the phobic situation and the patient is then induced to copy him.

**4. Operant conditioning.** Operant behaviour usually affects the environment and generates stimuli which 'feed back' to the organism. Any response or behaviour which is rewarding and therefore reinforcing increases the likelihood of further similar responses.

Shaping is based on operant conditioning principles. The patient is systematically instructed to do what he fears and is rewarded by the therapist with praise when he succeeds and with no response if he fails. This method is useful in the treatment of phobias and obsession.

**5. Aversion therapy.** Aversion conditioning is achieved by associating stimuli relating to the symptom to be treated with unpleasant effects following administration of apomorphine, emetine or by the administration of a painful electric shock. The latter enables a more precise timing in the presentation of the noxious stimulus and the stimuli related to the symptoms to be treated.

**6. Negative learning.** This has been used in the treatment of involuntary movements such as tics. It consists of getting the patient to adhere to a rigid schedule of massed practice of voluntarily carrying out the movements of the tic intervals throughout the day. This sets up a state of inhibition, which impairs or prevents the appearance of the movement.

## NON-DIRECTIVE PSYCHOTHERAPY

As a general rule psycho-therapy is divided into two categories directive and non-directive. In directive psychotherapy the psychiatrist or psychologist guides the patient, offering many directions and instructions while the patient is more or less passively involved. But in the present day world, non-directive psychotherapy is considered more efficacious than the older directive psychotherapy. In this, as is evident from the term, the doctor does not issue any direction or instruction, it is the patient himself who appears to be more active. He himself expresses his own thoughts and emotions, and resorts more to auto-suggestions. C.R. Rogers put forward this technique of non-directive psychotherapy in this book *Counselling and Psychotherapy*. This method is based on the contention that a patient has the right to solve his own problems and select his own goal in life, and if he is given the proper freedom he manages quite well. Hence, treatment does not involve doing anything to the patient, instead, it is aimed at helping the patient to develop and attain to maturity so that he may solve his own problem in the future. The psychiatrist fights shy of any advice, guidance or suggestion and does more than provide encouragement and explanation when and where he thinks them necessary. It is the patient who does most of the talking, the doctor only confining himself to recommittal but encouraging remarks. Superficially, at least, this method of curing people seems rather unusual and simple, but in fact it requires much skill and experience. The truth of the matter is that the doctor is never passive. He appears to be that merely because his aim and object is to let the patient understand his own problems and seek their solution. In the case of passive patients and patients who depend upon others such treatment becomes very difficult because this treatment requires the patient to realize his own real feelings and to find solutions for the problems that confront him, and in addition to decide when the treatment is to stop. Apparently, such a method requires much time to be really efficacious. But when compared with the psychoanalytic method-time taken appears to be not too long. But the technique of non-directive psychotherapy does not succeed with patients who have become used to their mental traits and characteristics. It proves to be more useful in the case of more intelligent patients who have the courage and enthusiasm to face the problems of life and to deal with them.

## MILD TYPES OF PSYCHOTHERAPY

There are certain mild methods of psychotherapy, in addition to special methods but all of them are not so important. Among them are the following :

(i) ***Relaxation :*** It is in fact a common experience that many mental diseases are the outcome of an extreme tension. Hence, from the mental and physical standpoint, it is possible to get rid of these diseases in a relaxed state. Concerning a method for achieving relaxation Jacobson has written that the patient is allowed to lie down on a couch where he consciously flexes the various muscles of his body systematically. This helps him achieve control on the individual muscles in the body, and then he can relax them at will. Now, when the physical tension is almost completely gone, the mind also relaxes. The patient can then sleep easily. While this process of conscious relaxation of body tissues is continuing, the psychiatrist can supplement it by suggesting to the patient that he is going to sleep. But, the patient is constantly encouraged to believe that he himself can achieve a condition of relaxation, can help in the removal of tension in the case of every mental disease, even if it may not be possible thereby to cure the patient completely of that disease.

(ii) ***Rest and isolation :*** S.W. Mitchell, in his book *Fat and Blood,* has laid considerable emphasis upon the importance of rest and isolation in the treatment of mental disease. According to his conception, at the root of all mental disease is fatigue, which can be eliminated by rest, complete social isolation and nutritious food. Mitchell succeeded in curing many female patients of their mental distress through the medium of rest, although Rose has expressed doubt whether the patients improved because of rest since there can be no doubt that Mitchell's powerful personality had not a little to do with the cure. It should further be remembered that a majority of his patients were women and that he himself had been very active in their treatment, care and cure. In fact, due to his mode of treatment, the disease became unattractive, painful and boring so that his patients thought it best to escape from it. Nowadays a majority of the psychologists do not treat fatigue as a cause of mental disease so that the rest and isolation method is no longer considered very important. Yet, it does have some beneficial influence.

(iii) ***Change of environment :*** In the case of mental disease, the individual's environment assumes a special importance. Due to some peculiar atmosphere or environment he turns a mental defective. Hence, it is only natural if his environment is changed, his cause should be influenced. This environment can be constituted of the behaviour to all people around him towards himself as well as of his family, social and financial level. Changes in the environment both human and material can help to remove many of the symptoms of disease in the patient, but nevertheless, modern psychologists do not set much store by the method because they consider it inadequate. Mere change in the environment cannot go a long way towards curing the patient of his disease. On the other hand, it is not possible for the doctor to change the environment.

## QUESTIONS FOR EXERCISE

1. Define Psychotherapy and discuss its process.
2. Explain the psychotherapy method of suggestion.
3. Write short note on Reassurance.
4. What is supportive therapy? Explain environmental manipulation and persuasion.
5. Write short note on Group Psychotherapy.
6. Write short note on Hypnosis.
7. Examine the psychoanalytic technique as a therapeutic method.
8. Write short note on Shock therapy.
9. Write short note on Psychosurgery.
10. Write short note on Muscular Relaxation.
11. Explain Biofeedback and Behaviour Therapy.
12. Explain Non-Directive Psychotherapy.
13. Explain mild types of psychotherapy.